29.99

The Practice of
Market and Social Research

An Introduction

We work with leading authors to develop the strongest educational materials in marketing, bringing cutting-edge thinking and best learning practice to a global market.

Under a range of well-known imprints, including Financial Times Prentice Hall, we craft high quality print and electronic publications which help readers to understand and apply their content, whether studying or at work.

To find out more about the complete range of our publishing, please visit us on the World Wide Web at:
www.pearsoneduc.com

The Practice of
Market and Social Research

An Introduction

Yvonne McGivern

Visiting Lecturer,
Trinity College, Dublin

FT Prentice Hall
FINANCIAL TIMES

An imprint of **Pearson Education**

Harlow, England • London • New York • Boston • San Francisco • Toronto • Sydney • Singapore • Hong Kong
Tokyo • Seoul • Taipei • New Delhi • Cape Town • Madrid • Mexico City • Amsterdam • Munich • Paris • Milan

To Granny Murphy
1902–1996

Pearson Education Limited

Edinburgh Gate
Harlow
Essex CM20 2JE

and Associated Companies throughout the world.

Visit us on the World Wide Web at:
www.pearsoneduc.com

First published in 2003

ISBN 0 273 65506 X

British Library Cataloguing-in-Publication Data
A catalogue record for this book is available from the British Library

Library of Congress Cataloging-in-Publication Data
McGivern, Yvonne.
    The practice of market and social research : an introduction / Yvonne McGivern.
        p. cm.
    Includes bibliographical references and index.
    ISBN 0–273–65506–X (alk. paper)
        1. Marketing research--Methodology.   2. Social sciences--Research--Methodology.
    I. Title.
    HF5415.2 .M3827 2002
    001.4--dc21   2002027884

10 9 8 7 6 5 4 3 2 1
06 05 04 03

Typeset in 10/12.5pt Sabon by 68
Printed in Great Britain by Henry Ling Limited,
at the Dorset Press, Dorchester, DT1 1HD

Contents

Part II Getting started

Contents

Foreword

Whatever else we can say about the twenty-first century from the vantage point of its beginning, we can predict with certainty that information technology will be at the heart of its neural networks. Computers, telecommunications, the Internet, e-mail and mobile phones are all transforming the way we communicate. Applying scientific methods to the gathering of information, and applying and exercising professional standards in its interpretation and presentation lie at the heart of the market and social research process.

As President of The Market Research Society, I represent the most professional body of market and social researchers in the world. Nine out of the world's ten leading market research firms have British origins. Here is a field where we can claim world leadership. It is entirely appropriate that we should offer internationally a qualification – the MRS Advanced Certificate in Market and Social Research Practice – that sets a standard and a source of insights into best practice. This book reflects that standard and is targeted at those who wish to understand the processes and, in many cases, to join the profession.

I started my career as a professional market researcher. At that time, no such book as this existed. I can without hesitation recommend this volume – it will become the passport to an internationally-recognised qualification.

In the twenty-first century, I predict that knowledge will be power as never before. Those who deal in information will have power. The quality of that information and its responsible interpretation and diffusion will be at the heart of both marketing and social policy decision making.

No matter where in the world you live and work, The Market Research Society will welcome you to its membership, knowing that you have absorbed and been tested on the contents of this book.

Michael Thomas, OBE, OM(Poland)
President, The Market Research Society
Emeritus Professor of Marketing
Strathclyde University
Past Chairman, The Chartered Institute of Marketing

The Market Research Society

With over 8,000 members in more than 50 countries, The Market Research Society (MRS) is the world's largest international membership organisation for professional researchers. All members agree to comply with The MRS Code of Conduct.

The UK government's Qualifications and Curriculum Authority officially recognises the MRS as the awarding body for qualifications in market research. This volume supports the MRS Advanced Certificate in Market and Social Research Practice.

The MRS offers qualifications and membership grades at several levels, as well as training and professional development resources to support them. These include publications and information services, conferences and seminars, and a range of networking opportunities.

As the 'voice of the profession' in its media and public affairs efforts, the MRS seeks to achieve for researchers the most favourable climate of opinion and legislative environment.

Tel   020 7490 4911
Fax   020 7490 0608
Website **www.mrs.org.uk**

Preface

■ The aim of this book

The aim of this book is to provide a comprehensive and straightforward account of the practice of market and social research – the techniques and the day-to-day tasks of the researcher – that is both easy to read and easy to understand.

■ Who should use this book?

This book has been written specifically with The Market Research Society's Advanced Certificate in Market and Social Research Practice in mind. Since it is intended to provide a thorough introduction to the practice of market and social research, it is also suitable for undergraduates or postgraduates on business studies or marketing courses with a research component. In addition, undergraduates in social science courses should find it useful in providing an understanding of research methods. Research practitioners in the early stages of their careers should find it useful as a reference text and source of information on both method and practice.

■ Distinctive features

Comprehensive coverage

The book is comprehensive in its coverage. It covers not only research methods and techniques, such as sampling and questionnaire design, but also the tasks involved in starting a project – preparing a brief and writing a proposal; managing a project – briefing interviewers, preparing a coding frame and a data processing specification, for example; and finishing it off – preparing a report and presentation and evaluating the findings. It contains a chapter (Chapter 12) on the analysis of qualitative data, which few other market research texts cover in any detail. It looks at ethics and the practice of research, and the implications of data protection legislation on research. It includes examples from both market and social research.

Clear structure

The book is divided into three parts: Part I, Introducing market and social research; Part II, Getting started; and Part III, Getting on and finishing up. Part I provides an introduction to market and social research; Part II deals with getting a project up and running, from thinking about the research problem through to designing the questionnaire or discussion guide; and Part III deals with getting on and finishing up, from getting the project into the field to analysing, communicating and reviewing the findings and thinking about the ethical aspects of research practice.

MRS Advanced Certificate Syllabus

At the start of each chapter we show how the material in that chapter relates to The Market Research Society Advanced Certificate Syllabus.

Chapter summaries

To help reinforce the main points made, and to act as a revision tool, a summary at the end of each chapter lists the main points made in that chapter.

Questions and exercises

At the end of each chapter there are a series of questions and/or exercises designed to test knowledge and understanding of the topics covered in that chapter, and which can be used by the reader for self-study and in in-class discussions.

Recommended reading

Each chapter ends with a list of recommended reading, which provides more detail on the topics or issues covered in that chapter; further reading is also included in the bibliography.

Website

A range of support materials is available to lecturers and students on the website for this book **www.booksites.net/mcgivern**. It also contains suggested solutions to the questions and exercises in the book.

Instructor's Manual

An *Instructor's Manual*, written by the author, is available on the website to lecturers and tutors adopting the book. It follows the text closely. Each chapter contains a chapter summary, which can be used as a handout for students, as well as detailed examples and cases. Additional, detailed case studies are presented to illustrate key processes, techniques and applications. There are also exercises to illustrate the use and workings of the statistics covered in Chapter 13.

A Companion Website accompanies

The Practice of Market and Social Research

by Yvonne McGivern

Visit *The Practice of Market and Social Research* Companion Website at
www.booksites.net/mcgivern to find valuable teaching and learning material including:

For Students

➢ Study material designed to help you improve your results
➢ Learning outcomes for each chapter
➢ Multiple choice questions to test your understanding
➢ A search facility for specific information within the companion website

For Lecturers

➢ A secure, password protected site with teaching material
➢ A downloadable *Instructor's Manual*
➢ A syllabus manager that will build and host your very own course web page

Acknowledgements

A lot of people have been enormously helpful to me while I was writing this book. I would like to thank Paula Devine at Queen's University, Belfast and Lizanne Dowds at the University of Ulster, not only for the use of the Life and Times Survey material that appears throughout the book but also for their help and support, lunches and coffee. I would like to thank my colleagues and students on the MSc in Applied Social Research at Trinity College Dublin, especially Catherine Conlon (now at the National University of Ireland, University College Dublin) and Dr Evelyn Mahon, for their support and encouragement.

I am very grateful to a number of people at The Market Research Society: David Barr and Ruth Martin for permission to use extracts from the *Journal of the Market Research Society*; Samantha Driscoll for her help with information about the syllabus of The Market Research Society Advanced Certificate in Market Research Practice; Debrah Harding of the Professional Standards Committee for her selection of the Codeline queries; Bruce Love, editor of *Research* magazine, for permission to use extracts from the 'Job Specs' feature; and Jackie Lomas for her help in providing journal articles and conference papers, and to her predecessors, Lisa Jones and Nicola Potts.

I am very grateful to Raehaneh Ghazni, Managing Director of Acuity Computing Enterprise Technology, for her help with data processing issues and preparation of charts, and for her support and encouragement throughout. I would also like to thank Kate Dann, Managing Director of kd consulting, for taking the time to talk to me about the research job market. I would like to thank Petra van der Heijden, Director, Network Research and Marketing Ltd, for allowing me to use the extract on the sampling decision in a telephone survey. I would like to thank Bob Carroll, Director, National Council on Ageing and Older People (NCAOP) for permission to use an extract from an NCAOP publication. I would like to thank Simon Wieremiej of the British Market Research Association for sending me industry statistics. I would like to thank Gill Wareing of The Market Research Quality Standards Association for sending me details of the Interviewer Quality Control Scheme. Thanks are due also to Alison Park, Director, National Centre for Social Research, for permission to reproduce questions from British Social Attitudes' surveys.

I would also like to thank the reviewers – their suggestions were invaluable. I would like to thank Jacqueline Twyman and the team at Pearson – Lynn Brandon, Ernestine Weller, and Liz Tarrant – for their patience, help and support.

I would also like to thank Peter Carter, Managing Director of Consumer InSight, and Jeremy Green, Chief Executive, Hall & Partners, USA, for their patience, guidance and humour during my formative years as a researcher at Millward Brown.

Finally, and not least, I would like to thank my friends and family for putting up with me (and my excuses) during the writing of the book. I am hugely grateful for the support and encouragement of all of them, especially my mother Cora and my husband Barry.

Yvonne McGivern

Part I

Introducing market and social research

Chapter 1

The practice of market and social research

Introduction

The aim of this chapter is to provide an overview of research and the research industry. First of all, we examine the role of market and social research in business and society, its uses and its limitations. We look at the nature of the research industry and, in particular, the roles of the in-house and the agency researcher. Lastly, we look at the impact that technology has had on the practice of research.

Topics covered

➢ Definition of research
➢ The use and value of market and social research
➢ The research industry
➢ The impact of technology on research

Relationship to MRS Advanced Certificate Syllabus

The material covered in this chapter is relevant to Unit 1 – Introduction and Problem Definition, specifically the following:

➢ the role of market and social research;
➢ the role of the agency and the client;
➢ the role of the in-house researcher.

Learning outcomes

At the end of this chapter you should be able to:

➢ define the contribution of research;
➢ understand the limitations of research;
➢ understand the roles of the research supplier and the person commissioning research;
➢ understand the impact of technological developments on practice.

What is research?

Research is the process by which we produce knowledge. It is founded on scientific methods, which are in turn supported by philosophical principles about the nature of knowledge and how we construct that knowledge.

Box 1.1 A definition of research

The Market Research Society (MRS), the United Kingdom-based professional body for research practitioners, defines research as:

> 'The application of scientific research methods to obtain objective information on people's attitudes and behaviour based usually on representative samples of the relevant populations.'

The MRS, *Market Research: Guidance for Members* (September 2001)

Market and social research is about gathering and analysing data to explore, to describe, to measure, to understand and to explain. The practice of research involves not only collecting and analysing data but defining the problem to be researched, designing research which will provide the necessary evidence to address that problem, drawing a sample from the relevant population, and interpreting and applying the findings to the original problem.

Box 1.2 Terminology

Market research

In some texts a distinction is made between *market research* and *marketing research*. The term *marketing research* is sometimes regarded as the broader of the two and is used to refer to the activities involved in the gathering, recording and analysis of facts relating to the *marketing* process. *Market research*, on the other hand, is often used to refer to the process of researching specific *markets*. In practice, however, the terms are used interchangeably. Indeed most practitioners in Europe tend to use the term *market research* to cover a very broad spectrum of industrial, business-to-business, consumer and social research. The Market Research Society includes in its definition of market research *'all forms of marketing and social research'* and goes on to mention *'consumer and industrial surveys, psychological investigations, observational and panel studies'*. With such narrow terms for such a wide variety of investigations, there are many who believe the terms *market research* and *marketing research* inadequate, a poor representation of the service provided by the research industry. The MRS has toyed with the idea of changing its name and, although there are no immediate plans to do so, the debate continues.

Social research

Although social research is included in the MRS definition of market research, there are some who make a distinction between the two, indeed the distinction is made in the title of

Box 1.2 continued

this book. The distinction is based solely on the subject matter addressed – the nature of the problem and the context of the problem – and not because there are differences in method or approach. Both market and social research require the same clear thinking to define the problem. Both require an understanding of research design and research methods. Both involve the systematic collection and analysis of data. Both require skill and knowledge to draw out the implications of the findings.

The use and value of market and social research

In the last 15–20 years or so research has become a much more widespread activity. Where previously it had been used largely in the fast-moving consumer goods sector it is now commonplace in, among others, financial services, the business-to-business arena, and pharmaceuticals and healthcare. Indeed you only have to look through The MRS Research Buyers' Guide (**www.rbg.org.uk**) to see the current scope of market and social research applications. Organisations are listed that specialise in research on transport and distribution, training and education, sports, leisure and the arts, property and construction, policing, the environment, agriculture and farming, local and central government, politics, housing, employment, and information communication technologies. Research is a worldwide activity. For example, from the United Kingdom, which is a hub for many international, multi-country research projects, you can commission research in the Caribbean, Central Europe, Japan or South America just as easily as you can commission research in Manchester or Melton Mowbray.

Organisations, not just those in the private sector but those in the public and not-for-profit sectors, rely on research to inform and improve their planning and decision making. In all organisations resources are scarce. For an organisation to survive and prosper it must use its limited resources wisely. To do this effectively it must understand the needs and opinions of both its customers and other stakeholders (employees and shareholders, for example, in the case of private sector organisations, and citizens – taxpayers and voters – in the case of public sector organisations). This is where the value of market and social research lies: in its ability to provide high-quality information for planning and decision making. Research is typically only one source of data in very complex decision-making environments in which all sorts of other information sources – whose quality and value are often harder to assess – vie for attention. Decisions based on robust and credible research evidence should lead to better quality decision making, better use of resources, better products and services, better policies and better relationships with customers and other stakeholders, increased customer and stakeholder satisfaction and ultimately greater longevity for the organisation than if research were not conducted. Thus research influences what is provided and the way in which it is provided. It connects people with organisations whose products or services they use, or whose policies affect their lives, and so gives them a voice, a role, a degree of influence.

There is not always a direct link between research and financial success, especially in the short term. There is, however, evidence that organisations which spend more on research are more successful in the long run. Research is therefore perhaps best viewed as an investment and not as a cost.

■ The use of market research

For what kind of planning and decision making does market research provide data? It is worth taking a quick look at the marketing process to help answer this question.

Marketing process

The Chartered Institute of Marketing (**www.cim.co.uk**) defines the marketing process as '*the management process responsible for identifying, anticipating and satisfying customer requirements profitably*'. Although this management process may not be formalised, or even recognised, as marketing in some organisations, the task of identifying, anticipating and satisfying the needs of the customer exists nevertheless. A marketer's job is to seek out (business) opportunities – opportunities that will serve the interests of the organisation. When an opportunity is discovered, the marketer's role is to develop a *marketing plan* to apply the organisation's resources to achieving measurable *marketing objectives*, and so contribute to the organisation's goals. Marketing objectives are statements of what is to be achieved. For example, a marketing objective might be to launch a new savings account into the online banking market and to achieve a 5 per cent market share within a year; or to launch a new cancer screening service and achieve an uptake of 80 per cent of the target market.

In order to develop a marketing plan and set marketing objectives, marketers need a clear understanding of the environment in which they operate. They need to understand the wider external environment that is made up of or influenced by social (and cultural), legal, economic, political and technological factors (you may have come across these factors under the acronyms *SLEPT* or *PEST*), and the internal environment and resources of the organisation. They need a clear picture of both the opportunities and threats posed by the external environment and also of their organisation's strengths and weaknesses. The process of examining the external environment and the resources of the organisation is referred to as a *marketing audit*. The analysis of strengths and weaknesses, opportunities and threats is called a *SWOT analysis*.

Once a marketing audit and a SWOT analysis have been completed and a business opportunity established and evaluated, a marketing plan can be developed and marketing objectives set. To achieve the marketing objectives a *marketing strategy* is developed – a plan for achieving the objectives. This plan will involve defining the *marketing mix*, which consists of the four Ps: the *product* (or service) – its design, its features, its packaging; its *price*; how it will be *promoted* – advertising, direct mail, public relations and so on; and *place* – the distribution and sales channels, and the level of customer service. The marketer's task is to implement the marketing plan and monitor and evaluate its success in achieving the marketing objectives.

Not only are individual products and services marketed to customers but the organisation itself is marketed to its customers and to a wider audience of stakeholders, including employees and shareholders, in the case of private sector organisations, and taxpayers and voters, among others, in the case of public sector organisations.

Think of all the information needs – the research needs – that this marketing process involves if it is to be done effectively, if the goal of marketing – to '*identify, anticipate and satisfy customer requirements profitably*' – is to be met. Market research can be used to achieve the following:

➢ understand the wider environment and how it affects the organisation;
➢ identify opportunities and threats;
➢ identify markets, competitors and customers;
➢ help with priority setting and direct the use of resources;
➢ build knowledge for longer-term benefit;
➢ understand customers and market dynamics;
➢ monitor customer and stakeholder satisfaction;
➢ understand how to build and enhance customer relationships;
➢ monitor and evaluate competitors/competitive activity;
➢ identify or monitor market changes and trends;
➢ develop marketing strategies;
➢ test different marketing strategies;
➢ monitor and control marketing programmes;
➢ understand how to influence customer attitudes and behaviour;
➢ understand how best to communicate with customers and stakeholders;
➢ develop advertising and communication strategies;
➢ develop and test advertising executions; and
➢ develop or select a product or service, a brand name, a pack design, a price point, a distribution channel.

More specifically, market research might be commissioned to do the following:

➢ measure customer satisfaction with the service provided by a bank;
➢ understand buying behaviour in the car market;
➢ describe the use of anti-perspirants and deodorants among men; or
➢ determine if there is a relationship between lifestyle characteristics and purchasing patterns of organic food.

■ The use of social research

Social research is commissioned for much the same reason as market research – to obtain information, to understand what is going on in the wider environment, to understand people's attitudes, opinions and behaviour – in order to provide data for effective planning and decision making in relation to policy development and implementation. In social research, the wider external environment is society, the attitudes of interest are 'social' attitudes, attitudes to 'social issues', and the behaviour of interest is how we live and behave in the 'social' world. Social research might be commissioned, for example, to describe the living standards of older people in the community, or to understand decisions taken during a crisis pregnancy, or to explore drug use in prisons or to establish the healthcare needs of homeless people.

The need for high-quality information is no less important in this arena than it is in the commercial arena. Plans and decisions have to made about how our society operates, about how we deal with 'social issues', about how we allocate scarce resources, about what services should be provided, how they should be designed and to whom they should be targeted. The plans and decisions might relate to provision of health services or education or environmental policy, for example. These plans and decisions about policy and public service provision are nowadays subject to scrutiny and may require justification. They should therefore be based on robust, defensible evidence; the best way of providing that evidence is via objective research.

Social research is commissioned by government departments, public bodies, public services, local government, non-governmental organisations, charities, policy studies groups, the media, think tanks, academia and research institutes. The topics are many and varied, and include social care, crime, transport, leisure and the arts, work and family life, housing, labour force participation, training and skills needs.

■ The limitations of research

The value of research depends on its providing actionable, insightful, high-quality information for the decision-making process. What limits its value? Research is only of value if it fulfils its purpose – if it provides information and knowledge that contribute to the planning and decision-making process. Research is a means to an end, not an end in itself. It will be of use only if it is based on a clear understanding of what problems or issues it is to address, and what kind of information is needed on which to make effective decisions. In fact, there are many factors that limit the value of a piece of research, including the following:

> poor definition of the problem;
> lack of understanding of the brief;
> poor or inappropriate research design;
> the limitations of the methods used;
> poor execution of the research itself;
> the interpretation of the results;
> the status of knowledge;
> the use or misuse of research evidence by the decision makers;
> the time that elapses between collecting the data and applying the findings.

Poor definition of the problem

A clear and accurate statement or definition of the problem is essential if the research is to provide useful information for the decision-making process (Bijapurkar, 1995). Good quality research is relatively easy to carry out but it all means nothing if it does not address the problem or issue under investigation. It will not be able to address the problem if it is not clear what the problem is. A key skill for a researcher is to be able to define or to help the client define the problem to be researched. To do this effectively the researcher must understand the wider context of the problem and the decision to be made on the basis of the research evidence, including the factors that may affect the implementation or action to be taken as a result of the research findings.

Lack of understanding of the brief

If the researcher fails to understand what the research must deliver, or misinterprets what is needed, he or she may design research that is inappropriate and so of little or no value. The researcher is responsible for making sure that he or she understands the brief (Pyke, 2000), and understands what evidence is needed from the research. The person commissioning the research has a responsibility to ensure that the brief is clear and unambiguous.

Poor or inappropriate research design

The value of any research will be limited by the research design – by its suitability in providing the kind of evidence needed to address the problem. If the research design is poor, the research will be of little value. Good research design is dependent on a clear and accurate definition of the problem and a clear understanding of the research brief. For example, if the client needs to know how effective its advertising campaign is in delivering messages about its brand to its target audience, conducting a one-off study after the first burst of advertising spend may not provide appropriate evidence. A more effective design, one that might provide more robust evidence, may be to track attitudes to the brand over a longer period of time.

The limitations of the methods used

The data collected will only be as a good as the methods used to collect them. If, for example, you need a detailed, in-depth understanding of women's facial cleansing routines, the data collected via a telephone interview may be limited; it may be more appropriate to use qualitative methods – interviews and observation – to get at the sort of understanding needed.

Poor execution of the research itself

Research can be badly executed. Errors can arise in questionnaire design, in fieldwork, in data processing and in data analysis. For example, a badly worded question, a failure to brief interviewers in the handling of probes and prompts to survey questions, a failure to brief coders in how to code respondents' answers may all lead to poor quality data.

The interpretation of the results

Research data and research findings can be misinterpreted, and any misinterpretation limits the value of the research. The researcher must guard against any possible misinterpretation by making sure that he or she clearly understands how to analyse and read the data (quantitative or qualitative) in an objective and systematic way, in a way that is free of bias.

The status of knowledge

Research does not produce 'right answers' – the findings from any research are always partial and contingent, and dependent on context (Shipman, 1997). Knowledge is not 'value free' – it is influenced by the social and cultural context in which it was collected, and by the view of the respondent and by the researcher designing the study and collecting and interpreting the data. Although we strive to conduct objective research we can never be completely objective – our ways of knowing and finding out about things are always filtered through our own way of thinking and our way of seeing and knowing the world. Throughout the research process – in designing and conducting research as well as interpreting and using it – we need to be aware of these possible sources of bias, and their influence.

The use or misuse of research evidence by the decision makers

The value of research also lies in how or whether the findings are used. They may be used well or badly, or they may be ignored. They may be ignored for a number of reasons – the decision makers may simply not believe them, or may not believe that they are valid or reliable; they may find them hard to understand, or unconvincing, or irrelevant; or they may fail to see how they could be used. Research findings are not always clear-cut – they can be inconclusive, which may limit their use, or lead to the wrong decision being taken. An organisation's internal political issues may affect the use, misuse or non-use of the research findings. In ensuring that the value of any research is maximised, these issues need to be addressed before the research begins. It is important to clarify with the decision makers at the outset what they want from the research, what they think it will deliver, what they plan to do with the research findings, how they envisage using them, and what decisions are to be made on the basis of the research. The researcher has a role in managing the expectations of the research buyer in terms of what the research can and cannot provide.

Time

The time that elapses between collecting the data and applying the research findings can limit the value of the research. Data become out of date – the passage of time erodes the value of research simply because the data are time dependent.

■ Research buyers' views of the research product

The environment in which research operates is constantly evolving. For the research industry to stay healthy and grow, to improve the service it offers, it should be aware of and understand its customers' needs, and their perceptions of the products and services it offers. So, what do research buyers think are the limitations or the weaknesses of the service provided by researchers? In discussions with research managers and research users, and from a review of the literature, Bairfelt and Spurgeon (1998) found that research often did not meet expectations. They found that research buyers perceived that it was not well managed, that findings were poorly presented, and that it failed to deliver value for money. Interviews with research users in

Spurgeon's organisation, Shell, revealed a perception that too few researchers are *'commercially oriented'* and most have little knowledge of or interest in the way the client's business works; they would rather focus on data than insights and implications. In addition, it was felt that the data produced are *'nice to know but not directly actionable'* and tend to be historical, not future focused. Research is perceived to be a discipline of *'black box techniques'* and the research process *'shrouded in mystery'*. It is viewed as lacking creativity in design and delivery – the output (and the way it is presented) seen as *'too often dull and uninspiring'*. Kreinczes (1990) believes that the market research industry holds *'a production rather than a marketing orientation, ...concentrated on selling what it makes, rather than on what its customers want to buy'*. He believes that researchers *'need a greater degree of insight, creativity, innovation and individual responsibility: a greater degree of pride of ownership in the results; a genuine, burning desire to champion the findings'*. Bijapurkar (1995) believes that market research is of less value in helping decision makers with more fundamental, strategic decisions. In order to contribute better to these sort of decisions, Bijapurkar argues that researchers should improve their problem-definition skills and their understanding of the business context of the decision, and learn to look to the future rather than describe the present.

So what is to be learnt from all this research on research? It is clear that the value and the perception of research can be enhanced by turning data into information and knowledge. This means paying attention to drawing out the implications of the research findings, and interpreting the findings in the context of the client's business environment, rather than just presenting data. This of course is predicated on the client and the researcher working together to provide a clear and accurate definition of the problem, and on the client providing the researcher with information about how the research findings are to be used. The client or research buyer should ensure that the researcher has access to the necessary information about his or her business that will allow the researcher to produce the level of insight expected (Pyke, 2000). The findings should be presented in an interesting way, a way that will engage the client's interest, and in a way that demystifies the research process.

The research industry

Research is a worldwide business. In 2000 the total market for market research was estimated at $15 billion or €16 billion, according to the European Society for Opinion and Market Research (ESOMAR). The world's three largest economies, the United States, Japan and Germany, account for more than half of this spend: the United States with 39 per cent and Japan and Germany with 8 per cent each. Despite being a smaller economy than either Japan or Germany, the United Kingdom is a bigger market for research – it accounts for 11 per cent of the total world market. France, the fifth largest economy, is also the fifth largest research market, with 6 per cent of the total. Overall, European Union (EU) member states account for 36 per cent of the research market; Europe as a whole accounts for 39 per cent; North America for 42 per cent; Asia Pacific for 14 per cent; and Central and South America for 5 per cent of the total.

■ Market structure

In recent years the trend in the research industry has been towards specialisation in techniques and fields of research, the development of branded products and services, and the ability to offer global, standardised services and products. This has led to a consolidation in the market, enabling organisations to benefit from economies of scale and allowing them access to capital to support the increasing levels of investment, particularly in technology, necessary to compete in the global market-place. This consolidation has meant that there is a relatively small number of very large research organisations. ESOMAR's annual industry study (2001) shows that in 2000 58 per cent of worldwide research revenues were captured by 25 organisations employing almost 73,000 full-time staff. The top six organisations in this ranking – ACNielsen Corporation, IMS Health Inc., The Kantar Group, Taylor Nelson Sofres plc, Information Resources Inc. and VNU Inc. – account for 45 per cent of the total revenue of the top 25 and employ almost 49,000 people full time.

■ Applications and methods

In the United Kingdom, according to British Market Research Association (BMRA) estimates for 2001, quantitative research takes the largest share of the market with about 85 per cent of total turnover among BMRA members. The top five applications of quantitative research were in the consumer research sector: advertising or brand awareness monitoring/tracking; new product development and concept testing; customer satisfaction; market measurement; and usage and attitude studies. The most common application of qualitative research was new product development and concept testing. In second place, but a long way behind in terms of turnover, were usage and attitude studies.

The most widely used methods in quantitative data collection, according to BMRA figures for 2001, were, in terms of the number of respondents interviewed, postal/self-completion, followed by face-to-face interviews, with telephone interviews in third place. The BMRA figures show that in 2001 about 77 per cent of telephone interviews were conducted using computer-aided rather than paper-based methods but only 9 per cent of hall or central location interviews and 20 per cent of other face-to-face interviews were conducted this way.

Group discussions were the most widely used qualitative method of data collection. Mystery shopping and other observation techniques, while they accounted for a sizeable proportion in terms of respondent numbers – more than double the number involved in groups and depth interviews – generated a much smaller turnover. According to BMRA figures web and Internet interviewing in 2001 represented 0.5 per cent of the total research turnover of its members and 1.5 per cent of all respondents interviewed.

■ Subject matter

BMRA figures show that the food sector spent the most on research in 2001, followed by non-over-the-counter pharmaceuticals, the financial sector, the broadcast media, health and beauty and vehicle manufacturers. Making up the rest of the top ten were retailers, public services, government and telecommunications. Combining public services research and government research, however, moves them up to second place.

■ Research roles

There are effectively three main roles in the research process – research supplier, research buyer and research user. The research supplier, as the name suggests, is the person who supplies the research. The supplier is typically responsible for the research design, for overseeing its execution and for reporting the findings to the research buyer and/or the research user. The research buyer, as the name suggests, buys or commissions research data or research expertise from a source either inside the organisation – for example from the marketing planning or marketing services department or the research department – or from outside the organisation – for example from a research agency or research consultant. In some organisations the research buyer is also the research user. For example, research may be commissioned by a brand manager or a marketing director, by a planner in an advertising agency, or by a policymaker in the public sector. In other organisations the research user might commission research via an intermediary, an internal or in-house researcher, for example, a research manager, a marketing planner or a consumer insight executive – someone from within the organisation who either conducts the research or briefs an external organisation to conduct it. Below we look at the role of the client or in-house researcher, the different types of research supplier, the roles within a research agency and, in particular, the role of a research executive.

Clientside roles

The clientside research role will depend on the type of organisation, the nature of its business and the way it views research. Some organisations no longer have a market research department. There may be several reasons for this; it may be as a result of any of the following:

> cost cutting and 'downsizing' in times of economic hardship;
> a merger or acquisition that led to excess capacity;
> changing business practices that have led to outsourcing research services; or
> the integration of the market research function into a broader function involving, for example, information or knowledge management, or product or brand management.

While in some organisations client researchers find themselves in a fairly traditional market research department, others now belong in this broader function and job titles (and roles) reflect this. A scan of the job advertisements in the trade press demonstrates the variety of clientside roles. There are still advertisements for market research managers, market research controllers, marketing planning managers, brand planners and information managers, but there are increasing numbers of advertisements for customer insight managers and insight analysts. Many organisations have reorganised to ensure that the customer is the focus of their business, with the result that research and market planning functions have been renamed and, to some extent, reconfigured, as customer or consumer insight. In some cases this may be a change in name only, in order to refocus or redefine the research role. In others it reflects a change in the traditional research role, in recognition of the need to manage and use data from a variety of sources, including scanner data and geodemographic data, for example, not just traditional market research data. In some organisations researchers are now involved in the earlier stages of the business or marketing process, at the development of ideas and opportunities, rather than at a later stage when formal research is being commissioned. A result of these changes is that those recruited to such roles need more than research and project management skills and an ability to work with information from a variety of sources besides market research. They also need an understanding of business practice and business processes, an understanding of how business objectives are formulated and how the information can be applied to formulating the objectives and developing the strategy to achieve these objectives.

The day-to-day job of an in-house researcher

The in-house researcher or the customer insight executive may be responsible for research and insight into a particular market or product or service area. The job is likely to involve liaising with or working alongside decision makers, for example in marketing, sales, production or policy formulation. It may involve an internal consultancy role, advising on the use of research and ensuring that research insights are integrated into the business planning process – in effect ensuring that research and other data are converted to information and knowledge and applied effectively to move the business forward. The role may involve providing guidance and advice to internal data analysts;

Box 1.3 Job Specs: the view from the clientside

Market research executive

Name: **Sarah Cosby**
Company: **Whitbread plc**
Job title: **Market research executive, group market research department**

How long have you been in the post? Just over two years

What previous posts have you held? After graduating I worked and travelled in Canada and the US for seven months. I then got a temporary post as research assistant at my old university...I took off for another 15 months, working and travelling in various countries.

What does the job entail? Group market research acts as a kind of internal market research agency. We refer to the internal Whitbread people as our 'clients' . . . With quant, upon receiving a brief from a client I write a full market research proposal. I then commission an outside agency to conduct the field and tab work. I spec the entire job and do the analysis, then present the findings back to the client. With qual, again I design and manage the entire research process. I write a proposal and discussion guide following a brief from a client. My research responsibilities include lager brands such as

Box 1.3 continued

Stella Artois and Heineken and restaurant brands including Bella Pasta and TGI Friday's. I am also responsible for the admin and *ad hoc* analysis of our continuous communications tracking study on behalf of Whitbread Beer Company.

What is the most enjoyable part of the job? I get most satisfaction when I am involved from the beginning of a project through to the final presentation. It's interesting to hear the client's interpretation of the market's issues and discovering how the consumers actually perceive them. The variety of brands and clients makes the job enjoyable as two days are never the same. As I work in a close environment with clients and colleagues, I have established good working relationships. It also allows for sharing knowledge, best practice and new ways of doing things.

Is there anything you would change about the job if you could? Time is the biggest frustration. I often find that I am carrying out a project to such short deadlines that I am unable to burrow deep into the data to discover if there are any alternative ways of interpretation. Although I enjoy working on a wide range of brands, it can also be frustrating having to switch attention between projects depending on clients' demands.

Source: *Research Magazine*, July 1999. Interview by Sylma Etienne. Used with permission.

On secondment

Name: **Annette Wright**
Company: **NOP Research. Currently on secondment at Ford Motor Company**
Job title: **SVC Speciality Products Insight Manager**

How long have you been at Ford? 20 months.

What were you doing previously? I was working on a major international continuous study with NOP Automotive.

What does your role involve? Working with internal clients from marketing and product development, planning and implementing research input to new product development.

What do you like about being seconded to a client? Working closely with my clients, getting to know them and what they need from research; seeing how the company uses research, and developing long-term research plans; seeing the bigger picture rather than just one research project at a time; and I love the work – being a part of developing the cars of the future is very exciting.

What do you hope to gain from the experience? I hope to know my clients better and what they want from the research; to be able to better support them, anticipate their needs, understand the pressures they face on a daily basis, and design research with actionable results and recommendations; and to gain the insight that will enable me to exceed my clients' expectations.

Source: *Research Magazine*, April 2000. Interview by Nathalie Watkins. Used with permission.

it may involve managing and developing databases and decision support systems. The role is also likely to involve providing and/or commissioning research, managing the research process, and managing the relationship with the research supplier. Have a look at the job descriptions in Box 1.3.

Types of research supplier

Research suppliers can be divided into three broad groups: full service agencies, specialist suppliers, and limited service suppliers. Full service agencies offer a full research service in qualitative research or quantitative research or both, supplying everything from research design, fieldwork and data processing to analysis and reporting of the findings and their implications. Specialist suppliers are those that specialise in a particular data collection method, for example telephone research; or those that specialise in a particular market sector, for example pharmaceuticals, media or business-to-business research; or those that specialise in a particular technique, for example consumer panels, mystery shopping or product testing. There is some overlap between categories – for example, qualitative research agencies may be considered to be specialist suppliers; those specialising in particular quantitative methods or in particular sectors or techniques may also be full service agencies. There are various kinds of limited service suppliers, suppliers that specialise in a particular part of the research process, usually fieldwork only (including recruitment for qualitative research) or data processing only or both – known as field and tab – or in statistical analysis. There are those – usually independent consultants – who provide research advice, research design, project management, qualitative fieldwork, data interpretation and reporting services.

Roles within a research agency

Most full service research agencies and most specialist agencies will have a client service department, a field department and a data processing department. Each of these services can be provided as a stand-alone service, and as we saw above limited service agencies are those that specialise in one or more of these. Within each of these departments or service functions there will be executives at different levels of seniority. These executives will have different titles depending on custom and practice within the organisation. The most common, in order of increasing seniority, are research executive or field or data processing executive; senior executive; research or field or data processing manager; associate director; perhaps even senior associate director; and director. Within an organisation's fieldforce there are interviewers, supervisors and area managers or area controllers. In the data processing department there are data entry and coding staff as well as data processing executives.

Box 1.4 The role of the agency research executive

The main duties of a research executive are to carry out the following:

➢ liaise with the client;
➢ help define the problem or issue to be researched;
➢ design the research;
➢ cost the research;
➢ write the proposal;
➢ discuss the proposal with the client and with colleagues;
➢ design the discussion guide or questionnaire;
➢ set up the research and manage it;

Box 1.4 continued

➢ conduct a pilot study;
➢ refine the research plan/questionnaire or discussion guide in the light of the findings from the pilot study;
➢ brief the fieldwork team or the recruiters;
➢ brief the data processing team including coders;
➢ prepare stimulus material (qualitative researchers);
➢ liaise with field staff on progress of the work;
➢ attend (or conduct, in the case of qualitative research) fieldwork;
➢ prepare an analysis plan;
➢ write the analysis specification for data processing;
➢ check the data tabulations for accuracy;
➢ analyse and interpret the data;
➢ prepare a report of the findings and/or a presentation;
➢ give the presentation, drawing out the implications for the client;
➢ take part in follow-up discussions with the client;
➢ organise archiving and storage of project documents.

The client service role

The job of the client service department and so the job of a research executive involves managing and being a part of the client's research business. Obviously, responsibility for various aspects of the business and the level of involvement will vary with seniority, and will depend on the size of the research team and the nature of the project. Basically, however, the job involves everything from the research briefing stage (and

Box 1.5 Job Specs: the view from the agency

The graduate trainee

Name: **Gemma Phillips**
Company: **ACNielsen**
Job title: **Account executive**

How long have you been in the post: Ten months

What does the job entail? Everyday client contact, helping to understand their business and key objectives in order to identify opportunities for ACNielsen products and services. I have responsibility for three accounts at present that I develop with the help of my other team members. I also give support on larger accounts as and when required . . .

Most enjoyable part of the job? I enjoy presenting . . . At the moment I am working towards my board presentation, which requires presenting internally as practice . . . Once I have passed the board I can then present to clients. Helping clients understand their position and being able to offer services to enhance their analysis is a satisfying area of the job and one that I enjoy developing. Working within teams is a good situation as it allows you to develop with others and feel constantly secure.

Box 1.5 continued

Anything about the job you would change if you could? There is a lot of company jargon and if there was any way of learning the terminology as quickly as possible I would love to know!

Source: *Research Magazine*, September 1999. Interview by Nathalie Watkins. Used with permission.

The senior research executive

Name: **Anne Kazimirski**
Company: **ORC International**
Job title: **Senior research executive, public sector**

How long have you worked for your employer? I have been in the Public Sector division of the company for over a year. Previously I was at Research International for just under two years. I started there as a graduate trainee.

What does your job entail? I am managing and helping to manage projects on education and employment for central government departments and agencies. I am also working on a project for the NHS. The research varies widely in methodology, from mystery shopping to qualitative interviews. Project management includes liaising with clients and our field-work departments, and conducting the interviews. I am often out of the office for client meetings or interviews.

What are the most enjoyable aspects of your job? Getting positive feedback from clients on completed work, the presentation of results and working with a variety of people.

Is there anything you'd like to change about it? We don't always find out what actions are taken in response to results. It would be nice to have more feedback, or have more time to follow up projects.

Source: *Research Magazine*, August 2001. Interview by Yvette Mackenzie. Used with permission.

sometimes before it) through to the delivery of the research findings (and sometimes beyond). In addition to this project management/client-facing role, the research executive may be involved in preparing new business sales pitches and in internal development work. Also, some of his or her time may be devoted to keeping up to date with developments in research practice.

Roles within the data processing service

The data processing (DP) department or DP service provider typically consists of a team of data processing executives or programmers (scriptwriters who write the questionnaires for computer-aided interviewing; specification writers who write the programs for running tables and analysis) and data entry and coding staff, all managed by a data processing manager, who in turn may report to a DP director. In addition, there may be executives with specialist statistical expertise and those with specialist IT knowledge.

The coding section of a DP department is responsible for the development of code lists or coding frames from the open-ended questions on a questionnaire. Most quantitative studies will include some open-ended questions, such as 'Please explain why. . . ' . The responses given to these questions must be coded – individual elements of a response to a particular question extracted from all questionnaires, listed under a heading and assigned a numeric code in order to be entered into the analysis package and appear in tabulations. We look in more detail at how to prepare a coding frame in Chapter 11. The research executive provides the coder with a brief on how responses are to be treated – guidance on how to construct the coding frame. The coder liaises with the research executive and the DP executive or manager about a study's coding needs in order to plan how the coding is to be organised and completed accurately and on time for the data processing schedule.

The next stage in data processing involves data entry and data verification. If data capture has involved computer-aided methods the data entry stage is not needed. During the data collection process the interviewer or the respondent enters responses directly into the computer. The data are therefore already held in electronic form and can be downloaded into an analysis package. If, however, paper-based methods are used to collect the data – data are recorded on a paper questionnaire – then the data must be transferred from the questionnaire to the computer analysis package. This data entry process is conducted either by computer operators experienced in touch-typing alphanumeric data or by electronically scanning the questionnaires. (To use scanning technology, however, requires that the questionnaire be designed in a way that the scanner can read.) Once the data have been entered verification takes place – to ensure that codes from the questionnaire have not been incorrectly entered.

Data processing executives write, test and implement the programs necessary for data capture, data entry, verification, and those for producing data tabulations and statistical calculations. The research executive prepares an analysis specification (sometimes called a tab spec or a DP spec) that sets out for the DP executive how the data are to be coded, tabulated and analysed and what statistical tests or special analyses are to be conducted. We look in detail at how to prepare a DP specification in Chapter 11. On the basis of this specification the DP executive writes the program that will produce the tables and the necessary analysis. In addition, in some larger agencies, DP executives may be involved in software development, including database design.

The role of the DP manager is to manage the workload of the DP department and liaise with clients and researchers about their needs. He or she may be involved in preparing costings for data processing tasks. The DP manager may be responsible for quality control and is likely to be involved in recruiting, training and supervising staff. He or she may have responsibility for managing a DP budget. The DP director is responsible for the success of the DP operation, for overall quality control, business development, keeping up to date with developments in technology and for implementing systems that will deliver to the needs of the clients and researchers.

Roles within the fieldwork service

The field executive's role involves preparing fieldwork costings, liaising with research executives on questionnaire design and on sample design and selection of sampling points, and setting up and managing fieldwork. Fieldwork management involves allocating work, setting quotas for the number of interviews to be completed per interviewer day, preparing briefing notes for interviewers, running briefing and training sessions, and checking on the progress of fieldwork. It may also include attending fieldwork or supervising fieldwork, administering interviewer pay, training and recruiting interviewers, and generally managing the fieldforce.

Depending on the size of the organization, the size of the fieldforce and the volume of fieldwork conducted, the field executive's role may be more differentiated, to the extent that some of these tasks are conducted by specialists. For example, there may be a dedicated interviewer trainer; a dedicated fieldwork allocator; there may be an administrator who deals mostly with interviewer pay claims and fieldwork expenses.

If international, multi-country research is involved an international fieldwork co-ordinator may be part of the field or client service team, or part of a separate international co-ordination unit. The role of a co-ordinator is to ensure that the fieldwork in each country is conducted to the same standards. This will involve liaising with in-market fieldwork suppliers, ensuring that those conducting the fieldwork are fully briefed about the project requirements and perhaps even training local in-market fieldworkers. It will involve checking that questionnaires and discussion guides are adapted to suit the market and that they, together with all related material, are translated accurately. Back-translation, that is, retranslating into the original language, is often carried out to ensure that any meaning is not lost or distorted as a result of translation. The co-ordinator will also check that question-naires and discussion guides in different languages are measuring the same thing. The role may also involve briefing research executives to ensure that they are aware of the environmental factors – cultural, social, economic, technological, legal and political – that will affect how the research is conducted or the data obtained. The co-ordinator may also be involved in overseeing the handling of the data at the end of fieldwork, and the processing of the data, including retranslation of responses to open-ended questions and translations of transcripts of focus groups and depth interviews.

■ Professional bodies and trade associations

The market research industry and the market research profession are served by a number of professional bodies and trade associations that aim to promote high standards in research practice and represent the research industry to the wider world.

The Market Research Society

The Market Research Society (www.mrs.org.uk), based in the United Kingdom, is the largest international membership organisation for professional researchers and those engaged in, or interested in, market, social and opinion research. It was founded in 1946 and has more than 8,000 researchers in more than 50 countries. It aims to ensure that professional standards are maintained, to offer members training and professional development services, and to represent the interests of the profession to the wider world. Its members agree to comply with the MRS Code of Conduct. The MRS offers various qualifications and membership grades, as well as training and professional development resources to support these. The UK government's Qualifications and Curriculum Authority officially recognises the MRS as the awarding body for qualifications in market research.

ESOMAR

The European Society for Opinion and Market Research (ESOMAR) (**www.esomar.nl**), founded in 1948, is the body that represents research professionals worldwide. It aims to promote the use of research for improving decision making in business and society. Its members agree to comply with the International Chambers of Commerce (ICC)/ESOMAR International Code of Marketing and Social Research Practice. It has about 4,000 members in 100 countries. Membership is open to anyone who is actively involved in marketing and opinion research.

The Association for Qualitative Research

The Association for Qualitative Research (**www.aqr.org.uk**) has almost 1,200 individual members. It aims to promote qualitative research within the research industry and in the wider business environment. It organises training in order to raise the standard of research practice.

The Social Research Association

The Social Research Association (**www.the-sra.org.uk**) has around 850 individual members. It aims to advance the conduct, development and application of social research.

The British Market Research Association

The British Market Research Association (**www.bmra.org.uk**) is the industry trade body for UK research organisations. It has a membership of some 220. It offers a service called Selectline that aims to match the needs of buyers with a suitable research supplier.

The Association of Users of Research Agencies

The Association of Users of Research Agencies is a body representing organisations in the United Kingdom that buy research on their own behalf. It has about 130 corporate members. It aims to promote the use of market research, and to exchange experiences and information about research agencies and services.

European bodies

There are several pan-European trade associations, including the Association of European Market Research Institutes (AEMRI) (**www.aemri.org**), which represents market research agencies in 36 countries; and the European Federation of Associations of Market Research Organizations (EFAMRO) (**www.efamro.org**), which includes the national associations of Sweden, Denmark, Germany, France, the Netherlands, Belgium, the United Kingdom, Italy, Spain, Portugal and the Czech Republic.

The impact of technology on research

The practice of research, concerned as it is with collecting, processing and communicating information, has been greatly affected by innovations in information and communication technologies. The successful implementation of technological innovations, in computing and telephony in particular, has led to greater efficiency in the use of resources. It has resulted in changes in work practices – from office to field functions, from setting up and administering research to processing the data and disseminating the findings. It has resulted in greater productivity and shorter project turnaround times, enabled multi-site and remote working and increased the ease of internal and external communication and co-ordination.

Box 1.6 The impact of technology

Technology has had the greatest impact on the following:

➢ project administration and set-up;
➢ communication and interaction;
➢ sampling;
➢ data capture;
➢ data management:
    ➢ data processing and analysis;
    ➢ data storage and retrieval;
    ➢ data fusion and data mining;
➢ research design.

■ Project administration and set-up

As computing power has increased and become cheaper to acquire, the impact on research has been the ability to process, and process more efficiently, greater volumes of data and to conduct more complex analyses. As more computing power is contained in ever smaller and more portable devices, there has been a move away from traditional paper-based data collection methods to computer-aided methods. As a result, fieldwork is easier to manage and co-ordinate, turnaround times have been reduced, and there have been improvements in the speed and accuracy of data processing.

■ Communication and interaction

User-friendly software and hardware have made it easier to produce high-quality documents – briefs, proposals, questionnaires, stimulus material, data tables, reports and presentations – and to alter these documents easily, leading to greater efficiency. In addition, technology that allows us to include spoken commentary from the researcher, and/or audio and video clips, for example from group discussions or of test advertisements, can enhance the value and impact of reports and presentations.

The standardisation of software and hardware, coupled with advances in transmission and communication capabilities (connectivity and interactivity), has led to an increase in access to and use of the Internet, intranets and peer-to-peer computing to disseminate data and documents, and to interact in real time via online conferencing and video links with anyone with a PC anywhere in the world. Rather than travel to presentations or group discussions (or interviews in the case of respondents) executives can join in from anywhere.

■ Sampling

Developments in the last 20 or so years in how census data are handled have had a major impact on sampling and survey techniques. Advances in technology have meant that census data are now more manageable and accessible than ever to researchers wishing to construct representative samples of the population. For example, via the UK Census Dissemination Unit (CDU) website (**http://census.ac.uk/cdu**) you can get access to census data and to data visualisation tools. Census data are available electronically on their own and, thanks to technological developments, in combination with other data, including geographic data. For example, small area statistics (SAS), data at the smallest geographic unit in the census (including data on housing type, age, social class and employment status, for example) are combined with data from geographic information systems (GIS), data that tell us where people live, to produce geodemographic data. Geodemographic classifications have proved particularly useful in sampling and analysis – they are often better at predicting consumer and social behaviour than single variables or combinations of variables that do not include a geographic component.

■ Data capture

Advances in technology based around optical mark readers or scanning devices and personal computers have had a major impact on data capture. Advances in voice recognition, wireless communication and the convergence of the PC, the television and the telephone in the form of interactive television are beginning to do the same.

Scanning technology and computer-aided data capture

The use of scanning technology (optical mark readers) has meant that data from specially designed questionnaires can be read directly into a computer, without the need for manual data entry. The use of computer-aided data capture technology – essentially programs that combine questionnaire, data entry and verification functions – has taken this a step further and made the data collection and data handling task more flexible, faster and more efficient, more accurate and easier to manage than paper-based methods. There is less manual work involved with no need to print or dispatch questionnaires, and no separate data entry or verification procedures. Until recently the capital investment in PCs and laptops on which to run such programs could be substantial. The cost of entry, however, has dropped as devices have become smaller and those of all sizes have become less expensive. Indeed, the use of handheld devices such as personal digital assistants (PDAs) and computer tablets is increasing.

Technological advances and the increased penetration of Internet users have led to growth in web and email data collection methods, including electronic observation and tracking. These methods, however, account for a relatively small proportion of all data collected. An increase in their use is likely to come from business-to-business and employee research, where access to the Internet or an intranet is relatively easy, where the method is a convenient and suitable one for approaching respondents, and where information on populations (from which to derive suitable samples) is more readily obtained.

Transmitting data

Transmission devices such as the modem, wireless technology and peer-to-peer technology mean that data captured by computer or PDA can be transferred or downloaded to a central server or processor at any time, regardless of the location of fieldwork. Fieldwork managers can thus check on progress, monitor strike rates and interview length, sampling and interviewer quotas, and interviewers' workloads. In addition, downloading data as work is in progress means that data processing staff can begin the coding process, and set up and run tables earlier than would be the case with traditional paper-based methods. Advances in wireless technology and its application in computer-aided wireless interviewing (CAWI) mean that there is no need for connections via modems or telephone lines in order to transmit data or fieldwork instructions: transmission can take place via an 'always-on' wireless connection to a server or local area network within a certain radius of the device. In addition, CAWI devices can be used to conduct research online without the need to be physically connected to a telephone line, giving increased flexibility in conducting this type of research.

Voice recognition technology

Voice recognition technology is available that enables automated, interactive voice response interviewing in which spoken responses are converted to text. Although advances have been made in recent years to improve recognition accuracy, the method is suitable only for very basic interactions. Until it improves further it is unlikely to gain wide acceptance as a method of data collection among respondents or researchers.

The software, however, is used by some to transcribe tapes from qualitative interviews, although it does not always produce transcripts of a very high quality. The availability of audio-engineering, especially noise reduction technology, is useful in cleaning up audio and video tapes, making the use of speech to text software and traditional transcribing easier. The technology works by removing or reducing background noise and enhancing speech. Recordings can be downloaded to a PC's hard drive or transferred to formats such as CD or DVD, allowing you, for example, to watch and/or listen to an interview or group via headphones on your PC while transcribing or preparing analysis. Audio or video extracts from interviews can be included in presentations.

Wireless technology

Members of consumer panels and interviewers compiling audits currently scan bar codes on product packaging using electronic scanning devices. The data are then transmitted via modem to a central computer. Wireless and 'silent' technology, however, is already available that enables the products themselves to transmit information (Accenture, 2001), which is likely to affect the collection of panel and audit data in the future. The packaging of some products already contains radio frequency identifier tags (RFIDs) or microprocessors that allow manufacturers to track products through the supply chain. More advanced processors, such as micro-electro-mechanicalsystems (MEMS), enable the item in which they are embedded to 'talk' to the retailer or manufacturer, not only about where it is but what the environment is like (the temperature in the fridge, for example) and what condition it is in (for example the amount of shampoo left in the bottle). Manufacturers and retailers will be able to access real-time information about speed of use, for example, and frequency of purchase.

RFIDs and MEMS also have applications for employee health and safety and could be used in fieldwork management. They can be embedded in clothing or in other devices used by employees to track and monitor them in real time.

Interactive television

Advances in and the convergence of computer, telephone and television technology (set-top computers, always-on telephone connection) mean that interactive television is likely to become a medium for data collection. The increase in penetration of digital and interactive television also presents researchers and clients with issues in relation to effective audience measurement.

■ Data management

Advances in data capture technology and in data storage capabilities have meant that it is relatively easy to collect and store large amounts of data. But more data does not always translate into more information or greater insight. Although a dataset or database is a valuable commodity, because of its mass and/or its complexity, it is sometimes difficult to access, understand or use to good effect. Advances in technology, however, mean that data management – from processing and analysis through search and retrieval to output and presentation – is easier, more efficient and more user friendly.

Data processing and analysis

Developments in software for the analysis of qualitative data make the analysis and interpretation of relatively large-scale qualitative research projects more manageable. Tabulations from quantitative research, once provided on paper in the days when few researchers had access to a personal computer, are now provided (and transmitted) electronically as standard. Developments in data handling and data analysis software, making it more user friendly and easier to understand, have meant that end users can manipulate and analyse data and pull out reports without having to involve a specialist data processing executive. Technology is available that allows access to data in real time, as it is being collected by interviewers or respondents.

Storage and retrieval

It is relatively inexpensive to store large amounts of data – as data tables and datasets – on CDs, on a network server, on the organisation's intranet. If archived and indexed in an effective way in a database or a data warehouse data, as well as the project report and presentation, can be accessed quickly and easily.

Data fusion and data mining

Standardisation of operating platforms, software applications and conventions for labelling and formatting data across the research industry means that there is a common interface between data collected and stored in different formats; readability problems across datasets are thus minimised or avoided. This has led to an increase in data fusion, the process by which data from a variety of sources or suppliers, internal and external, including survey data, customer data from loyalty cards, and data from geographical information systems and the census, are linked or integrated. The software and hardware exist that enable large databases and data warehouses to be structured and mined or searched, thus increasing the usability of the data they contain for decision making and decision support. As a result, the value and the long-term benefits to the organisation of all data, including market research data, are increased. We look in detail at what is involved in data fusion and data mining in Chapter 5.

■ Adoption of technology

Advances in technology and their adoption have disadvantages as well advantages, sometimes creating as many problems as they solve. For example, the increased adoption of relatively new methods of communication – mobile phones over traditional land lines, interactive television, digital broadcasting and the proliferation of channels that results – all offer challenges to researchers. Technology has enabled us to collect more data in shorter periods of time. With more and more data being generated it is necessary to have more time to devote to the analysis and interpretation of that data, in order to convert the data into actionable information. The speed with which data are gathered, however, seems to feed the desire to see the findings as soon as data collection has finished, if not before. This means that the amount of thinking time becomes as compressed as the fieldwork period, which has implications for the quality of the output. Because we have the technology to process, mine and analyse large amounts of data, there is increasing pressure to do so, sometimes regardless of whether it will produce anything of real interest or value.

Not everyone is comfortable with all aspects of technology, especially communications technology, and the 'at a distance' feel that it gives. People like human interaction and in the use or overuse of technology there is a risk of losing out on the valuable relationship building that is part of communicating face to face and by telephone. It is unlikely that new methods of communication and interaction – virtual meetings and presentations – will overtake traditional ones just yet. In fact, although the pace of change is likely to increase, the rate of adoption of technology will continue to vary.

The pace of change and the rate of adoption

Given that there is likely to be more change in the next three years than in the last three, keeping up with and implementing technology can give rise to problems and impede progress. Adoption of technology does not happen at the same rate in every country, nor at the same rate throughout a country, which has implications for how international and multi-country studies are conducted. Cape Town and other large cities in South Africa, for example, are technologically well developed; the rest of South Africa is not. The speed of adoption of technology is influenced by a whole range of factors, not least social and cultural attitudes. There is, for example, far greater interest in and far greater speed of adoption in the Nordic countries than in most of the rest of Europe; adoption is much slower in the countries of southern Europe. Economic factors – national wealth and degree of deregulation in telecommunications markets, for example – have an influence. Existing technological infrastructure plays a large role – even across Europe there is a great deal of variation in telecommunications infrastructure, in the level of PC and Internet penetration, in the availability of broadband access.

Adoption and use of technology also relies on customer demand and on the ability of the organisation to develop profitable business models to meet it. This in turn depends on, among other things, access to the capital necessary to fund the investment in technology and the continuing customer interest in the outputs – the products and services that result. Adoption of new technology also requires new skills, which means investment in training and recruitment, and can be influenced by skills shortages.

■ Putting technology to work

The pace of change has been rapid and is unlikely to diminish. Research organisations must adapt in order to remain competitive. There is a danger, because of the level of investment needed to keep up with and benefit from technological change, that smaller organisations will be left behind or will disappear, acquired by larger organisations. We saw above that there has already been a consolidation in the industry in recent years, driven in part by the need for capital to invest in and keep up with technological developments, and to benefit from the economies of scale in developing and marketing products and services.

Research is dependent on technology, and the technology should be used to its benefit – to improve efficiency and quality and reduce costs; to create new products and services; to improve existing products and services and how they are delivered; to tailor them to meet, if not exceed, the needs and expectations of customers; and to strengthen relationships with customers and other stakeholders, including the general public.

Chapter summary

➤ Research plays a vital role in providing robust and credible evidence for the planning and decision-making processes in organisations in the public, private and not-for-profit sectors.

➤ The value of research can be limited by many things, including the following:
  ➤ poor problem definition;
  ➤ lack of understanding of the brief;
  ➤ poor or inappropriate research design;
  ➤ the limitations of the methods used;
  ➤ poor execution of the research itself;
  ➤ the interpretation of the results;
  ➤ the status of knowledge;
  ➤ the use or misuse of research evidence by the decision makers;
  ➤ the time that elapses between collecting the data and applying the findings.

➤ The research industry is made up of research suppliers and those who buy and/or use research. There are several kinds of research supplier, including the full service agency, the specialist agency and the independent consultant.

➤ The role of the in-house client researcher varies from organisation to organisation. It can involve an internal consultancy role, advising decision makers on the use of research and ensuring that research and other data are converted to information and knowledge and applied effectively. The role may also involve providing and/or commissioning and managing external research.

➤ The role of the agency researcher is to manage a research project from the initial client briefing, through research design and set-up, fieldwork and data processing to analysis, interpretation and presentation of the findings and their implications to the client.

➤ Various professional bodies, including The Market Research Society and ESOMAR, represent researchers and the research industry to the wider world and aim to ensure that research is conducted in a professional and ethical manner.

➤ Technological developments have had a major impact on research practice, not least in the areas of project management, data capture and data processing and analysis.

Questions and exercises

1 What is research? Describe what is meant by 'market' or 'marketing' research. What is social research?

2 Describe the main uses of market research.

3 Describe some of the uses of social research.

4 What is the value of research?

5 What limits the value of research?

6 Describe the role of professional bodies such as The Market Research Society.

7 What does the role of client or in-house researcher typically involve?

8 Describe the roles of the data processing provider and the fieldwork provider.

9 What are the day-to-day duties of a research executive in an agency?

10 What impact has technology had on the following aspects of research practice:
(a) data capture;
(b) data management; and
(c) project administration, communication and interaction?

References

Accenture (2001) *The Unexpected eEurope*, London: Accenture.

Bairfelt, S. and Spurgeon, F. (1998) *Plenty of Data, but are we doing enough to fill the Information Gap?* Amsterdam: ESOMAR.

Bijapurkar, R. (1995) *Does Market Research Really Contribute to Decision Making?* Amsterdam: ESOMAR.

ESOMAR (2001) *Annual Study on the Market Research Industry*, Amsterdam: ESOMAR.

Kreinczes, G. (1990) 'Why research is undervalued', *Admap*, March.

Pyke, A. (2000) 'It's all in the brief', *Proceedings of The Market Research Society Conference*, London: The Market Research Society.

Shipman, M. (1997) *The Limitations of Social Research*, London: Longman.

Recommended reading

The *Research Works* series: papers from the AMSO (now BMRA) Research Effectiveness Awards, Henley-on-Thames: NTC. For accounts of the use and value of a wide range of research.

Marks, L. (ed.) (2000) *Qualitative Research in Context*, Henley-on-Thames: Admap. For detail on the use of qualitative research in a wide variety of settings, including social research.

Chapter 2

Introducing types of research

Introduction

Research can be described or classified in a number of ways. For example, you might hear a piece of research described as exploratory, as quantitative research or as continuous research, or in some combination, such as exploratory qualitative research or syndicated continuous research. The purpose of this short chapter is to introduce you to some of the ways in which research is described and the uses to which the different types of research are put.

Topics covered

➢ Exploratory, descriptive and causal research
➢ Continuous and *ad hoc* research
➢ Qualitative and quantitative research
➢ Primary and secondary research
➢ Face-to-face, telephone, postal and Internet research
➢ Syndicated and customised research
➢ Consumer, industrial, business-to-business and social research

Relationship to MRS Advanced Certificate Syllabus

This chapter introduces topics covered in several units, specifically:

➢ Unit 2 – Primary and secondary data collection and exploratory research;
➢ Unit 3 – Research and survey design (including continuous and *ad hoc* research);
➢ Unit 5 – Data collection methods (qualitative, quantitative and observation).

Learning outcomes

At the end of this chapter you should be able to:

➢ understand the terminology used to describe different types of research;
➢ understand the basics of each type;
➢ be aware of the main uses of each.

Types of research

Research can be described or classified according to the following:

➢ the nature of the research enquiry – exploratory, descriptive and explanatory or causal research;
➢ the mode of data collection – continuous and *ad hoc* research;
➢ the type of data – qualitative and quantitative research;
➢ the status or source of the data – primary and secondary research;
➢ the method of data collection – face-to-face, telephone, postal and Internet research;
➢ the way in which the research is bought or sold – syndicated or customised research; and
➢ the nature of the market or population under investigation – for example, consumer, industrial, business-to-business or social research.

■ Type of research enquiry: exploratory, descriptive and causal research

Research can be classified according to the nature of the research enquiry and the type of evidence it aims to produce into three categories – exploratory, descriptive and causal or explanatory. Descriptive and explanatory research enquiries are sometimes referred to as conclusive research. Each of these types of research enquiry can involve primary or secondary, qualitative or quantitative research. Below is a summary of the nature and uses of each of these types of enquiry; we look at each type in greater detail in the context of research design in Chapter 4.

Exploratory research

Exploratory research is, as its name suggests, research undertaken to explore an issue or a topic. It is particularly useful in helping to identify a problem, clarify the nature of a problem or define the issues involved. It can be used to develop propositions and hypotheses for further research, to look for new insights or to reach a greater understanding of an issue. For example, you might conduct exploratory research in order to understand how consumers react to new product concepts or ideas for advertising, or what business executives mean when they talk about 'entrepreneurship', or to help define what is meant by the term 'elder abuse'.

Descriptive research

A lot of market and social research is about description as well as exploration – finding the answers to the questions Who? What? Where? When? How? and How many? While exploratory research can provide description, the purpose of descriptive research is to answer more clearly defined research questions. Descriptive research aims to build a picture – of a market, a set of customers, a social phenomenon, a set of experiences, for example. It aims to identify, describe and in some cases count things. It can be used to examine some of the key issues facing marketers and policy makers.

Box 2.1 Examples of questions addressed in descriptive research

Market research

➤ How big is the market?

➤ Who are the main suppliers of product X?

➤ Which brands compete in which segment?

➤ What volume of sales did brand A achieve in Year 2 compared to Year 1?

➤ Who is buying brand B?

➤ What do customers think of the new advertising?

➤ How satisfied are customers with the new product formulation or service offer?

➤ How many organisations are using the technology and what are they using it for?

Social research

➤ How many people were the victims of a crime in the last year?

➤ What is the profile of those who stay in hostels for the homeless?

➤ What is the decision-making process of a woman with a 'crisis' pregnancy?

➤ What is the pattern of drug use among prisoners (who uses drugs, which drugs, when, where, how often)?

➤ How satisfied with the service are the users of a government employment service?

Causal or explanatory research

Causal or explanatory research addresses the 'why' questions: Why do people choose brand A and not brand B? Why are some customers and not others satisfied with our service? Why do some prisoners and not others use drugs? What might explain this? We design explanatory or causal research to answer these types of questions, to allow us to rule out rival explanations and come to a conclusion, to help us develop causal explanations.

Nature of data collection

■ Continuous and *ad hoc* research

Continuous research, as its name suggests, is research done on a continuous basis or at regular intervals in order to monitor changes over time, for example in a particular market or among a particular population. *Ad hoc* (Latin for 'for this special purpose') research is research that is conducted on a 'one-off' basis, to provide a snapshot at a particular point in time.

Continuous research

The most common way of conducting continuous research is to use a panel of respondents chosen to represent the target population; data are collected from panel members at regular intervals. The panel can be made up of individuals or households, often called a consumer panel, or it can be made up of businesses or other organisations; for example, retail panels are made up of a sample of retail outlets.

Continuous data can also be derived from independent samples of the same population, samples that are recruited anew for each round of fieldwork. For example, omnibus studies and advertising tracking studies, or product tests where the same methodology is used on similar or identical samples, can provide continuous data. Examples of this type of continuous or regular research include the General Household Survey and the National Food Survey, both conducted on behalf of the UK government.

Ad hoc research

Ad hoc research is usually designed to address a specific problem or to help understand a particular issue at a certain point in time. For example, you might commission *ad hoc* research among employees to determine satisfaction with their new office accommodation, or to understand the issues faced by overseas students in their first few months at university, or to gauge whether your latest television advertisement is communicating key product messages to the target market. The types of studies that come under the heading *ad hoc* research include advertising pre-tests and communication testing, usage and attitudes studies, hall tests, store tests, market mix tests and brand/price trade-off research.

The type of data: quantitative and qualitative

One of the major distinctions in research is between quantitative and qualitative research. The differences between the two are summarised in Table 2.1.

■ Quantitative research

Quantitative research involves collecting data from relatively large samples; the data collected are usually presented as numbers, often in tables, on graphs and on charts. Quantitative research is used to address the objectives of conclusive (descriptive and explanatory) research enquiries; it can also be used for exploratory purposes. It provides nomothetic description – sparse description of a relatively large number of cases. Qualitative research, on the other hand, provides ideographic description, that is, description that is rich in detail but limited to relatively few cases.

Quantitative data are collected via sample surveys or panels. Quantitative interviews are structured and standardised – the questions are worded in exactly the same way and asked in the same order in each interview. Qualitative interviews, on the other hand, are more like conversations, on a continuum from semi-structured and semi-standardised to unstructured and non-standardised. Quantitative interviews can be conducted face to face (in the street, in a central venue, often called a 'hall test' or central location test, or at the respondent's home or place of work), over the telephone, by post, or via the Internet (email or the web). We look in detail at quantitative methods of data collection in Chapter 7.

Quantitative research is useful for describing the characteristics of a population or market – for example household spending patterns, market and brand share, use of technology, voting behaviour or intention, levels of economic activity. It is useful for measuring, quantifying, validating and testing hypotheses or theories. It has some

Table 2.1 Differences between quantitative and qualitative research

Topic	Quantitative research	Qualitative research
Research enquiry	Exploratory, descriptive and causal	Exploratory and descriptive
Nature of questions and responses	Who, what, when, where, why, how many?	What, when, where, why?
	Relatively superficial and rational responses	Below the surface and emotional responses
	Measurement, testing and validation	Understanding, exploration and idea generation
Sample size	Relatively large	Relatively small
Data collection	Not very flexible	Flexible
	Interviews and observation	Interviews and observation
	Standardised	Less standardised
	More closed questions	More open-ended questions
Data	Numbers, percentages, means	Words, pictures
	Less detail or depth	Detailed and in-depth
	Nomothetic description	Ideographic description
	Context poor	Context rich
	High reliability, low validity	High validity, low reliability
	Statistical inference possible	Statistical inference not possible
Cost	Relatively low cost per respondent but relatively high project cost	Relatively high cost per respondent but relatively low project cost

limitations. It is not as flexible as qualitative research – data collection is structured and standardised (although this offers reliability in return). The structure and standardisation can produce superficial rather than detailed description and understanding. The use of closed questions does not allow us to collect responses in the respondent's own words, and so we may lose out on 'real' responses, and on detail and context; the standardisation means that we may miss the subtleties, the slight differences in response between respondents. Both can contribute to low validity. We look at the concepts of reliability and validity in Chapter 4.

■ Qualitative research

Qualitative research typically involves relatively small sample sizes. The techniques used include interviewing, via group discussions (also known as focus groups) and in-depth interviews, observation and accompanied visits (for example to a doctor, a supermarket or bar and involving interviewing and observation). The findings are expressed as words (or pictures), rarely (but sometimes) as numbers.

Qualitative research is concerned with rich and detailed description, understanding and insight rather than measurement. It aims to get below the surface, beyond the spontaneous or rational response to the deeper and more emotional response. It is often used to gain insight into and understanding of the 'what' and particularly the 'why': what people do, what they think, what they feel, what they want; and why they do and think and feel and want. It seeks to discover what accounts for certain kinds of behaviour, for example drug use in prison, or what makes customers loyal to a particular brand. It is good at uncovering a range of responses, and the subtleties and nuances in responses and meanings. It is both less artificial and less superficial than quantitative research and can provide highly valid data. It is suitable in exploratory and descriptive research enquiries. It is more flexible than quantitative research – the researcher has the scope during fieldwork to modify or adapt the interview guide or the sample to suit the way in which the research is developing. The less structured and less standardised approach can, however, mean that is relatively low in reliability. This is something that qualitative researchers acknowledge and take steps to address (via training, addressing one's own feelings, opinions and biases before undertaking fieldwork, discussing approach and findings with other researchers or team members, for example). It is possible using qualitative research to tackle complex issues, for example understanding the decision-making process in a crisis pregnancy. The findings from a qualitative research study cannot be said to be representative in the statistical sense, because of the small sample sizes involved and the nature of the sampling techniques, but it is possible nevertheless to generalise the findings from the sample to the wider population. It is not advisable to use qualitative research if your objectives are to validate or measure.

Qualitative research is used in a wide variety of settings. It is used to generate, explore and develop ideas for products, services and advertising, for example, and for understanding social issues. It is used to provide information to help guide and develop policy and strategy – for business, for marketing, advertising and communications, and for development of social policy. It is used to evaluate policies and strategies, and their implementation. It can be used in conjunction with quantitative research to great effect. At the beginning of a study it can be used to generate and develop ideas or hypotheses; to define the issues under investigation; and to find out how people think and feel and behave, how they talk about an issue or a product. This type of information is particularly useful in helping to structure quantitative research and design the questionnaire. Qualitative research is also useful at the other end of a study – in exploring the findings of a quantitative study in greater depth, providing a wider context in which to understand and interpret them. While the cost per respondent is greater in a qualitative study than in a quantitative one, the relatively small overall sample size often means that the total project cost can be smaller. We look at qualitative methods of data collection in Chapter 6.

The source of the data: primary and secondary research

Primary research is designed to generate or collect data for a specific problem; the data collected – primary data – do not exist prior to data collection. Secondary data are data that were originally collected for a purpose other than the current research objectives – in revisiting them you are putting the data to a second use. Searching for, analysing and using secondary data is called secondary research.

■ Primary research

The role of primary research is to generate data to address the information needs in relation to a specific problem or issue. For example, imagine you are interested in understanding how customers have reacted to changes to the service you provide. There are no pre-existing data available – you need to conduct primary research. Primary research may be exploratory, descriptive and/or causal; qualitative or quantitative; syndicated or customised. Primary data can be collected face to face, by telephone, by post, via the Internet or via observation; on a one-off or on a continuous basis; and in almost any market or on any issue.

■ Secondary research

The role of secondary research is very often exploratory and/or descriptive. For example, secondary research might be used to explore the background to a problem or issue, to describe its wider context, to help define the problem or issue, or to generate or test hypotheses or ideas. To illustrate: consulting the data from a study you conducted the last time you made changes to your product or service – to help you understand or set in context issues related to current changes – is a form of secondary research. Analysing sales data to determine the impact of the changes is secondary research. Searching the literature on a topic to reach a greater understanding of the issues involved, or to help develop interview questions or a framework for analysis, is secondary research. You will see secondary research referred to as desk research – the sort of research or data collection you can do without leaving your desk. In contrast, primary research is sometimes referred to as field research – you have to go into the field, do fieldwork, to collect the data. Secondary data may be data from outside the organisation – external data, for example government-produced statistics; or, as we saw above, data generated by the organisation – internal data, sales data or findings from previous research, available from the organisation's in-house management information system or decision support system. Of course, secondary data started life as primary data. In order to evaluate their quality, and suitability to your research objectives, you need to know about their previous life – for example why they were collected, who collected them, how they were collected, what sampling technique was used and so on. We look at secondary research and the evaluation and analysis of secondary data in more detail in Chapter 5.

The method of data collection

Research is often classified into interviewing and observation according to the method of data collection used. Interviewing is further classified into personal interviewing – face-to-face and telephone – and self-completion formats delivered typically by post, email or via the Internet. We look in detail at qualitative methods of data collection in Chapter 6 and quantitative methods in Chapter 7.

■ The way the data are bought: syndicated and customised research

Syndicated or multi-client research refers to research that has been put together by an organisation (usually a specialist research organisation) and sold to a number of different clients, to whom it may be equally relevant. For example, a financial services organisation with a small research budget may buy into a syndicated advertising tracking study along with several other financial services organisations as a cost-effective way of finding out how its advertising is being received by its target market. Omnibus surveys are a form of syndicated research, with clients buying space for their questions (for which it may not be feasible to conduct an *ad hoc* survey) alongside questions placed by other clients. Continuous research can be expensive and is often syndicated in order to spread the cost. Customised research is research that is commissioned by a single organisation, usually to meet their research objectives alone. Most *ad hoc* projects are customised.

The type of respondents: consumer, industrial, business-to-business and social research

Research can be classified according to the nature of the topic under investigation (we saw this in Chapter 1 with the distinction between market and social research). It can also be classified according to the type of respondents involved in the research.

■ Consumer research

Consumer research, as its name suggests, is conducted among consumers – individuals and households. The purpose of consumer research is usually to understand consumer behaviour and consumer attitudes and opinions in relation to products and services and the marketing activity that surrounds them.

■ Industrial and business-to-business research

Business-to-business (B2B) research and industrial research are conducted among individuals who are involved in or represent organisations. The topics researched relate to the issues faced by such organisations, the nature and dynamics of the markets in which they operate, the attitudes and behaviour of buyers and of employees, for example.

■ Social research

As we noted in Chapter 1, social research involves researching aspects of society, the social world, social life and social issues. Topics that fall under the social research heading tend to be those associated with health, education, law and order, religion, politics, policy and culture.

Chapter summary

➤ Research can be described or classified according to the following:

  ➤ the nature of the research enquiry – exploratory, descriptive and explanatory or causal research;
  ➤ the mode of data collection – continuous and *ad hoc* research;
  ➤ the type of data – qualitative and quantitative research;
  ➤ the status or source of the data – primary and secondary research;
  ➤ the method of data collection – face-to-face, telephone, postal and Internet research;
  ➤ the way in which the research is bought or sold – syndicated or customised research; and
  ➤ the nature of the market or population under investigation – for example consumer, industrial, business-to-business or social research.

➤ One of the most important distinctions is between qualitative and quantitative research. Quantitative research involves collecting data from relatively large samples; description of this large number of cases tends to be sparse. Qualitative research involves relatively small samples; description of these relatively few cases is rich and detailed. Quantitative research tends to be used in conclusive (descriptive and explanatory) research enquiries; qualitative research in exploratory and descriptive enquiries.

Questions and exercises

1 In what ways can research be classified?

2 Describe briefly what is meant by the terms exploratory, descriptive and causal research.

3 Describe what is meant by the terms primary and secondary research. Give examples of the use of each type.

4 What are the main differences between qualitative and quantitative research? What are the strengths and weaknesses of each type? For what sorts of research enquiry is qualitative research most useful? Give examples.

5 Describe what is meant by the following terms, giving examples of the use of each type of research:
  (a) continuous research;
  (b) *ad hoc* research;
  (c) syndicated research; and
  (d) customised research.

Recommended reading

The *Research Works* series: papers from the AMSO (now BMRA) Research Effectiveness Awards, Henley-on-Thames: NTC. For accounts of the use of a wide range of research.

Chisnall, P. (1997) *Marketing Research*, Maidenhead: McGraw-Hill. For detail on specific research applications including continuous research, advertising research and industrial market research.

Marks, L. (ed.) (2000) *Qualitative Research in Context*, Henley-on-Thames: Admap. For detail on the use of qualitative research in a wide range of areas from advertising, broadcasting and design to politics, religion and social policy.

The Research and Development Sub-committee on Qualitative Research (1979) 'Qualitative research – a summary of the concepts involved', *Journal of the Market Research Society*, **21**, 2, pp. 107–24. A useful run through the nature of qualitative research, the practice of it and its uses.

Part II

Getting started

Chapter 3

Starting a research project

Introduction

The aim of this chapter is to take you through the process of initiating a research project. We look at what is involved – from defining the problem to writing the research brief, choosing a supplier and responding to the brief with a research proposal. The initiation stage of a project is crucially important. If the problem is not clearly defined, the information needs not clearly identified, the use of the information not clearly established, or the problem not accurately communicated to the research supplier, any research that follows will be a waste of time and money.

Regardless of the nature or context of the problem, the steps in the process are largely the same:

➢ Identify and define the problem clearly and accurately.
➢ Identify the information needs.
➢ Establish the end use to which this information will be put.
➢ Communicate the problem clearly and accurately to the researcher via a research brief.
➢ Describe the approach to the research via a research proposal.

The way in which the process is described here assumes that the tasks involved are fairly distinct and separate: the client identifies and defines the problem and prepares the research brief; the researcher questions the brief, further defines and refines the problem, and prepares the research proposal. This is only for ease of explanation, however, and you will know from your own experience that these tasks are not always so clear-cut. The roles that the client and the researcher take in the process, and so the process itself, are influenced by a range of factors. These include the type of problem (its complexity, how similar it is to previous research, for example), the type of organisations involved and their preferred ways of working and, perhaps most significantly, the relationship between the client and the researcher. It is important to bear all this in mind when reading the chapter. It is not intended as an account of how things are always done, nor is it a prescription for how things should be done. It is a guide to good practice for designing effective research that you can adapt to the situation in which you are involved.

Topics covered

➢ Defining the problem
➢ Preparing a research brief
➢ Choosing a research supplier
➢ Questioning a brief
➢ Preparing a research proposal
➢ Evaluating a proposal
➢ Responding to a proposal
➢ The client–researcher relationship

The topics covered in this chapter are part of Unit 1 – Introduction and Problem Definition, more specifically:

➤ problem definition;
➤ the research brief;
➤ the research proposal.

Learning outcomes

At the end of this chapter you should be able to:

➤ understand the importance of the problem definition stage in designing effective research;
➤ understand the process involved in starting a research project;
➤ develop and write a research brief;
➤ understand what should be covered in a research proposal;
➤ evaluate a research proposal.

Defining the problem

The importance of defining the problem clearly and accurately cannot be overstated. Everything follows from this. It does not matter how good the research is (how robust the sample, how well designed the questionnaire or discussion guide); if the problem has not been clearly and accurately defined the research will not measure what it should be measuring and is likely to be a waste of time and money. You may end up wrongly advising your client, which may lead to a wrong and costly decision being taken.

Box 3.1 What kind of problems are we talking about?

Selling cars

A large car dealership has found that although the number of inquiries it is handling and the number of visitors to the showroom have remained the same compared to the previous year, sales have fallen dramatically (as has market share). It realises that external economic factors may be affecting this. It is particularly concerned about the rise in the number of purchases of imported cars. It wants to understand what is happening among the car-buying public in order that it can take some action to at least halt the sales decline.

Launching a new service

An airline has launched a new service to the United States. The launch was accompanied by an advertising campaign that had been used successfully in several other markets. It was used in this new market with very little modification. The client has several questions: How is the advertising working among the airline's target market? Is it communicating the message intended? Is it creating the right image for the airline? Should it be run unchanged during the next phase of the campaign or should new advertising be developed especially for this new market?

Box 3.1 continued

Making use of technology

A government department with responsibility for economic development set out an action plan to help businesses speed up their adoption of information technology. The action plan set objectives that were to be achieved by a certain date. In order to develop policy for the coming year, and to set new objectives, the department wants to review the current situation. It would like to know how successful organisations have been in meeting the original objectives. It also wants to gauge what effect the use of technology has had on their business in particular and on their industry and their markets in general. Is it increasing competition? Is it reducing the cost of market entry? Is it making new markets or industries more accessible?

Providing for the whole community

An inner city community with a large number of illegal drug users has, with the help of a voluntary trust, received funding to set up a resource centre. The role of the centre will be to provide services for the whole community, including drug users. The community representatives are, however, unsure about the type of services to offer drug users, and the way in which the services should be provided.

■ From problem to research objectives

Look again at the car dealership example in Box 3.1. The issue is a decline in sales over time. The manager needs to take action to stop the decline in sales. But what action should she take? Deciding what action to take – this is the management or decision maker's problem. The researcher and the decision maker must be clear about what action might be taken because the aim of the research is to deliver the information that will allow the decision maker to take the most effective course of action.

In the car dealership case, the answer to the question '*What action should we take to stop the decline in sales?*' depends on understanding why sales are declining. To understand why sales are declining we need to examine the wider context or setting of the problem. What is going on in the external environment that might be affecting the sales of cars? What is going on in the car dealership itself that might be affecting sales? This is where background or exploratory research can be very useful. We discover via some informal exploratory research (interviews with the sales staff and key account customers; a review of recently published reports on the car industry) that external factors, particularly the cost savings to be had in buying an imported car, and internal factors, such as customer service, are having an impact on sales. We now have an idea about what might be going on. We are making predictions – that the cost savings to be had in buying an imported car are affecting the sales of the dealership's non-imported cars; that the perceptions of the service that the dealership offers is affecting sales. These ideas or statements about connections between things are called hypotheses. The aim of the research is to gather evidence that will allow us to test these hypotheses. At the beginning of the research process, an hypothesis is likely to be a fairly vague statement – for example that there is a link between perception of customer service and sales. Later in the process, when we have collected data, we may develop and test more specific hypotheses – for example that those with a higher score on a customer service rating scale, indicating a positive view of customer service, are more likely to buy from the dealer than those with a lower score.

Box 3.2 The role of background research

In defining and refining the problem, in understanding the issues and narrowing the focus of the research, background or exploratory research is very useful. It may help to uncover information that helps define the problem and develop hypotheses to be tested; it may help to identify information gaps and so help decide whether primary research is necessary; it may uncover information on ways of approaching the research.

Depending on the information needs and the stage of development of the project, this exploratory research may be a formal stage in the research project, requested in the research brief or recommended in the proposal, and requiring a structured approach, or it may be more informal and less structured. It might involve primary data collection, for example informal interviews with experts or sales and marketing staff; or it might involve secondary research – a search of published data sources, analysis of existing internal data, a review of previously commissioned research on the topic. We look at secondary research in more detail in Chapter 5.

With the information now available to the manager she identifies some possible courses of action to halt the sales decline: a move to selling imported vehicles; a price promotion on selected marques and models currently stocked; a training programme to improve customer service; an advertising campaign focusing on quality of customer service.

Now that we have a fairly clear idea of the decision maker's problem and the possible courses of action open to her, we are in a much better position to specify what information we need to help the manager take appropriate action. Gaps in knowledge remain – the manager realises that she knows very little about how the dealership is perceived by its target market in general and its customers in particular, and how it compares to its competitors. She is also unsure, given the changes in the market (the popularity of importing a car), about who her competitors really are. After further discussion client and researcher agree on the research problem: research is needed to identify what factors are influencing consumers in the car-buying process, and to determine the perceived strengths and weaknesses of the dealership compared to its competitors. The information provided by the research will be used to decide the best course of action to take to halt the decline in sales.

Now that we have a clear definition of the research problem we need to pin down the specifics. We need to move from the fairly broad research objective, '*Identify what factors are influencing consumers in the car-buying process, and determine what the dealership's strengths and weaknesses are compared to its competitors*', to the specific research objectives – in other words, what we need the research to tell us. This is a crucial stage – it will give us a framework on which to build the research design. Research objectives should be as specific and precise as possible. In the car dealership example we need the research to tell us:

➢ What factors are involved in an individual's buying decision?

➢ Who is involved in the decision-making process?

➢ What range of marques and models is considered?

➢ What influences the range of marques and models considered?

➢ What sales options are considered, e.g. new or used; dealership or private buy; import or domestic?

➢ What criteria are used in selecting which sales option to take?

➢ What likes and dislikes do buyers have about the buying situation?

➢ How do they rate the chosen option in terms of customer service?

➢ What is the profile of those who buy:

➢ from approved dealers

➢ new cars

➢ dealer-approved used cars

➢ imported cars?

It is important during the 'project scoping' phase to make sure that the focus of the research is neither too broad nor too narrow. The research should tackle what we *need to know* – providing information that is relevant to the problem and that will be used to address the problem – and should not be expanded to include what would be *nice to know*. In preparing a research brief this may mean setting out the information needs in order of priority so that if there are time and budgetary constraints the research can focus on delivering the information most relevant to the problem. In narrowing the focus, however, we need to be careful not to define the problem or the information needs too narrowly, and so run the risk of failing to collect the data needed to understand or interpret the findings or take action.

Defining the decision maker's problem and the research problem, and getting to the specific research objectives – as we have done above – can involve several rounds of discussion with the owner of the problem, the decision maker, or the organisation's

Box 3.3 Roles in the problem definition stage

The role of the research supplier (the researcher) is to design effective research that will deliver the information needed by the person commissioning the research (the client) and present this clearly in the research proposal. To do this properly the researcher must have a clear understanding of the problem and its wider context, the type of information needed by the client to address the problem, and how this information will be used. The role of the client, typically, is to define the problem, identify what information is needed to address the problem and communicate this clearly to the researcher via the research brief. Depending on the client's background and experience, the way in which the client organisation works, or the nature of the relationship between client and researcher, the client may involve the researcher in either the problem definition or information needs assessment stage (Pyke, 2000). This is one way in which the researcher can 'add value' to the process – working with the client to define or refine the problem, helping the client reach a clear understanding of his or her information needs, and showing how research can address these.

internal researcher (if there is one). Most of this discussion may take place between the decision maker and the internal researcher before an external researcher is involved; on the other hand, the external researcher may be involved at this early stage. Some of the discussion may be revisited if, upon receipt of the brief, the external researcher finds that some elements of it are not clear.

■ Investing in research: the practicalities

There are two important issues to be considered in deciding how to proceed: how much time is available in which to complete the research and what resources (people and money) are available with which to undertake it. Both will have a bearing on the type and scope of research that can be conducted. For example, if a decision must be made within a week of identifying the problem, it may be that primary research is not feasible; the budget may not stretch to the proposed tailor-made survey but it might accommodate including questions in an omnibus survey. A decision must be made as to the importance of the research in the decision-making process and enough time and resources should be set aside to reflect this. In deciding on the budget (and to some extent the time available for the research) the client should consider the value of the information that the research will provide to the organisation and to the decision to be taken. The value of the information (the benefit) should be greater than the money spent to get it (the cost). One way of doing this is to assess the risk (and the cost) involved in making a decision without the help of the information generated by the research: is the risk (and the cost) of making the wrong decision greater than the cost of the research? If, for example, you are planning to spend €3 million on the launch of a new service, the decision to spend €50,000 researching the effectiveness of the launch campaign may be relatively straightforward. The risk is that you spend the €50,000 to find out that the launch campaign is highly effective. If you do not spend the €50,000 on research you take a bigger risk – the risk of spending €3 million on an ineffective launch. In the car dealership case, if the business is losing sales equivalent to €4 million annually, the decision to spend €20,000 on research to determine the most effective action may be relatively easy. Determining the value of the information is, however, not always so straightforward. In some cases, depending on the nature of the decision, the type of organisation or the size of the potential investment, more formal risk assessment or cost-benefit analyses, for example using decision tree theory or Bayesian statistical theory, might be made.

Box 3.4 The key questions: a summary

➤ What is the issue or problem?

➤ What decision is to be made?

➤ What information is needed to help make an effective decision?

➤ What specific objectives must the research address?

➤ How much should be invested to gather the information needed?

■ Going on: from research objectives to research design and method

Now that we know what the research must deliver we are in a position to start thinking about the most appropriate way of going about it. This is the subject of the next chapter, Chapter 4. Once we have decided on a research design we can build a research plan, addressing questions relating to the sample (Chapter 8), the method of data collection (Chapters 6 and 7) and the design of the data collection instrument (Chapters 9 and 10). It is at this stage – designing the data collection instrument – that we will return to the research objectives, in order to translate them into questions that will allow us to gather the information we need. The point to remember from this section is that, to produce effective research, decisions about research design and research method must be founded on a clear and accurate definition of the problem.

The rest of this chapter is devoted to two very important documents in the research process: the research brief and the research proposal. We deal with each document from the point of view of the person responsible for it: in the case of the research brief, the client or decision maker; in the case of the proposal, the research supplier.

Preparing a research brief

If you are commissioning research it is your responsibility to ensure that the potential research supplier understands the decision maker's problem, the context of the problem, the information needed to address it, and the nature of the constraints (time and money) within which the research must be designed. The research brief is the document in which these things are set out. It is circulated to potential research suppliers with a view to eliciting a research proposal. Verbal research briefings – either by telephone or face to face – are common but are usually accompanied by a written brief. Preparing a written brief is good practice – having to commit ideas to paper usually enhances the quality and clarity of the thinking behind them. A written brief is a valuable aid to communication and acts as a record for consultation and discussion. A draft version can be circulated to all involved in the project for comment. Several versions may be prepared before agreement is reached on the definition of the problem and the way in which it is to be addressed. For much of its

Box 3.5 Writing to improve the quality of thinking

The earlier ideas are committed to paper the better. Having to write things down forces us to think about what we know (and to sort out our ideas and present them in a logical way) and what we do not know – it should serve to highlight gaps in our thinking. For example, it should become apparent in the writing process if you have clearly defined the problem – it is difficult to write clearly about something that you do not understand or which you are unsure about. The writing process should uncover questions about the problem and the first draft of the brief should act as a stimulus to early thinking, or as a focus for further discussion, depending on the stage at which it is first prepared.

early existence the brief may be circulated internally only. However, once the final version is agreed it is sent to potential research suppliers. It provides all those involved – client, decision maker, research supplier – with a record of what is required, and can reduce the chance of a dispute arising about what is delivered. It can be used at the end of the research project to review or evaluate the process and determine, for example, if the research objectives were met and if the research provided useful information for the decision maker.

The brief is usually accompanied by a letter that sets out the deadline for response to the brief with client contact details, should the research supplier want to discuss the brief further. It is good practice to set up a face-to-face briefing meeting. It gives the researcher a chance to ask further questions about the brief, and perhaps test the reaction of the client to some early ideas about the shape of the research. It gives the client a chance to determine whether the researcher understands the issues involved. Thus all parties have the opportunity to assess if a working relationship is possible or desirable.

■ Contents of a research brief

Below is a guide to preparing a detailed brief. Not all briefs contain or need to contain all of this information. In cases where the research is a repeat of a similar job, or where there is an established relationship between client and researcher, some of the information may not be included. A more comprehensive brief is, however, recommended in cases where either party is fairly new to research, where the relationship between client and researcher is new, or where the project is unusual or complex.

Title

A title is important – it informs the reader immediately of the main focus of the project and draws attention to the key issue. A title may not be obvious until you have thought through exactly what it is you want – so it may be the last thing you decide upon. Here are two examples: 'A study of preferences for employment and retirement among the over 55s'; 'An evaluation of the effectiveness of an advertising campaign for X'.

Definition of the problem

Get to the heart of the issue immediately with a clear, accurate and precise definition of the problem. This may be harder to write than you imagine. If you do have trouble writing it down it may be that you are not clear about it yourself, and if you are not clear about it it is unlikely that the researcher will be. Use clear, jargon-free language. Avoid ambiguous words and phrases. Be as specific and precise as possible. Look back at the car dealership example. The dealership is experiencing a decline in sales; the management wishes to take action to address the decline but is unclear what action to take. It suspects – but it has no robust evidence – that the availability of cheaper, imported cars, which it does not sell, is a factor; it also suspects that perceptions of its customer service may be an issue. To make a decision on the most effective action to take to address the sales decline, the management needs accurate and robust information about these issues and their impact on sales. It therefore wishes to commission research to '*Identify what factors are influencing consumers in the car-buying process, and determine what the dealership's strengths and weaknesses are compared to its competitors.*'

Background to the problem

Give some background information about the product, service or issue to which the problem relates, and its wider setting within the organisation. It might also be useful to provide some information on the external conditions within which the organisation operates. In addition, especially if it is the first time that the researcher has been asked to prepare a proposal, you might include some background information about the organisation – its role, its aims, its responsibilities, its mission statement or business strategy – something to give a flavour of the organisation's work. This will not only help the researcher formulate the most effective research design but will be useful for interpreting the research findings and understanding the implications for the organisation.

Why research is necessary

State why you think research is necessary and, briefly, how you came to this conclusion. For example, '*Although existing data tell us that there has been a sharp decline in sales, we have no evidence as to why … .*'

Statement of research objectives

State the research objectives – what it is you want the research to tell you. Be as specific and unambiguous as possible. Avoid vague statements such as '*To research the market for imported cars*' or even '*To conduct a study of the image of the car dealership among its target audience*'. Have a look again at the main objectives of the car dealership project, to '*Identify what factors are influencing consumers in the car-buying process, and to determine what the dealership's strengths and weaknesses are compared to its competitors*'. This is further specified in a series of more precise objectives, for example, '*What factors are involved in an individual's buying decision?*' and '*Who is involved in the decision-making process?*'

Use of the information

To ensure that the research is focused and to help the researcher determine the type and scope of information or evidence needed, and the robustness of it, state what the information will be used for, who will use it and how it will be used. For each research objective ask yourself, '*How will the information I get here be used in the decision-making process?*'

Target population

Give as much detail as you can about the target audience or the target population. This will help the researcher decide not only on the sampling approach but on the type of research and the method of data collection. It will also help to cost the project more accurately. Be as specific and as precise as possible. For example, if you have information on the incidence of the target market in the wider population, include it.

If you have specific requirements, for example if you want to compare 25–34-year-old users and 35–44-year-old users; or those in employment and those not; or frequent users, occasional users and non-users; or those with children and those without, state this in the brief. This information will guide the researcher in designing the sample, in determining the number of focus groups or the number of interviews necessary for these comparisons to be made. In addition, it is important to clarify what you mean by terms such as 'frequent', or 'in employment'. Does employment mean paid employment only, for example, or would you include those in voluntary work or on home duties? Does it include those working part time as well as those working full time? Does it include those on paternity or maternity leave? Be as specific and unambiguous as possible.

Suggested approach

The amount of detail you give here may depend on your knowledge of research, or on whether you prefer the research supplier to put forward ideas that are not influenced by your own. Tell the researcher if the decision makers have a preference for a particular type of research or research evidence, for example qualitative or quantitative. If the research needs to be comparable with a previous piece of research mention this and give details. If you want the researcher to suggest a range of possible options and the pros and cons of each, say so.

Analysis required

Set out clearly what type of analysis you need. In a quantitative study you might want to give the researcher an idea of the complexity of the analysis required. For example, do you want a set of standard cross-tabulations with descriptive statistics (e.g. means, standard deviations, standard error) and/or inferential statistics (significance tests)? Will you want to run a factor analysis, cluster analysis or conjoint analysis? The researcher needs this sort of information in order to make decisions about research design, design of the sample, sample size, type and level of resources to be assigned to the project, time needed to complete it and so on.

Outputs

Data tables, summary reports, full reports and presentations of findings are often referred to as 'deliverables' or outputs – the products of the research. Specify exactly what deliverables you expect during and on completion of the research. Typically they will consist of a presentation of the findings and either a written summary report or a full report, handed over at the end of the project. For some projects – especially large-scale ones – you may want interim reports of the findings. You may want to comment on a draft report before the final report is produced. In a qualitative project you may want copies of the videotapes or audiotapes of the interviews or group discussions and copies of the transcripts, or a summary of the findings from each group. Whatever your requirements, mention them in the research brief so that the researcher can cost them and include them in the work plan.

Liaison arrangements

Set out clearly the contact or liaison arrangements you want. For example, if you have a project team or advisory group with which the researcher must meet to discuss progress give details in the brief – frequency of meeting, type and detail of reporting needed – so that the researcher can build this into the work plan and the costing.

Timings

Give the date by which you need the research to be completed and highlight any interim deadlines (for completion of fieldwork, say, before an advertising campaign breaks or a product or service is launched). This information will not only allow the researcher to plan the work but it will also affect how he or she designs the research. For example, the time frame may put constraints on the number of interviews, or the method of data collection. Make sure the time frame is reasonable and make sure you can meet any obligations you might have – for example to approve the questionnaire, attend the fieldwork, provide samples of product or stimulus material.

Budget

If the research design and the research method are specified in detail in the brief, which is rare, then it may not be necessary to provide details of the budget – the researcher should have everything he or she needs to cost the work. In cases where the client does not specify design and method (the more common situation) the budget may not be stated. The reason often given is that the researcher will design the research to use up this budget, whether the problem calls for it or not. This of course would not be ethical on the part of the researcher. If you have asked for more than one proposal the absence of a budget can make it more difficult for you to compare them. Different researchers will interpret a brief in different ways, making different assumptions that will impact on the cost. It is therefore worthwhile to give at least some idea of the budget so that the researcher can avoid proposing research that does not meet it and is better placed to design research that will maximise value for money.

Form of proposal

Specify clearly the way in which you want the supplier to present the proposal. For example, you might specify the headings under which the proposal should be written, the order of the headings, the nature and detail required, even the appearance of the document, method of delivery (on paper and/or electronically) and the number of copies to be submitted. Here is an alternative set of headings to the ones outlined in Box 3.6.

> **Box 3.6 Headings for research brief**
>
> ➤ Title
> ➤ Definition of the problem
> ➤ Background to the problem
> ➤ Why research is necessary
> ➤ Use of information
> ➤ Research objectives
> ➤ Target population
> ➤ Suggested approach
> ➤ Analysis required
> ➤ Outputs
> ➤ Timings
> ➤ Budget
> ➤ Form of proposal
> ➤ Selection criteria

➤ Understanding of the problem and the client's requirements
➤ Details of the approach
➤ Any difficulties that might be anticipated and how these might be overcome
➤ Timetable
➤ Separate costing for all options proposed
➤ Pricing schedule outlining staff inputs and daily rates
➤ Details of relevant experience of organisation and proposed project staff.

Selection criteria

It is common in the tendering process for government contracts for the researcher to be told on what basis the research contract will be awarded – in other words on what basis the proposals will be evaluated. The selection criteria might include the following:

➤ suitability of proposed methodology;
➤ relevant experience in this area;
➤ cost;
➤ demonstration of understanding of the brief.

Each proposal is rated on the extent to which it meets these selection criteria. A weighting or score may be given to each of them – for example, demonstration of understanding of the brief may be judged to be the most important, and cost the next most important.

Choosing a research supplier

Once you decide that research is necessary you must decide who is to carry it out. It may be that you can handle it internally. If you do not have the resources or the particular expertise to do so you must select an external supplier. To choose a supplier think first of all about the type of project it is and the type of supplier you might need. You may have several options, ranging from a full service agency, to a supplier of fieldwork and tabulation, to a consultant to write up the findings from data you have collected. You can obtain information on agencies and consultants from the directories of organisations representing the research industry, such as The Market Research Society (www.mrs.org.uk) and ESOMAR (www.esomar.nl). The British Market Research Association (www.bmra.org.uk) runs Selectline, a free service designed to help you find a supplier with the expertise you need. The directory of the Association for Qualitative Research (www.aqr.org.uk) is a useful source of information on qualitative research organisations and independent qualitative research practitioners. The Social Research Association (www.the-sra.org.uk) can provide details of those who specialise in social research. MrWeb is a web-based service that lists independent research consultants (www.mrweb.co.uk); Fieldwork Exchange (www.fieldex.net) lists fieldwork suppliers.

From the suppliers you have identified you may want to draw up a shortlist. The shortlist can be selected against a number of criteria including the following:

> *experience in the general subject area* – for example consumer, social or business-to-business issues;
> *experience in the particular area* – for example pharmaceutical products, older people's issues, office equipment; or advertising research, new product development, employee research;
> *services available* – for example full service or limited service; computer-aided interviewing or paper-based methods;
> *expertise in particular research methods or techniques* – for example qualitative, quantitative; omnibus, continuous research, mystery shopping.

You can determine whether researchers meet your criteria by examining their entries in directories or their advertising, by talking to those who have used their services and by talking to them directly. You can invite prospective candidates to make a 'credentials' pitch to you – a presentation outlining their experience and expertise. Once you have established your shortlist you can send out the brief.

It is preferable not to ask more than four research suppliers to tender for a project. Proposals take time and money to prepare but are provided free of charge to clients requesting them, on the understanding that the researcher has a reasonable chance of winning the job. It is judged unfair by The Market Research Society to ask suppliers to tender for projects for which they have less than a one in four chance. This guideline was developed in order to protect research suppliers from being used by clients as a source of free research advice. The cost of preparing proposals is of course built into the researcher's overhead and so ultimately affects the cost of research. The more proposals requested, the more research costs will rise. If more than four suppliers are involved in a pitch individual suppliers may decline to tender, or may ask the client to pay for the proposal.

Questioning a brief

We now switch to the research supplier side. When you receive a brief make sure to read it through several times and, as you start to formulate your ideas about how to structure the research, ask yourself the following:

> Is the problem clearly defined? What assumptions, if any, have been made?
> Why is the research needed?
> Is it clear what the information needs are?
> Will research help?
> Do I have all the information I need to design effective research?
> > Are there any gaps in my knowledge about the problem?
> > Are there any gaps in my knowledge about what the research is required to provide?
> If a research approach is suggested, is it feasible? Will it deliver what is needed?

> ➤ Are the research objectives clear and unambiguous?
> ➤ Are the research objectives relevant to the problem?
> ➤ Is it clear what the client expects from the research?
> ➤ Is it clear how the research will be used?
> ➤ Is the budget adequate?
> ➤ Is the time frame feasible?
> ➤ Are there any gaps in my knowledge about what the proposal should contain?

Even in a well-prepared brief the client may have made some assumptions about what is known or not known, or may not have fully explained some points – as a result of being too close to the problem, for example – and so some gaps or ambiguities might remain. If there is anything that is not clear go back to the client for clarification.

Preparing a research proposal

You should now have all the information you need to write the proposal, having received the brief and clarified any issues with the client. The research proposal is the document that sets out what type of research is to be conducted, why this is suitable, how it is to be conducted, the time frame in which it will be completed and the cost that it will incur. It should demonstrate that you have a clear understanding of the problem, its context and the need for research. In writing the proposal do not assume that those reading it will be research experts or particularly research literate. Explain things clearly and simply and avoid trying to impress the reader with unnecessary jargon or technical language. Remember your aim is to show that you:

> ➤ Understand the problem and the issues involved.
> ➤ Understand the implications of the problem in research terms and in the wider business context.
> ➤ Have the expertise to design, set up, manage and deliver good quality research that will help in the decision-making process.

■ Types of research proposals

Not all projects start with the sort of formal, detailed research proposal described below. The work being commissioned may be similar to, or a repeat of, a previous study and may not warrant a full proposal; or the researcher and client may have an established relationship and so the client may not require the detail of a full proposal. Time may be a factor, limiting what can be produced. About a week to two weeks' notice is needed to prepare a proposal – giving the researcher time to fit it into the work plan, arrange for costings to be prepared and so on. About one or two days will be spent thinking and writing, depending on the complexity of the project. It is good practice to prepare some sort of a written proposal – it will avoid confusion and misunderstanding. Sometimes a one or two pager, a short, less formal proposal covering the basics – introduction, a statement of the problem, the need for research, research objectives, recommended approach, reporting, timings, costs and relevant experience – is all that is needed.

■ The contents of a research proposal

Here is a guide to what should be covered in a full proposal.

Background to the problem

Show the client that you understand the nature and setting of the problem. Do some background research – do not just reproduce the background information that the client gives you in the brief. Add in information that shows you understand the issues and the client's business problem. This can add value to the proposal, and shows the client that you are interested and willing to do that little bit extra.

Research objectives

The research objectives should state what the research will do and so should be relevant to the research problem. They may not be fully or clearly stated in the brief, so you may need to do some work to draw them out. It is crucial that your understanding of these objectives and the client's understanding of them are one and the same; and you both should agree that they will deliver the necessary information. From the research objectives, and from other information provided in the brief, you may be able to set out what general questions will be addressed in the research.

Approach to the research

Set out the research design and why this approach is the most suitable for collecting the evidence needed. Whatever you suggest, explain your reasoning and set out the limitations that the approach may have. We look in detail at the elements of research design in Chapter 4.

Sampling

State clearly the target population for the research. For example, it might be all those aged 18–64 living within a 15 km radius of the car dealership who have bought a car in the last six months or who plan to buy a car in the next six months; all those aged 55 and over living in the community; or all users of a particular Internet Service Provider (ISP). Note your assumptions about the incidence of the target population in the wider population and the basis of the assumption. Explain how you intend to draw a sample from this population, for example using quota sampling or random sampling. (We look at sampling in detail in Chapter 8.) State the intended sample size, or the number of group discussions or depth interviews, and the size of any sub-samples that are relevant to the research objectives (for example those who bought their current car from the car dealership). Explain the reasons for these choices, and the implications they have. Point out if you envisage any problems in either contacting the sample or achieving the interviews and explain how you propose to overcome these.

Method of data collection

Specify the way in which you plan to collect the data, for example whether you plan to use accompanied visits (to the car showroom or on test drives), group discussions, individual or paired depth interviews; face-to-face or telephone interviews; pen and paper methods or computer-aided methods. Mention the reason why you are recommending a particular method. Specify the expected interview length, its content or coverage and its style. You do not need to include a fully worked-up discussion guide or questionnaire but you may want to show the client that you understand what topics or question areas need to be covered in order to address the research objectives. You may even want to give examples of the type of question to be used. In a qualitative project mention whether you plan to use stimulus material or projective techniques. To provide an accurate costing you will need to use the information you have been given in the brief to estimate question-naire or interview length. You should make this, and the assumptions on which it is based (for example an estimate of the number of open questions and the number of closed questions), clear in the proposal so that the client can see how you reached the cost. Set out the implications of using the method suggested: what are the advantages and dis-advantages? For example, if you have suggested telephone interviews it is worth pointing out that this will limit the interview length to about 20 minutes. Include information on how fieldwork is to be organised. You could explain that respondents for the group discussions will be recruited by specially trained qualitative recruiters; that the fieldforce for the quantitative survey meets the standards set by the Interview Quality Control Scheme; that work is conducted in accordance with the MRS or ESOMAR Code of Conduct.

Data processing and analysis

Set out how the data will be handled. For qualitative research note whether the group discussions and individual interviews will be recorded on audio or videotape; whether tapes will be sent to the client; whether full transcripts of all interviews will be made; whether these will be sent to the client. Mention how the analysis will be tackled: will the data be analysed using specialist analysis software? If full transcripts are not made will analysis be based on the moderator's notes and the tapes? For quantitative research you may want to provide details about data processing – the extent and nature of the editing process, the verification procedure after data entry, the cleaning of the dataset, the procedure for coding responses to open-ended questions. Confirm the analysis package that will be used and the format in which the data will be made available, for example as cross-tabulations or as a datafile; hard copy or electronic, or both. Give details of any weighting that might be applied to the data. Set out the type of analysis that will be pro-vided – cross-tabulations, significance tests, specialised statistical techniques, for example.

Outputs

Make it clear what outputs you will provide, the format, the number of copies, the dates on which they will be provided. Set out the cost of additional deliverables, for example interim summary reports, so that the client can take account of the cost implications if these are required.

Timetable

Include a draft timetable or work schedule, highlighting key dates, especially those that are dependent on input from the client. Two different formats are shown below. Figure 3.1 is set out as a table showing the dates associated with key tasks or 'milestones' (you could add a third column to show the outputs associated with the tasks). Figure 3.2, a Gantt chart, shows the individual activities or tasks as bars with week numbers or days, so that it is clear when different phases begin and end and where they overlap. At this stage you may not be able to include exact

Week	Tasks
1	Project start meeting Identification of population and selection of sample for in-depth interviews Design and approval of discussion guide for in-depth interviews
2	Recruitment for in-depth interviews In-depth interviews ongoing Transcription of interviews
3	In-depth interviews completed Transcription of interviews Analysis of interviews
4	Analysis of interviews Progress meeting to discuss findings from in-depth interviews and development of survey questionnaire
5	Design of draft survey questionnaire Meeting to discuss draft questionnaire Amendments to draft questionnaire Approval of survey questionnaire for pilot interviews
6	Survey questionnaire briefing and pilot interviews Feedback from pilot interviews Amendments to questionnaire Fieldwork planning and set-up
7	Final agreement on survey questionnaire Fieldwork set-up completed Specification for analysis of tables Fieldwork start
8, 9, 10	Fieldwork Data processing set-up Data processing – editing and data entry
11	Data processing
12	Standard tables produced Table checking Tables and datafiles available
13	Preparation of report and presentation Informal discussion of findings
14	Delivery of summary report and presentation Follow-up queries

Figure 3.1 Example 1 of a draft project timetable

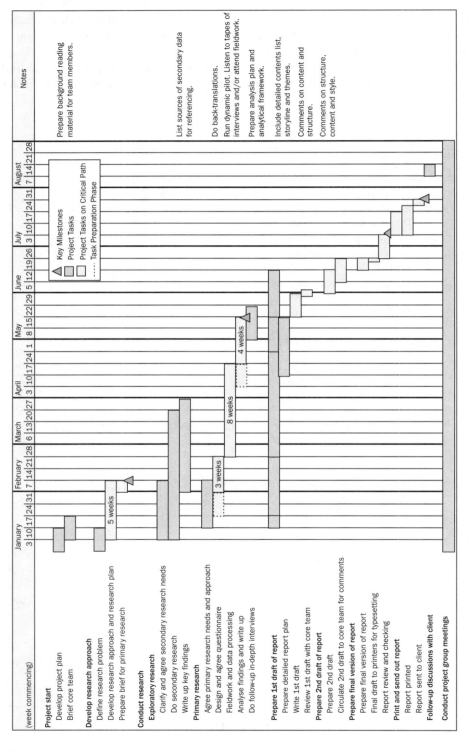

Figure 3.2 Example 2 of a draft project timetable

dates – this will depend on the client giving the go-ahead – but you can put in week numbers and add in the dates when the details have been confirmed. In drawing up the timetable think of the practicalities. If possible, and it is not always possible, build in some contingency time; if the timetable is tight, mention this to the client.

Box 3.7 Working out project timings

Working out precise project times can be difficult – there are so many elements involved that impact on timings, for example:

- ➢ the nature of the research - whether qualitative or quantitative or a combination;
- ➢ the size, scope and complexity of the project;
- ➢ the method of data collection and data capture;
- ➢ the nature of the population under study – ease of accessing the population or sample, the strike rate or speed and ease of recruitment;
- ➢ the length of the interview;
- ➢ the number of interviews;
- ➢ the geographic scope of the research;
- ➢ the time of year (the impact of holidays);
- ➢ data processing and analysis needs;
- ➢ reporting requirements;
- ➢ thinking time – time needed for interpretation, comparison with other data;
- ➢ the extent of liaison required with the client during the project.

Table 3.1 below gives a rough idea of the time involved from briefing to reporting for a range of different projects.

Table 3.1 Guideline to approximate turnaround times for domestic research

Method	Sample	Sample size	Turnaround time
Group discussions	Consumer	6 groups	4 weeks
In-depth interviews	Business	12	4 weeks
Street survey (pen and paper interviewing)	Consumer	300	4 to 6 weeks
Face to face/in-home (computer-aided personal interviewing) using random sample	Consumer	600	4 to 6 weeks (depending on response rate)
C-aided self-interviewing (15-min interview)	Business	400	3 to 4 weeks
CAPI hall test (20-min interview)	Consumer	400	2 weeks
Postal survey	Business	300	2 to 3 months (depending on response rate)
Email or web survey	Business	300	3 to 4 weeks (depending on response rate)

Costs

Include details of the cost of conducting the research proposed and the assumptions on which these costs are based. The detail in which you present the costs may vary depending on custom and practice within your organisation, or on the level of detail requested by the client, and by the nature of the project. Some clients want to see an over-all cost plus an estimate of expenses; others want to see the number of hours each staff member will spend on the project and his or her daily or hourly charge-out rate. A quantitative costing might be presented on a task-by-task basis, or as a client service cost plus a 'field and tab' cost. An example of a project costing grid for client service time for three staff grades is given in Table 3.2. The daily rates included are for illustrative purposes only.

A qualitative costing might be presented in terms of the cost per group or depth inter-view, or as one total cost, or it may be broken down into recruitment costs, fieldwork costs (venue hire, refreshments, transport, incentives), moderator's fee and report writ-ing fee. Box 3.9 is an example of how a cost for a qualitative project might be presented in a proposal. Again, the costs presented are for illustrative purposes only.

Table 3.2 Example of a costing grid for client service time

Task	Estimated time (days)	Daily rate (€)	Cost (€)
Project team briefing and set-up	$\frac{1}{2}$	1,000	500
	$\frac{1}{2}$	700	350
	$\frac{1}{2}$	350	175
Questionnaire design	$\frac{1}{2}$	1,000	500
	3	750	2,250
	1	350	350
Discussion/client approval	$\frac{1}{2}$	1,000	500
	$\frac{1}{2}$	750	375
Fieldwork briefing	$\frac{1}{2}$	1,000	500
	$\frac{1}{2}$	700	350
	$\frac{1}{2}$	350	175
Fieldwork visit	1	700	700
	$\frac{1}{2}$	350	175
Design of analysis specification	$\frac{1}{2}$	700	350
Data checking	$\frac{1}{2}$	350	175
Interpretation and preparation of report	1	1,000	1,000
	5	750	3,750
	2	350	700
Preparation of presentation	1	1,000	1,000
	2	750	1,500
	1	350	350
Presentation/discussion of findings	$\frac{1}{2}$	1,000	500
	$\frac{1}{2}$	750	375
Administration	2	350	700
Total	–	–	17,300

Box 3.8 Working out costs

The cost of a project is closely related to the expenditure of time. In particular, it will depend on the degree of difficulty obtaining respondents, the length of interview, and so number of interviews possible per shift, the total number of interviews, the location of the interview, the type of interview, the analysis requirements, and the project management and reporting requirements. Costing procedures vary. For example, the data processing and client service costs for a quantitative project may be worked out by those departments in an agency, or by the supplier, on the basis of an hourly rate for the grades of staff involved and the number of hours it is likely to entail. Hourly (and daily) charge-out rates are calculated on the basis of employee costs and overheads – the cost of office space, the cost of equipment and so on – and include a profit margin. The field department or fieldwork supplier may work out fieldwork costs. The strike rate or number of interviews achievable in an interviewer shift, the cost of that interviewer shift and its associated expenses (equipment and venue hire, travel and subsistence costs and so on) plus the cost of managing the project – the cost of supervisor time and administrative time – will all be used in reaching a total cost.

Box 3.9 Example of a qualitative research costing

The cost for completing six group discussions, from recruitment to reporting, would be €25,200 plus respondent incentives (at €65 per person and assuming eight per group) of €3,120, giving a total cost of €28,320. The cost for the four and five group options, as requested, is given in Table 3.3.

Table 3.3 Group costs

Option	Cost (€)	Cost per group (€)	Incentives (€)	Total cost (€)
Six groups	25,200	4,200	3,120	28,320
Five groups	23,000	4,600	2,600	25,600
Four groups	19,800	4,950	2,080	21,880

The costs include the following:

➤ briefing of recruiters;
➤ recruiters' fees (for recruitment and hosting of groups);
➤ recruitment costs (preparation of sampling frame, printing of recruitment question-naires etc.);
➤ venue hire;
➤ respondents' refreshments;
➤ consultant fees for project management, moderating, analysis and reporting;
➤ presentation;
➤ three copies of presentation charts and management summary report.

The costs quoted here are exclusive of VAT and do not include moderator's travel and subsistence expenses, which would be agreed when the location of the groups is decided. The cost does not include respondents' travel costs. We would recommend a contingency of €20 per respondent (€160 per group) should we need to arrange transport for respondents.

Be clear about the length of time for which the costs you quote are valid. The time that elapses between submitting the proposal and being commissioned to do the work may be considerable and costs may rise (or fall) in the interim. Be clear also about the costs for which the client will be liable if he or she cancels. See the paragraph on terms and conditions of business below. Make sure

> ### Box 3.10 Headings for a research proposal
>
> ➢ Introduction
> ➢ Background to the problem
> ➢ Research objectives
> ➢ Approach to the research
> ➢ Outputs
> ➢ Timetable
> ➢ Costs
> ➢ Relevant previous experience
> ➢ Project team CVs
> ➢ Terms and conditions of business

you state whether the cost you have quoted includes or excludes any relevant sales tax. Costing international projects can be difficult, especially with fluctuating exchange rates. In costing an international project make it clear in which currency you are billing the client and, if exchange rates apply, what range of fluctuations in the rates (typically ±10 per cent) will be acceptable before it is necessary to recalculate the cost.

Relevant previous experience

This is your chance to sell, to show your credentials, to tell the client why *you* should conduct the research. Rather than presenting a standard credentials pitch, tailor it to the particular research brief. Think about what you bring to this subject matter, to this type of research, to this project. The client may request details of project team members. Whether this is the case or not, it is useful to include a set of short CVs or résumés of key staff designed to show experience and expertise in the area.

Terms and conditions of business

The proposal is an important contractual document as well as a selling tool. It is important to include information on your terms and condition of business, including notice of your adherence to the MRS Code of Conduct or ICC/ESOMAR Code of Practice; how you plan to bill the client; the exchange rate to be used in converting foreign currencies; an assertion of the right to amend the project cost if the client changes the specification; what payment is due if the client cancels the project after commissioning it. Here is a basic example:

Statement of Terms and Conditions of Business
We invoice 50 per cent of the total cost upon commission of the project with the final 50 per cent due on delivery of the presentation and report. All invoices are payable within 30 days. We place a 5 per cent per month surcharge on unpaid invoices. In the event of a project being cancelled after commission a cancellation charge of 30 per cent of the total cost will be charged.

Meeting the proposal submission deadline

The research proposal should be submitted on time. It creates a poor impression if the research proposal arrives late. In government tendering a deadline is set – for example 1500 hours on 17 October – and no proposal will be accepted after that time, even one minute after it. Other clients are less precise – close of business on Thursday or Tuesday morning may be the instruction. A deadline is a deadline and you should use it as an opportunity to show that you can complete a piece of work on time.

Evaluating a proposal

How do you know if a research proposal you have received will produce effective research? Read the research proposal thoroughly, several times. Meet with the research suppliers (at your office or at theirs – meeting at their place may give you more insight into their working practices). Asking the suppliers to present or discuss the proposal is a useful way of gauging their ability to undertake the work and will help you determine whether you can develop a working relationship with them. Box 3.11 is a guide to the sort of questions you might ask as you read the proposal or as you discuss it with the supplier.

Box 3.11 Useful questions in evaluating a proposal

The problem and the research objectives

➢ Has the researcher demonstrated that he or she clearly understands the problem?
➢ Has the researcher shown that he or she clearly understands the context of the problem and the decisions to be made on the basis of the research?
➢ Has the researcher clearly identified the key research objectives and the research questions?
➢ Has the researcher made any incorrect assumptions?

The research design

➢ Will the research design or approach suggested deliver the right kind of evidence?
➢ Has the researcher made a solid and credible case for the approach suggested?
➢ Has the researcher identified any limitations of this approach?
➢ Will the data produced be credible?
➢ Has the researcher clearly and precisely identified the target population?
➢ Has the researcher made a plausible case for the proposed sampling strategy?
➢ Is the sampling strategy appropriate to the aims of the research?
➢ Is the method of data collection suitable?
➢ Has the researcher identified any limitations of this method?
➢ Has the researcher addressed quality control issues?
➢ To what standard is fieldwork conducted?
➢ Is it clear how the data are to be analysed and presented? Is this approach suitable?
➢ Can the researcher provide normative data for comparison?
➢ Has the researcher suggested a framework for interpretation of the findings?
➢ Have any ethical or legal issues been dealt with appropriately?

Box 3.11 continued

Timing and costs

➤ Is the timetable suggested in line with your own and is it manageable?

➤ Is the cost justified and is it clear where the costs arise? Is it value for money?

➤ Have all contingencies been allowed for?

Experience

➤ Has the researcher the right level and kind of experience to deliver the research specified?

➤ Is the staffing suggested appropriate? Do the personnel have the right amount and type of experience?

➤ Has the researcher added any value, provided useful insights, done more than you expected?

➤ Is the proposal clearly set out, well written and easy to follow?

Responding to a proposal

Once you have chosen the proposal that best meets your needs the next step is to inform the supplier in writing and agree to meet to discuss it in detail. This meeting is sometimes called a Project Start meeting. It gives all parties the chance to bring up any outstanding issues, to talk through how the research will happen and to clarify what each expects of the other. Any amendments to the original brief or the proposal or subsequent research plan should be agreed and put in writing. For example, it may be that the research proposed is outside your budget. You may want to discuss with the supplier what changes could be made to meet the budget (one less group discussion, a smaller sample size) without of course sacrificing or compromising the objectives.

It is good practice to inform those who have not been successful with their proposal, and to tell them why they were not successful. This allows the supplier to learn from the experience, address any weaknesses they may have and so improve the service they offer.

The client–researcher relationship

To be able to deliver, and to commission, good research it is important that client and supplier establish a good working relationship. A good working relationship is characterised by a rapport between the parties – a sense of being on the same wavelength. The client has certain expectations of the researcher. He or she expects the researcher to be competent in the design and management of a research project. Yet the client does not want someone who is merely good at the mechanics of research but rather someone who can see the 'big picture' and who can put the research findings into this picture. Failure to do this is a common criticism of researchers: clients often report that researchers are too focused on the research process and the data and not focused enough on what the data say about the problem (Bairfelt and Spurgeon, 1998). The client expects the researcher to have a sound understanding of and an interest in his or her business and the issues facing him or her, to think about the context of the problem, the wider issues involved and how the research can help address these. The researcher should not ignore the question of what is to be done with the information provided by the research.

It is here that we come full circle: as a researcher you must always keep in mind why the research was commissioned in the first place; you will not be able to deliver effective research if you have not paid attention to the front end of the research process. If you have not fully understood the nature of the problem, the context of it, or what the client needs from the research, you will have problems at the delivery stage. Always think of the end result at the beginning. This can be difficult – it may not be possible to get access to the decision maker or the information end user, or information about them, particularly the sort of information that might help you understand the decision-making process and the culture and politics of the organisation. You therefore rely on your relationship with the client. From the researcher's point of view, for the relationship with the client to work best there should be no hidden agendas; the client should help establish an atmosphere in which the researcher feels able to explore or question the brief and reach a full understanding of the issues. In order to improve service delivery, the researcher should ask for (and the client should provide) open and honest feedback about the service.

Chapter summary

➢ The start of a research project typically involves the following:
   ➢ identifying and defining the problem clearly and accurately;
   ➢ identifying the information needs;
   ➢ establishing the end use to which this information will be put;
   ➢ communicating this information to a researcher via a brief;
   ➢ describing the approach to the research via a proposal.

➢ The importance of spending time identifying, defining and clarifying the problem to be researched cannot be overstated. It is essential if good quality, actionable research is to be produced.

➢ In deciding on the resources to be allocated for the research the client should consider the value of the information the research will provide.

➢ A detailed research brief should contain the following information:
   ➢ definition of and background to the problem;
   ➢ why research is necessary;
   ➢ use of information;
   ➢ research objectives;
   ➢ target population;
   ➢ suggested approach;
   ➢ analysis required;
   ➢ deliverables, timings and budget.

➤ It is important that the researcher understands the brief fully. Anything that is not clear should be clarified with the client.

➤ In preparing a proposal the aim is to show that you understand the problem and its implications in the wider business context and that you have the expertise to deliver good quality research that will provide the information to address the problem.

➤ A research proposal should include:
  ➤ an introduction and background to the problem;
  ➤ statement of the research objectives;
  ➤ approach to the research;
  ➤ deliverables, timetable and costs;
  ➤ relevant previous experience and project team CVs;
  ➤ terms and conditions of business.

➤ The proposal should be evaluated to ensure that the research approach described will deliver the information required.

➤ Once a supplier has been chosen the client and supplier should meet to discuss in detail how the research is to be conducted. It is good practice to inform those who have not been successful with a proposal why they were not successful.

➤ To deliver, and to commission, good quality research client and supplier should establish a good working relationship.

➤ The client expects the researcher to be competent in designing and managing the research and to be able to understand the implications of the findings in the wider business context.

Questions and exercises

1 What are the steps leading up to the preparation of a research brief?

2 Discuss the importance of clearly defining the problem to be researched.

3 What is the purpose of a research brief? Why is it important to prepare one?

4 What information should a comprehensive research brief contain?

5 Prepare a checklist based on your answer to question 4 above. Examine an existing research brief, checking off what it contains and what is missing.

6 What questions should you ask in examining a brief?

7 What is the purpose of a research proposal? What information should it contain?

8 Prepare a checklist against which to evaluate a proposal. Use this checklist to evaluate an existing research proposal.

9 Describe the process of choosing a research supplier.

10 What makes a good client–researcher relationship?

References

Barfelt, S. and Spurgeon, F. (1998) *Plenty of Data, but are we doing enough to fill the Information Gap?*, Amsterdam: ESOMAR.

Pyke, A. (2000) 'It's all in the brief', *Proceedings of The Market Research Society Conference*, London: The Market Research Society.

Recommended reading

Bijapurkar, R. (1995) 'Does market research really contribute to decision making?', Amsterdam: ESOMAR. A very clear account of the importance of defining the problem.

Hedges, A. (1994) *Commissioning Social Research: A Good Practice Guide*, London: Social Research Association. A useful guide for those involved in commissioning or tendering for social research.

Moser, C. and Kalton, G. (1971) *Survey Methods in Social Investigation*, Aldershot: Dartmouth. A very useful overview of the issues to be considered in planning a survey.

Punch, K. (2000) *Developing Effective Research Proposals*, London: Sage. A detailed, practical guide aimed at social researchers but just as useful for those in other fields.

Pyke, A. (2000) 'It's all in the brief', *Proceedings of The Market Research Society Conference*, London: The Market Research Society. A very useful look at the roles of researcher and client in the briefing process.

Smith, D. and Fletcher, J. (2001) *Inside Information: Making Sense of Marketing Data*, London: Wiley. A very useful account for those involved in commissioning and using research and a very useful insight for researchers preparing proposals.

Chapter 4

Designing research

Introduction

In this chapter we look at research design – what it is, why it is important and what it involves. We look at the concept of validity and its importance in research design. We examine the nature of research enquiry and we look at four types of research design – cross-sectional, longitudinal, experimental and case study.

Topics covered

➤ Research design
➤ The importance of good research design
➤ The nature of the research enquiry:
  ➤ exploratory
  ➤ descriptive
  ➤ explanatory or causal
➤ Research designs:
  ➤ cross-sectional
  ➤ longitudinal
  ➤ experiment
  ➤ case study

Relationship to MRS Advanced Certificate Syllabus

The material in this chapter is relevant to Unit 3 – Research and Survey Design, specifically:

➤ exploratory research;
➤ descriptive research;
➤ conclusive research.

Learning outcomes

At the end of this chapter you should be able to:

➤ understand what is meant by research design, what it involves and why it is important;
➤ understand the concept of validity and its importance in research design;
➤ understand the nature of research enquiry (exploratory, descriptive or explanatory/causal) and how this relates to research design;
➤ understand the main types of research design (cross-sectional, longitudinal, experimental and case study), their features and their strengths and weaknesses.

What is research design?

Some people confuse research design with choice of research method, seeing it as a decision to use qualitative or quantitative methods, for example, or to use face-to-face interviews rather than telephone, or an omnibus survey rather than a tailor-made one. All these decisions are part of the research design process but they are not the whole of it. It is easiest to think of research design as having two levels. At the first level, research design is about the logic of the research, its framework or structure. It is at this level, given what we know about the nature of the research enquiry (exploratory, descriptive or explanatory), that we make decisions about whether to use a cross-sectional, a longitudinal, an experimental design or a case study – or a combination of these. At the second level it is about the 'mechanics' of the research – what type of data (primary or secondary, qualitative or quantitative or a combination), what method of data collection, what sampling strategy, and so on. The first level is about designing the overall structure of the research so that it delivers the evidence needed to answer the research problem; the second level concerns decisions about how to collect that evidence. The steps in the research design process are set out in Box 4.1.

Box 4.1 The research design process

First level design issues

➤ Defining the research problem
➤ Thinking about the end use of the data
➤ Deciding on the sort of evidence you need
➤ Deciding on the logic and structure of the research
➤ Choosing the research design that will deliver the evidence you need

Second level design issues

Deciding on the type of data and the method of data collection:

➤ Primary or secondary or both
➤ Quantitative or qualitative or both
➤ Face to face, telephone, groups, in-depth interviews and so on.

Designing a sampling strategy:

➤ Identifying the target population
➤ Identifying the sampling units and the sample elements
➤ Choosing a sampling approach
➤ Choosing a sample size.

Designing the data collection instrument:

➤ Defining the concepts, choosing indicators, operationalising the concepts
➤ Designing the questionnaire or discussion guide.

The importance of good research design

The purpose of research design is to deliver the evidence necessary to answer the research problem as accurately, clearly and unequivocally as possible. A sound research design is the framework on which good quality research is built. Validity is a key concept in assessing the quality of research. It refers to how well a research design (and the research method and the measures or questions used) measure what it claims to measure, in other words, gives us clear and unequivocal evidence with which to answer the research problem. There are two types of validity: internal and external validity.

■ Internal validity

Internal validity in the context of research design refers to the ability of the research to deliver credible evidence to address the research problem. Put another way, the job of the research design is to ensure that the research has internal validity. In causal or explanatory research, for example, it is about the ability of the research design to allow us to make links or associations between variables, to rule out alternative explanations or rival hypotheses and to make inferences about causality. Internal validity must also be considered when designing the data collection instrument and constructing questions. In this context, internal validity refers to the ability of the questions to measure what it is we think they are measuring.

■ External validity

When a piece of research has external validity it means that we can generalise from the research conducted among the sample (or in the specific setting) to the wider population (or setting). The ability to generalise from the research findings is a key aim in almost all research enquiries and must be considered at the research design stage as well as at the sample design stage. For example, in a longitudinal or panel design, it is important to decide how to deal with drop-out and replacement in order to ensure that the panel sample remains representative of the population throughout its life.

We started the process of research design in Chapter 3, showing you how to get to grips with the research problem and how to determine what sort of evidence you need to address it. The next step is to think about the nature of the research enquiry and the structure or the design of it. This is the main focus of the chapter. The second level design issues outlined in Box 4.1 – choice of data collection method, sampling strategy, design of the data collection instrument – are dealt with in subsequent chapters. We start, first of all, with a brief look at the nature of the research enquiry; we move on to look at the four classic research designs: cross-sectional, longitudinal, experiment and case study.

The nature of the research enquiry

In choosing a research design, you need to ask the following questions:

➢ What is the *nature* of the research enquiry?
➢ What kinds of answers are we looking for?
➢ What sort of evidence do we need?

As we saw in Chapter 2, research is often categorised according to its purpose into three types of enquiry: *exploratory, descriptive and explanatory* or *causal*. (Sometimes descriptive and explanatory research appears under the heading of *conclusive* research.) In some texts all three types – exploratory, descriptive and explanatory or causal – are referred to as research designs; it is perhaps easier to think of them as types of research enquiry that help inform the choice of research design.

■ Exploratory research

As we saw in Chapter 2, an *exploratory research enquiry*, as its name suggests, aims to explore. It is particularly useful in helping to identify a problem, clarify the nature of it and define its scope. It is useful in looking for insights, developing propositions and hypotheses for further research, and reaching a greater understanding of an issue, for example. In all of these applications exploratory research can contribute to the development of a research design. In fact it should be thought of as a first stage in the research design process, undertaken as part of almost every research project (there are exceptions, of course – for example, repeat studies may not require any exploratory research).

Box 4.2 Examples of exploratory research studies

Telecommunications

Brief: to find out about use of the Internet among the general public (in the early days of the Internet) including level of awareness, profile of users, extent of use, place of use, attitudes.

End use of data: to help decide about the nature and shape of further research.

Research design: cross-sectional.

Research method: quantitative, structured questionnaire administered face to face.

Drug use

Brief: to understand the issues involved in methadone maintenance programmes; to identify the issues around methadone use; to explore users' perspectives; to identify the terminology involved.

End use of data: to clarify the issues involved in preparation for a major study.

Research design: case study of a methadone maintenance clinic.

Research method: qualitative in-depth interviews.

Research design and method and exploratory enquiry

Depending on the objectives of an exploratory enquiry, any of the four research designs – cross-sectional, longitudinal, experiment or case study – may provide an appropriate structure for gathering evidence, for example:

➤ A cross-sectional design would enable you to explore the current market situation.
➤ Primary or secondary analysis of longitudinal or panel data would provide evidence of market or social trends.
➤ A case study of an organisation would provide in-depth understanding of roles and process.

Nor is exploratory research restricted to a particular type of data or method of data collection – it can involve collecting primary data or analysing secondary data, or both; it can involve quantitative or qualitative research, or both; and any method of data collection may be appropriate, depending on the research context.

■ Descriptive research

As we saw in Chapter 2, much market and social research is about description: finding the answers to the Who? What? Where? When? How? and How many? questions. The difference between exploratory research and descriptive research is that, while exploratory research can provide description, in *descriptive research* we usually have a clearer idea of what is needed and are looking for answers to more clearly defined questions.

Before designing descriptive research, think carefully about the information you need and how you are going to use it. Imagine, for example, that you have been asked to design research to help a manufacturer of bricks decide whether or not he should target a new market:

➤ What exactly do you need to describe? What is the scope of the research?
   ➤ Do you need to know the size of the market? If so, do you need to know the size of the market for all bricks, standard bricks only or for special kinds of bricks? Do you need to know the size in terms of volume and value?
   ➤ Do you need to know the market structure – who the main manufacturers are, who the main suppliers (retailers or wholesalers) are, for example?
   ➤ Do you need to know about the specifying or buying process – who decides what type of brick to use, who orders or buys the bricks?
➤ Do you need to look at developments in the market over time or do you want to focus on the size and structure of the market at this particular point in time?
➤ Where is this new market?
   ➤ Does it have a geographical boundary? Are you interested in comparing regions or cities within this geographical area?
➤ Who makes up this market?
   ➤ Are you interested in those who specify what bricks to use, for example quantity surveyors or architects, or those who order or buy them, for example builders' merchants or builders?
   ➤ Do you need to look at any of these particular sub-groups in detail?

Box 4.3 Example of descriptive research study

Building products

Brief: to find out about market size and structure in country X.

Research questions:

➢ How big is the market for standard and special bricks (in value and volume terms)?
➢ Who are the main manufacturers and the main suppliers?
➢ What are the most popular products?
➢ What is the nature of the supply chain?
➢ Who makes the buying decision?
➢ What form of marketing communications do buyers prefer?

End use of data: to decide whether or not to enter a new market.
Research design: cross-sectional.
Research approach: secondary research to gather market size and structure data; quantitative, semi-structured telephone interviews with sellers of bricks – DIY retailers, builders' merchants; qualitative in-depth interviews with specifiers (architects, quantity surveyors, structural engineers, builders).

Research design and method and descriptive enquiry

What sort of research design – cross-sectional, longitudinal, experiment or case study – is suitable for a descriptive enquiry? With the exception of experimental designs, which as we see later are limited in the descriptive data they can deliver, all research designs can produce descriptive data. We look in detail at the features of each and their suitability for different sorts of enquiry later in the chapter. Suffice to say at this stage that the choice of a particular design, or combination of designs, depends on the precise requirements of the descriptive research enquiry. Descriptive research (and the design you choose for it) is not limited to a particular research method or technique, as the example in Box 4.3 shows. It can involve analysis of secondary data or the collection of primary data, or a combination of both. Quantitative or qualitative methods or both can be used. Any method of data collection, from observation to interviewing, is suitable.

■ Causal research

Descriptive research aims to build a picture – of a market, a set of customers, a set of experiences, for example. But what if you want an explanation of what you found? Research that provides explanations (for example of why people buy brand A and not brand B, why some people are in favour of capital punishment and others are not), which helps identify causes (for example of increased sales of brand A) or even helps predict behaviour, is known as *explanatory* or *causal research*. Explanatory or causal research allows you to rule out rival explanations and come to a conclusion – in other words to help develop causal explanations. But what exactly are 'causal explanations'?

Causal explanations

A causal explanation might be that sales of brand A are affected by price (or that income is related to level of educational attainment). In other words a causal explanation says that one thing, call it variable Y (sales of brand A, say, or income), is affected by another thing, call it variable X (price of brand A or educational attainment), or that there is a relationship or association between variable X and variable Y.

Covariance and correlation

It is relatively easy to see if there is a relationship or an association between two variables (by plotting graphs of one thing against the other or by using the statistical techniques of covariance and correlation, which we look at in Chapter 13). Sales of brand A might indeed increase if the price is reduced, for example, or income may be greater among those with higher levels of educational attainment. In a relationship between two variables there may be a direct causal relationship – the change in Y (sales of brand A) is caused directly by X (price of brand A). On the other hand, there may be an indirect causal relationship – in the link between X and Y there may be an *intervening* variable or variables that produce the change in Y. For example, occupation may be the intervening variable through which educational attainment and income are related.

However, because we see a relationship or an association between variables, it does not mean that there is a causal relationship – that one causes the other. The two things might *co-vary*, that is, one thing might follow the other – a change in X is accompanied by a change in Y. X and Y might even be strongly correlated. It is possible to observe covariation and correlation *without there being any causal relationship between X and Y at all*. For example, the correlation between advertising spend and sales may be *spurious* (that is, not causally related at all); it may be that the correlation we see is the result of another variable, an *extraneous* (or confounding) variable (competitor activity, for instance.)

Inferring causation

We can see covariance, association and correlation but we cannot see causation – we have to infer it. In order to make sound inferences about cause we must make sure that the research design allows us to do the following:

➤ look for the presence of association, covariance or correlation;
➤ look for an appropriate time sequence;
➤ rule out other variables as the cause;
➤ come to plausible or common-sense conclusions.

Presence of association, covariance or correlation

If there is a causal relationship between X and Y then we should expect to see an association between them – a change in X associated with a change in Y. In assessing the evidence for cause we should take into account the degree of association between X and Y. We might make one inference on the basis of a strong association and another on the basis of a weak one. For example, we might see a strong association between temperature and sales of ice cream – as the temperature rises, sales of ice cream rise – and we might infer from this that there is a causal relationship between the two. *But remember even if there is an association, no matter how strong, it does not mean that there is causation.*

Appropriate time sequence

The effect must follow the cause. If we think that X causes Y and we find that Y in fact precedes X then we have no evidence for causation. If, however, we observe that Y does indeed follow X then we have some evidence for causation. But in real-life research situations, especially when we are dealing with attitudes and behaviour, it can be very difficult to establish a time sequence.

Ability to rule out other variables as the cause

Although we see an association between X and Y it might be the case that a third variable is responsible for both, and that the relationship we observe exists because of the effect of this third variable. For example, occupation may be 'the cause' of income levels rather than educational attainment. In fact there may be a whole causal chain of other variables linking X and Y. The ability to rule out other variables rests to some extent with our ability to identify what other variables might be involved. But even if we identify the key variables – we live in a complex world so it is unlikely that we would ever be able to identify all the variables in the marketing or social environment of the research – how do we rule them out? For example, it is unlikely that sales of brand A are determined by price alone – other elements of the marketing mix as well as competitor activity are likely to have had some effect. In the prison example mentioned earlier (Box 2.1), a range of other factors is likely to have played a role in affecting drug use (type of drug use, addiction, reaction to being in prison, pressure from other prisoners, lack of desire to conform to prison regulations, availability). Thus a more realistic, 'real-world', causal explanation is that variable Y is affected, directly or indirectly, by a number of variables besides X.

Plausible or common-sense conclusions

We also need to ask: Is it possible that one thing might have caused the other? How likely is the explanation? Does it pass the common-sense test? What does other evidence tell us?

Knowing that this is the type of evidence we need to make inferences about cause, we need to make sure that the research we design delivers it. This means understanding the research problem clearly and in detail; thinking about what relationships might exist between variables, and what the obvious explanations and the alternative explanations for these relationships might be; and thinking about what interpretations we might place on the data. This front-end thinking is crucial. If all of these things are clearly thought out – possible relationships, explanations and interpretations – it is much easier to design research that will deliver the evidence needed to make sound causal inferences. At the same time, we need to recognise that we will never be able to collect 'perfect information' and that our inferences

Table 4.1 Design and method and the nature of research enquiry

Design and method	Nature of research enquiry		
	Exploratory	Descriptive	Causal
Design			
Cross-sectional	✔	✔	
Longitudinal	✔	✔	
Experiment			✔
Case study	✔	✔	
Type of data			
Secondary	✔	✔	✔
Primary	✔	✔	✔
Qualitative	✔	✔	✔
Quantitative	✔	✔	✔
Method of data collection			
Observation	✔	✔	✔
Interviewing	✔	✔	✔

will be only that, inferences and not fact. Research will always be constrained by the complexities of the social and marketing environment and those of human behaviour and attitudes.

Research design and method and causal research

Causal research requires a research design that allows us to infer causation. As we saw above, this means the research should be structured so that we can look for association, covariance or correlation between variables, establish if the appropriate time sequence exists, rule out other variables as the cause and come to plausible or common sense conclusions. Although cross-sectional, longitudinal and case study designs can take us some of the way towards this, they do not provide the structure for proving causation. The experimental design is the one used most often in causal research. Any type of data or method of data collection can be used.

Research designs

As we noted above, there are four main types of research design:

➢ the cross-sectional study;
➢ the longitudinal study;
➢ the experiment;
➢ the case study.

In this next section we look at what each of them involves, and how to choose a design that will deliver the sort of evidence you need for your research enquiry.

■ Cross-sectional research design

Cross-sectional research design is probably the most common type of design in market and social research. It allows you to collect data from a cross-section of a population *at one point in time*. A *single cross-sectional design* involves only one wave or round of data collection – data are collected from a sample on one occasion only. A *repeated cross-sectional design* involves conducting more than one wave of (more or less) the same research with an *independent* or fresh sample each time. The use of an independent sample at each round of data collection is what distinguishes repeated cross-sectional design from longitudinal research. In longitudinal research, data are collected from the *same sample* on more than one occasion.

Uses

A cross-sectional design can be used to provide data for an exploratory or descriptive research enquiry. It can also be used to look for and examine relationships between variables; to test out ideas and hypotheses; to help decide which explanation or theory best fits with the data; and to help *establish causal direction* but not to *prove cause*.

Box 4.4 Examples of the use of cross-sectional design

Single cross-sectional design: buying a car

Aim: to describe and understand the decision-making process involved in buying a car.

Research method: qualitative – mini group discussions, paired (family) and individual in-depth interviews.

Analysis: comparisons made between those who took a test drive and bought a car and those who took a test drive and did not buy.

Single cross-sectional design: assessing needs

Aim: to determine the health and social services needs of older people.

Research method: quantitative survey – face-to-face, in-home interviews.

Analysis: comparisons made (*inter alia*) between sexes; between those living alone and those living with family members; and between those on state pension only and those on state pension plus private pension or other income.

Repeated cross-sectional design: pre-and post-advertising test

Aim: to determine the effect of an advertising campaign on attitudes to brand A.

Research method: quantitative pre- and post-advertising surveys with independent samples using face-to-face interviews.

Analysis: comparisons made (*inter alia*) between regular buyers of brand A, occasional buyers and rejectors of brand A, pre- and post-advertising.

Repeated cross-sectional design: social attitudes

Aim: to determine the prevalence of a range of social attitudes.

> **Box 4.4 continued**
>
> *Research method*: quantitative survey using CAPI in-home interviews, repeated annually among a 'fresh' nationally representative sample.
>
> *Analysis*: trends in social attitudes over time; comparisons made (*inter alia*) between men and women, those with children and those without.
>
> Examples of social surveys using a repeated cross-sectional design include the European Social Values Survey; in the United Kingdom, the General Household Survey, the Family Expenditure Survey; in the United States, the General Social Survey.

With a cross-sectional design, and this is something that distinguishes it from experimental research design, we rely on there being differences within the sample in order to be able to make comparisons between different groups. For example, if we need to compare attitudes of buyers and non-buyers of brand A, we depend on these differences existing within the sample. In experimental research design, we create differences within the test sample by manipulating one of the variables – the independent or explanatory variable – in order to see if it causes a change in another variable – the dependent variable.

■ Longitudinal research design

Longitudinal research is common in market and social research, where it is often referred to as panel design. It involves collecting data from the same sample (of individuals or organisations, for example) on *more than one occasion*. Whereas the cross-sectional design provides a 'snapshot' of a situation, the longitudinal design provides a series of snapshots over a period of time that can be joined together to give a moving image. The number and frequency of the snapshots or data collection points depend largely on the research objectives. For example, if the purpose of the research is to look at the immediate, short-term impact of an advertising campaign, a relatively small number of data collection points, fairly closely spaced in time, may suffice; to examine the longer-term impact of advertising on a brand may require a relatively large number of data collection points over many years.

What distinguishes longitudinal designs from repeated cross-sectional designs is that in longitudinal designs data are collected from the *same sample* on more than one occasion, rather than from *independent* or fresh samples each time. There is some overlap in the definitions of longitudinal and repeated cross-sectional designs, best illustrated by the way in which tracking studies or trend studies are classified. In some texts, tracking studies are classified as a longitudinal design, the argument being that the sample at each wave is effectively the same (albeit composed of different individuals). In others, and in this one, tracking studies are classed as a cross-sectional design because although the samples are matched at each wave they are nevertheless independent samples.

Although panel designs are associated with quantitative research, they can be and are used in qualitative research, as the examples in Box 4.5 show. Secondary analysis of panel data is also commonplace.

Uses

The main application of longitudinal design is to monitor changes in the marketing or social environment, changes that occur in the normal course of things and events that are planned, for example changes as a result of an advertising campaign, a new product launch or an election. Longitudinal design can be used to provide data for descriptive research enquiry. Although it cannot be used to prove cause, it can be used to achieve the following:

➢ explore and examine relationships between variables;
➢ establish the time order of events or changes, and age or historical effects;
➢ help decide which explanation or theory best fits with the data;
➢ help establish causal direction (rather than prove cause).

Box 4.5 Examples of the use of longitudinal or panel research

Voters' attitudes and intentions

Aim: to determine reactions to events; to understand the decision-making processes in relation to voting intentions in the run-up to an election; to observe the impact of events on attitudes and intentions; to gain reaction to the content and wording of campaign messages.

Design: three rounds of fieldwork with the same sample of voters over a three-month period, each round timed to follow key political events and decisions.

Method: qualitative mini-depth interviews.

Attitudes to developments in new technology

Aim: to determine attitudes to developments in new technology and the implications these developments might have in daily life.

Design and method: a series of nine qualitative online discussions over a one-year period with the same sample.

Behaviour in the convenience meals market

Aim: to understand buying behaviour – frequency, brands, type of meal and usage data.

Design and method: quantitative computer-aided self-completion questionnaire/diary recording meal type, time of day, meal accompaniments and so on; continuous with weekly downloading of data.

Drop-out and replacement in panels

As time passes the universe or population from which the panel is recruited changes – this is especially so in fast-moving markets and in new markets (for example the Internet) as penetration and use increases (or declines). Also, the panel members themselves change – for one thing, they get older. It may therefore be necessary to replace panel members – refresh the panel – in order to maintain its representativeness (and its external validity).

The longer a panel lasts the greater the chance that panel members will drop out. A key question in panel design and management is whether or not to replace them. If you do not, you may end up with a very small sample and one that is likely to be unrepresentative (and so poor in terms of external validity) – those who drop out being in all likelihood different from those who stay.

If you decide to replace the drop-outs, how do you go about it? There are two approaches to replacement. The first is to find out the characteristics or profile of the drop-outs and recruit replacements with exactly the same profile. It is of course important to be aware that you can never know all the characteristics of an individual (there may be characteristics that we do not use in recruiting respondents but which nevertheless have a bearing on other characteristics). The second approach is the use of a rolling panel design, a technique used in most market research panels, indeed in any long-term panel which puts a fairly heavy burden on respondents and so results in respondent fatigue and high drop-out or attrition rates. The advantage of the rolling panel method is that it smoothes out drop-out. It also smoothes out conditioning (the phenomenon of responding to questions in a way that is 'conditioned' by having responded to the same or similar questions in previous rounds of data collection), which affects the quality of the data.

Data quality is also an issue with new recruits to the panel: joiners will not have provided data in the same time period as those already on the panel (which has implications for looking at data at the individual rather than the aggregate level); they are likely to be more enthusiastic (less conditioned) than established panel members and so the data they provide will be different and not comparable with that of established members. The solution here is to ignore data from new panel members for the first one or even two data collection periods of their membership.

■ Experimental research design

The purpose of an experimental research design is to examine *in isolation* the effect of one variable (*the independent or explanatory variable*) on another (*the dependent variable*). The idea is that the effects of all other variables will be removed or *controlled* in order to see clearly the effect of this one variable. The main application of experimental research designs is to determine if a causal relationship exists and the nature of the relationship, to rule out the effects of other variables and to establish the time order or sequence of events (which is the cause and which the effect). It is the most effective research design in determining causal connections. It is used in marketing experiments, for example, to make decisions about elements of the marketing mix, to evaluate effectiveness of advertisement A or B, the weight of advertising spend or the combination of media to be used in a campaign.

Experimental design works like this. Two identical samples or groups are recruited: one is known as the *test* group, the other is the *control* group. The test and control groups are matched on key criteria – in other words the two are the same on all key characteristics. The independent variable – the one that is thought to cause or explain the change – is manipulated to see the effect that this change has on the dependent variable. This is referred to as the *treatment*. The treatment is applied to the test group but not to the control group. The purpose of the test group is to observe the effect of the treatment; the purpose of the control group is to act as a comparison. Since the treatment is not applied to the control group any changes that take place will not be due to the independent variable but to some other factor(s). The design of the experiment should be such that the effect of other factors is limited or controlled. Comparison of the test and control group allows us to determine the extent of the change that is due to the independent variable only. This type of experimental design is called the 'after with a control group'. There are variations to this design: when the independent variable and the dependent variable are measured in both groups *before* the treatment takes place the design is called a 'before and after'; if a control group is used it is called, not surprisingly, a 'before and after with a control'.

The purpose of the 'before measurement' is to ensure that both the test and control groups are similar on the key measures. These before measurements, however, do not need to be taken if we are satisfied that the test and control group samples are the same on all measures (if, for example, each was chosen using random sampling). The post-treatment differences between the test and control groups should be sufficient to determine the change due to the action of the independent variable. We can take several post-treatment measurements, depending on the objectives of the research – for example, some effects may take longer to manifest or we may want to observe the longer-term impact of the independent variable.

The experimental designs described above deal only with the effect of one variable. This can be impractical (and expensive) if we want to look at several variables and inappropriate if we need to determine how sets of variables might interact or work together. To look at the effect of more than one variable at a time *factorial design* is required. This type of design allows us to examine the main effects of two or more independent variables and to look at the interaction between the variables (for example gender and age on quality of life; or price and pack size on sales).

The clinical terminology used in experimental design reflects its origin in the laboratory-based sciences. Experiments can, however, be carried out in the field – for example sensory testing, test marketing (including simulated test markets) and advertising tests, as well as tests about research practice, as the example in Box 4.6 shows.

Experimental designs are difficult (and expensive) to use in the real world – it is not always possible to isolate or account for the complexity of variables. Care must be taken in interpreting the results, especially if the experiment has been applied to real-world marketing and social issues. It is always possible that other uncontrolled external factors may be exerting an influence. For example, imagine you need to determine the effect of advertising on sales of brand A. You could set up an experiment: choose three areas of the country that are matched in terms of key (demographic) characteristics – non-overlapping television regions, if you want to test the effects of television advertising, or separate distribution channels if you want to test the effect of press or magazine advertising. In each area you could advertise with a different weight of spend. You are manipulating the advertising variable – the causal or independent variable – and you want to see if sales of the advertised brand (the

Box 4.6 Example of an experimental design

The effects of monetary incentives on response rate to a mail survey

One of the objectives of this experiment was to examine the relative effectiveness of prepaid cash incentives, a prize draw for cash and a prize draw for an equivalent value non-cash prize, as methods of increasing mail survey response rates.

The sample was made up of 900 New Zealand residents randomly selected from the 57 electoral rolls representing the main urban centres. Approximately equal numbers of respondents from each socio-economic level were assigned to each of nine groups – one control group and eight treatment groups; each group contained 100 respondents:

1 control – no incentive;
2 20 cent coin in first mailout only;
3 50 cent coin in first mailout only;
4 $1 note in first mailout only;
5 20 cent coin in second mailout only;
6 50 cent coin in second mailout only;
7 $1 note in second mailout only;
8 prize draw for $200 cash offered in each mailout;
9 prize draw for $200 gift voucher offered in each mailout.

All respondents were sent the same questionnaire, a covering letter and a reply-paid return envelope. The letters to the different test groups varied only in the wording of a single sentence that drew attention to the incentive.

The response rates were monitored. The results provide qualified support for the claim that monetary incentives are an effective means of increasing response rates in mail surveys; 50 cents sent with the first mailout was very effective in this regard. However, after three mailouts, this was the only incentive that produced a statistically significant result when compared to the control group, indicating that some monetary incentives are not necessarily any more effective than two reminder mailouts.

Source: Adapted from Brennan, M., Hoek, J. and Astridge, C. (1991) 'The effects of monetary incentives on the response rate and cost-effectiveness of a mail survey', *Journal of The Market Research Society*, **33**, 3, pp. 229–41. Used with permission.

dependent variable) are affected: does a difference in the weight of advertising spend affect sales? You are controlling the effect of some other variables by matching the samples in each of the three test areas – but what about other uncontrollable or unknown variables such as competitor activity? Can you rule out the effect of these variables?

It is useful to be sceptical about the extent to which a causal relationship is proven. Even with a control group external factors (known and unknown) may influence one group disproportionately. It is also important to think about the external validity of the results. The very fact of being studied makes people act differently (the Hawthorne Effect). Think about how artificial the experiment was, and whether you can generalise from the findings to the wider population.

As with panel design, in a before and after experimental design you need to go back to the same people for an 'after' measure. You might find that some drop out. It is important to bear in mind the effect this change in the sample will have on pre- and post- and test and control comparisons. Some problems may be overcome using statistical manipulation of the data. Conditioning is also an issue in experimental design – respondents can become sensitised to the research topic, and they may remember the answers they gave in the pre-stage and offer their post-answers accordingly. Timing of the post-stage measure is critical so that you do not miss the effects of the test variables (by collecting the data too early or too late); it is possible to under- or overestimate the length of the effect. Also, you have to bear in mind that the longer the time lag between the tests the more likely it is that respondents will drop out.

■ Case study research design

A case study is an in-depth investigation of a 'case' for exploratory, descriptive or explanatory research purposes, or a combination. A 'case' might be, for example, a household, an organisation, a situation, an event, or an individual's experience. Case study research may involve examining all aspects of a case – the case as a whole and its constituent parts. For example, a case study of a particular household may involve data collection from individual members; in an organisation the elements of the case might be departments and individuals within departments. A case study design might be made up of several case studies, not just one. A variety of methods of data collection can be used in a case study, including analysis of documents, observation and qualitative and quantitative interviewing.

Box 4.7 Examples of the use of case study designs

Drug treatment centre

Aim: to understand the reason for the level of success of a particular drug treatment centre and whether lessons in relation to policy and practice could be transferred to other centres.

The case study included a review of the brochures and other documentation drawn up by the centre; a review of policies, procedures and guidelines; and interviews with management, staff, volunteers, and clients and their families.

A university programme

Aim: To evaluate the effectiveness of a pre-admission university programme.

The case study included a review of the documents related to the programme; a review of the recruitment practice of the programme; qualitative in-depth interviews with experts involved in the policy-making decisions, programme staff, students on the programme; and a self-completion survey among students on the programme.

Uses

The main application of a case study design is to get the full picture, to achieve an in-depth understanding and to get detailed (idiographic) description. It is also useful in understanding the context of attitudes and behaviour in order to reach a greater understanding of their meaning. It can be used to establish a sequence of events; to examine relationships between variables; and to understand which explanation best fits a hypothesis or theory. Case studies are common in educational and organisational research and in evaluation research.

If the findings from a particular case study are to be used to make generalisations about the wider group or population to which the case belongs, some care must be taken in ensuring that the particular case is representative of the wider population of cases. In some instances generalisation may not be the aim of the research – the aim may be to understand fully the particular case.

Table 4.2 Summary of key features of research designs

Feature	Single cross-sectional	Longitudinal	Experiment	Case study
Suitable for exploratory research	+	+	−	+
Suitable for descriptive research	+	+	−	+
Suitable for causal research	+	+	+	+
Exploring relationships between variables	+	+	+	+
Establishing time sequence	−	+	+	+
Establishing association, covariance and correlation	+	+	+	−
Ruling out other variables/ explanations	−	−	+	−
Understanding why one thing causes or affects another	+	+	−	+
Ability to deal with complexity	−	+	−	+
Making comparisons between groups	+	+	−	+
Ability to detect change	−	+	+	−
Representativeness	+	−	−	−
Ability to look at data at the level of the individual	−	+	−	+
Relative cost	+	−	−	−
Ease of set-up	+	−	−	+
Ease of management	+	−	−	+
Burden on respondents	+	−	−	−

+ indicates a relative strength; − indicates a relative weakness.

Chapter summary

➤ Research design is about deciding on the structure the research will take in order to deliver the evidence needed to address the research problem clearly and unequivocally.

➤ There are two levels of research design. The first level involves getting to grips with the research problem, defining it and clarifying the nature of the evidence needed to address it; it also involves deciding on the structure of the research that will deliver the evidence. The second level involves decisions about how to collect the evidence: decisions about sampling and method of data collection.

➤ Validity is an important concept in judging the quality of research. Two types of validity are important in the context of research design: internal validity and external validity. Internal validity refers to the ability of the research design to deliver the evidence needed to address the research problem clearly and unambiguously; external validity refers to the representativeness of the research findings, the ability to generalise from the research gathered from the sample or setting to the wider population.

➤ There are three types of research enquiry: exploratory, descriptive and explanatory or causal. Descriptive and causal research are also known as conclusive research.

➤ Causal research is about seeking causal explanations. We can see (and measure) association, covariance and correlation; we have to infer cause. To make sound inferences about cause the research design must enable us to look for the presence of association, covariance or correlation, and an appropriate time sequence, to rule out other variables as the cause and to come to plausible or common-sense conclusions.

➤ There are four main types of research design: cross-sectional, longitudinal, experimental and case study.

➤ Cross-sectional research design is probably the most common type of design in market and social research. In a *single cross-sectional design* data are collected once only from a cross-section of a population *at one point in time*; a *repeated cross-sectional design* involves conducting more than one wave of (more or less) the same research with an *independent* or fresh sample each time.

➤ The use of an independent sample at each round of data collection is what distinguishes repeated cross-sectional design from longitudinal research. In longitudinal research, data are collected from the *same sample* on more than one occasion.

➤ The purpose of an experimental design is to examine *in isolation* the effect of one variable (*the independent or explanatory variable*) on another (*the dependent variable*). The effects of all other variables are removed or *controlled* in order to see clearly the effect of this one variable. The main application of experimental research design is to determine if a causal relationship exists.

> A case study is an in-depth investigation of a case (or cases), for example a household or an organisation, for exploratory, descriptive or explanatory research purposes, or a combination of these.

> A research design can use any method of data collection.

Questions and exercises

1 What is research design? What is involved in:
   (a) first level of research design;
   (b) second level of research design?

2 Why is research design important?

3 What do the following terms mean: internal validity and external validity?

4 Describe what is meant by exploratory and descriptive research. Give examples of each type of enquiry.

5 What is the aim of causal research?

6 To make sound causal inferences what sort of evidence must a research design provide?

7 Describe:
   (a) what is involved in a cross-sectional research design – give examples;
   (b) what is involved in a longitudinal research design – give examples;
   (c) what distinguishes a repeated cross-sectional design from a longitudinal design.

8 Describe the main stages in an experimental research design. Give an example of the application of an experimental design.

9 What is case study research? What methods of data collection are suited to a case study approach?

10 What type(s) of research design are suitable for a descriptive research enquiry?

Recommended reading

De Vaus, D. (2001) *Research Design in Social Research*, London: Sage. An excellent account of all aspects of research design.

Chapter 5

Doing secondary research

Introduction

The aim of this chapter is to introduce you to secondary data and secondary research. Secondary data are a useful source of information and should not be overlooked. An exploration of secondary data is especially useful in the early stages of a project, helping with problem definition and research design and planning and, at the later stages, providing a context for the interpretation of primary data, for example. In this chapter definitions of the terms secondary data, secondary research and secondary data analysis are given and examples of useful sources of secondary data provided. We also look in some detail at the use of databases and data warehouses for storing secondary data, and the techniques of data fusion and data mining in analysing these data.

Topics covered

➤ Secondary research
➤ Secondary data analysis
➤ Sources of secondary data
➤ Data storage – data archives, databases and data warehouses
➤ Analysing data – data fusion and data mining

Relationship to MRS Advanced Certificate Syllabus

The topics covered in this chapter are part of Unit 2 – Primary and Secondary Data Collection and Exploratory Research, more specifically:

➤ the role of secondary data;
➤ how to source secondary data;
➤ the use of in-house data;
➤ the use of databases;
➤ the concepts and problems of data fusion;
➤ the use of data mining.

At the end of this chapter you should be able to:

➤ understand the nature of secondary data;
➤ evaluate the usefulness of secondary data;
➤ understand what is meant by secondary data analysis;
➤ demonstrate knowledge of secondary data sources;
➤ understand the concepts of marketing information systems and decision support systems;
➤ understand the principles of data fusion and data mining.

Secondary data

As we saw in Chapter 2, secondary research involves looking for data and analysing data that already exist in some form. These secondary data have not been created specifically for the purpose at hand (unlike primary research data) but were originally collected for another purpose. Secondary research is also known as *desk research* – you can do it without leaving your desk, making use of published sources, data available on an internal database, or via online databases and the Internet.

Box 5.1 Uses and benefits of secondary research

➤ Answers the research problem without the need for primary research.
➤ Leads to a better understanding of the issues and the wider context of the problem.
➤ Helps define the problem.
➤ Helps in the development and formulation of hypotheses.
➤ Helps determine the nature of the evidence required to address the problem.
➤ Helps formulate an effective research design.
➤ Enriches the interpretation of the primary data.
➤ Sets the findings from the primary research into a wider context.

■ Why use secondary data?

The value or usefulness of a set of data is rarely exhausted on its initial or primary application. The data may be useful in the same context at a later date, or in a different context. One dataset may be combined with others – from very different sources – making the combined set more valuable and of greater use than the individual elements. Using information already collected can be much cheaper than carrying out primary research. Secondary data are also relatively quick and easy to get hold of – unlike primary data they are already available and relatively easy to access, especially using online internal and external databases. Consulting existing data – doing secondary research – should be the first step in answering any query or researching any topic. You may discover that there is no need for expensive primary research, that the secondary data answer the research or marketing problem. If, however, you discover that gaps in your knowledge or understanding remain, exploring the secondary data may help you define more clearly the problem or issue you need to research. A clear definition of the problem will help you define the scope of the research and the nature of the evidence you need, and help you with research design and planning. For example, it may uncover relationships and suggest hypotheses to be tested in primary research. Secondary data also provide a very useful context for the interpretation of primary data, and will increase the richness and depth of interpretation and reporting.

■ Evaluating the quality and usefulness of secondary data

It is important to evaluate the quality and usefulness of secondary data. The data may be limited in their suitability – by definition the data are not specific to the problem in question, they were gathered for another purpose and so may not directly or adequately address the problem. The definition of variables may not match your definition, reducing the usefulness of the information and the scope for comparability and data fusion. It may be possible to reanalyse or manipulate the data in order to increase comparability but this may erode any time and cost savings in using secondary rather than primary data. The data may have been collected some time ago and so may be out of date. There is also a likelihood of bias – those who produced the data may have had a particular agenda, which may have led to bias in how the data were collected, analysed or interpreted. The data may be of poor quality – error can creep in at almost any stage of the research process, for example as a result of an inappropriate research or sample design, a poorly designed or executed questionnaire. You need to be aware of the source of any potential errors, and the scope for compounding these errors in your use of the data.

In order to evaluate the quality of secondary data, and their usefulness to your research objectives, you need to investigate their background and previous life. Make sure you ask the following questions:

➤ Why were the data collected? What were the original research objectives?
➤ Who commissioned the research?
➤ Who conducted the research?
➤ How accurate are the data?
➤ What quality standards were employed in the research process?
➤ What was the research design?
➤ What sampling procedure was used?
➤ What was the sample size?
➤ What method(s) of data collection were used?
➤ What was the response rate?
➤ How good was the design of the questionnaire or discussion guide?

➤ How were the parameters or variables defined (for example, definition of social class, income and family as well as other key variables may vary)?

➤ How were the data processed and analysed?

➤ Are the data weighted? If so, what is the basis of the weighting procedure?

➤ How were missing values handled?

➤ How old is the data? When was it first collected? Is it out of date?

➤ How useful is the information?

Secondary data analysis

Secondary data can be used in their 'raw' form, as they are, without being manipulated in any way; they can also be used in further or secondary analysis. Hakim's (1982) definition of secondary data analysis is:

> *any further analysis of an existing dataset which presents interpretations, conclusions or knowledge additional to, or different from, those presented in the first report on the inquiry and its main results.*

The aim of secondary analysis therefore is to extract new findings and insights from existing data. Secondary analysis became an important part of social research in the United Kingdom and elsewhere in the 1970s when the type of data collected by government changed from statistics derived from administrative records to data collected via sample surveys. At the same time there was an increase in access to computers for data analysis and archives were created to store and preserve computer-readable data, thus making the process much easier than it had been.

■ Evaluating data for secondary analysis

The factors affecting the quality and usefulness of a dataset for secondary analysis are the same as those for the use of raw secondary data. If you are planning to conduct secondary analysis on a dataset it is important to know the source of the data and to have at least a copy of the original survey questionnaire or discussion guide and a description of the sampling techniques used. You may also find it useful to have a copy of the instructions that were given to the interviewers or moderators who conducted the fieldwork. It is also important to know the definitions and clarifications they may have given respondents. From a data processing point of view you should have a detailed description of how the data were coded and analysed. You may want to know how the dataset is structured, what technical tools were used in processing and analysis and what weighting, if any, was applied. In addition, a list of the variables and values and the coding and classification schemes used, including non-response codes, as well as any derived variables that were constructed, can be invaluable. A list of the publications produced from the data will give a better insight into the study; it will highlight the ground already covered and point to interesting questions still waiting to be answered.

Sources of secondary data

Secondary data are often classified according to their source as internal and external secondary data. Internal data are those generated by the organisation, for example data from previous research, financial data and, crucial to the marketing function, sales data. External data are data gathered by those outside the organisation.

■ Internal sources of secondary data

Technological developments in the last ten years or so have meant that it is possible to capture, store and analyse huge volumes of sales and transaction data. Data can be captured at the point of interaction with the customer, whether it is in person via EPOS (electronic point of sale) scanners or remotely via telephone, wireless and Internet technology. The data collected can be stored in and retrieved from databases and data warehouses designed to function as management information systems (MIS) or marketing information systems (MkIS). Such systems are often referred to as decision support systems (DSS), and are structured in a way that allows users to search for and retrieve the data they need for planning and control, and for strategy development, for example.

■ External sources of data

External data, which can also be integrated into an organisation's DSS, are data generated by those outside the organisation. There are two main sources of external secondary data: those produced by government departments, agencies and related bodies and sometimes referred to as *official statistics*; and those produced by trade bodies, commercial research organisations and business publishers, and sometimes called *unofficial statistics*. Most of these data are available in hard copy format, from the publisher, source or a library, or via online and offline (CD-ROM) databases.

Government published data

Governments and related bodies collect a wide range of social, economic and business data, from the Census of Population and the demographic characteristics of the population, through their spending habits, lifestyle and attitudes, to information about different market sectors, from agriculture to tourism, and information on domestic and international trade and key economic indicators. The quality and usefulness of government produced data should be assessed in the same way and with the same rigour as data from other sources.

Research data and information on the EU and its member states can be accessed via the EU information website (<u>http://europa.eu.int/geninfo/info-en.htm</u>) and from databases located at CORDIS, the Community Research and Development Information Service (<u>www.cordis.lu</u>). A web-based subscription service called 'eurotext' provides full text versions of key EU documents from 1950 (<u>http://eurotext.ulst.ac.uk/</u>).

The Resource Centre for Access to Data on Europe (r-cade) provides online access to European statistics from Eurostat, the EU Official Statistical Office, as well as access to United Nations' data sources (**http://www.r-cade.dur.ac.uk/**).

In the United Kingdom, the Government Statistical Service (GSS) – an organisation spread among 30 or so government departments and bodies – is responsible for providing *'Parliament, government and the wider community with the statistical information, analysis and advice needed to improve decision making, stimulate research and inform debate.'* Within the GSS it is the role of the Office for National Statistics (ONS), a body independent of any other government department, to collate research and statistical publications produced by government departments and related bodies in compendia publications and databases. These publications can be bought, accessed in hard copy form via libraries or accessed online via the ONS website (**www.statistics.gov.uk**). The British Official Publications Current Awareness Service (BOPCAS) offers access to a database of abstracts, summaries and, in some cases, the full text of recent official publications and provides an email alerting service (**http://soton.ac.uk/~bopcas**).

Government statistical services exist in most countries. In Ireland the body responsible is the Central Statistics Office (**www.cso.ie**); in Australia it is the Australian Bureau of Statistics (**www.abs.gov.au**); in India it is the Ministry of Statistics and Programme Implementation (**www.nic.in**); in the United States it is the US Census Bureau (**www.census.gov**). Most of these sites provide links to equivalent sites in most other countries. Government departments for trade and foreign affairs and the embassies of foreign governments are useful sources of data on international business environments, providing information on political, legal, economic and cultural aspects of doing business or research.

Non-government published data

Sources of non-government data abound. They include newspapers, journals, magazines, newsletters, pamphlets, books, directories, guides, catalogues and databases. Material is produced by trade associations and professional bodies, chambers of commerce, regulatory bodies and pressure groups, academic and research institutions, as well as by commercial organisations, including market research companies and business information publishers. Much of this material can be tracked down via the source organisation's website, via specialist information host sites that list catalogues, directories, guides and databases and via information gateway sites. One such site is SOSIG, the Social Science Information Gateway (**www.sosig.ac.uk**). It provides an extensive list of links to online databases worldwide – bibliographic, numeric and full text databases – covering most subjects relevant to market and social research. The Resource Discovery Network (RDN) provides a gateway to other subject areas including health, medical and life sciences (**www.rdn.ac.uk**). COPAC is a free access service to the unified online catalogues of some of the largest university libraries in the United Kingdom and Ireland and includes access to documents in around 300 languages (**http://copac.ac.uk/**).

Other useful sources of international data include the United Nations (www.un.org), which has a wide range of links to online catalogues, bibliographic databases and directories relating to social, economic and market data; the World Bank (www.worldbank.org), the OECD (Organisation for Economic Co-operation and Development (http://www.oecd.org) and the World Economic Forum (www.worldeconomicforum.org).

There are several commercial organisations that supply (secondary) research data on a range of topics, including Mintel (www.mintel.co.uk), Data Monitor (www.datamonitor.com), Kompass (www.kompass.com) and www.business.com. Forrester Research (www.forrester.com), Nua (www.nua.ie) and eMarketer (www.eMarketer.com) among others specialise in new media research. Through the Financial Times Discovery Service (http://ftdiscovery.ft.com) you can access a wide range of information on organisations, industry sectors and countries.

Data storage

There are several types of data stores: data archives, databases and data warehouses. Although they have much in common – they are all databases of one sort or another – there are some differences.

■ Data archives

A data archive is a store or repository for data. Commercial organisations have their own data archives in the form of internal databases and data warehouses that form the basis of DSS and MIS. External organisations also maintain data archives that can be accessed by anyone interested in using the data stored there. A vast amount of data relating to social and economic life in the United Kingdom is held at the UK Data Archive, which is administered by the Economic and Social Research Council (ESRC) and the University of Essex. The Archive contains data collected by the ONS on behalf of the UK government from regular, repeated surveys such as the Labour Force Survey, the General Household Survey and the Family Expenditure Survey. Besides government produced data, the Archive holds academic research data – data produced with funding from the ESRC itself as well as material from other (international) archives and data from market research, independent research institutes and public bodies. The Archive website (www.data-archive.ac.uk) contains full descriptions and documentation of datasets (including qualitative data) and supports several methods of searching for information. The Archive's main online retrieval system, known as BIRON, can be used for subject and topic searches as well as searches by name of person or organisation associated with a study, or the dates and geographical location of data collection. BIRON is in effect a catalogue consisting of descriptive information (the metadata) about studies held in the Archive.

Another useful archive is the Central Archive for Empirical Social Research at the University of Cologne (www.gesis.org/en/za/index.htm). It houses German survey data as well as data from international studies and is the official archive for the International Social Survey Programme (ISSP), of which the European Social Values Survey is a part. The ISSP collects data on key social and social science issues in over 30 countries worldwide. The Central Archive provides access to the data collected from each individual country and to the file containing data from all participating countries for each year of the survey.

The archive at the Inter-University Consortium for Political and Social Research (ICPSR) at the University of Michigan (**www.icpsr.umich.edu/**) provides access to social science data from over 400 member colleges and universities worldwide. It also has a series of archives relating to particular topics, for example the Health and Medical Care Archive, the International Archive of Education Data and the National Archive of Criminal Justice Data.

Box 5.2 Accessing data from archives

Until relatively recently those interested in using data from an archive were sent the data on magnetic tape, floppy disk or CD, or via file transfer protocol (FTP). Developments, especially in web technology, have meant that researchers can now use the archive's website to access individual tables, or to download the data on to their personal computer. One such development is NESSTAR server software. The services it offers include facilities for searching and browsing information about the data stored in the archive, for doing simple data analysis and visualisation over the web, and for downloading data. NESSTAR makes use of developments from the Data Documentation Initiative (DDI), an initiative that aims to establish international standards and methodology for the content, presentation, transport and preservation of metadata, the data that describe the datasets. As a result of the DDI metadata can now be created with a uniform structure that is easily and precisely searched, and which means that multiple datasets can be searched.

Source: Paula Devine, Institute of Governance, Queen's University, Belfast.

■ Databases

We mentioned earlier that in recent years there has been a huge increase in the amount of data collected and stored about customers and their transactions with suppliers, especially in retail and financial services markets. Developments in data capture and data storage technology have meant that it is relatively easy and relatively cheap to collect and store the details of every query or contact made with a customer helpline, and every transaction at the point of sale, for example, in databases. The use of 'loyalty' cards, sometimes called 'reward' or 'club' cards, means that these transactional data can be tied to the record of an individual customer. (You apply for the card in order to benefit from the organisation's promotion schemes. When you apply you give the organisation, a retailer or an airline, for example, your personal details. Your card details are logged against each transaction you make, so the organisation can record your buying behaviour in your personal record in its database.)

These databases are a rich source of secondary data, providing detailed current and historic information about consumer behaviour, giving the decision maker a different view of the market from that provided by traditional market research. Databases can be analysed in order to identify sales patterns by different outlet types and by different regions and patterns of buying behaviour among customers. Analysis can also reveal the characteristics, demographic or geodemographic for example, that are associated with different behaviour patterns. These patterns and characteristics can be used to build profiles of customers and outlets and to identify market segments and gaps in the market.

'Shopping basket analysis' can show what sets of products or brands are bought together among the different segments, for example, and which ones rarely occur together. By examining trends in behaviour over time the researcher can build models to predict behaviour, sales volumes and revenue. This information can be used to understand, for example, how profitable different groups of customers or different types of outlet are, and what type of promotion works best for which group. Loyalty card data, however, can be limited. For example, while they give information about customer behaviour in the store, they do not give information on behaviour outside it (for which data from traditional consumer panels may be useful); the demographic information provided may not in all cases be accurate; and people may hold more than one card for the same store (Passingham, 1998).

The Market Research Society (**www.mrs.org.uk**) publishes Guidelines for Handling Databases. These guidelines provide a framework for researchers who must adhere to the MRS Code of Conduct (and data protection legislation) in working with databases containing personalised data.

■ Data warehouses

A data warehouse is a repository for data, in effect it is a very large database that contains data from one but usually more than one source. It is a central storage facility that takes the concept of a data archive one step further, in that different datasets within the warehouse are integrated and elements in one set can be related to elements in another set (known as a relational database). Data stored in the warehouse are data that are useful for supporting management decision making, for example for marketing and sales management or customer relationship management. Data warehouses (and the tools used to extract information from them) are sometimes called decision support systems. The data warehouse is designed or structured, and data in it given context, in order to enhance this decision support role and to make access to the data in the warehouse fast and efficient. The technology used in data warehousing allows quick and easy retrieval of data derived from different internal and external sources, even those using different formats or platforms. As with a data archive, data can be retrieved remotely from the warehouse via a networked workstation and interrogated and analysed using tools designed to deal with very large volumes of data.

Building a data warehouse

Data are sent to the warehouse from what is called the *operational field* – from scanner data of transactions at the point of sale, from a geodemographic information system or from the data tables of a survey. Once in the warehouse they are referred to as being in the *informational field*. Data sent to the warehouse should be good quality: they are the raw material that will be used to support key management decisions and any inaccuracies or inconsistencies will impact on the quality of the decision making. It is good practice to clean the data before sending them to ensure that they are accurate and complete, that definitions of terms and variables, and the coding procedures used for these, are consistent so that data can be fully integrated or fused with other data in the warehouse. In addition, only data relevant to the needs of the DSS should be sent to the warehouse. Irrelevant or unnecessary data will only clog up the system and slow down access and processing time.

Structure of a data warehouse

The end use of the warehouse should dictate its structure. The data should be stored and organised in a way that allows the analyst to look at the data from relevant perspectives, for example by customer type, by brand and by market. Current data and historic data may be stored in a way that facilitates faster access to the more frequently used current data but allows older data to be called up for comparison, for examining trends or making predictions. In effect, the data warehouse contains lots of shelves or rooms. Different datasets can be stored on different shelves or in different rooms within the warehouse.

The warehouse contains information telling users about its structure and how to find their way around the shelves and the rooms. This information is called *metadata*. Besides being a map of the warehouse, it also acts as a contents list, providing the user with details of the databases or datasets in the warehouse, the elements contained in them, and how these elements relate to elements in other datasets in the warehouse. Data in the warehouse may have been transformed in some way (changes to coding or to format) and they exist in the warehouse at different levels of detail – from what is called 'detail' through 'lightly summarised' to 'highly summarised'. The metadata also give the user this information – telling him or her how the data were transformed, what changes were made to make them consistent, and on what basis the data are summarised.

The key characteristics of a well-designed data warehouse are as follows:

➢ It can store ever-increasing volumes of data without affecting processing performance.
➢ It is user friendly.
➢ Everyone has access to it regardless of location.
➢ Lots of users can use it at once with little effect on processing speeds.
➢ It facilitates analysis of data from a variety of perspectives.
➢ The speed of analysis and query answering is so fast that the search does not get in the way of thinking about the problem.

Analysing data

With an increase in the use of databases two techniques for analysing and making use of data in them have become more popular: data fusion and data mining.

■ Data fusion

Technological developments have meant that it is possible to build an even more detailed picture of the market and the consumer by merging the data held in databases with data derived from other sources, including surveys and consumer panel data, and by merging the findings from separate surveys. The aim of data fusion is to obtain insights that could not be obtained from the sources individually (Leventhal, 1997). The process of merging or integrating data from separate sources is known as data fusion. The process of fusion depends on being able to match individual records in one dataset, usually according to demographic or geodemographic details, with comparable records in another dataset. The idea is that data collected from person X1 about attitudes or buying behaviour, say, can be combined with data collected from person X2 on media usage, who is similar in his or her demographic or geodemographic characteristics to person X1. The fused data record (X1 plus X2) contains details of attitudes or behaviour and media usage for what is assumed to be the same person.

Merging datasets from different sources, however, can be problematic. Besides issues of format and software platform, which can be overcome with technology, there are also issues with the content of the datasets. If two sets of data are to be fused it is essential that there are variables common to each set. Common variables, say on demographics or product purchase, should be defined in the same way, so that they are measuring the same thing, and coded in the same way, so that the analysis program takes them to mean the same thing. This has implications at the research design stage, in particular for the design of the data collection instrument. If you know that two sets of data may be merged it is important to identify and define common variables before data collection starts. If this is not possible variables can sometimes be manipulated and redefined at the processing or analysis stage.

Geodemographic data

Geodemographic data are a form of fused data – geographic data, information on addresses from the postal service, for example, can be combined with demographic data from the Census of Population to produce a geodemographic database. The combined information can be transferred to and held in a geodemographic information system, and displayed on maps or in standard tables. Consumers can be classified according to their geodemographic characteristics. Indeed such geodemographic classifications have been found to provide a better understanding of consumer behaviour than demographic data alone. They are often used as the basis of market segmentation systems, for targeting marketing activity, planning store locations and distribution patterns and the location of public services (Baez Ortega and Romo Costamaillere, 1997).

Geodemographic information systems are available for most European countries as well as for the United States, Canada and Australia. Several commercial organisations specialise in providing these systems, including CACI, which produces a product called ACORN – A Classification of Residential Neighbourhoods; CCN, which produces MOSAIC and EuroMOSAIC; CDMS, which produces SuperProfiles; and Pinpoint, which produces Finpin. The basis of most of these GIS is more or less the same: they relate the demographic characteristics of the residential population, derived from the Census at the Enumeration District (ED) level, the smallest geographical unit within the Census for which data are available, to geographic information about that area. The sources of information used to construct the system may also include the electoral register, postal address files, car registration information, data from surveys on media use or attitudes, and data from customer databases. The end product is a classification of neigbourhoods or areas within which consumers with certain characteristics live. The classification or segmentation of the neighbourhoods is based on a cluster analysis. Each 'cluster' or type of neighbourhood will be different from every other cluster or neighbourhood – because the type of consumers living in that neighbourhood will be different. A neighbourhood in one town may be classified as belonging to the same cluster or type of neighbourhood in another town, because the characteristics of consumers in that neighbourhood are the same or similar. CACI's ACORN system divides the population of Great Britain into 54 types, which are grouped together into 17 groups spread across six clusters or categories:

A. Thriving
B. Expanding
C. Rising
D. Settling
E. Aspiring
F. Striving

Within the Rising category, for example, which represents 8.5 per cent of the population, there are three groups covering ten types: Affluent Urbanites, Town and City Areas; Prosperous Professionals, Metropolitan Areas; and Better-off Executives, Inner City Areas. CCN has developed a classification system known as EuroMOSAIC that divides consumers in European countries into ten clusters or lifestyle groups:

1 Elite suburb
2 Average areas
3 Luxury flats
4 Low-income inner city
5 High-rise social housing
6 Industrial communities
7 Dynamic families
8 Low-income families
9 Rural/agricultural
10 Vacation/retirement

There are other segmentation systems and products available that classify consumers at the individual level, according to income, buying behaviour and life stage, and which can be tied into a GIS. There are also segmentation systems that classify online customers according to their behaviour on the Internet.

Geodemographic classifications are used primarily to identify and target different types of consumers. Using geodemographic information can help organisations to gain a more in-depth understanding of their customers' habits, preferences, attitudes and opinions. This information can be used to develop strategy and to target products, services and marketing communication more effectively. Applying geodemographic codes to, say, existing sales data on customers derived from loyalty cards will help give you information on their demographic and lifestyle characteristics. If you know the geodemographic profile of your customers you can use a GIS to find where other people with similar profiles are located. This information can be useful in planning store location, store type and size, product mix within the store and so on; and in targeting marketing and advertising campaigns.

Since geodemographic classifications are rooted in a geographic location, knowing a person's post code or postal address is enough to allow us to assign them to a particular geodemographic group. As a result each record held on a customer database can be assigned to a geodemographic cluster; if we know the area from which a sample, sub-sample or respondent was drawn, individual cases from a survey can be assigned to a geodemographic cluster. This means that data from different sources – from a customer database or from any type of survey – can be analysed in terms of its geodemographic profile. Thus data from a survey on buying behaviour, survey data on attitudes and values, and data from a customer database can be linked – the geodemographic classification of each unit or case being the common variable for fusing the data. The database created by this fusion allows us to examine relationships between different types of consumers, their attitudes and their behaviour.

■ Data mining

The databases and data warehouses created to house data are enormous – hundreds of thousands, even millions of rows, and thousands of variables. Until relatively recently, however, whilst the potential value of the information contained in them was widely recognised, there were problems extracting it. The lack of suitable tools to explore and analyse such vast datasets meant that little use was made of them: standard computer techniques could not process or analyse the volume of data fast enough or comprehensively enough for it to be of use. This is where the techniques of data mining came in.

Data mining, also known as knowledge discovery in databases (KDD), is the process by which information and knowledge useful to decision makers are mined or extracted from very large databases using automated techniques and parallel computing technology. Some of the techniques used in data mining are similar to those used in standard and multivariate data analysis. A data mining program can manipulate the data, combining variables, for example, and allowing the user to select elements or sections of the database for analysis; it can provide basic descriptive statistics, look for associations and relationships between variables, and perform cluster analysis. Where data mining differs from other data analysis techniques is in the volume of data it can process and analyse, and in its ability to discover patterns and relationships that cannot be detected with standard analysis techniques. And it does this at high speed, producing answers to queries or searches almost immediately, by using parallel computing technology. The data mining system divides the workload between a set of parallel processors, enabling streams of data to be processed simultaneously, in parallel. Speed of processing can be further enhanced if the database is structured in a particular way, for example if it is divided up or 'partitioned' into smaller units or packets; the data mining program works on each partition in parallel.

Approaches to data mining

There are two approaches to data mining: verification and discovery. In the verification approach you already have an idea about patterns of behaviour or relationships between variables – you have formulated a hypothesis, and you want to test the hypothesis in the data. You take the discovery approach, on the other hand, if you have no clear idea about patterns and you want to find out what hidden treasures exist among the mass of data. You get the computer to search and explore the database in order to find patterns and relationships. The computer program searches the database for these patterns and relationships by getting to know the data, and by learning the rules that apply within the database, identifying how all the elements relate to each other, what networks exist within the data. The mining metaphor is a good one – it is often necessary in data mining to sift through large volumes of dross before finding the high value material. It is possible to use data mining techniques on very large and complex databases containing data from several sources that would defy conventional analysis techniques. The database can be analysed at the individual level – the level of each transaction or individual customer – and at the aggregated level. And because the database is dynamic – data from the operational field are being added to it on a regular basis – information is always timely.

Box 5.3 Techniques used in data mining

➢ Summarising
➢ Learning classification rules
➢ Cluster analysis and segmentation
➢ Analysing changes
➢ Searching for anomalies
➢ Searching for dependency or neural networks

Data mining techniques

A data mining system can examine the data and automatically formulate 'if x, then y' classification rules from its experience working with the data. For example, if the customer has a certain set of characteristics, say living in a single-person household in a large town or city with annual income greater than 60,000, then the classification rules show that he or she will be interested in range X food products. The system can build the classification rules into a model, displaying them in a hierarchical structure, such as a decision tree (similar to the output of the multivariate technique, AID analysis). For example, in searching the database of a bank it might find those customers who took out a personal loan in the last three years and those who did not. Among those who took out a personal loan it might split out those who repaid the loan early and those who did not.

The system can also look for associations between elements or variables in the data and can formulate rules about associations. For example, it might discover that on 84 per cent of occasions when a customer buys brands S and R he or she also buys brand M. It has sequence/temporal functions that can search the data for patterns that occur frequently over a period of time. For example, it might discover what group of products is bought before buying a personal digital organiser, or what type of purchases follow the purchase of a desktop PC.

Data mining systems also run cluster analysis, working in more or less the same way as the cluster analysis or segmentation techniques used in standard analysis. The computer searches the database for cases that are similar on a characteristic or range of characteristics and it groups or clusters similar cases together. Cluster analysis can be used to identify different types of buying behaviour, for example. Besides being useful for their own sake, clusters are often used as the basis for further exploration.

Data mining can use neural networks to interrogate databases. A neural network is a mathematical structure of interconnected elements, analogous to the neural pathways in the brain, a sort of non-linear, non-sequential computer program. It is a sort of complex 'black box' technique that works by looking for all the interdependencies between a set of variables or elements in a database. It can be used to uncover patterns and trends in a very large database that standard sequential computing techniques cannot see because they are so complex. The neural network can learn from the database – in fact it can be 'trained' to be an expert in the data it has to analyse. Once trained it can be asked to make predictions by investigating 'what if' scenarios.

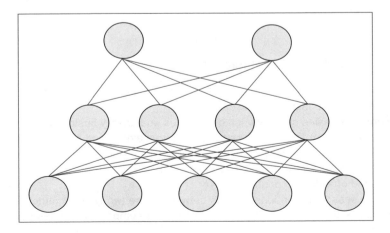

Figure 5.1 Diagram of a neural network

Criticisms of neural networks centre on the 'black box' approach, which means that there is little or no explanation of the method by which the findings are obtained. It can also take time to train the neural network in the database. The network learns by experience, by tracking back and forth between elements in the database, and so with very large databases this can be time consuming.

Data visualisation is often used with data mining techniques to help understand the data. It can help at the initial exploratory stage, by making relationships and patterns in the data easier to understand, and at a later stage for presenting or illustrating the findings.

OLAP

Online analytical processing or OLAP is a form of data mining suitable for very large databases and those that contain elements that are interrelated and multidimensional. Multidimensional means that the database is structured in a hierarchical way, so that the data and the relationships between data are structured and stored in a logical way. For example, the database might contain aggregated data on sales; it will also contain a multidimensional cell with data on sales classified or categorised according to different dimensions relevant to the needs of the organisation, dimensions such as brand, sales outlet, market and so on. A single cell will contain data at the most granular level – for example, sales of brand X in Week 32 in bars in Ireland. A variety of analyses can be performed on an OLAP database. Data can be aggregated or consolidated into larger sets – for example weekly sales into monthly sales, monthly sales to quarterly, quarterly to annual; sales via the website can be aggregated with sales via traditional retail outlets to produce total sales, or sales in each EU country can be aggregated into an EU total. Aggregated data can be disaggregated or broken down into smaller units, even down to the individual level, in a process known as 'drill-down'. Data can be examined across a range of perspectives, for example by volume, by volume within market, or by volume within outlet type by market, in an operation known as 'slicing and dicing'.

Box 5.4 Examples of OLAP queries

➢ How many units of brands W and R did we sell in Ireland, the United Kingdom, France and Germany in the last financial year?
➢ How were these sales split between direct sales and agency business?
➢ What is the gross profit on direct sales and agency sales based on these sales figures?
➢ On the direct sales side, how were sales split between wholesalers and retailers?
➢ Among the retailers in the United Kingdom and Ireland, what was the split between on-sales and off-sales accounts?
➢ Were there seasonal variations in sales between these two types of outlet?
➢ How do sales per quarter in the last financial year compare with sales per quarter in the last two years?

Chapter summary

➤ Secondary research, also known as desk research, involves looking for and analysing data that already exist – data that have not been created specifically for the purpose at hand but were originally collected for another purpose.

➤ Secondary data are a useful source of information, especially in the early stages of a project, helping with problem definition and research design and planning, and at the later stages, providing a context for the interpretation of primary data.

➤ It is important to evaluate the quality of secondary data before using them.

➤ Secondary data can be found inside the organisation (internal secondary data) or outside the organisation (external secondary data).

➤ The two main sources of external secondary data are those produced by government departments and related bodies (*official statistics*); and those produced by trade bodies, commercial research organisations and business publishers (*unofficial statistics*). Most are available in hard copy format, from the publisher or source, from a library, or via online and offline (CD-ROM) databases.

➤ Data archives and data warehouses are very large databases that contain data from one or more than one source. Management information systems or decision support systems are databases or data warehouses in which internal and external data are stored. They are useful sources of secondary data and are designed with the information needs of end users in mind.

➤ Data fusion is the process of merging or fusing data from different datasets or databases and can be used to build a detailed picture or profile of the consumer. If two sets of data are to be fused it is essential that there are variables common to each set.

➤ Demographic data from the census are merged with geographic data to produce geodemographic data. Geodemographic classifications can provide a better understanding of consumer behaviour than demographic data alone, and are often used as the basis of market segmentation systems.

➤ Data mining, also known as knowledge discovery in databases, is the process by which information and knowledge are extracted from very large databases using automated techniques and parallel computing technology. Its advantages over standard techniques are in the volume of data it can handle, its ability to discover patterns and relationships otherwise undetectable, and the speed at which it works.

Questions and exercises

1 What are secondary data?

2 What is meant by the term 'secondary data analysis'?

3 Describe the main uses of secondary data.

4 What questions would you ask in evaluating the usefulness of secondary data? Take a look at the 'Internet Detective tutorial' at the Social Science Information Gateway (SOSIG) website (**www.Sosig.ac.uk/desire/internet-detective.html**). The aim of the tutorial is to raise awareness of the quality of information found on the Internet and to encourage you to evaluate it critically before using it in your work.

5 Describe the main sources of secondary data useful to the market or social researcher.

6 What is a data warehouse? What are the key characteristics of a well-designed data warehouse?

7 Why are databases and data warehouses useful to market and social researchers?

8 What is data fusion? What are some of the potential problems you might come across in fusing data from different sources?

9 What is geodemographic classification? Why might such a classification be useful?

10 What is data mining? What are the main uses of data mining? Give examples.

References

Baez Ortega, D. and Romo Costamaillere, G. (1997) 'Geodemographics and its application to the study of consumers' *ESOMAR Conference Proceedings, The Dynamics of Change in Latin America*, Amsterdam: ESOMAR.

Hakim, C. (1982) *Secondary Analysis in Social Research*, London: Allen & Unwin.

Leventhal, B. (1997) 'An approach to fusing market research with database marketing', *Journal of the Market Research Society*, **39**, 4, pp. 545–58.

Passingham, P. (1998) 'Grocery retailing and the loyalty card', *Journal of the Market Research Society*, **40**, 1, pp. 55–63.

Recommended reading

Dale, A., Arber, S. and Proctor, M. (1988) *Doing Secondary Analysis*, London: Unwin Hyman.

Hakim, C. (1982) *Secondary Analysis in Social Research*, London: Allen & Unwin.
Two excellent accounts of how to do secondary analysis.

Leventhal, B. (1997) 'An approach to fusing market research with database marketing', *Journal of the Market Research Society*, **39**, 4, pp. 545–58. An account of an approach to data fusion in the financial services sector.

Baez Ortega, D. and Romo Costamaillere, G. (1997) 'Geodemographics and its application to the study of consumers', *ESOMAR Conference Proceedings, The Dynamics of Change in Latin America*, Amsterdam: ESOMAR. An account of the use of geodemographic segmentation systems.

Dilly, R. (1996) *Data Mining: An Introduction*, **www.qub.ac.uk/pcc**. An excellent introduction to data mining, it includes tutorials and illustrations of the uses of data mining.

Chapter 6

Collecting qualitative data

Introduction

In Chapter 2 we looked briefly at the nature of qualitative research and the way in which it differs from quantitative research. The purpose of this chapter is to describe the methods of collecting qualitative data, and the applications of these methods.

Topics covered

➢ Observation
➢ Qualitative interviewing:
  ➢ in-depth interviews
  ➢ group discussions
  ➢ online qualitative research
  ➢ panels, juries and workshops

Relationship to MRS Advanced Certificate Syllabus

The material covered in this chapter is relevant to Unit 5 – Data Collection Methods and Unit 7 – Qualitative Information Collection, specifically:

➢ group discussions, depth interviews, paired depths, observation (Unit 5);
➢ planning for qualitative information collection, role of the moderator and outline of techniques (Unit 7).

Learning outcomes

At the end of this chapter you should be able to:

➢ understand what is involved in the main data collection methods used in qualitative research;
➢ choose the most appropriate method for a given research proposal.

Observation

Observational techniques, based on ethnographic methods used in anthropology and sociology, are well established in social research and are increasingly used in market research. The main advantage of observation over interviewing is that in an interview the respondent is recalling and recounting his or her behaviour to the researcher whereas in observation the researcher sees it at first hand – without the filter of memory or selection.

There are two kinds of observation: simple observation and participant observation.

■ Simple observation

Simple observation involves watching and recording people and activity, for example in a supermarket, a bar, a café or a hospital waiting area, whatever setting is relevant to the research. If the researcher is present, he or she makes notes about the behaviour, about incidents, routines and body language (and may record the activity on video). For example, in a bar, the researcher might note the demeanour and body language of a person coming into the bar, the way in which the bar staff greet her, the time taken to choose a drink, the drink chosen, the seat chosen and so on. If the researcher is not present, the activity may be taped and this record viewed and analysed later. Observation allows the researcher to gather data on what people do rather than what they say they do. In order to understand why the respondent behaves in a particular way, the recording of the observation may be played back to the respondent as a reminder, and the researcher may ask about the activity, and the respondent's thoughts and feelings at the time.

■ Participant observation

Participant observation is when the researcher is involved in or part of the activity or task being observed. Accompanied shopping is an example of participant observation – the researcher goes with the respondent on a shopping trip, listening, observing and/or recording his or her behaviour on audio or videotape, and making notes. The researcher may ask questions for clarification or understanding and to note the respondent's thoughts and feelings – collecting data relevant to the research objectives.

■ Uses

Observation is useful in providing detailed and in-depth understanding of how and why people do things, in the context in which they do them – how and why they choose brands at the point of sale, for example, or how they use them at home. It is also useful in understanding how they think and feel at the time. It is, however, more time consuming and so more expensive than interviewing. The decision to use observation should be determined by the objectives of the research, and by the practical constraints of time and budget. It is particularly useful in the exploratory phase of a project – when it is necessary to get to grips with an unfamiliar activity or process or setting. It is also useful when we need to challenge the assumptions we make about everyday activity that appears all too familiar, and when we need to see and understand things from the perspective of the respondent. It is useful in providing insight in situations where respondents might find it difficult to describe their behaviour. It is also useful for providing the context needed for understanding and interpreting other data.

Interviewing

Observation is often accompanied by interviewing. As we saw in Chapter 2, what distinguishes qualitative interviewing from quantitative interviewing is the style of the interview. Quantitative interviews are standardised – the questions are worded in exactly the same way and asked in the same order in each interview – and most of the questions are structured rather than open ended and non-directive. Qualitative interviews are more like 'guided conversations' (Rubin and Rubin, 1995) or 'conversations with a purpose' (Burgess, 1984).

■ Why choose qualitative interviews?

Qualitative research lends itself in particular to exploratory and descriptive research enquiries. You might choose to collect data using qualitative interviews if the following apply:

➤ you want to find out about people's experiences, the way they do things, their motivations, their attitudes, their knowledge, the way in which they interpret things, or the meanings they attach to things;
➤ you want in-depth accounts, detailed (ideographic) descriptions, context-rich data, an understanding of the issue, the processes or the behaviour;
➤ you believe that this is the best (or the only) way of getting the type of evidence you need to address your research problem, the best (or the only) way of finding out what it is you want to know.

Qualitative interviews are more flexible (Sampson, 1967 and 1996) than quantitative interviews. The interviewer has the freedom to react to what the respondent is saying and adapt the interview accordingly. He or she can alter the way the questions are asked, the order in which they are asked, and can insert follow-up questions if the respondent mentions something that the researcher would like to clarify or explore in greater detail.

The choice of interview rather than observation, while driven to some extent by he nature and objectives of the research, often comes down to the practicalities of time and cost – interviewing tends to be more cost effective. Interviewing is also more suitable when the objectives of the research are clearly defined, and when it is necessary to gather data from a greater range and number of people or settings.

■ Individual in-depth interviews

In-depth interviews are conducted by a qualitative researcher on a one-to-one basis with a respondent who has been chosen according to the agreed recruitment criteria for the project. As the name suggests, the aim is to explore a topic in depth, and most in-depth interviews will last from about 45 minutes to two hours, depending on the topic and what has to be covered. In most cases the researcher will use an open-ended interview approach. Interviews may take place in the respondent's home, workplace, central location or viewing facility. Typically the interview is tape-recorded.

In-depth interviews are not an alternative to group discussions (see Box 6.1 below) – they generate very different types of data. They are appropriate for more sensitive subjects, for understanding in detail without the views of the respondent being influenced by what members of the group say, or what other members of the group might think of them if they were to report a particular attitude or behaviour. Of course similar problems can arise in an individual interview situation but they are easier to read and disentangle when there is less contamination.

The number of interviews conducted will depend on the research objectives, the complexity of the topic, the sample requirements and the practicalities of time and cost. For example, to assess the effectiveness of a television advertisement, 8 to 12 in-depth interviews might be conducted alongside a quantitative advertising test; to understand the issues involved in adopting new technologies, 20 to 30 in-depth interviews with business executives might be required; to understand the perspectives of those involved in a drug rehabilitation programme, it may be necessary to conduct 50 to 60 interviews.

Box 6.1 Individual interviews or groups?

Choose in-depth interviews if:
➢ your topic is of a sensitive or intimate nature;
➢ you need to get detailed information on individual attitudes and behaviour;
➢ you need to get beyond the socially acceptable view;
➢ you need 'time-line' or longitudinal information (for example, to follow a decision-making process);
➢ your sample is difficult to find.

Choose group discussions if:
➢ you need to see a wide range of attitudes and opinions;
➢ you need to determine differences between people;
➢ you do not need minority views or views not influenced by the group;
➢ you want to understand social and cultural influences;
➢ you need to draw out creative thinking/solutions.

■ Variations on the in-depth interview

There are several variations on the standard individual in-depth interview, including mini-depths, paired depths, triads and family interviews.

Mini-depths

A mini-depth is a shorter version of an in-depth interview, lasting usually about 20 to 40 minutes, and is used to explore a specific, bounded topic.

Paired depths (duos)

As the name suggests, paired depths are when two people are interviewed together. The pair may consist of two friends; two family members – partners, siblings, fathers and sons; two work colleagues – whatever is suitable for the topic being researched. Paired depths are useful for two reasons. First, some people, particularly children and teenagers, find it less intimidating and embarrassing to be interviewed with someone rather than alone. Secondly, the research objectives of a particular study may mean that it is necessary to determine what goes on during a decision-making process that involves more than one person – for example, in buying a car. It may be important to find out who takes on what role, for example who is the purchase influencer and who is the buyer or the financier?

Triads (trios)

Triads involve interviewing three people simultaneously, and may be suitable for the same reasons as paired depths.

Family interviews

In-depth interviews are sometimes conducted with all or some of the family group, either together or separately, or in combinations. The purpose of family interviews is often to find out about elements of family life, decision-making patterns, rules and relationships governing food, clothes, holidays and leisure, for example.

Semi-structured interviews

Semi-structured interviews are a sort of half-way house between qualitative in-depth interviews and more fully structured quantitative interviews (Young, 1966 quoted in Sampson, 1967). They are often used in industrial and business-to-business research. The interview guide is more structured than is usual in qualitative research and interviews are carried out by interviewers trained in qualitative probing and prompting techniques but who are not necessarily qualitative researchers.

■ Group discussions

A standard group discussion or focus group is usually made up of 8–10 people (10–12 people in the United States) – small enough for a manageable discussion and large enough to have a range of views represented. Respondents are recruited for the group according to criteria relevant to the topic under investigation. A skilled qualitative researcher, known as a moderator or facilitator, guides the discussion. In some circumstances, depending on the nature of the topic and the objectives of the research, the group may consist of 6–8 participants, rather than

8–10. The smaller group allows the moderator to get a greater depth of response from group participants. Smaller groups are often used to research sensitive topics, or when the group consists of children or teenagers – smaller groups are less daunting for participants and allow the moderator to spend more time on each participant.

A group usually lasts about an hour and a half to two hours (although in some countries, India for example, the group may happily continue for about four hours), giving enough time to explore a range of issues related to the research topic in some depth. Should it be necessary to research the topic in greater depth, the duration of the group may be extended.

Groups usually take place in a central location, for example a meeting room in a hotel or, more commonly nowadays, at a viewing facility; some groups take place in the home of the person who recruited the respondents.

The number of groups will depend on the research objectives, the complexity of the topic, the range of views or types of respondent needed, and the constraints of time and budget. It would be unusual to conduct fewer than four groups; projects involving 10–12 groups are common.

■ Variations on the standard group discussion format

Mini-group

A mini-group, as its name suggests, is a cut-down version of a group, with usually about 4–6 respondents rather than 8–10. It lasts an hour to an hour and a half – rather than an hour and a half to two hours. Mini-groups are often used if the topic is a sensitive one, or if it is particularly difficult to recruit respondents.

Extended group

An extended group, again as its name suggests, lasts about four hours (and sometimes longer) rather than the usual one and a half to two hours. The extra time means that the topic can be explored in greater detail. A wide range of stimulus material can be examined and a variety of projective and enabling techniques can be used. The moderator may also devote a greater amount of time, in comparison to a standard group, to the group forming process, ensuring that the atmosphere created is relaxed and safe – this often leads to a greater level of disclosure from the group.

Reconvened group

A reconvened group is one that is recruited to take part in at least two discussions, usually separated by about a week. The first deals with the basics of the topic, explores the background to it and the more straightforward aspects of it. Participants are briefed on a task that is to be completed in time for the next meeting. The task might be to prepare something on a topic, for example, 'Can you live without . . .' The group reconvenes for the second discussion to impart their thoughts, feelings and experiences about the topic under investigation.

Friendship group

A friendship group, consisting of pairs or groups of friends or family members, is another version. This sort of group is often used when researching children or teenagers, or when examining a buying decision in which two or more people are involved (for example a mortgage or a car).

Sensitivity panel

A sensitivity panel (Schlackman, 1984) is a series of group discussions using the same group of people and making use of the psycho-dynamic processes within the group. Panel members attend a number of groups at which they learn how to access thoughts and feelings that in normal everyday circumstances would be hidden or difficult to access. They do this using a variety of techniques including free association, analogy generation and stream of awareness. Another dimension of the panel is that over the course of its existence members get to know one another and so the level of trust and rapport grows, allowing disclosure and 'sharing' to take place. Sensitivity panels can be enormously useful but to run them effectively requires the moderator to have a great deal of training and experience in group psychology and psychoanalytical theory.

■ Group processes

Group discussions tend to go through a number of different stages. These stages have been described as forming, storming, norming, performing and mourning. They usually occur in this order, although some stages may be repeated during the discussion.

Forming

The forming stage of a group is the inclusion stage, and it is very important that the group passes through this stage if it is to function properly as a group. The moderator must get everyone to speak during the first few minutes. This helps respondents to get rid of their anxiety about speaking and contributing to the group, and allays their fears about being included and being a useful member of the group. It is also important that group participants talk to each other and not just to the moderator and so it can be very useful at the beginning of a group to run a warm-up or forming exercise. One way of doing this is to ask respondents to pair off and introduce themselves, then introduce each other to the group. Depending on the size of the group, this paired introduction can be expanded to groups of three or four.

Storming

Storming is the stage the group works through in order to establish how to relate to one another and how to relate to the task. At this stage respondents will be sizing each other up, testing the water, and trying to establish the boundaries of what is acceptable in the group. Storming can happen later in the group when new tasks or new material are introduced.

Norming

Norming is when the group settles down, when respondents see that they have something in common with other members of the group. A sign that it has happened is when there is a general air of agreement, and when the atmosphere is noticeably relaxed. This is the stage at which the main work of the group can begin.

Performing

The performing stage is when the work is done. When the group reaches this stage it is task oriented, co-operative and happy to get on with things.

Mourning

Mourning is the wind-down stage of the group. To make sure that this phase is worked through properly the moderator must signal the end of the group clearly and build in a wind-down period. If respondents are not given time to go through this stage they can feel used – they may be left with the feeling that the moderator wanted them to complete a task, get information from them and get rid of them. Signal the end of an hour-and-a-half-long discussion with about 20 minutes to go. With about 5 or 10 minutes to go, ask some winding-up questions, such as, 'Anything you'd like to say that you haven't mentioned?' or 'Anything you've said that you wish you hadn't?'

Box 6.2 Practical aspects of qualitative data collection

Recruitment

Specialist interviewers, known as recruiters, are responsible for finding and inviting people to take part in interviews. The recruiter is briefed by a fieldwork manager or by a researcher involved with the project and aims to find people who match the criteria specified for the project. In the United States this process is sometimes called 'screening'. Guidelines for good recruitment practice are contained in the Qualitative Research Guidelines published by The Market Research Society and available at its website (**www.mrs.org.uk**). In Chapter 15 we look at researchers' ethical responsibilities to respondents.

Incentives or participation fees

When respondents are being recruited for market research they are told that they will receive a 'thank-you' payment or a participation fee. In being told of it up front, it is a form of incentive to attend (and is usually called an incentive). Anecdotal evidence suggests that this is a useful strategy – it saves money on recruitment costs by ensuring that those recruited will attend and avoids the need for excessive over-recruitment and rescheduling. Although the size of the incentive does not cover the total cost of taking part in a group it shows the participants that you value their time and realise the inconvenience they have

Box 6.2 continued

experienced in attending. It is fairly common nowadays to find that people expect to be paid. Some clients or funders, however, particularly in social and academic research, do not have a tradition of paying attendance fees or incentives.

The venue

Qualitative research interviews are conducted in a variety of settings, including the recruiter's home, the respondent's home or workplace, a central venue such as a hotel, or in a specialised research venue. In the United States, most are conducted in these specialised venues, known as viewing facilities, and in Europe they are becoming more and more popular. A viewing facility comprises a room in which the group or the individual sits (set up to look like someone's living room – although in the United States they have more of an office look) and an adjoining viewing room, where the client sits to view the interview through a one-way mirror. The equipment used to record the group, either on audio or video-tape (usually both) is built in in such a way that it is unobtrusive.

The choice of venue for the research will be determined by a number of factors, including the following:

➢ the availability and/or accessibility of a viewing facility or central venue;
➢ whether the client or funder wants to watch the interviews;
➢ the suitability of the venue for the topic under investigation or the type of respondents – for example, a study of household products among a sample of women may be more suited to a home environment; IT use among business people may be better suited to a more formal environment such as a viewing facility or a hotel;
➢ the type of interview – respondents in individual interviews can feel uncomfortable in a viewing facility, knowing that they are being observed;
➢ the acceptability of inviting respondents to a private home – in some cultures this may not be appropriate;
➢ cost – hiring a viewing facility can add considerably to the cost of a project.

Whatever venue you choose for the research, make sure that respondents have no difficulty in getting to it (this may involve organising transport for them). Also make sure that the physical environment is comfortable – neither too hot nor too cold, with adequate lighting, that it is not noisy, has comfortable seats and so on. If necessary (and possible), rearrange the furniture so that there are no barriers between you and the respondent(s).

Recording the discussion

The interview or discussion is usually recorded, with the respondents' permission, so that it can be revisited (and transcribed) for detailed analysis. In most cases and in most settings interviews are recorded on audiotape. If it is important to capture visually what took place – the dynamics or interactions in a group discussion, non-verbal communication, reaction to stimulus material – then the session will be recorded on videotape. Make sure that the equipment works before you start.

■ The interview guide

The style of the interview guide (also known as the discussion or topic guide) – the equivalent of the quantitative researcher's questionnaire – varies from a simple list of topics that the interviewer plans to discuss or explore with the respondent to one that has more structure, with a series of questions listed under headings or topics. The style depends on a number of factors, including the following:

➤ the objectives of the research, for example an exploratory study may mean a less structured approach;

➤ the need for comparability between interviews or groups, for example if field-work is shared between a number of researchers or is conducted in a number of countries;

➤ the experience and knowledge of the interviewer – for example, an experienced interviewer with an in-depth knowledge of the topic may find it easier to work from a topic guide, whereas a less experienced interviewer might prefer to have a more detailed guide;

➤ the house style or preference of the researcher or client – some clients, for example, prefer a more detailed and structured interview guide.

Box 6.3 Examples of interview guides

Example 1: Topic style group discussion guide

Subject: Customer satisfaction with problem handling and resolution for a utility company

Introduction
General attitudes towards the service and the service provider
Experience of any problems or areas of concern
Experiences of how provider dealt with problem(s)
Reaction to/feelings about how provider dealt with problem
Feelings about resolution of the problem (satisfied/dissatisfied – probe for detail)
Suggestions for improvement
Close

Example 2: Extract from topic style in-depth interview guide

Subject: Evaluation of a health care service

Perceptions of the service
The location
The physical layout
The atmosphere
Experience of other services
Nature of other services
How this service and other services compare
Advantages and disadvantages
The staff
Contact with the staff

Box 6.3 continued

Staff attitudes
Relationship with the staff

Example 3: Extract from a more detailed group discussion guide

Subject: Retail store development

Warm up
How often do you visit [type of shop]?
How do you decide which one(s) to visit?
Which do you really like going into? (Probe fully for reasons.)
Are there any you dislike visiting? (Probe fully for reasons.)

Attitudes to target shop
Check – have you ever visited X?
Have you ever bought anything from X?
When was that?
What did you buy?
What do you like/dislike about buying from the shop?
How would you rate it for the following:
   – the range of products and brands;
   – keeping the products you want;
   – keeping the brands you want;
   – prices (including offers);
   – service (including staff attitudes, follow-up service);
   – layout (including displays, lighting, signs, atmosphere/feel etc.);
   – overall image?

What could X do to make you want to go there (more often)/buy more?

■ Questioning style

The style of questioning used in qualitative interviews differs from that used in quantitative research (although many of the principles outlined in Chapter 10 can be applied to the design of questions and interview guides for qualitative research). Where most questions in a quantitative interview are closed or pre-coded, questions in a qualitative interview tend to be open ended and non-directive; projective and elicitation techniques are also used – we look at these in more detail later in the chapter. This style or model of interviewing is called the 'psycho-dynamic' model – that is, it is 'based on the assumption that public statements may be rationalizations dictated by what respondents believe interviewers want to hear, or believe they "ought" to say' (Cooper and Tower, 1992). The aim of qualitative interviewing is to get below the surface, beyond the rational response, to encourage respondents to talk in depth and in detail about their experiences, their attitudes and opinions and their thoughts and feelings (Cooper and Branthwaite, 1977; Cooper and Tower, 1992).

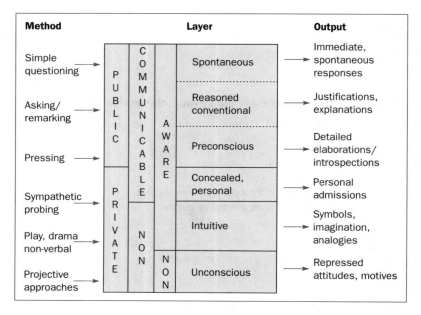

Figure 6.1 A qualitative interviewing model

Source: Cooper, P. and Tower, R. (1992) 'Inside the consumer mind: consumer attitudes to the arts', *Journal of the Market Research Society*, **34**, 4, pp. 299–311. Used with permission.

Open-ended and non-directive questions allow respondents to relate to the topic in their own way, to use their own language (and not that of the pre-coded response) with little or no direction in how to answer from the interviewer. Probing – using follow-up questions to clarify meaning or to encourage the respondent to answer in more depth or detail – for example, 'Exactly what happened next?' and 'Tell me more about that' – is used extensively. Closed or more precise questions can be used to establish clearly the context or ascertain particular facts – for example 'How much did you pay for it?' or 'How many times did you use it?' Prompting is another way of encouraging the respondent to answer: techniques include repeating the question or rephrasing it; using non-verbal cues – encouraging looks, nods of the head and pauses and silence, for example. It is important, of course, to keep a balance between encouraging the respondent to answer and leading him or her, or putting words in their mouths, for example 'I suppose you are sorry that you bought it'.

It is important in a qualitative interview to listen to exactly how things are being said so that you can ask useful follow-up questions. Listen out for sweeping claims and generalisations, for example 'I always use that' or 'I would never buy that' and think of questions to challenge these claims in a gentle but probing way, for example asking 'Is there any exception?' or restating 'Never?' or 'Always?' Here are some more examples:

➢ *Response*: 'That's impossible' or 'I couldn't do that.' *Probe*: 'What makes it impossible?' 'What prevents you … ?' or 'What if … ?'
➢ *Response*: 'They must/should/need … ' *Probe*: 'What would happen if they did not … ?'
➢ *Response*: 'That just doesn't work.' *Probe*: 'What doesn't work?'

Other useful questioning techniques include summarising and restating or reflecting what the respondent has said to clarify meaning, help increase understanding and build empathy, for example 'You feel upset about how they handled the problem.'

■ Structure of the interview

The structure of the interview or group discussion is important. There should be a clear introduction and 'warm-up' phase and a clearly signalled ending or 'wind down', in line with the group processes of forming and mourning described above.

The introduction

A clear introduction is vital – from an ethical point of view and in order to put the respondent(s) at ease. It is likely that they will be nervous (Gordon and Robson, 1980), and it is the interviewer's or moderator's job to allay any fears about what is involved and help the respondent relax. In the introduction you should do the following:

➢ say something about yourself (your name, the organisation you work for);

➢ tell respondent(s) about the topic and state the purpose of the research;

➢ tell the respondent(s) how long the interview is going to take;

➢ tell the respondent(s) about your role as interviewer or moderator (independent, there to guide the discussion or interview, and to listen);

➢ tell the respondent(s) how and why they were chosen;

➢ give assurances about confidentiality and/or anonymity;

➢ ask the respondents' permission to tape the interview;

➢ tell the respondent(s) whether the interview is being observed and by whom and obtain their consent;

➢ tell the respondent(s) how the information will be used;

➢ let the respondent(s) know that their participation is voluntary and that they are free to leave and free to refuse to answer any questions;

➢ mention the 'ground rules' (that there are no right or wrong answers, that it is not a test, that it is the respondents' experiences, feelings, opinions you are interested in, that all views are valid, that they can talk to each other, that they do not have to agree with each other's views).

Box 6.4 Example of an introduction to an in-depth interview

'My name is [name] from [research organisation]. I am carrying out research on [topic]. The aim of the research is to [brief description]. It has been commissioned by [organisation]. The interview will last about an hour. All the information you give me will remain strictly confidential. Extracts from the interview may appear in the final report but under no circumstances will your name or any identifying characteristics be included. Your participation is entirely voluntary, you are free to end the interview at any time or decline to answer any of the questions.'

The main body of the interview

It is a good idea to start the interview with relatively straightforward, general questions or topics that respondents will find easy to answer or talk about – this helps create a relaxed atmosphere and helps establish rapport between interviewer and respondents. It is possible then to move on to more specific questions or more difficult topics. This technique is known as 'funnelling'. For example, you might ask this sequence of questions:

> ➤ *Broad, open-ended questions*: 'Tell me about shopping' or 'Tell me about a really satisfying shopping experience.'
> ➤ *Pressing and probing questions*: 'What do you particularly like/dislike about shopping?' 'You mentioned X. Tell me more about that.' 'What did you do about that?'
> ➤ *Questions narrowing in on particular topics or issues*: 'How did she react when you made the complaint?' 'What happened next?' 'What was the end result?' 'How does that compare to the way X handled it?'
> ➤ *Clarifying questions*: 'What exactly did you do then?' 'How did that make you feel?'
> ➤ *Summarising statements or questions*: 'You said that they sent you a letter of apology, explaining what the problem had been and offering you your money back. I get the impression that the apology meant the most to you.'

The wind down

It is important to signal the end of the interview or discussion – about 10 minutes before the end of an hour-long session, and about 15 minutes before the end of a one and a half to two-hour session. Some useful wind-down strategies include presenting a summary of the main points and asking for final comments; asking respondents if there is anything that they have not said that they would like to say, or anything they have said and wish they had not; and asking what one thought or idea the respondent(s) would like the client to take from the session.

In putting together an interview or discussion guide, check that the questions:

> ➤ give you the information you want;
> ➤ are meaningful and relevant to respondents (and are within respondents' frame of reference);
> ➤ are in an order that helps the flow of the interview.

■ Projective and enabling techniques

Projective and enabling techniques – indirect forms of questioning that are deliberately vague and ambiguous – are often used in qualitative research, and in particular in attitude resesarch, to get beyond the rational response to the 'private' and the 'non-communicable' (Cooper and Branthwaite, 1977). The idea is that respondents will 'project' their ideas, feelings, emotions and attitudes in completing the task. In doing so, responses are elicited that respondents may not have been able or willing to give via direct questioning.

Types of projective techniques

There are several types of techniques – techniques of association, completion, construction and expressive techniques. Examples are given in Table 6.1.

Table 6.1 Examples of projective techniques and their uses

Name	Description	Uses
Word association	Respondent asked for first word that comes to mind when given a particular word (spoken or written down).	To explore connections, get at language used, uncover product or brand attributes and images.
Picture association	From a large and varied collection of pictures respondents asked to choose which best suit a brand or a product or its users.	
Thought bubble completion	Respondents fill in what the person depicted in a drawing or picture might be thinking or feeling.	To uncover thoughts, feelings, attitudes, motivations and so on associated with different situations.
Sentence completion	Complete incomplete sentences, for example, 'If X [name of organisation] was really interested in protecting the environment it would ... '	
Collage	Respondents create a collage from a pile of pictures; or a collage or picture board is compiled in advance of fieldwork.	To uncover a mood, an image or a style associated with a product, a service, a brand, an experience and so on.
Projective questioning	'What do you think the average drinker might think of this bar?'	To uncover beliefs, attitudes, feelings, ideas that the respondent may not want or be able to express directly.
Stereotypes	Develop a story about a person in a picture.	
Personalisation of objects/brand personality	'If this brand were a person, what would he or she look like? What would he or she do for a living? What type of house would he or she live in?'	
Mapping	Sort or group brands or organisations according to key criteria; sort again on a different basis.	To see how people view a market; to understand positioning; to identify gaps.
Choice ordering techniques	Given the ends of a scale, put brands or products where they fall along the scale.	To understand how people see a range of products or brands in relation to certain characteristics and in relation to each other.

Table 6.1 continued

Name	Description	Uses
Visualisation	Interviewer guides the respondent in thinking back to the last time he or she did X or tried Y, to visualise the scene in all its details.	To allow respondents to recall in detail an experience or a situation and to bring to mind thoughts and feelings about it.
Psycho drawing	Draw a brand or a process.	To bring to mind thoughts and feelings about a brand or a process that could not be articulated or were not top of mind.

Using projective techniques

When using projective techniques make sure that the technique you choose fits the research objectives. If you plan to use projective techniques in international research make sure that the techniques chosen are suitable for the particular culture. If you are conducting a multi-country study make sure that the technique used works in the same way in each country. Those suitable for multi-country work include collage (make sure that the pictures chosen are relevant to the country or market and check the meaning of signs, symbols and colours in each country); word association; bubble and sentence completion; mapping; and personification.

For a technique to work well it must be introduced at the right time, when respondents are relaxed and the interview or group is working well. The task should be simple and straightforward: explain clearly and precisely exactly what is to be done. Make any instructions – whether it is to be done individually or in small groups, whether respondents can talk to each other during the task, whether they can ask questions, the amount of time available, what will be required at the end of the task and so on – as clear as possible. Reassure participants that it is not a test. As they work on the task, give them plenty of encouragement. Remind them when the time is coming to an end and reassure them that it does not matter if they have not finished. Invite them in turn to explain the end product to you (in an individual interview) or the group. Follow this up with a discussion about what conclusions they would draw from what has been done.

Box 6.5 Semiotics and qualitative research

Semiotics is the study of signs and symbols (including words and images) and their use and meaning in all forms of communication. Kaushik and Sen (1990) describe, for example, how the colour yellow, which in India is associated with 'life-giving, auspiciousness and ... vibrancy', used in a sunflower oil advertisement in India 'becomes the signifier that connects the goodness and the light quality of the cooking oil with the life and health-giving qualities of the sun's rays and the sun-kissed flowers'. Semiotics is used in qualitative research to explore, understand and interpret or 'decode' the meaning of signs and symbols, in particular those used in advertising and brand imagery, and is thus useful in gaining the cultural understanding necessary for developing effective cross-cultural communications (Harvey and Evans, 2001).

■ Listening, building rapport and observing

Of course qualitative interviewing is not just about asking questions and applying techniques – it is just as much, if not more so, about listening and observing. Much of what is communicated is communicated via tone of voice and body language. It is important that you listen not only to what is said but to how it is said – the words used, the pauses, the style of speech and the tone of voice, and the non-verbal cues of body language (Colwell, 1990). This will give you a fuller understanding of the meaning of what is said. This is easier said than done. During an interview or a group you are having a conversation with the respondent or respondents – asking questions, listening, asking the next question. You are also having a conversation with yourself, in your head. You are doing the following:

➤ thinking about how what the respondent has said or not said fits with the research objectives, or the ideas you have developed about the issue;

➤ deciding whether or not you should follow it up, or clarify, or move on;

➤ formulating the next question;

➤ watching the body language;

➤ taking account of the dynamics of the interview and what they mean for what should happen next;

➤ thinking about the time you have left and what else needs to be covered.

Box 6.6 NLP and qualitative research

Neuro-linguistic programming (NLP) is a technique that is applied in a range of fields including qualitative research. Developing a sensory acuity – being alert to what you are hearing and seeing and feeling – is one of the pillars of NLP practice. NLP also focuses on building and maintaining rapport for effective communication and on developing multiple perspectives in order to obtain the maximum amount of information and insight from an interview or group.

Listening

Despite this internal conversation, you must listen actively and attentively to the respondent and you must show that you are listening (in a non-judgemental, empathetic and respectful way) and show that you are interested in what is being said. To do this well:

➤ remove physical barriers between you and the respondent(s), if possible;

➤ make eye contact;

➤ lean slightly forward towards the respondent(s);

➤ keep a relaxed posture;

➤ use encouring responses (nods, 'mm'ing).

Do not:

➤ use a desk or other object as a barrier;

➤ sit too close;

➢ stare or avoid eye contact or look away;
➢ look around the room or stare at the floor or at your discussion guide;
➢ look tense, anxious or ill at ease;
➢ look at your watch;
➢ fidget or make unnecessary movements;
➢ frown or look cross;
➢ yawn or sigh or make discouraging responses or use a discouraging tone of voice;
➢ interrupt.

Building rapport

The whole interviewing process can be a nerve-wracking experience for respondents – meeting someone (or several people) they have never met before; being questioned and asked to talk about subjects that, sometimes, they may not even discuss with friends. It is vital that the researcher is able to put respondents at ease, and establish rapport – without rapport the quality of the interaction between interviewer and respondents (and the quality of the data) will be poor. Rapport is about getting the respondent's attention and creating trust. You can build rapport by actively listening, as described above, by giving the respondent your full attention and by showing the respondent that you are interested in understanding his or her perspective by going back over what was said. In addition, you can 'mirror' or 'match' – (subtly and genuinely) adopting aspects of the respondent's verbal and non-verbal behaviour – the pace and tone of speech, facial expression, posture, for example.

Observing

To build and sustain rapport you need to observe as well as listen. You need to be aware of and sensitive to respondents' body language in order to interpret what they are saying correctly and in order to run the interview well. For example, you need to know whether the respondent understands the question or the issue, you need to know whether they are anxious or interested and so on. Body language will help tell you these things. The key elements of body language include the following:

➢ movements (of the head and other parts of the body, including hand gestures);
➢ facial expressions;
➢ direction of gaze (including eye contact);
➢ posture;
➢ spatial position (including proximity and orientation);
➢ bodily contact;
➢ tone of voice;
➢ dress.

If you are involved in international research, remember that gestures and body language may mean different things in different countries (Morris, 1994). In addition to observing respondents' body language you need to be aware of your own and the messages that it might be conveying to respondents.

Managing yourself

It is important to think about your role in the interview process, about what assumptions you make about the people you are interviewing, and about the topic, and to make these explicit to yourself before fieldwork begins. An open mind and high degree of self-awareness are important ingredients in qualitative interviewing. At the outset of a study you should examine your own feelings and views on it. For example, ask yourself what assumptions you have made about the topic or what you think you might hear from respondents about it; examine what prejudices you have, what your views on it are; ask yourself how prepared you are to hear a view different from your own or to hear something shocking. Remember, one of your skills as a qualitative interviewer is not to give your own opinion or appear judgemental.

Box 6.7 summarises the tasks of the qualitative researcher and the skills needed to carry out the role effectively. It is widely accepted (Research and Development sub-committee, 1979) that the skill and experience of the qualitative researcher 'is the most important determinant of the value. ... of the study'.

Box 6.7 The job of the qualitative interviewer or moderator

Key tasks

➢ Understanding the research brief
➢ Briefing and liaising with recruiters
➢ Managing the fieldwork process
➢ Designing the interview guide
➢ Conducting the interview or discussion
➢ Creating an atmosphere in which respondents are willing to talk and share
➢ Listening attentively
➢ Relating what is being said to the research brief
➢ Deciding what to explore and in how much detail
➢ Deciding when to probe or challenge, ask for clarification, or summarise

Key skills (Research and Development sub-committee, 1979)

➢ Personal capacity for empathy, sensitivity, imagination and creativity
➢ Ability to become involved and yet remain detached
➢ Articulate but a good listener
➢ Intellectual ability but common sense
➢ Capacity for logical analysis
➢ Conceptual ability and eye for detail
➢ Think analytically yet tolerate disorder
➢ Verbal skills
➢ Confidence to handle verbal presentations

The role of the assistant moderator

In some circumstances, and more so in social research than in market research, an assistant moderator is involved in a group discussion. If, for example, there is a lot of material to cover or a lot of stimulus material to get through, it can be useful to have the help of an assistant, even if it is to take charge of the recording, the catering or the paper work. If the project deadline is particularly tight it can be useful to have someone to take detailed notes – this can speed up the analysis process. The assistant moderator may be a trainee researcher and, besides his or her role in assisting or note taking, is there to learn. In some cases the discussion may be split between the moderator and an assistant moderator, with one maintaining the discussion and the other introducing new topics and handling stimulus material.

Online qualitative research

Qualitative data can be collected online using a variety of techniques, including web-based group discussions, bulletin board groups and email groups. Recruitment for online research can take place online (via websites or email) or via traditional methods.

Web-based group discussions

Web-based groups can be conducted in real time via a specially set up chatroom. They consist of between six and eight participants and last between an hour and an hour and a half. The technology allows the moderator to communicate with the group and with individual group members. The client can observe the group output and can communicate with the moderator. Stimulus material can be shown. Depending on the complexity of the task and the number of participants, it is not uncommon to have two moderators.

Another way of running a group discussion online is to use a bulletin board to which the moderator posts questions and respondents post replies and comments on other members' contributions; respondents can be sent or directed via links to view stimulus material. The discussion can run over several days, weeks or even months and involve a 'community' of 20–30 respondents. The moderator briefs respondents about frequency of viewing and responding to questions and comments, which can vary depending on the nature of the research and the duration of the discussion group. The technology allows the moderator to see who logs on when and for how long, and to track their comments and their viewing of the stimulus material.

One of the advantages of web-based discussion is that at the end of the process you have a detailed written record of the discussion for analysis. Web-based methods are useful if your topic relates to the virtual world, or if your sample is hard to access in other ways. The drawbacks are obvious – you cannot see the people taking part, so you have no way of using or seeing body language and you have no way of verifying that the participants are who they say they are. Using traditional recruitment practices (face to face and telephone) is one way round this; another is to use a form of back-checking, telephoning respondents after a group session; also, quality and consistency checks can be made on the data themselves. Further advantages and disadvantages are outlined in Box 6.8.

Email groups

Email groups are group interviews rather than group discussions. There is no direct interaction between group members; the interaction is with the moderator and with the moderator's account of the group's responses. In effect, they are more like one-to-one interviews operating in parallel. These 'moderated email groups' work like this (Comley, 1999): the moderator emails questions to each of the group participants, between 10 and 20 per group, who send back their replies within an agreed time. The moderator collates and analyses these responses (often with input from the client) and produces a summary document, which is sent out to the group for comment. There may be a further wave of questions and interaction with the moderator, depending on the nature of the project and the time frame, which can be up to two or three weeks.

Box 6.8 Advantages and disadvantages of web and email groups

Advantages
➤ Access to low penetration samples
➤ Access to geographically widely dispersed populations
➤ Heterogeneous groups are not a problem
➤ No group interactions to manage
➤ All participants have an equal chance to contribute
➤ Easy to keep to topic
➤ Participants can answer at own pace in own time
➤ Can get more considered responses
➤ Anonymity can mean that respondents are less inclined to give socially desirable responses
➤ Suitable if a more structured approach is needed

Disadvantages
➤ Not being face to face – some communication lost
➤ Verification of respondents difficult
➤ Respondents can adopt personas
➤ Interaction between participants is limited
➤ Interaction with moderator is limited – cannot always probe for detail and clarification
➤ Requires participants with computer literacy and email access
➤ Requires moderator with computer literacy skills and ability to interpret responses
➤ Compatibility of software between moderator and participants
➤ Administration and set-up (respondent agreement, commitment, availability)
➤ Time required longer than in traditional face-to-face groups
➤ Costs can be relatively high compared to traditional methods

Panels, juries and workshops

Qualitative methods of data collection can be used to gather data from respondents on panels or juries and in workshops or clinics.

■ Panels and juries

A qualitative panel or jury is made up of a number of individuals (about 10–12, typically) who meet at intervals and may stay together for an extended period (up to 12 months, or longer in some cases). The panel or jury may have a theme – consumer or community consultation, for example. At each session a topic relevant to the theme may be discussed. Participants may be briefed about the topic in advance of the session.

■ Workshops

Workshops can be used to explore issues in detail, to solve problems and come up with ideas and solutions using techniques such as brainstorming. Most workshops consist of about 15–20 people, sometimes including clients as well as consumers or those with an interest in the topic, and can last for seven or eight hours. During the workshop session smaller sub-groups may break away from the main group to work on different aspects of an issue or problem.

Chapter summary

➢ There are two main ways of collecting qualitative data – observation and interviewing.

➢ Simple observation involves watching and recording people and activity; participant observation is when the researcher takes part in the activity that he or she is observing.

➢ The main advantage of observation over interviewing is that in an interview the respondent is recalling his or her behaviour whereas in observation the researcher sees it at first hand – without the filter of memory or selection.

➢ Qualitative interviews have been described as 'guided conversations' (Rubin and Rubin, 1995). They are less standardised and more flexible than quantitative interviews. They use a more open-ended and non-directive approach.

➢ Qualitative interviews are suitable if you want in-depth accounts, detailed descriptions, context-rich data and understanding of the issue, the processes or the behaviour.

➢ The choice of interview over observation will be dependent on the nature and objectives of the research and the practicalities of time and cost. Interviewing is more cost effective, and suitable when the objectives of the research are clearly defined, and when it is necessary to gather data from a range of people or settings.

➢ The main forms of interviewing in qualitative research are the one-to-one in-depth interview lasting about one hour and the group discussion consisting of 8–10 respondents and lasting about one-and-a-half hours.

➢ Individual interviews are used if the topic is sensitive or intimate; if you need detailed information on individual attitudes and behaviour; if you need to get beyond the socially acceptable view; if you need 'time-line' information; or if your sample is difficult to find.

➢ Groups are appropriate if you need to see a wide range of attitudes and opinions; you need to determine differences between people; you do not need minority views or views not influenced by the group; you want to understand social and cultural influences; or you need to draw out creative thinking/solutions.

➢ The interview or discussion should have a clear introduction and a clearly signalled wind-down period towards the end of the interview.

➢ There are variations on both the individual interview (paired depths, triads, for example) and the group discussion (mini-groups, extended groups, for example).

➢ The style of interview or discussion guide varies from a simple list of topics to one that has more structure, with a series of questions listed under headings. The choice depends on the objectives of the research, the need for comparability between interviews or groups, the experience of the interviewer and the house style of the researcher or client.

➢ Projective and enabling techniques – techniques of association, completion, construction and expressive techniques (indirect forms of questioning that are deliberately vague and ambiguous) – are used to get beyond the rational response.

➢ Listening and observing and the ability to build rapport with respondents, as well as questioning skills, are vital in qualitative interviewing. Other (related) skills include the capacity for empathy, sensitivity, imagination and creativity and the ability to become involved and yet remain detached.

➢ Group discussions can be recruited and conducted online, in two ways: on the web, usually at a prearranged, private chat room or bulletin board, or via email.

➢ There are advantages and disadvantages to online data collection. Advantages include access to low penetration samples and widely dispersed populations; lack of problems associated with heterogeneous groups and group interactions; suitability if a more structured approach is needed; all participants have an equal chance to contribute, they can answer at their own pace and in their own time and responses can be more considered; and the anonymity can mean that you get fewer socially desirable responses. Disadvantages include loss of non-verbal communication and limited interaction between participants and with the moderator; it requires that participants are computer literate and have Internet access; time and costs can be high compared to traditional methods.

➢ Qualitative methods are also used to collect data from panels and juries and in workshops.

Questions and exercises

1 What are the main methods of qualitative data collection?

2 What does qualitative observational research entail? What are the advantages of observation over interviewing?

3 How does a qualitative interview differ from a quantitative interview?

4 How should a qualitative interview be structured? Why is it important to have a clear introduction and a wind-down period towards the end of the interview?

5 Describe the role of the qualitative interviewer or moderator. What skills are needed to undertake the role?

6 What is the role of an assistant moderator? In what circumstances might it be useful to have an assistant moderator?

7 Describe what is meant by an in-depth interview. For what reasons would you choose to use in-depth interviews? In what circumstances would it be useful to use paired depth interviews?

8 Describe what is involved in a group discussion. For what reasons would you choose group discussions as your main method of data collection? In what circumstances would you use mini-groups?

9 Why are projective techniques useful? Describe three different projective techniques and give examples of the sorts of studies in which they might be used.

10 What are the advantages and disadvantages of online qualitative research?

References

Burgess, R. (1984) *In the Field: An Introduction to Field Research*, London: Allen Unwin.

Colwell, J. (1990) 'Qualitative market research: a conceptual analysis and review of practitioner criteria', *Journal of the Market Research Society*, 32, 1, pp. 13–36.

Comley, P. (1999) 'Moderated Email Groups: Computing Magazine case study', *Proceedings of the ESOMAR Net Effects Conference*, London.

Cooper, P. and Branthwaite, A. (1977) 'Qualitative technology: new perspectives on measurement and meaning through qualitative research', *Proceedings of The Market Research Society Conference*, London: The Market Research Society.

Cooper, P. and Tower, R. (1992) 'Inside the consumer mind: consumer attitudes to the arts', *Journal of the Market Research Society*, 34, 4, pp. 299–311.

Gordon, W. and Robson, S. (1980) 'Respondent through the looking glass: towards a better understanding of the qualitative interviewing process', *Proceedings of The Market Research Society Conference*, London: The Market Research Society.

Harvey, M. and Evans, M. (2001) 'Decoding competitive propositions: a semiotic alternative to traditional advertising research', *Proceedings of The Market Research Society Conference*, London: The Market Research Society.

Kaushik, M. and Sen, A. (1990) 'Semiotics and qualitative research', *Journal of the Market Research Society*, **32**, 2, pp. 227–42.

Rubin, H. and Rubin, I. (1995) *Qualitative Interviewing: The Art of Hearing Data*, London: Sage.

Morris, D. (1994) *Bodytalk: A World Guide to Gestures*, London: Jonathan Cape.

The Research and Development sub-committee on Qualitative Research (1979) 'Qualitative research: a summary of the concepts involved', *Journal of the Market Research Society*, **21**, 2, pp. 107–24.

Sampson, P. (1967 and 1996) 'Commonsense in qualitative research', *Journal of the Market Research Society*, **9**, 1, pp. 30–8 and reprinted in **38**, 4, pp. 331–9.

Schlackman, W. (1984) 'A discussion of the use of sensitivity panels in market research', *Proceedings of The Market Research Society Conference*, London: The Market Research Society.

Sykes, W. (1990) 'Validity and reliability in qualitative market research: a review of the literature', *Journal of the Market Research Society*, **32**, 3, pp. 289–28.

Recommended reading

Adriaenssens, C. and Cadman, L. (1999) 'An adapation of moderated e-mail focus groups to assess the potential for a new online (Internet) financial services offer in the UK', *Journal of the Market Research Society*, **41**, 4, pp. 417–24. An account of the use of online research.

Gordon, W. (1999) *Goodthinking: A Guide to Qualitative Research*, Henley-on-Thames: Admap. A detailed guide to the techniques and practice of qualitative market research, including a very useful section on the psychology of groups.

Hammersley, M. and Atkinson, P. (1995) *Ethnography: Principles in Practice*, London: Routledge. A useful account of the practice of ethnography.

Harvey, M. and Evans, M. (2001) 'Decoding competitive propositions: a semiotic alternative to traditional advertising research', *Proceedings of The Market Research Society Conference*, London: The Market Research Society. A detailed account of the application of semiotics.

Kaushik, M. and Sen, A. (1990) 'Semiotics and qualitative research', *Journal of the Market Research Society*, **32**, 2, pp. 227–42. A description of the value of semiotics in understanding advertising and brand imagery.

Lee, R. (1992) *Doing Research on Sensitive Topics*, London: Sage. A very useful guide for those involved in research on sensitive issues.

Rubin, H. and Rubin, I. (1995) *Qualitative Interviewing: The Art of Hearing Data*, London: Sage. An excellent guide to interviewing.

O'Connor, J. and Seymour, J. (1993) *Introducing NLP*, London: HarperCollins. For those interested in finding out more about NLP.

Rose, J., Sykes, L. and Woodcock, D. (1995) 'Qualitative recruitment: the industry working party report', *Proceedings of The Market Research Society Conference*, London: The Market Research Society. A review of the issues in recruitment.

Sampson, P. (1985) 'Qualitative research in Europe: the state of the art and the art of the state', ESOMAR Congress, Weisbaden. An excellent overview.

Chapter 7

Collecting quantitative data

Introduction

Quantitative research is about collecting data from a relatively large sample or population in a structured and standardised way. In this chapter we look at the main methods of collecting such data – via interviewing (interviewer-administered and self-completion) and observation.

Topics covered

- Interviewing:
  - the role of the interviewer
  - face-to-face interviews
  - telephone interviews
  - computer-aided interviewing
  - self-completion (postal and Internet) data collection
- Panels and omnibuses
- Observation

Relationship to MRS Advanced Certificate Syllabus

The material covered in this chapter is relevant to Unit 5 – Data Collection Methods, specifically:

- face-to-face interviews;
- telephone interviews;
- postal surveys;
- computer-aided interviewing;
- internet data collection.

Learning outcomes

At the end of this chapter you should be able to:

- show awareness of the range of different methods of data collection used in quantitative research;
- understand the uses of each method;
- understand the limitations of each method;
- select the appropriate method or combination of methods for a given research proposal.

Interviewing

Quantitative data can be collected via interviews using standardised structured or semi-structured 'forms' – interview schedules or questionnaires and diaries. There are two ways of getting your sample to complete these 'forms'. You get the respondent to do it themselves – this is called 'self-completion'; or you get an interviewer to ask the questions of the respondent, either in person face to face or via the telephone, and record his or her answers on the 'form' – this is called 'interviewer administered'. The option you choose will depend on a number of things. You will need to determine how suitable the method is for the following:

➤ the study and its objectives;
➤ the topic or issues under investigation;
➤ reaching the right sample;
➤ achieving the right numbers;
➤ the time and budget available.

For example, if you have a subject of a very sensitive nature the telephone may be the best option as it offers the respondent a degree of anonymity and distance that a face-to-face interview does not. If you have a sample that is hard to reach in person – a sample of business executives, for example, the telephone or a postal or email survey may be the only way of contacting them. If you need to show respondents stimulus material, for example an advertisement, or get them to try a product, a face-to-face approach may be the only feasible one. If you need to achieve a particular sample size you may decide against a postal survey or an email survey unless you are fairly sure that the return or completion rate (which can sometimes be hard to predict) will give you the numbers (and the sample) you need. If you are working to a tight budget you might consider a postal survey – with no interviewer costs it can be cheaper than a telephone or face-to-face survey. If you are working to a tight deadline a postal survey may not be appropriate – turnaround times are often relatively long – therefore a telephone or email survey might be considered.

Before we look in detail at the different methods of interviewer-administered data collection, it is worth looking at the role of the interviewer.

The role of the interviewer

The interviewer has two jobs to do – he or she must contact people who match the recruitment criteria of the survey and encourage them to take part in an interview, and he or she must administer the interview. This is a skilled job. It requires a high level of interpersonal skill, a sound understanding of the data collection and research processes, including responsibilities under data protection legislation as well as those set out in the MRS Code of Conduct or the ICC/ESOMAR Code of Practice. Indeed the MRS publishes guidelines for interviewers, which you can view at its website (www.mrs.org.uk).

■ The effect of the interviewer

Interviewers are not all the same and nor are respondents. An interviewer may react to or interact differently with different respondents, and respondents will react differently to different interviewers. Much research has been done on the effect an interviewer has on response rates and on the quality of data collected. There is evidence to show that appearance, age, gender, social grade, ethnic background, religion and attitude or personality have an effect on the interviewing process and on the outcome of the interview. This is not confined to face-to-face interviews. Research shows that respondents in telephone interviews make judgements about an interviewer's characteristics on the basis of his or her voice. To minimise the effects of interviewer variance interviewers are trained to carry out interviews according to the instructions provided and to do so in a professional, courteous and objective way.

■ Uniformity of approach

A questionnaire will have been designed to gather data from a relatively large number of people that make up the sample or population under study. Due to the number of interviews needed it is likely that more than one interviewer will be involved in the data collection process. Uniformity or consistency of approach is a key aim in structured and standardised quantitative research – data must be collected in the same way across the sample and any possible bias or errors in asking questions or recording responses must be kept to a minimum. It is important therefore that each respondent is asked the questions on the questionnaire in exactly the same way. This means that the interviewer must read out instructions and ask the questions exactly as they appear on the questionnaire, and in the way that they were briefed to do (a change of emphasis on a word can change the meaning). With closed, pre-coded questions the interviewer selects or records the code that applies to the respondent's answer. For some questions, such as those with an 'other' code in the list of pre-coded responses, or where the respondent says 'Don't know' or 'Not sure', the interviewer may need to probe (depending on what it says in the briefing notes or instructions given during training). Where there are open-ended questions, questions that require the respondent to answer in his or her own words, the interviewer must record the answers verbatim. If probing is needed, to elicit a more detailed response, the interviewer must follow the specified probing/prompting procedure set out on the questionnaire or specified in his or her training and in the briefing for the particular study. He or she must record the result of the probing/prompting.

All this means that the interviewer must be familiar and comfortable with the questionnaire and the interviewing process. Two things are vital here: interviewer training and briefing. Questionnaire design also has a role to play: the person designing the questionnaire has a responsibility to the interviewer to ensure that the questionnaire is clear, logical, easy to follow and set out in such a way that makes it easy for the interviewer to record responses. We return to this in Chapters 10 and 11.

■ Training

Typically the interviewer will have been trained by the research agency or fieldwork company for whom he or she undertakes work. This training will usually have involved one or two days of 'theory' in the classroom covering the following:

➢ how to find the right respondent;
➢ how to obtain and record information to determine the respondent's social grade;
➢ how to get the respondent to agree to an interview;
➢ explaining the nature of the interview and the time needed to conduct it;
➢ explaining about confidentiality, and the use of the personal details collected;
➢ the importance of asking questions and reading out instructions exactly as they appear on the questionnaire;
➢ the importance of coding pre-coded responses accurately;
➢ the importance of recording responses to open-ended questions verbatim or as close as possible;
➢ the extent of probing allowed or required and the manner in which probing is to be done (and how this should be recorded);
➢ how to use the data collection equipment;
➢ how to complete all paperwork accurately.

Office-bound training is followed by some practice interviews in the field under the supervision of a senior interviewer for face-to-face interviews, on the telephone with a supervisor or senior interviewer listening. Further on-the-job training takes place at regular intervals. Interviewers may be accompanied or listened to by a senior interviewer, supervisor or area manager from time to time to check on the quality of their work, especially if they are assigned a type of job of which they have little experience. This is part of the overall quality control procedure that is part of the management of a fieldforce. Fieldwork quality control also includes checking and monitoring the interviewers' completed work.

Interviewer Quality Control Scheme

In 1978 the MRS established the Interviewer Quality Control Scheme (IQCS) to address the issue of quality in fieldwork. The IQCS outlines a minimum standard (now part of British Standard BS7911) for the quality of interviewers and interviewing in consumer, social and business-to-business research. Any company wishing to join the scheme must meet these minimum standards in a number of areas including recruitment, training, quality control, survey administration and office standards. The aim of the scheme is to assure clients that all data are collected to acceptable and ethical standards. In terms of training, for face-to-face interviews individuals must receive a minimum of 12 hours' training; for auditing and telephone interviewing the minimum is 6 hours. As part of the training individuals are accompanied and/or assessed on their first job. Once trained interviewers are assessed on an ongoing basis depending on the number and type of jobs they conduct in a year.

MRS accredited interviewer training

the MRS has introduced a scheme of accreditation for interviewers. The aim of this scheme is to set national professional standards for interviewing and to provide a recognised qualification. To become an accredited interviewer, interviewers must complete a training scheme run by an accredited trainer – either an employer such as a research agency or a third party training provider.

■ Interviewer briefing

Interviewers are briefed in detail about the requirements of each particular job. The aim of briefing interviewers on each job is to ensure overall consistency of approach – by making sure that they understand clearly how to administer that particular questionnaire, and to address any concerns or questions that they may have about it. The briefing may be given by the client service or field executive or the supervisor or area manager, although it may sometimes involve the person commissioning the work (the client). Most briefings for telephone surveys take place face to face – mainly because the interviewers work from a central telephone unit and those involved with the project are usually on hand. In-person briefings for central location face-to-face surveys are common; those for street and in-home or at-work surveys often less so because of budget restrictions – it is expensive to gather together geographically dispersed interviewers and supervisors and client service or field staff. In such circumstances briefings are typically given by post, email or telephone. We look in detail at what is involved in a briefing in Chapter 11.

Face-to-face interviews

Depending on the nature of the survey, face-to-face interviews can take place in the respondent's home, in the street, in a central location, for example in a hall or in a shopping centre or mall, or at the respondent's place of work. Thus, if you need a quota sample of consumers, the interview is about product preferences and is likely to last no more than about 10 minutes, you could recruit and conduct interviews in the street or in a central location such as a shopping centre. If, however, you are conducting a random sample survey on household spending that lasts up to 35 minutes, a face-to-face, in-home interview may be more appropriate.

■ Street interviews

Street interviews are conducted in busy streets with a lot of pedestrian traffic. The interviewer approaches people who he or she thinks fit the sampling criteria, if the research is being conducted using a quota sample; if a random sample is required, he or she approaches the nth passer-by and requests an interview. Street interviews usually last no more than ten minutes – people will not stand around answering questions for any longer. The topic of the interview must be one that most people are content to talk about on the street. The amount of stimulus material that can be shown is limited.

■ Shopping centre/hall tests

The main advantage of interviewing in shopping centres (or rooms or halls on high streets) compared to street interviews lies in the comfort of the environment – interviewer and respondent are protected from the weather and the centre is traffic free. This allows a slightly longer interview, up to about 15 minutes. In addition, the layout of the centre may be such that it is possible to set out an interviewing station with tables and chairs at which to seat the respondent. As a result the shopping centre or hall may be used for what are known as 'hall tests' – longer interviews that would not be feasible in the street, lasting up to about 30 minutes. This format also allows scope for exposing the respondent to stimulus material – for example tasting a product or viewing advertisements.

Shopping centres and halls are private property and permission must be obtained in order to conduct fieldwork; a fee for their use is usually payable. Where necessary and relevant interviews can also take place inside shops, but permission must again be obtained.

■ In-home interviews

In-home interviews are conducted in the home of the respondent or on the doorstep. In-home interviews may be necessary for several reasons. It may be necessary to recruit the sample by going door to door to specific addresses (for example addresses chosen at random from a sampling frame such as the Electoral Register or the Postal Address File) or by going to specific areas or streets identified under a geodemographic classification system as containing the type of people likely to meet the sampling criteria. It may be that the home environment is the most suitable place for the interview – it may be necessary to refer to products used in the home or it may be a sensitive topic and the home may be the most relaxed environment for asking such questions. It may require the interviewer to record observations, for example the brand and model of video recorder – something that the respondent is unlikely to remember in detail. Interviewing in-home allows a longer interview to take place, usually about 45 minutes to an hour.

■ Workplace interviews

Workplace interviews are suitable when the subject matter of the interview is related to the respondent's work. The interview is conducted in the respondent's office or in a suitable meeting room or in a quiet area – somewhere where, if possible, interruptions – from the telephone ringing to people knocking at the door – can be kept to a minimum.

■ Strengths of face-to-face interviews

Face-to-face data collection has a number of advantages. The interviewer has the chance to build rapport with the respondent, which can help achieve and maintain co-operation and increase the quality of the data. Response rates can be relatively high in comparison to other methods. Face-to-face methods allow for a relatively high degree of flexibility in the interviewing process – the interview can last up to an hour; stimulus material can be used; complex questions explained and administered; and probing and prompting carried out. In central location or hall tests the environment of the interview can be controlled.

■ Weaknesses of face-to-face interviews

There are some disadvantages with face-to-face data collection, particularly in relation to in-home interviews. It is relatively expensive and time consuming. Finding respondents at home (or at work) at a suitable time (and willing to take part) can be difficult. To overcome this it is often necessary (and almost essential for business-to-business interviews) to make an appointment with the respondent, either by telephone or in person, to set a suitable time. Interruptions from other members of the household or workforce or the presence of someone else in the room during the interview can impact on the quality of the data collected. It is difficult to cover remote or rural locations. Cluster sampling methods, which serve to reduce travel time and costs, risk introducing sample bias. Representativeness of the sample can be affected in other ways: interviewers may be reluctant to interview in some (socially deprived) neighbourhoods; they may find it difficult to obtain interviews in higher income areas; potential respondents in any neighbourhood may be unwilling to open the door to a stranger. There is a greater tendency in face-to-face methods for the respondent to give socially desirable responses – showing him- or herself in the best possible light. With quality control procedures at more of a distance than in telephone interviewing (where interviewers' work can be continuously monitored) there is greater scope for interviewer bias or cheating.

Box 7.1 Computer-aided data capture

Data can be captured and recorded electronically via a PC, laptop computer, handheld tablet or personal digital assistant:

> CAPI – computer-aided personal interviewing;
> CATI – computer-aided telephone interviewing;
> CASI – computer-aided self interviewing;
> CAWI – computer-aided wireless interviewing.

In computer-aided methods the questionnaire (and in some cases the stimulus material), data entry and data editing and verification procedures are programmed into the computer. To start a new interview the interviewer calls a new questionnaire up on screen and enters responses into the computer using the keyboard or touch screen. The program is designed so that it automatically brings up the next question relevant to that respondent as soon as the response to the previous question is entered. All completed questionnaires are stored in the computer's memory and can be downloaded via modem or wireless connection to a central computer at the agency's data processing centre. There are many advantages in using computer-aided methods.

Box 7.1 continued

Fieldwork management
➤ No printing of questionnaires required
➤ Review of quotas and sample
➤ Monitoring of interviewer performance and strike rates
➤ Data on interview length
➤ Electronic access to all questionnaires

Use of stimulus material
➤ High quality images embedded in the questionnaire
➤ Multi-media capabilities – can embed and play high-quality video and audio material

Data processing
➤ Checking and editing done automatically
➤ No manual data entry – data downloaded via modem or wireless connection to central processing
➤ Interim results easily obtainable
➤ Fieldwork to tabulation time greatly reduced

Data quality
➤ Smooth flow of interview
➤ Digital recording of verbatim responses
➤ Automatic routing reduces errors
➤ No separate data entry eliminates keying errors

   The main disadvantage is the capital investment required to buy and maintain the equipment and the software (although this is becoming less of an issue as devices become smaller and cheaper) and to train and support interviewers and other staff to use it. Piloting questionnaires is strongly advised as mistakes in the program cannot be as easily rectified as paper questionnaires once interviewing begins.

Telephone interviews

Most data collection via telephone interviewing is conducted from specialist telephone units or centres, most of which use CATI systems. Traditional telephone interviewing, in which the interviewer records responses to questions on a paper questionnaire, is, however, still used. Telephone interviews typically last about 15–20 minutes, although if the subject matter is of interest to the respondent longer interviews are possible.

▪ Strengths of telephone interviews

Telephone interviewing, and especially CATI, has a number of advantages over face-to-face methods. A geographically dispersed sample (including those in remote and rural areas) can be obtained more easily. It may be the only way of reaching some populations – such as the business community. It is possible to use a pure random sampling approach rather than the cluster sampling approach that is common in face-to-face methods, thus reducing the chance of sampling error, and all at a greatly reduced cost because interviewer travel time is not an issue. A telephone survey may also make it easier to reach a wider spectrum of respondents – for example in socially deprived areas where interviewers may be reluctant to work and in higher income areas where access to homes may be difficult. It is possible to record digitally answers to open-ended questions in full. Greater quality control is possible (and so cheating is minimised), with interviewers being monitored 'live' rather than after the event, via back-checking. Clients and research executives can listen in, enabling them to get a feel for the findings.

It is relatively easy to monitor interview length and the time taken for individual questions – this can facilitate a dynamic or rolling pilot study and questions can be altered if necessary. It is also relatively easy to determine the strike rate and refusal rate and so monitor the sample and control quotas. Call-backs are easily managed so that bias towards those more often at home is reduced. Centralised, face-to-face briefings are more common than on face-to-face projects and supervisors and executives may be on hand to answer queries during fieldwork. Multi-country studies can be conducted from a central telephone unit, enabling greater control over administration and increased consistency. Telephone interviews offer respondents a greater degree of perceived anonymity than do face-to-face interviews. As a result, it is a useful method for collecting data on sensitive or intimate subjects, and it is useful in reducing social desirability bias. Telephone interviewing is faster than face-to-face – more questions can be asked in a shorter period of time and project turnaround times are faster. It can therefore be more cost effective than face-to-face interviewing.

■ Weaknesses of telephone interviews

There are some disadvantages. Although fixed line telephone ownership in the United Kingdom is almost universal this is not the case in other parts of the world – even among EU member states. Those who do not have a fixed line telephone are different from those who do – they are more likely to be from lower income households and they tend to be older. This has implications for obtaining a truly random sample of these populations – not everyone has the same chance of being selected and not all of them are in the sampling frame or universe. This problem – of sampling error and bias – is exacerbated if the telephone directory is used as a sampling frame. Not all telephone numbers (and so individuals and households or businesses) are listed. In addition the problem is further exacerbated by the fact that many people (particularly in younger age groups) have mobile rather than fixed line phones. The incidence of telephone answering machines, call screening, lines being used to access the Internet and more than one line per household add to the problems of access and sampling. The rise in the use of telemarketing has made people suspicious of bona fide telephone research and this has impacted on response rates.

In a telephone interview some of the benefits of social interaction and the chance to build rapport with a respondent are lost. It can be easier for the respondent to refuse an interview or end it early and harder for the interviewer to encourage the respondent to take part. It is difficult to include stimulus material, although this can be overcome by sending material out to respondents in advance of the interview. Long and complex questions are best avoided.

Self-completion methods of data collection

Self-completion surveys are one of the most cost-effective ways of collecting data, mainly because no interviewers are involved. They can be administered by post (the most common method) or electronically via email or the web or handed out in person. They can be included as part of a personal interview – to collect data on sensitive subjects, where the respondent might be embarrassed to provide answers to an interviewer; and in situations where it is not necessary to have an interviewer ask the questions, during a product or advertising test, for example. Diaries are a specialised form of self-completion survey – they can be used, for example, to gather data on respondents' product usage or eating or shopping habits. Self-completion surveys are an effective way of reaching people who would not otherwise take part in research – for example those in industry or busy professionals such as lawyers and doctors.

Self-completion surveys are an effective method of collecting data if you ensure that:

➢ the nature of the research and the topic are suited to this method of delivery;
➢ the topic is relevant and of interest to the target population;
➢ the method is a suitable way of reaching and achieving a response from the target population;
➢ the questionnaire is well designed – clear and easy to follow – and presented in a professional manner.

Success in encouraging response – on which the representativeness of the sample relies – depends on all of these. Before deciding to use this method it is worth asking whether the subject matter is interesting enough to the sample, and worth finding out (from the literature or from previous research) the response rate you might expect.

■ Techniques to increase the response rate

Other techniques or procedures that can help to increase the response rate include use of a personalised covering letter, sponsorship, pre-notification, reminders, incentives and, for postal surveys, a return envelope.

Covering letter or email

Postal, email and web questionnaires may be accompanied by a 'covering' letter or email, personalised if possible, as this has been found to increase response rates (Yu and Cooper, 1983). The aim of the letter is to do the following:

➢ explain the nature of the survey and why it is being conducted;
➢ explain why and how the recipient was chosen;

➢ reassure the recipient about the confidentiality and/or anonymity of the information they provide;

➢ state that participation is voluntary and that they can refuse to answer any question;

➢ give details of any incentive for completing the questionnaire (such as free entry to a prize draw);

➢ give details of the date by which the completed questionnaire should be returned;

➢ give details of how it should be returned (a pre-paid envelope is usually included).

Advance or pre-notification

Depending on the sample and the nature of the research, it may help to inform the sample in advance of the arrival of the questionnaire. This has also been found to improve the response rate (Yu and Cooper, 1983). Pre-notification can take the form of a letter, an email or a telephone call.

Sponsorship

It can be helpful in encouraging participation and response to include on the questionnaire or mention in the covering letter the name of the organisation sponsoring or involved in the research.

Reminders

In most postal, web and email surveys at least one reminder is sent – usually only to those who have not returned the questionnaire after a specific period of time. With postal surveys a reminder is usually sent after two to three weeks; with email or web surveys it depends on the time frame for the survey but a week is fairly typical. The reminder usually takes the form of a letter – carefully worded to encourage response and not deter it – and in most cases a second copy of the questionnaire is attached, in case the first one has been misplaced, destroyed or deleted.

Incentives

Incentives are used to encourage response and to thank respondents for the time taken to complete the survey. You can choose between pre-paid incentives and those sent on receipt of the completed questionnaire; monetary incentives and non-monetary ones, for example a pen, a book, a copy of the research report and entry in a prize draw.

Return envelopes

For postal surveys a stamped or reply-paid envelope is usually included to encourage and facilitate response.

■ Strengths of postal and Internet data collection

Postal, email and web surveys have a number of strengths. They are relatively easy to set up and administer, although email and web surveys do require specialist knowledge. They enable you to reach a widely dispersed population, and one that may not be amenable to research by other methods. They are relatively cost effective as there are no interviewers to pay. And with no interviews they are free of interviewer bias or error. They are an effective way of asking questions that need time for consideration or involve the respondent in checking or consulting documents. They are also effective in collecting data on sensitive topics and for reducing the risk of social desirability bias as they offer respondents a high degree of perceived anonymity.

■ Weaknesses of postal and Internet data collection

There are drawbacks to postal, web and email surveys. Although postal surveys in particular can be relatively cheap in comparison to other methods, the cost per completed interview, especially if a survey of non-responders is conducted, may be greater. Response rates vary – they can be as low as 15 per cent in postal surveys; web and email surveys can fare better (50–80 per cent). With a poor response rate, or one that is hard to predict, there is a chance that the sample will not be representative of the population: those who respond may differ from those who do not. The lower the response rate the less representative the sample. In addition, the sample is *self-selecting*. Although you might choose a sample relevant to the research and send questionnaires and reminders out to that sample, you have no control over who fills in the questionnaire (or how many do so). The recipient decides whether or not he or she will take part; he or she may pass the questionnaire on to someone else or someone else other than the intended recipient may complete it.

Another drawback to postal, email and web surveys is the lack of control over the data capture process, which has a knock-on effect in terms of data quality:

➤ The respondent can consult with others before answering the questions.
➤ Respondents may not answer all the questions they were supposed to or in the way required.
➤ You may get little detail in open-ended questions.
➤ There is no opportunity to probe or clarify answers – you must accept the response written in by the respondent.
➤ Questions requiring spontaneous answers do not work well.
➤ The respondent can skip ahead or indeed read the whole questionnaire before filling it in, so any 'funnelling' of questions and topics does not work.
➤ There is no opportunity to observe, for example, or to read body language or hear tone of voice.

■ Web surveys

Web surveys are conducted on the World Wide Web, usually at a specially designed private web address to which the sample is directed and/or given a password to access. Recruitment or sampling can happen in several ways. Traffic (people browsing the web) can be intercepted on a website – it is useful here to think of the analogy of the interviewer stopping people in the street – by alerting them via advertising banners,

Box 7.2 Summary of strengths and weaknesses of self-completion methods

Strengths

> Easy to set up and manage
> Cost – no interviewers to pay
> No interviewer bias or error
> Ability to reach a widely dispersed sample
> Can ask questions that need considered answers
> Can ask questions on sensitive topics

Weaknesses

> Poor response rates and so problems with representativeness
> Reliant on availability of relevant and up-to-date sampling frame
> Lack of control over data capture
> Concerns about data quality
> Not good for open-ended/complicated questions and instructions
> Not always the most cost-effective route

which scroll across the screen, or via 'pop-ups', which pop up on the screen. A sample can be recruited offline and given details – by telephone, post or email – of the web address at which the survey is posted. To achieve an acceptable response rate it is advisable to keep the interview length to no more than about 15 minutes. The questionnaire must be simple and straightforward – easy to follow and easy to fill in.

■ Email surveys

Email surveys are sent out to the respondent's email address with the survey questionnaire either embedded in the email or provided as an attachment. Pre-notification is important – email questionnaires sent to respondents who have not agreed to take part may be rejected, and the sender stopped from sending others. The sample may be notified about the survey by email, telephone or post. All the good practice recommended for a covering letter or email outlined above also applies here. The sample for an email survey may be recruited via traditional routes or via the web. As with web surveys, an interview length of about 15 minutes is recommended in order to achieve a reasonable response rate. And as with all self-completion data collection methods, it is essential that the questionnaire looks good and is easy to fill in.

■ Online panels

Online panels are a popular way of achieving a sample that represents a specific population, for example a nationally representative sample of the online population, or a representative sample of users of a bank's online facilities. Online panels work in the same way as traditional panels. A pool of people is recruited (using traditional techniques or online) who are willing to take part in research over a specified period of time.

Issues around keeping the panel together and minimising the attrition or drop-out rate are similar to those in traditional panels, although often more work is needed in building rapport and establishing the feeling of a community online. To this end it is essential to make sure that there are clear lines of communication between the panel members and the panel administrator, including telephone contacts as well as email contacts.

■ Issues in Internet data collection

Data collection using the Internet offers many of the advantages of postal surveys. It can, however, be more expensive to commission. It also has most of the disadvantages of postal surveys. Sampling and representativeness of achieved samples are key issues and the suitability of the method for the population you wish to research must be considered in the light of these issues. The need for an accurate and up-to-date sampling frame is even more crucial than it is in other methods of data collection. Email, for example, does not tolerate wrong addresses. In addition, people tend to change ISPs and email addresses more often than they change postal addresses. As Internet access, email use and web activity increase, it is important to bear in mind that the make-up of the population under study may be changing rapidly – samples drawn from even slightly out-of-date sampling frames may be unrepresentative.

Web and email data capture offer advantages over the postal method not unlike those offered by CAPI and CATI over traditional paper data capture. Large-scale surveys are relatively easy to set up and manage. Response rates can be monitored easily – for example there is automatic notification if an email is undelivered. Turnaround times from end of fieldwork to production of tables are fast compared to postal surveys: data (including verbatim responses) are captured directly, which also reduces data processing errors. You can show multi-media stimulus material (pictures, audio and video clips). You can programme the software to skip automatically to relevant questions; and in web surveys you can control to some extent how much of the questionnaire the respondent sees before filling it in. In addition, you can set up the questionnaire in different languages and allow respondents to choose the language in which they wish to answer.

There are potential pitfalls, however. Surveys can take more time to set up and, for web surveys and panels especially, specialist skills are needed. Pilot studies are important, if not essential, in order to ensure that the questionnaire works in different computing environments and on different platforms – the browser type or screen size can affect the format of the questionnaire and thus how it looks to the respondent. It is also important to take into account the size of the questionnaire file and the length of time it takes to download to the respondent's computer (this will depend on modem speeds and connection type). From the sender's point of view (and the receiver's, if the survey is being sent to one organisation or to those using the same server or ISP), it is crucial to think about what effect the size of the mailing and the likely size of return traffic will have on server capacity. If a large mailing is required it is best to spread it out over a period of time in order not to swamp the server. Some ISPs block mailings over a certain size and most organisations have firewalls to protect them against unsolicited mailings and viruses, which can stop large-scale mailings. It may therefore be necessary to encrypt the questionnaire or email in order to comply with security requirements.

> ## Box 7.3 Things to think about when considering Internet data collection
>
> ### Suitability, representativeness and quality of data issues
>
> - ➤ How suitable is the population for this method of data collection?
> - ➤ How representative will the sample be over time?
> - ➤ Can you achieve a sample that is representative of the population?
> - ➤ Do you have a good quality, accurate and up-to-date sampling frame?
> - ➤ What is the likely response rate?
> - ➤ What about non-response bias?
> - ➤ Can you survey the non-responders?
> - ➤ How good is the recruitment process?
>
> ### Technical issues
>
> - ➤ How widespread is Internet access among your target population – what are the levels of PC penetration, telephone line access, use of ISPs?
> - ➤ Think of the respondent's set up – the firewall, speed of connection, bandwidth, browser type and operating system.
> - ➤ Think of the survey administrator's set-up – server capacity.
>
> ### Design/layout issues
>
> - ➤ Think of the respondents – you need to make it easy for them and need to keep them engaged with the subject.
> - ➤ Keep it simple – remember download times and the effect of the browser type and screen size on layout.
> - ➤ Keep the interview length to about 15 minutes.

Web and email methods are particularly popular in business-to-business and employee research – Internet access is almost universal among medium and large organisations in the United States and Europe. They are also effective in popular online business-to-consumer markets such as financial services, retailing (especially food, books and music) and travel services. For research among the general public, where sampling is more difficult and response rates poorer, online panels are the most popular approach.

Specialised data collection formats

In this section we look at two types of specialised data collection formats: panels and omnibuses.

■ Panels

Panels are an example of a longitudinal research design (see Chapter 4) – they are a way of collecting data from the same pool of individuals, households or organisations over time, either on a continuous basis (every day) or at regular intervals. The data can be used to monitor changes in the market, short-term changes – for example reaction to price changes or promotions – as well as long-term trends, for example in brand share. The data can also be used to examine *ad hoc* issues such as the effect of a new advertising campaign.

The panel is recruited to be representative of a particular population, for example subscribers to a particular ISP, owners of particular makes of car, all households in Ireland or all off-licences. As people drop out of the panel and the population from which the panel is drawn changes, new members are recruited so that the panel remains representative over time. This is particularly important in a new or rapidly developing market, for example the Internet and online panels. Newly recruited panel members tend to behave differently from longer-established members. For this reason data from new members are usually excluded for their first few weeks on the panel.

Recruiting and maintaining panels is a relatively expensive business. Panel owners use a number of techniques to encourage panel members to stay with the panel and to prevent members dropping out before their time. Incentives include prize draws, competitions and reward points that can be redeemed against gifts. Panel newsletters are often used as a way of building on the community feeling of a panel as well as a way of keeping panel members informed.

Panels can be designed to gather all sorts of data. They are best for recording data about what, how many, how much – what people have done rather than the attitudes or opinions they hold. Many panels are set up to gather information about market characteristics in order to determine things like brand share or media usage, details of TV viewing, radio listening, newspaper and magazine reading habits – what, where, when, how long for. Panels in which individual consumers are the respondents are called *consumer panels*. For example, there are panels of motorists and panels of mothers of babies and small children as well as panels representative of all households. Panels made up of a sample of retail outlets are called *retail panels* and are used to collect *retail audit* data such as stock held, brand coverage, rate of sale, promotions, price and so on in order to determine distribution and sales patterns of different brands, pack sizes by type of outlet, sales by location/region.

Capturing panel data

Data from panel members or panel outlets are collected using questionnaires, diaries and electronic and wireless devices, including bar code scanners. Consumer panel members recording grocery purchases, for example, used to do so in diaries; nowadays the same information is captured by scanners, handheld devices that read the black and white bar codes that appear on product packaging. The panel member scans each item purchased. The information captured by the scanner can be sent by the respondent down the telephone line via a modem to the agency's computer. Data from media panels measuring television viewing or radio listening can be collected electronically, using meters attached to the television or radio. Retail panel data are often collected by an interviewer who visits the store and counts and records, either on paper or in an electronic notebook, the number of items on the shelves and in storage, and checks delivery dockets for items received in the period since the last audit.

Accuracy of panel data

Recruiting and in particular maintaining the representativeness of a panel can be difficult to achieve. The data can be weighted to bring the sample more in line with the population characteristics. Other errors that can affect panel data apart from sampling error include pick-up errors, when the respondent (or the data collector in a retail audit) omits to record or scan in an item, which can be accounted for when making estimates of market size in a process similar to weighting the sample to population estimates.

■ Omnibus surveys

Omnibus surveys are surveys that are run by research agencies on a continuous basis. Clients can buy space on these surveys to insert their own questions – they are usually charged an entry fee and a fee per question that covers fieldwork and standard data analysis. They can be used to generate continuous or longitudinal data by repeating the same questions in each round, or they can be used to gather cross-sectional data on an *ad hoc* basis – to collect data on specific issues as the need arises.

Depending on the number of questions included, using an omnibus survey can be very cost effective – fieldwork costs are shared and set-up time is minimised because of the ongoing, pre-set nature of the survey. The law of diminishing returns, however, kicks in at about eight to ten questions – it is likely that for this number of questions a customised survey is just as cost effective.

The omnibus may survey a representative sample of the general public or it may target a more specialised population or group. For example, omnibus surveys are run among samples of general practitioners, motorists, teenagers, older people, Internet users, European consumers and independent financial advisers.

Omnibus surveys are usually conducted face to face or by telephone. Nowadays (almost) all use computer-aided interviewing (CAPI or CATI). Respondents are recruited anew for each round of an omnibus survey using random or quota sampling techniques. Many omnibus surveys take place weekly, some twice weekly and others once every two weeks. Sample sizes vary: for general public omnibus surveys the sample is usually around 1,000 respondents per week but can be up to 3,500; for more specialised target groups it may be 500 every two weeks. To achieve a robust sample of a low incidence target group, for example hearing aid users, may mean that questions are included on more than one round of the omnibus. Turnaround times – from close of fieldwork to delivery of the tables – is often a matter of two to three days, if the data are captured electronically (using CAPI or CATI) and if there are few open-ended questions to code; for international work it is about two weeks.

Variations on the omnibus survey

A variation on the omnibus survey is when the agency designs the questionnaire, collects the data on a continuous basis or at regular intervals, processes the data and

Box 7.4 Advantages and disadvantages of omnibus surveys

Advantages

➤ Cost effective
➤ Available at short notice
➤ Speed of delivery of results
➤ Good for collecting data from low incidence groups
➤ Produce robust, quality data
➤ Results confidential to client who inserted the questions

Disadvantages

➤ Position effects – at beginning or end of interview, subjects tackled before your questions
➤ Not good for gathering open-ended data, or if probing necessary
➤ Not cost effective if more than eight to ten questions

sells it on in whole or in part to whichever client wants it. None of the data is confidential to a particular client since all the questions were included by the agency itself. An example of this type of continuous survey is the British Market Research Bureau's Target Group Index (TGI) which collects data on consumer purchases and media habits.

A tracking study is a survey that runs on a continuous basis with a fresh sample each time but in this case the client designs the questionnaire and so the data collected are confidential to the client. The syndicated tracking study is a variation on this. Several clients interested in the same product field or topic commission a continuous study. The questionnaire includes questions common to all clients – all clients see data on these – each client has some space in which to ask his or her own questions, for which only he or she sees the data.

Observation

Structured observational techniques can be used to collect quantitative data. Observations are recorded on a data collection instrument similar to a questionnaire. Collecting data in an audit is a form of structured observation. Data can be collected in person or electronically – television-viewing meters are a form of electronic observation, as are the scanners used to record purchases in shops. As we saw in Chapter 6, there are two forms of observation: simple and participant. In simple observation the observer does not interact with the activity, the people or the things he or she is observing (as in the audit example). In participant observation the observer interacts with the subjects. Mystery shopping is a form of participant observation. As we noted in Chapter 6, the main advantage of observation over interviewing is that it enables us to record actual rather than reported behaviour; the main disadvantage is that in most cases we are unable to determine the reason for the behaviour. Observational techniques are often used in conjunction with interviewing.

■ Mystery shopping

Mystery shopping involves a trained observer posing as an everyday shopper. He or she goes through the shopping experience, asking the sort of questions a real customer might ask. As soon as the mystery shop is complete the mystery shopper fills in the details of his or her experience on a questionnaire. For a personal visit the information recorded might include, for example, length of time in the queue; number of service points or tills open out of the total available; details of the greeting and exchange with the member of staff; handling of questions; information or advice offered and so on. For a telephone mystery shopping exercise the information recorded might include number of rings before the phone was answered, length of time on hold, as well as information on the exchange between shopper and staff member.

Chapter summary

➢ Quantitative data can be collected via interviewing and observation using standard-ised structured or semi-structured 'forms' – questionnaires and diaries.

➢ The method of data collection chosen depends on its suitability for achieving the research objectives; the topic or issues under investigation; its ability to reach the sample and achieve the right numbers; and the time and budget available.

➢ The interviewer has a vital role to play in collecting good quality data. Interviewing is a skilled task requiring a high level of interpersonal skill and a sound under-standing of the data collection process.

➢ Face-to-face interviews can take place in the home, in the street, in a central location or at the respondent's place of work, depending on the nature of the survey. Face-to-face data collection has a number of advantages over other methods. It enables the interviewer to build rapport with the respondent, which has positive effects on data quality; and it allows for a degree of flexibility in the interviewing process. It is, however, relatively expensive and time consuming; cluster sampling methods, which serve to reduce travel time and costs, risk introducing sample bias; with quality con-trol procedures at a distance there is greater scope for interviewer bias or cheating.

➢ Telephone interviewing, especially CATI, has a number of advantages over face-to-face methods. Geographically dispersed and other samples that are hard to reach can be obtained more easily; it is possible to use a random sampling approach, thus reducing sampling error; greater quality control is possible with interviewers being monitored 'live'; and it is faster and more cost effective. There are some disadvantages related to sampling and representativeness, including the increased incidence of mobile rather than fixed line phones and telephone answering machines, call screening, lines being used to access the Internet and more than one line per household.

➢ Data can be captured and recorded electronically. The questionnaire, data entry, editing and verification procedures are programmed into the computer. There are advantages from fieldwork management to data processing – fieldwork to tabulation time is reduced and data quality is enhanced. The main disadvantages are the capital investment and training required.

➢ Self-completion surveys – postal, email and web – are effective if the topic is relevant and of interest to the target population and the method is a suitable way of reaching the target and achieving a response. Response rates may be increased by the use of a personalised covering letter, sponsorship, pre-notification, reminders, incentives and, for postal surveys, a return envelope. They are easy to set up and manage, can be cost effective as there are no interviewers to pay, and are suitable for reaching widely dispersed and otherwise hard to reach samples. Web and email surveys offer the advantages that come with electronic data capture. All methods, however, can suffer from poor response rates and thus problems with representativeness; and there is lack of control over data capture.

➢ Panels are a way of collecting data from the same pool of individuals, households or organisations over time, either on a continuous basis (every day) or at regular intervals. The data can be used to monitor changes in the market over time.

➢ Omnibus surveys are run on a continuous basis. Clients buy space to insert their own questions for an entry fee and a fee per question that covers fieldwork and standard analysis. They can be used to generate continuous or longitudinal data by repeating the same questions in each round, or they can be used to gather cross-sectional data.

➢ Structured observational techniques can be used to collect quantitative data, in person or electronically. Mystery shopping is an application of personal observation; television-viewing meters are a form of electronic observation.

Questions and exercises

1 Describe the role of the interviewer in the data collection process.

2 Why are interviewer training and interviewer briefing important in the collection of good quality data?

3 How do you decide on the most appropriate method or methods of data collection for a particular research project?

4 What are the advantages and disadvantages of face-to-face data collection? Give examples of the types of study in which face-to-face data collection is appropriate.

5 What are the advantages and disadvantages of data collection by telephone? For what types of research is the method particularly suitable?

6 Describe what is meant by the term 'computer-aided interviewing' and its advantages and disadvantages over the traditional pen and paper survey methods.

7 For what types of study is data collection via the web or email particularly suitable? Give reasons.

8 What are the advantages and disadvantages of using a postal survey?

9 What steps would you take to ensure that you get a reasonable response rate from:

(a) a postal survey?

(b) an email survey?

10 Describe what happens in a mystery shopping exercise.

Reference

Yu, J. and Cooper, H. (1983) 'A quantitative review of research design effects on response rates to questionnaires', *Journal of the Market Research Society*, 20, 1, pp. 36–44.

Recommended reading

The Market Research Society publishes a range of Guidelines on data collection, all of which are available at the MRS website (**www.mrs.org.uk**). These aim to interpret and expand on the MRS Code of Conduct in relation to data collection and the MRS recommends that they are read alongside its publications (also available via the website) on the use of databases and on the Data Protection Act.

Moser, C. and Kalton, G. (1971) *Surveys in Social Investigation*, 2nd edn, Aldershot: Dartmouth. An excellent account of the design and use of surveys and just as applicable to market research.

Chapter 8

Sampling

Introduction

In this chapter we look at the ideas behind sampling and the issues involved in developing a sampling plan and choosing a sampling technique.

Topics covered

➤ Developing a sampling plan
➤ Sampling theory
➤ Probability or random sampling methods
➤ Semi-random sampling
➤ Non-probability sampling methods
➤ Sampling in qualitative research

Relationship to MRS Advanced Certificate Syllabus

The material covered in this chapter is relevant to Unit 6 – Sampling, specifically:

➤ the theory of sampling;
➤ sampling techniques and their uses and limitations;
➤ determining sample size;
➤ sampling frames.

Learning outcomes

At the end of this chapter you should be able to:

➤ demonstrate knowledge and understanding of sampling theory and practice;
➤ develop and implement an appropriate sampling plan;
➤ understand the implications of the sampling plan for data accuracy and generalisability of research findings.

Developing a sampling plan

Sampling is about selecting, without bias and with as much precision as resources allow, the 'items' or *elements* from which or from whom we wish to collect data. In market and social research projects these elements are usually people, households or organisations, although they may be places, events or experiences. Drawing up a sampling plan is one of the most important procedures in the research process. It involves the following:

➢ defining the target population;
➢ choosing an appropriate sampling technique;
➢ deciding on the sample size;
➢ preparing sampling instructions.

Box 8.1 Sampling units and sampling elements

The elements of the sample – the people, the organisations – may be 'contained' in a *sampling unit*. For example, imagine you are commissioned to gauge the attitudes of the general public to a range of social issues. To achieve the sample you decide to use a sample source (a *sampling frame*) that provides you with details of households. You select a sample of households from this sampling frame and from each household you select an individual. In this case the household is a sampling unit and the individual is the sample element. You may have decided, on the other hand, to select a sample of individuals directly, and not from within households. In this case the individual is both the sampling unit and the sample element.

■ Defining the population

In research terminology the term *population* has a broader meaning than its common usage in reference to human populations of particular countries. In a research context it refers to the *universe of enquiry* or, put another way, to the people, organisations, events or items that are relevant to the research problem. It is important to define the population of interest as precisely as possible. Any flaws in the definition of the population will mean flaws in the sample drawn from it.

For example, if you are investigating the health and social welfare needs of older people, then you might say that older people are the population of interest. But what do you mean by 'older people'? What age limits do you impose? For the lower age limit, do you use retirement age, that is 60 years of age for women and 65 for men? Or do you have one lower age limit for both sexes? Should you impose an upper age limit or not? Do you include only older people living independently in the community or do you include those living in sheltered or residential care accommodation or those in nursing homes or hospitals? If you decide that it is only those living independently in the community, how do you define that? Should you include those living in the home of a relative or only those living in their own home?

The way in which the population is defined depends on the issues the research aims to address. If, for example, the study of the health and social welfare needs of older people has been commissioned to help develop policy in relation to community health initiatives, you may decide that those in residential care, nursing homes or hospitals are not part of the relevant population. In defining the population, think of the aims of the research.

Box 8.2 Examples of criteria used in defining the population

Organisations and employees

➤ *Type of organisation* – for example private sector (privately owned or stock market listed), public sector or not for profit; those selling mainly to consumers or mainly to other businesses or both; or those selling to more than one country or to one country only.

➤ *Geographic area* – for example all organisations with a head office (or any office) in a particular region or country.

➤ *Market or industry sector* – for example all organisations in the financial services sector or those in the financial services sector selling to private individuals only.

➤ *Size of organisation* – for example in terms of annual turnover or number of employees.

➤ *Type of experience and/or time* – for example all organisations involved in an Initial Public Offering (IPO) on the stock market in the last financial year.

➤ *Type of department or office within the organisation.*

➤ *Job title or role or responsibilities of an individual employee.*

➤ *Type of experience of an employee* – for example all those receiving merit pay awards or promotions in the last six months.

Households and people

➤ *Geographic area* – for example all households within a particular region or country or telephone area code.

➤ *Demographic profile* – for example age, sex, social class, presence of children.

➤ *Geodemographic profile* – those living within a particular geodemographic cluster or type of residential neighbourhood.

➤ *Time* – for example all those visiting a pharmacy between 10 am and 1 pm on weekdays; all those who bought a new car in the last three months.

➤ *Type of experience and/or time* – for example women who gave birth in the last six months in a private hospital; regular users of brand X.

Target population and survey population

Moser and Kalton (1971) make the distinction between the *target population* and the *survey population*. The target population is the population from which the results are required; the survey population is the population actually covered by the research. As Moser and Kalton point out, in ideal circumstances the two should be the same but, for practical reasons, they may not be. For example, people or organisations in places that are remote or difficult to access using a face-to-face survey, such as those on islands, may not be included in a survey population. In a survey of older people's health and social welfare needs it may be difficult to get permission to interview those living in sheltered or residential accommodation. So, although you may have identified them as part of the target population, they may be excluded for the sake of expediency from the survey population.

If there is a difference between the target and the survey population, to avoid misrepresentation of the research and its findings it is important that the difference is made clear to all involved with the research and in any documents relating to the research.

Census or sample?

Once the population is clearly defined you must decide whether to collect data from every member or element of that population (usually referred to as a *census*) or from a representative sub-set or *sample* of it. In most market and social research the population of interest is too large for a census to be practicable, either in terms of the time it would involve or the cost. There are some circumstances, for example research among members of a professional body or employees of an organisation, where the population may be small enough, and accessible enough, for a census to be feasible. In other cases it may be necessary or desirable to collect data from all elements of a population. For example, in research to help with a decision about changes in working practices it may be important (and politic) to ensure that all employees' attitudes and opinions are surveyed.

There are other disadvantages in conducting a census besides those of time and cost. The level of non-response may mean that the results are less representative than might have been achieved with a well-designed sample of the same population. Furthermore, the size and scope of the census undertaking may result in an increase in the amount of non-sampling error as scarce administrative, field and data processing resources are stretched to the limit. In the end, a census may deliver data of poorer quality than a well-designed sample. Some of the cost and time savings that arise from using a sample rather than a census could be directed to reducing non-response and non-sampling error.

The argument for using a well-designed sample rather than a census rests on two issues: on the practical issue of the time and cost involved in administering it; and on the methodological issue of the ability of a sample to be *representative* of the population (to deliver *external validity*). By 'representative' we mean that the results provided by the sample are *similar* to those we would have obtained had we conducted a census. Of course it is unlikely, no matter how carefully we choose a sample, that it will deliver results that match exactly the values in the population. Sampling theory tells us that a sample design is sound if it delivers results each time it is repeated that *on average* would have been achieved with a population census. Producing representative results is an important aspect of actionable research. It would be pointless if a study of a *sample* of older people's health and social welfare needs could not be used to generalise about the health and social welfare needs of *all* older people; or if, from a study of the brand preferences of a sample of 18–24 year olds we could not make reliable and valid inferences about the brand preferences of *all* 18–24 year olds.

■ Sampling techniques

How do you design a sample that is representative of the population from which it is drawn? It is important to restate what we mean by representative. When a sample is representative of the population it should deliver results close to the results we would have obtained if we had surveyed the entire population. The results are not biased in any way – the sample estimates of the characteristics we set out to measure (for example the incidence of cinema attendance among 16–24 year olds) closely match the value of these characteristics in the population. So what kind of sampling technique produces a representative sample?

Types of sampling technique

There are two categories of sampling techniques:

➢ random or probability sampling;
➢ purposive or non-probability sampling.

Random or probability sampling is where each element of the population is drawn at random and has a known (and non-zero) chance of being selected. The person choosing the sample has no influence on the elements selected. The random selection process should ensure to some extent that the sample is representative of the population. There are certain conditions that need to apply, however, for random selection to produce a truly representative sample:

➢ For true randomness in the selection process to take effect the sample size must be at least 100.
➢ The population should be homogeneous or well mixed – if it is not (if it is stratified or layered in any way or there is a tendency for similar elements within it to cluster together) a simple random selection process may not deliver a truly representative sample.
➢ The sampling frame, which represents the population from which the sample is chosen, must be complete, accurate and up to date.
➢ Non-response must be zero or, put another way, all those selected as part of the sample must take part in the research.

Of course, in real-world research situations, the last three conditions may not hold. We come back to this in more detail later.

The theory that underpins *probability or random sampling* allows us to calculate how accurately a sample estimates a population characteristic and how likely or probable it is that the sample estimate lies within a certain range of the population characteristic. This leads us to the concepts of sampling distributions, sampling error, standard error and confidence intervals, which we return to in more detail in the section on sampling theory.

In *non-probability sampling* there is no random selection process, and we do not know what probability each element has of being selected because the person choosing the sample may consciously or unconsciously favour or select particular elements.

So how do we ensure that the sample chosen in this way is representative of the population? We address this issue when we look in detail at non-probability sampling methods later in the chapter. Suffice to say at this stage that quota sampling, the method of non-probability sampling most widely used in market research, can produce results that closely resemble those that would have been achieved with a probability sample.

In qualitative research, notions of *statistical* representativeness do not apply because of the small sample sizes involved. But representativeness is still an important goal and later in the chapter we look at ways in which sampling in qualitative research sets out to achieve this.

Choosing a sampling technique

How do you decide which type of sampling technique to use? For qualitative studies, which in most cases involve relatively small sample sizes, non-probability techniques are the most suitable. We look at various approaches to sampling for qualitative studies, including theoretical or judgement sampling, 'lurk and grab', list sampling, snowball sampling, and piggy-backing or multi-purposing, later in the chapter. The decision about which technique to use in a quantitative study is more complicated. It will be influenced by both methodological issues, such as the nature and aims of the study, and by practical concerns, including the nature and accessibility of the study population, the availability of a suitable sampling frame and the constraints of time and budget.

Box 8.3 Example: the sampling decision in a consumer telephone survey

The aim of the survey is to produce a comprehensive overview of consumers' use of product X. The sampling units are households (in the United Kingdom). It is crucial to the aims of the research that the sample is representative of all telephone households. A problem arises in terms of how to achieve a representative sample, however, because there is no list of all domestic telephone numbers commercially available: telephone directories (or their electronic equivalent) do not contain non-listed numbers – the sample drawn would not therefore be representative of all telephone households.

A random sample could be drawn using random digit dialling. This involves dialling numbers at random within 'blocks' of numbers that are known to be issued. A disadvantage of this method, however, is that it results in many calls being made to numbers that do not exist or that are fax or business numbers. Another approach might be to use telephone numbers from previous surveys or from commercial databases as a 'seed' sample. New numbers are created for the sample by adding one (known as 'digit plus 1') to the original number. A potential problem with this method, however, is that there may be biases in the original database from which the sample was drawn, and these are carried over into the new sample.

This problem can be avoided by using a directory sample combined with 'digit plus 1'. The first step is to select a representative sample of private households from the telephone directories for the whole of the United Kingdom using a fixed sampling interval from a random start point in each area directory. This will give us a representative sample of all households whose numbers are listed in the directory. Instead of calling the selected households, this sample is used as the 'seed' sample to create new numbers to

Box 8.3 continued

call by adding one to the final digit of each telephone number. Thus the number generated by the random selection from the directory, say, 0123 123456 will become 0123 123457. This will ensure that the numbers called will include non-listed numbers as well as listed ones. These households should be similar in location and type of household to the number originally selected but will still under-represent non-listed numbers in areas where non-listed numbers are particularly prevalent (Foreman and Collins, 1991).

During the interview the respondent is asked whether his or her number is listed or non-listed. This enables us to estimate, for each directory area, the proportion of non-listed households. At the analysis stage a weight may be applied to each household (if necessary) to correct for any differences in the incidence, and therefore the probability of selection, of non-listed numbers within each directory area.

This sampling plan should produce a reasonably representative sample of private telephone households. It is, however, worth noting the following:

➤ it will not represent any mobile telephone-only households; and
➤ it may overrepresent households with two or more land lines since these have a greater chance of being selected (this is a problem with all of the common methods of selecting domestic telephone samples).

Initial calls will be made to the selected 'digit plus 1' numbers during evenings and weekends in order to avoid overrepresenting households where people are at home during the day. It may be that households with only one line and who are heavy Internet users may be difficult to reach. The only practical solution to this problem is to ensure that subsequent calls are made at different times of day and on different days of the week.

Source: Network Research and Marketing Ltd. Used with permission.

In deciding what sampling technique to use, think first of all about the nature and aims of the study. If the purpose of the research is exploratory and not conclusive (that is, neither descriptive nor explanatory), in other words if it is not necessary to obtain highly accurate estimates of population characteristics in order to make inferences about the population, then a non-probability sample is appropriate. If, on the other hand, it is necessary to obtain measurements from the sample of known accuracy or precision (in order to make statistical inferences or generalisations from the sample to the population), then a probability sampling technique should be used.

Random sampling, however, does not always produce more accurate estimates of population characteristics than non-probability techniques. In fact, in certain circumstances, non-probability (quota) sampling may provide a more representative sample. Where there is little variability within a population, that is when the population is homogeneous, a non-probability sample can be effective in achieving a representative sample; with a great deal of variability in the population a random sample is likely to be more effective. When the non-sampling error (errors arising from question wording, interviewer bias, recording error, data-processing error) is likely to be greater than the sampling error, non-probability techniques may be just as good at producing a representative sample.

In terms of the practicalities, if there is no suitable sampling frame from which to select the sample, then random methods are not feasible. We look at sampling frames in more detail later. In addition, probability sampling, especially for face-to-face research, can be difficult, time consuming (not only in terms of drawing the sample but in conducting the fieldwork) and expensive; it is more straightforward and easier to manage in a telephone survey. If time and budget are limited in a face-to-face study, it is likely that a non-probability method such as quota sampling will be used. We look in more detail at various random or probability and non-probability techniques later in the chapter.

Box 8.4 Applications of sampling techniques

Probability or random sampling

➤ Descriptive and explanatory (conclusive) research enquiries
➤ Surveys conducted to provide accurate estimates of sales, market share, usage, incidence of behaviour or attitudes (for example employment, household spending, social and political attitudes or opinion)
➤ Telephone surveys

Non-probability sampling

➤ Exploratory research enquiries
➤ Surveys conducted to provide guidance, for example on product/service design and development, advertising development
➤ Qualitative research studies
➤ Street interviewing and hall tests
➤ Absence of a suitable sampling frame
➤ Hard to reach or inaccessible populations

■ Choosing a sample size

The sample size is the number of elements that will be included in the sample. The size of the sample is important, particularly in terms of the precision of the sample estimates, but on its own does not guarantee that the results will be accurate or unbiased; the way in which the sample is chosen (the sampling technique used, the sampling frame) will affect this.

Deciding on the sample size involves thinking about the nature and purpose of the research enquiry, and the importance of the decisions to be made on the basis of the results. In exploratory research the sample size (for qualitative or quantitative methods) may be relatively smaller in comparison to that used in a conclusive study. In conclusive research enquiries the aim is often to provide precise estimates of population characteristics (also called population parameters) – for example the proportion of 25–34 year olds using brand X. The sample size therefore needs to be big enough to provide such estimates. The research may be commissioned to provide conclusive evidence that, for example, a greater proportion of 16–24 year olds compared to 25–34 year olds prefer brand X, and to provide that evidence with a certain degree of confidence that the findings are an accurate reflection of the situation in the wider population. The sample size in this case needs to be large enough to provide the evidence with the specified degree of confidence. If we know the level of precision required of the sample estimates, or the size of the confidence level or interval required, we can work out the sample size needed to achieve these. We look at this in more detail later, in the section on sampling theory.

It is also important to consider the way in which the findings will be analysed. We may need to look at (and compare) the findings among particular sub-groups within the sample, for example particular age groups, or organisations of different sizes or in different industry sectors. It is therefore important to consider how big these sub-groups need to be in order to provide precise estimates of their characteristics and to allow robust analysis. Also, we need to think about the type of analysis needed – if, for example, we plan to use multivariate statistical techniques, we need to think about what implications this has for sample size. In planning the sample it is helpful to know the incidence in the population of any groups of interest, as this may affect the decision about the overall sample size and the choice of sampling technique. Finally, and arguably in practice the most important factor in the choice of sample size, we must take into account the time, budget and other resources available. Generally speaking, for any given sampling approach, the bigger the sample size the greater the cost.

■ Preparing sampling instructions

Once a sampling approach and a sample size have been agreed it is important to set out how the actual sampling process is to be conducted. This will involve drawing up a sampling plan that should include the following:

➣ the definition of the study population;
➣ the sample size required;
➣ the sampling method to be used, including the way in which the units and elements are to be selected;
➣ details of the sampling frame, if one is available.

■ Checking the sample achieved

As the fieldwork progresses the sample is monitored to ensure that the units and elements selected meet the sample criteria. Once sampling and fieldwork are completed, the sample achieved is checked to ensure that it matches the sample requirements. If any discrepancies are found (high rates of non-response, under- or over-representation of particular elements and so on) it will be necessary to address them (for example by conducting further sampling and fieldwork, or statistical manipulation). It is also important to check key sample statistics against the relevant population parameters, if that information is available (for example from a recent census) or against sample statistics from other surveys. This serves as a validation check on the representativeness of the sample.

Box 8.5 Sample details from the Life and Times Survey 2000

➤ Target population: men and women aged 18 and over in Northern Ireland
➤ Required sample size: 1,800
➤ Sampling frame: Postal Address File (PAF)
➤ Sampling units: households
➤ Sample elements: individuals aged 18 and over; eligible individuals at the selected address chosen randomly using a Kish grid
➤ Sampling technique: to ensure adequate representation in areas of lower population density, Northern Ireland was stratified into three areas and using a simple random sampling approach addresses were selected from each of these areas
➤ Number of sampling units selected: 2,850 selected in order to provide reserve addresses
➤ Number of sampling units in scope: 2,808 (42 were found to be vacant, derelict or commercial properties)
➤ Sampling/data collection procedure: pre-selected addresses; advance letter notification; Kish grid for random selection of eligible individuals; CAPI and self-completion
➤ Number of calls: interviewers to make five calls or to have received a refusal or other information confirming that an interview would not be obtained before being given a reserve address
➤ Response from 2,808 addresses: 1,800 interviews; 428 refusals; 554 non-contacts; and 26 others, giving a response rate of 64 per cent
➤ Sample checks: key characteristics of households (housing tenure) and individuals (including age, sex, marital status and economic activity) are compared to characteristics from previous surveys in the Life and Times series, from the Office of National Statistics' *Continuous Household Survey* (1999/2000) and with the 1991 Census figures

Source: Adapted from Devine, P., *User Documentation* (**http://www.ask.ac.uk/nilt**). Used with permission.

Sampling theory

Before discussing the details of the various sampling techniques we need to look at the theory that underpins probability sampling. This is important because it will help you to understand better a number of related issues, including those of precision, accuracy and bias, and the rationale behind confidence intervals and inferential statistical tests.

■ Terminology

First of all we need to introduce some more terminology. The things that we want to talk about in the population, for example the proportion of 18–24 year olds who drink brand A, or the average income of a particular group, are known as *population parameters*. The corresponding figure derived from the sample is an estimate of this population parameter and is known as a *sample statistic*. For example, in a survey of the brand preferences of 18–24 year olds, the proportion who drink brand A is the sample statistic, or the estimate of the proportion who drink brand A in the population. Here is another example: you are conducting a survey among organisations in the financial services sector to determine the average pay of women. The average obtained from the sample is called the sample statistic. It is an estimate of the population parameter, the unknown value of average pay among women in the wider population of financial services organisations.

The purpose of a survey may be to provide such estimates. The important thing to remember is that the findings provided by a sample are only *estimates* of the population values. Statements based on findings from a random or probability sample are always *probability statements*. We *cannot* make claims about the value of population parameters based on sample data *with absolute certainty*. What we do is rely on an effective sample design to ensure that the sample estimates accurately reflect the population values *most of the time*, and with a known *margin of error*. This brings us to sampling theory.

■ Sampling distribution of the mean

You are interested in knowing the weekly food spend of single person households in Sweden. You select a sample at random from the population of all single person households and from the sample data you note the average (or mean) of the particular value that interests you – weekly spend on food. You then select another sample at random and note the value of weekly food spend from this sample. You continue this process ad infinitum; you plot the value of the average weekly spend on food from each sample on a graph. Once you have plotted this value for your infinite samples you should have a graph like the one in Figure 8.1, the bell-shaped curve of a normal distribution. This graph is known as the *sampling distribution of the mean*.

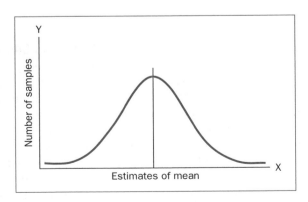

Figure 8.1 Sampling distribution of the mean

Sampling variability

The graph shows that each sample does not produce the same value: a range of samples produces a range of values for the same measure (in this case the average weekly food spend). This variation is known as *sampling variability*. In real-world research, however, we do not take repeated samples from a population to measure a value; usually we take only one sample and we estimate the population value on the basis of this one sample. But given the amount of variability between samples that the sampling distribution shows, how can we know how accurately our sample measure reflects the true population value? We can do this with a fairly simple calculation – called the *standard error of the mean* – from one randomly selected sample made up of at least two sampling units.

Standard error of the mean

The standard error of the mean is a measure of the variability within the sampling distribution – the variability or spread in the values of the measures we have taken from each sample. It is the standard deviation of the sampling distribution. We can use it to measure the probable accuracy or precision of a particular sample estimate. To work out the standard error of the mean we need to know the standard deviation of the population (S) and the size of the sample (n). There is a small complication – it is very unlikely that we will know the value of the population standard deviation. In its place we use the standard deviation of the sample (s).

Box 8.6 Formula for calculating the standard error of the mean

For numerical data:

$$\text{Standard error } (\bar{x}) = \frac{s}{\sqrt{n}}$$

For % data:

$$\text{Standard error } (p\%) = \sqrt{\frac{p\%(100 - p\%)}{n}}$$

From the information needed to calculate the standard error of the mean we can see that what it measures – the precision of a sample estimate – depends on two things: sample size and the level of variability in the population, which is measured by the standard deviation. It makes sense that these two factors have an impact on precision. If you think about sample size, it makes sense that a bigger sample will deliver results that are more precise. The formula for calculating the standard error shows the relationship between precision and sample size: to increase the precision of an estimate by a factor of two – in other words, to halve the standard error – you need to increase the sample size by a factor of four. It also makes sense that variability within the population will have an impact on the precision of a sample estimate. If, for example, there is very little variability – say, for example, that the average weekly food spend of all single person households in Sweden is €200, then the standard deviation and the standard error would be zero. We can say that the sample provides a precise estimate of the population value. If, however, the average weekly food spend varies from, say, €50 to €500, the standard deviation will be relatively large and so will the standard error. As a result, the sample will provide a less precise estimate of the population value.

■ Confidence intervals

You saw in Figure 8.1 that the sampling distribution of the mean closely resembles a normal distribution. In fact, the larger the sample, the closer the sampling distribution will be to a normal distribution. The normal distribution has a number of useful properties that can be applied to sampling. It is symmetrical in shape, with 50 per cent of observations or measures lying above the mean and 50 per cent lying below the mean. If we divide the normal curve up into segments delineated by standard deviations, we find that about 68 per cent of all observations lie within one standard deviation either side of the mean; 95 per cent lie within two; and 99 per cent are within 2.6 standard deviations.

If a sampling distribution closely resembles a normal distribution then we can use the properties of the normal distribution to obtain some very useful information about our sample estimates. The first thing we need to do is to convert the standard deviations into standard errors. This allows us to say that 95 per cent of our sample estimates lie within 1.96 standard errors of the population mean; and 99 per cent lie within 2.58 standard errors. To put it another way, we can say that a sample mean or sample statistic has a 95 per cent chance of being within 1.96 standard errors of the population mean or the true mean; or a 99 per cent chance of being within 2.58 standard errors.

Calculating the accuracy of the sample estimate

An example makes all this a bit less abstract and a bit more real: imagine that you have completed your survey on weekly food spend among single person households in

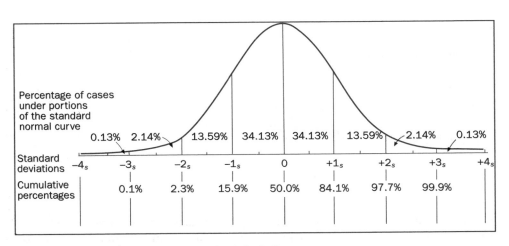

Figure 8.2 Normal curve with standard deviations

Table 8.1 Symbols for population and sample values

Value	Population	Sample
Mean	μ	$\bar{x}$
Proportion	π	p
Variance	σ^2 or S^2	s^2
Standard deviation	S	s
Size	N	n

Sweden. You have found that the average weekly spend is €250. The first question you ask is, how accurate an estimate is this of the population value? In other words, how big is the standard error? To work this out you need to know the standard deviation and the size of the sample.

The first step in working out the standard deviation is to calculate the variance (which is a fairly simple measure of the spread of values within the sample). To do this, you subtract the sample mean from each of the individual observations, which in this case are amounts of money spent on food. Next, you square each of the deviations from the mean (to get rid of any negative values), then add them all up and divide by the sample size. This last figure is the variance of the sample. Take the square root of the variance to get the standard deviation. To calculate the standard error, divide the standard deviation by the square root of the sample size. The calculations are slightly different if you have proportions or percentages rather than means, for example if you want to look at the proportion of buyers of brand A in the sample.

Box 8.7 Formulae for variance and standard deviation

Using means

Variance $s^2 = \dfrac{\Sigma(x - \bar{x})^2}{n}$

Standard deviation $(s) = \sqrt{s^2}$

Using percentages

To calculate the standard deviation using percentages:

Standard deviation $(s) = \sqrt{\dfrac{p\%(100 - p\%)}{n}}$

Of course, you would use a computer program to calculate these figures – in a real research project it would not be practicable to calculate them by hand. From the formulae, however, you can get some idea of the underlying logic. The second column in

Table 8.2 Calculations involved in determining the standard deviation

Sampling unit Household	Observation (x) Weekly food spend (€)	Sample mean (x̄) Average spend (€)	Deviation from the sample mean (x − x̄)	Square of the deviations (x − x̄)²
1	247	250	−3	9
2	253	250	+3	9
3	247	250	−3	9
4	248	250	−2	4
5	259	250	+9	81
6	242	250	−8	64
7	250	250	0	0
8	252	250	+2	4
9	244	250	−6	36
10	258	250	+8	64
Total	2,500		Total	280

Table 8.2 shows the weekly food spend from the ten households in the sample (in reality, of course, the sample would be much bigger). Column three shows the average spend across all ten households; column four shows the deviation of the actual spend from the average spend; and the final column shows the square of that deviation.

The sum of the squared deviations – the total of the figures in the final column of Table 8.2 – is 280. To calculate the variance you divide by the sample size, which in this example is ten. The variance therefore is 28. The standard deviation, that is the square root of the variance (28), is 5.29. The standard error, which is the standard deviation (5.29) divided by the square root of the sample size (3.16), is 1.67. What does this figure tell you? You can say that you are 68 per cent confident that the true (population) value of average weekly food spend lies within the range €250 ± €1.67 (the mean plus or minus one standard error). In other words, you are 68 per cent confident that the average weekly spend among the population is somewhere between €248.33 and €251.67. You can say that you are 95 per cent confident that it lies within the range 250 ± 1.96 standard errors (1.96 × 1.67) – that is, between €246.73 and €253.27. You can be 99 per cent confident that it lies within the range 250 + 2.58 standard errors (2.58 × 1.67), that is, between €245.69 and €254.31. These limits on the range of a value are called *confidence limits*. The size of the difference or the margin of error is called the *confidence interval*.

You can look at this another way – in terms of the probability that the claims you make about your findings are correct. This is where significance levels come in. If you claim that the average weekly food spend among the population lies somewhere between €246.73 and €253.27, the probability that you are right in this assertion is 95 per cent (the confidence limit is 95 per cent). There is a 5 per cent or 1 in 20 chance that you are wrong (this is known as the significance level). If you want to make sure that there is less chance that your assertion is wrong, say, 1 in 100 or 1 per cent chance (a greater significance level), you are setting a wider confidence interval, which means the margin of error will be larger.

Box 8.8 Significance levels and the risk of error

Significance levels are the level of probability at which you accept that a difference is statistically significant or real – that is, not due to chance. They are sometimes referred to as the p or α (alpha) value. The level of significance is the point at which the sample finding or statistic differs too much from the population expectation for it to have occurred by chance – the difference cannot be explained by random error or sampling variation and is accepted as a true or statistical difference. Decisions about whether a hypothesis is accepted or rejected are based on these significance levels.

The three significance levels used most often are the 5 per cent or the 0.05 level of probability (sometimes written as $p = 0.05$ or $p <= 0.05$); the 1 per cent or 0.01 level; and the 0.001 or 0.1 per cent level. At the 5 per cent significance level there is a 5 per cent probability or a 1 in 20 chance that the result or finding has occurred by chance. This is the lowest acceptable level in most market and social research projects. At the 1 per cent significance level you are setting a higher standard by saying that there is a 1 per cent or 1 in 100 probability that the finding has occurred by chance. The 0.1 per cent level indicates that there is a 1 in 1,000 probability that the finding has occurred by chance. As the significance level falls, in other words, the more confident you can be in the results (the confidence level is greater). So in using significance levels to judge results you are giving a probability that the results are sound and at the same time saying that there is a chance that they may not be.

The significance level you choose will depend on the amount of risk you are prepared to tolerate in drawing the wrong conclusions from the research. If, for example, the research involves evaluating a product, it might be best to set the significance level at $p = 0.001$, as the impact on the client's business of launching a product that might be rejected 5 per cent of the time (if $p = 0.05$) could be costly.

Type I and Type II errors

Every time you make a decision to accept or reject a null hypothesis you risk making an error. There are two types of error – Type I or α (alpha) and Type II or β (beta) errors. If you make a Type I error you reject the null hypothesis when in fact it is true and you should have accepted it. An example of a Type I error is when an innocent person is found guilty. You make a Type II error when you accept the null hypothesis when in fact it is false and should have been rejected. A Type II error is when a guilty person is acquitted. The chance of committing a Type I error is no greater than the level of significance used in the test (which is why the significance level is sometimes called the alpha value, the value associated with an alpha error). If you use the 5 per cent level you can only make a Type I error 5 per cent of the time. You can reduce the probability of making a Type I error by setting the significance level at 1 per cent or 0.1 per cent. If you drop the significance level (in effect increasing the stringency of the test and raising the confidence limits to 99 per cent or 99.9 per cent) you increase the chances of making a Type II error. In setting significance levels therefore you need to reach a compromise between the types of error. If making a Type I error (accepting as true something that is really false) is deemed worse than making a Type II error (accepting something that should be rejected and is not), then you should set the significance level low (say 0.1 per cent). If, however, the risks associated with a Type II error are greater, then it might be best to set the significance level at 5 per cent. To lower the risk of either type of error arising, you increase the sample size.

In conducting a piece of research you may want to specify at the outset how precisely you want the sample measures to reflect the population values – in an opinion poll, for example. In other words you may want to specify the confidence limits and the margin of error that will be acceptable. For example, in the survey of weekly food spend among single person households, you may want to set the confidence limits at the 95 per cent level (the level most commonly used in market and social research) and you might want the estimate of average weekly spend to be accurate to within €1 of the population values. The question is, what sample size do you need to achieve this? The formula for calculating the sample size is given in the example in Box 8.9.

Box 8.9 Calculating the sample size for a given level of precision

The 95 per cent confidence interval means that the sample estimate will lie within 1.96 standard errors of the mean. So 1.96 = z
The standard deviation of the sample is 5.29. So s = 5.29
The margin of error we want is €±1. So d = ± 1

Formula for working out sample size:

$$n = \frac{z^2 s^2}{d^2}$$

$$= \frac{(1.96 \times 1.96) \times (5.29 \times 5.29)}{(1 \times 1)}$$

$$= 107.5$$

$$= 108 \text{ (rounded up to the nearest whole number)}$$

So you need a sample of 108 to ensure that you can be 95 per cent confident that our estimate of average weekly food spend is within €1 of the population value.

In research we deal with percentages as well as averages. To work out the sample size necessary to ensure that a particular percentage is within an acceptable margin of error, the formula is similar. For example, in the survey of weekly food spend, imagine that you asked whether people had bought fresh fruit. You expect that about 60 per cent will have done so and you want a confidence interval of ±2 per cent and a confidence level of 99 per cent. The calculation is shown in Box 8.10.

If you were to reduce the confidence level from 99 per cent to 95 per cent, what effect would this have on the sample size needed to achieve the same confidence interval of ±2 per cent? Lowering the confidence level would mean that a sample of 2,305 would deliver a ±2 per cent confidence interval. If you were to reduce the confidence interval by half to ±1 per cent, keeping the confidence level the same, what would this mean for sample size? You would need a sample size of some 9,220 – in other words, to halve the confidence interval you need a fourfold increase in sample size.

In deciding on sample size it is not just the total sample that is important; you need also to think about the size of sub-groups within the main sample. For example, it may be crucial to the research objectives to examine the views of women and

Box 8.10 Sample size calculations using percentages

Confidence interval $d\% = \pm2$ per cent
Standard error for 99 per cent confidence level $z = 2.58$
Estimate of percentage being measured $p = 60$

Formula

$$n = \frac{z^2 p\%(100 - p\%)}{d^2}$$

$$= \frac{(2.58 \times 2.58) \times 60(100 - 60)}{2 \times 2}$$

$$= \frac{15,975.36}{4}$$

$$= 3,993.84$$

men separately, or to look at regular users of a service or occasional users. You need to make sure that these sub-samples are large enough to allow you to comment at the chosen confidence level and within an acceptable confidence interval.

Caveat – For ease of explanation, all of the above is based on the use of a simple random sampling approach. Most sample designs in real-world market and social research are more complicated than this, with the result that calculating margin of error and confidence intervals is also more complicated. We have also made assumptions about using standard deviation of the sample rather than the standard deviation of the population.

Probability or random sampling methods

A random or probability sample is one in which each member of the population has a known and non-zero chance of being selected. There are several kinds of random sampling methods, from the fairly straightforward simple random sampling approach to the more complex cluster sampling methods.

■ Simple random sampling

Simple random sampling works like this: imagine we have a population of 1,000 (denoted $N = 1,000$). The population might consist of people or organisations, whatever is relevant to the research investigation. Before making any selection from the population, we know that each item in it has a 1 in 1,000 chance of being selected. Once an item is selected as part of the sample we do not return it to the population. This is known as *sampling without replacement*. The reason for using sampling without replacement is to make sure that no item (a person or organisation, for example) is chosen more than once. In a market or social research survey we would not (usually) interview the same person twice. This makes simple random sampling slightly different from the sampling associated with probability theory, which is sampling with replacement. In this *unrestricted random sampling* approach (Kish, 1965) a selection is made from the population and that item is replaced before the next selection is made.

There are two main ways of selecting a simple random sample. The first will be familiar to anyone who has watched numbers being selected in a lottery game. Each item in the population is represented by a ball. All balls are placed in a drum, thoroughly mixed, and a sample of them is drawn at random. The second method of simple random sampling involves numbering each item in the population, from 1 to N. A sample is drawn at random by selecting numbers from a random number table or by generating a random number using a computer program.

■ Systematic random sampling

Systematic random sampling is a variation of simple random sampling. The items in a population are numbered from 1 to N and arranged in a random order. We decide what size of sample we need (n) and we work out what is known as the sampling interval (k) by dividing the population size (N) by the sample size (n). We select every N/n item from the randomised list of the population. For example, say we have a population of 6,000 and we need to draw a sample of 200. We calculate the sampling interval to be 30 (6,000/200) and starting at a random point between 1 and 6,000 (N) in the list we select every 30th item from the list until we get the required sample size of 200. The reason that this method is referred to as *systematic* random sampling is because a system is in operation for selecting the sample and using the system means that the sampling interval and the randomly chosen starting point on the list will determine which items in the sample are selected. For example, if our random start point is 37, then using the sampling interval of 30 the next item to be selected will be 67, and the item after that will be 97, then 127 and so on until all 200 sampling units are selected. So each item selected is dependent on the previous item. In simple random sampling there is no such dependence – each item is selected independent of all other items in the population.

The results produced by a systematic random sample will be very similar to those produced by a simple random sample if the list used to generate the systematic sample is randomised. If, however, the list is ordered in some way – for example names in alphabetical order, employees in order of their staff grade, or students ranked in order of examination results – then a systematic sample may produce a better sample because it will ensure a spread of sample units from right across the list. The only problem that might arise is if the list has an inherent pattern or is sub-divided into categories. For example, if users and non-users of a service are listed alternately on the list, an even-numbered sampling interval will miss odd-numbered items. Or if items on the list are grouped in some way, depending on the size of the groups and the size of the sampling interval, some groups may be missed out or underrepresented. As a result, the systematic approach may not deliver a good sample.

For practical reasons it may not be possible to use either simple random sampling or systematic random sampling. In many market and social research situations lists of the target population may not be available. Where they are available population size may make it difficult to number all of the items, although with computerised lists and databases this is less of a problem that it was in the past.

■ Stratified random sampling

Stratified random sampling is one of the most widely used methods of sampling in research. In sampling a population for a market or social research project it is very likely that we know something about that population which we can use to improve the quality of the sample and the precision of the results derived from it. For example, in a population of employees, we may know which staff grade each holds. We can use this information to make sure that employees from each staff grade are properly represented in the sample. To do this we must divide the population into the relevant groups or strata, for example all who belong to staff grade 1, all who belong to grade 2, all from grade 3 and so on. In this case staff grade is what we call the *stratification factor*. Which stratification factor to choose will depend on what you believe to be most relevant to the research objectives. From each of the strata we choose the required sample size – using a simple random or a systematic random sampling approach.

Proportionate and disproportionate stratified sampling

If you choose the sample from within each stratum using a systematic sampling approach and you select sample units from each stratum in proportion to the size of the stratum, this is known as *proportionate allocation*. Using the same sampling interval for each stratum will produce a proportionate allocation to the strata and achieve a *stratified sample with proportionate allocation*. Put simply, this means that in the sample the strata are represented in the same proportion as they appear in the population.

If for some reason you want to over- or under-represent particular strata in the sample, then you use *disproportionate allocation*. For example, it might be important to examine the views of a low incidence group within the population. The best way of achieving a robust sub-sample for analysis is to make sure that the group or stratum is overrepresented in the sample in comparison to the population. To achieve such a *disproportionate stratified sample* you use a different sampling interval for each stratum. An approach known as *optimum allocation* is common in industrial and business-to-business research, where sampling units – the organisations – vary in size and you want to ensure that you include a greater proportion of the larger organisations. The sampling fractions for each size of stratum within the population (for example, the small, medium and large organisations) are calculated to provide the best sample (with the lowest sampling error for a given cost) using the statistical theory of optimum allocation. You might end up sampling 1 in 40 small organisations; 1 in 20 medium sized; 1 in 10 large organisations and 1 in 5 very large organisations.

■ Cluster and multi-stage sampling

Populations can often be divided up into groups. The national population is easily divided up into administrative areas, states or regions, electoral constituencies, wards and post code areas, for example; organisations have departments and so on. We can make use of these natural *clusters* in a sampling strategy. It is also possible, if no natural clusters exist, to create a cluster by, for example, imposing a grid on to a map.

In a study of attitudes to the redevelopment of a park among the population of a large town, you might first select a sample of the electoral wards (administrative districts made up of a relatively small number of streets) that make up the town. You could then draw a sample of households from within each of the selected wards. This is an example of a cluster sample – the households, the sampling units, are clustered together in wards. You could add further stages before selecting individuals for interview. You could select particular streets within each ward.

Box 8.11 Selecting individuals: the next birthday rule and the Kish Grid

Where there is more than one eligible person for interview, and to ensure that each has a roughly equal chance of selection, individuals can be selected using the 'next birthday rule', choosing the individual with the next birthday, or by using a Kish Grid.

Table 8.3 Example of a Kish Grid

Serial number of contact	Number of eligible individuals					
	1	2	3	4	5	6 or more
1	1	2	1	4	3	5
2	1	1	2	1	4	6
3	1	2	3	2	5	1
4	1	1	1	3	1	2
5	1	2	2	1	2	3
6	1	1	3	2	3	4
7	1	2	1	3	4	5

A sampling approach in which you first of all select a sample of groups such as an electoral constituency or a department, and then go on to select a sample from within each group, is known as *multi-stage sampling*. The first stage groups are known as *primary sampling units* or *PSUs*. If the units within each of the PSUs are clustered together, the sample is known as a *cluster sample*. But it is not necessary in multi-stage sampling to begin with clusters – the first stage groups may be widely dispersed.

Using clusters of the target population and selecting a sample from within each cluster is often a more cost-effective approach than that of simple or systematic random sampling where the sample may be more widely spread. The interviewer travel time needed to complete a set number of interviews in a cluster sample is usually much less. There is a disadvantage with multi-stage sampling. The standard error is greater than if a simple random or a stratified random sample were used. At each stage of a multi-stage sample we are introducing sampling error and, as a result, sample estimates may be less precise than those from a single stage probability sample.

Sampling with probability proportional to size (PPS)

It is possible, even very likely, that PSUs (for example electoral constituencies, or organisations) will vary greatly in size. In a random selection of these PSUs each has an equal chance of being chosen. For example a small PSU, say a small organisation with 50,000 customers, has the same chance of being selected as a large organisation in the same market with 100,000 customers. This could lead to an unrepresentative sample. If both the large and the small organisations were chosen as PSUs, then at the second stage sampling, any one of the smaller organisation's 50,000 customers has a greater chance of being selected than any one of the 100,000 in the larger organisation. You could overcome this by using the same sampling interval for both sizes of organisation. For example, with a sampling interval of 500, we would achieve a sample of 100 from the smaller organisation and a sample of 200 from the larger one. Again, this may not be satisfactory since we may not achieve a robust enough sample size for analysis of different sub-groups of customers from the smaller organisation. You could use disproportional allocation, in the manner outlined above.

Another solution is to use sampling with *probability proportionate to size* or *PPS*. Using this approach, the PSUs are chosen in proportion to their size. So, for example, the larger organisation, at twice the size of the smaller one, would have twice the chance of selection. At the second stage of the sampling process the same number of items is chosen from each PSU. This means that overall the chance of any item being chosen is the same, regardless of the size of the PSU to which it belongs. So, in our example, each customer has the same chance of selection.

The advantage of using PPS is that it delivers a sample with a smaller standard error (or greater precision) than does a simple random sample of PSUs followed by second stage sampling with a constant sampling interval. Although the larger PSU is more likely to appear in the sample using PPS, the number of second stage units taken from it are fixed, so its 'members' are unlikely to dominate in the total sample. The only drawback with this approach is that in order to set the probability proportional to size we need to have accurate and up-to-date information about the size of the PSUs.

■ Sampling frames

In order to choose a random sample you need a sampling frame. A sampling frame can be a database, a list, a record, a map – something that identifies all the elements of the target population. To be effective as a sampling frame, to allow you to draw a sample that is representative of the population, it must be accurate, complete and up to date. The famous and much quoted example of the consequences of using an inappropriate sampling frame (the poor response rate, 22 per cent, also played a part) is that of the *Literary Digest* 1936 opinion poll. The magazine's poll predicted that in the United States presidential election Alf Landon would beat the incumbent Franklin Roosevelt by a landslide. In fact Roosevelt won a second term by the largest majority in history. The poll sample of 10 million was drawn from two sources: car registrations and telephone listings. Remember, the year was 1936, the effects of the Depression were still much in evidence. Choosing a sampling frame that overrepresented the relatively well off (those who could afford cars and telephones) and underrepresented the relatively poor section of the electorate produced a biased sample.

In terms of practicality, the sampling frame must be easily available, convenient to use, and contain enough information to enable us to find the elements listed on it. Kish (1965) identifies four main problems with sampling frames: missing elements; clusters of elements; blanks or foreign elements; and duplication.

Missing elements

Missing elements are elements that belong to the population but do not appear on the sampling frame. It can often be difficult to detect whether a sampling frame has missing elements. An incomplete sampling frame will mean that the sample derived from it will not be representative of the population. One way round this is to look for another source of information about the same population and compare and/or combine the two. For example, a list of dentists may be obtained from a subscription list to a professional association or to a journal or magazine. If it appears to be incomplete – some dentists may not subscribe – the list could be checked against the listing of dentists given in the telephone directory.

Clusters of elements

A sampling frame may list elements not as individuals but as groups or *clusters of elements*, for example individuals at the same address. In our dentist example, rather than listing individual dentists, the sampling frame might list dental practices. A dental practice may be one dentist or it may be several dentists. How do we treat this? We have a number of options:

➢ Include all the dentists from the cluster in the sample. *Drawback* – dentists in the same practice may be similar in attitudes, age and so on.
➢ Choose one at random from the cluster. *Drawback* – this means that all elements of the population do not have an equal chance of selection.
➢ Take a sample of all the clusters in the sampling frame, list all the elements of each one and take a random sample from this list. *Caution* – need to take a large enough sample of clusters and an appropriate sampling interval to ensure that each of the elements in the final sample comes from a different cluster.

Blanks or foreign elements

An element may be included in a sampling frame that does not belong there. Such elements are known as *blanks* or *foreign elements*. The incidence of blanks or foreign elements may be relatively high in a sampling frame that is out of date. For example, between the compilation of the sampling frame and its use individuals listed may have died, retired, left the country, or no be longer eligible to be considered as part of the target population. The sampling frame may cover a wider population than the population of interest and so contain elements that are not relevant to the target population. For example, a subscription list for a dental journal may be a useful sampling frame from which to draw a sample of dentists but it may also include non-dentists, such as dental equipment sales people, dental technicians or dental nurses.

The best way of treating blanks or foreign elements when drawing a sample is to omit them and continue selecting sample units in the appropriate way. A substitution of the next item on the list is not a suitable way of dealing with them. That approach means that an item next to a blank or foreign element has two chances of being selected, once in its own right and once as a replacement for a blank or foreign element.

Duplication

An element may be *duplicated* in a sampling frame, appearing more than once. For example, in a subscription list, an individual may appear twice if he or she subscribes to two or more products. Duplication is relatively easy to deal with when the sampling frame is held electronically. A *de-duplication* program is run which eliminates the reoccurrence of an element.

■ Examples of sampling frames

For selecting samples of households and members of the general public, the most commonly used sampling frames in the United Kingdom include the Postal Address File (PAF) and the Electoral Register. Several commercial organisations specialise in designing samples from the PAF and the electoral register. Sources of sampling frames for industrial and business-to-business research include Census of Employment List (UK) and commercial directories such as Kompass (**www.kompass.com**), Dun and Bradstreet (**www.dnb.com**) and, in the United Kingdom, the Yellow Pages (**www.yell.co.uk**).

Box 8.12 Dealing with non-response

Non-response error occurs when those included in the sample do not respond. This is an important issue in research – it can lead to serious concerns about the representativeness of the sample and so the validity of the data. If the responders and the non-responders to a survey differ the data – the sample estimates – will be biased.

The main causes of non-response are refusals and 'not at home'. Refusal rates can be reduced by good questionnaire design and good research administration (including training and briefing of interviewers, pre-notification and follow-ups, use of appropriate incentives and so on). There are two main approaches to managing 'not at homes': varying the times at which contacts are made (weekends and weekdays, daytime and evening) and making 'call backs' or return visits. Non-response can also be addressed by providing substitutes or replacements for the non-responder. Taking a sample of the non-responders (and using the results to project to all non-responders) can help in understanding the differences between respondents and non-respondents and the final sample may be adjusted accordingly.

Semi-random sampling

In all of the sampling methods described above, the interviewer is not involved in selecting a subject for interview or observation – the sample performs this task and the interviewer's job is to get hold of that subject. This can be an expensive process, especially in face-to-face surveys. Generating the sample, a detailed list of addresses for each interviewer to visit and completing the fieldwork can be time consuming and expensive. One way of reducing the time and cost involved without giving the interviewer greater discretion in selecting locations, households or individuals (and thus introducing selection bias) is to use a *semi-random* sampling procedure known as *random route sampling* or *random walk*. This method does not involve the time and expense incurred in drawing a full random sample from a sampling frame. A list of random starting addresses is selected using a multi-stage stratified random sample, for example to ensure a mix of urban and rural locations or towns of varying size. Each interviewer is given one random address at which to conduct the first interview (and instructions for choosing which individual to select within that household). Along with the random starting address the interviewer is given a set of instructions for selecting subsequent addresses at which to interview.

As with random sampling methods, no substitutes for the chosen subject are allowed and a number of call backs may be necessary to achieve an interview. This may mean that there is little difference in fieldwork costs. In order to achieve cost savings call backs may be scrapped in favour of a quota-based approach. We will look at quota sampling next.

Non-probability sampling methods

It is not always possible or feasible to use probability sampling methods. The time and cost involved may be prohibitive, a sampling frame may not be available, or the type of research may not require it. In this section we look at the alternatives to probability sampling – *non-probability* sampling methods. With non-probability sampling the interviewer or observer has some control over the selection of elements for the sample. We do not know what chance any item has of being selected and we cannot use probability theory to make inferences about a population based on the sample or make calculations about precision of sample estimates.

■ Quota sampling

Quota sampling is perhaps the most widely used sampling technique in quantitative market research. In most markets the researcher or the client will have extensive knowledge of the target population, especially on key variables or characteristics. This knowledge will have been derived from primary and secondary sources, including customer databases, geodemographic or national census data and other research. This information is used to design a sampling framework that will reflect the make-up of the population on these key characteristics. For example, the research might require a nationally representative sample of the adult population of the United Kingdom in terms of age, gender and socio-economic group. A sampling framework or *quota* based on these characteristics can be drawn up. Quotas are allocated to interviewers and the interviewers' task is to select the individuals who fit the characteristics set out in the quota.

In designing a quota sample we have two options. We can have an independent quota or an interlocking quota. In an independent quota the interviewer is free to select anyone who fits a particular quota criterion, independent of any other criteria. There is no instruction to obtain, for example, specific numbers of male respondents within a particular age band, or a specific number of women in each socio-economic group. Within the age quota 18–34, for example, we assume that the interviewer will choose individuals at random but he or she could choose women and not men. Since this may lead to an unrepresentative sample it is likely that the interviewer will be instructed to select a 'spread' of the sexes within each age group, and a spread on socio-economic group. An example of a sample with independent quota controls is given in Table 8.4. The advantages of independent quota controls are that they are easier to set, easier for the interviewer to achieve and so less expensive in comparison to a sample with interlocking quota controls. The disadvantage is that, in leaving the interviewer so much leeway in the selection process, a representative sample is not always achieved.

When the interviewer is asked to find an individual who meets several of the quota controls in combination, for example so many women within each age band and within each SEG, the quota is known as an interlocking quota. An example of an interlocking quota is given in Table 8.5. Designing an interlocking quota sample is more difficult than designing an independent quota, and it can be more difficult and time consuming for interviewers to achieve. It may, however, limit selection bias, and so give more control over the composition of the final sample and a greater chance of the sample being representative of the population.

In setting quotas for consumer surveys, the population characteristics most often used include age, gender, social class, region, working status, and characteristics directly appropriate to the research study, for example buyers or non-buyers of a particular product or brand. In a study in which organisations rather than people are the sampling units the quota controls may include organisation type or sector, size (number of employees or turnover), or region.

Table 8.4 Example of independent quota controls

Characteristics	Proportion in the target population %	Number necessary for sample of 400
Age		
18–34	30	120
35–54	35	140
55+	35	140
Gender		
Male	48	192
Female	52	208

Table 8.5 Example of an interlocking quota control

	Age 18–34		Age 35–54		Age 55+	
	Male	*Female*	*Male*	*Female*	*Male*	*Female*
Buyers	30	30	50	60	30	25
Non-buyers	20	20	50	40	20	25
Total	50	50	100	100	50	50

The quality of a quota sample will depend on two factors: the degree of random-ness, or extent of bias, with which the interviewer makes selections (which can be influenced by interviewing training, clear briefing instructions, variation in interview-ing times and locations); and how accurate and up to date is the information on which the quota controls are based. In choosing which characteristics to use in setting quota controls it is important to think of the research objectives and to choose char-acteristics that are relevant to these. In many ways quota sampling resembles strati-fied sampling – on the basis of what we know about the population we are able to divide it up into strata and determine what proportion we need in each stratum to ensure that the sample represents the population. The main difference between strati-fied sampling and quota sampling lies in the choice of individuals (or items) to fill the quota. In a stratified random sample these items are chosen at random and the inter-viewer's task is to interview them, even if this means completing a number of call backs. A substitute is not accepted if the specified individual is not available. In a quota sample the characteristics of individuals (or items) are specified by the quota but a particular individual is not specified. The interviewer's task is to interview someone (anyone) who fits the quota criteria, not a particular individual chosen at random. If a person is not available for interview call backs may be made but it is more likely that the interviewer will look for someone else more readily available or easier to find to fill the quota. In other words, with a quota sample the choice of the final sampling unit is not random.

Research has been carried out in which the results obtained by random sampling and quota sampling have been compared and found to be different (Marsh and Scar-brough, 1990). Many research organisations, however, argue (from experience) that quota sampling can produce a quality, representative sample, especially if care is taken to limit bias at the final selection stage. To this end particular care is taken to ensure that hard-to-find individuals, for example those at work, those who travel a lot, are included in the sample. While however, a well-designed probability or random sample should be representative of the target population in all aspects (because of randomness), a well-designed quota sample may only be representative of the popu-lation in terms of the characteristics specified in the quota. It may be unrepresentative in other ways. With probability samples we are able to estimate representativeness; with quota sampling we are not able to estimate representativeness, or even gauge the possible biases that exist.

Quota samples have a number of points in their favour, however, which account for their popularity in market research. In comparison to probability methods they are relatively quick and inexpensive to set up and administer. Call backs can be avoided, saving on interviewer travel time and expenses. A quota sample is often a more practicable alternative if a sampling frame does not exist. If a research project, however, demands that results be underpinned by statistical theory, probability sampling is the only choice.

Sampling in qualitative research

In qualitative research sample sizes are generally small and so probability theory and notions of statistical representativeness do not apply. But, as we noted earlier, this does not mean that representativeness is not important. Neither does it mean that selecting a sample is not a rigorous or systematic process.

In choosing a sample for a qualitative research study it is important, as in a quantitative study, to define clearly the target population. It is crucially important to define clearly what relationship the sample has with this population. For example, the sample may aim to be broadly representative of the wider population in terms of key characteristics such as age, gender and social class but it will be difficult, if not impossible, to achieve a truly representative sample with a small sample size. In many cases true representativeness is not the aim. The sample may be chosen to encapsulate a range of characteristics relevant to the topic under study, or to provide a detailed view of behaviour, experiences or events that are seen in the wider population. As in the quantitative research context, it is important to think ahead to the analysis and interpretation of the findings. Choosing sample units or elements on the basis of their relevance to the research problem, the analytical framework or the explanation you hope to develop is known as theoretical sampling. The best-known version of this sampling approach is that developed by Glaser and Strauss (1967).

The sampling process

In qualitative market research sampling is usually referred to as *recruitment* and the specially trained interviewers who undertake it are known as *recruiters*. Recruitment can take a number of forms. Usually a grid or matrix or a detailed list is drawn up identifying the types of people or organisations relevant to the research. For example, they might be defined in terms of demographic characteristics (age, gender, social class, working status and so on) or they might be defined in terms of usage of a particular product or service, or in terms of their attitude or experience of an event – whatever is relevant to the aims of the research. A combination of factors may be used to describe the target population and so the sample required. Care should be taken not to over-specify, however, as this is usually unnecessary and can make recruitment difficult and expensive.

If necessary, a *recruitment* or *screening questionnaire* can be used and recruiters are asked to find individuals who match the recruitment or sample criteria. The recruitment questionnaire may be administered face to face by contacting people at home or on the street, or at a specific place where the incidence of those likely to fit the recruitment criteria is relatively high. Recruiting at a specified site is another form of convenience sampling, sometimes known as *outcropping* or '*lurk and grab*'. For example, if we were looking for church-goers, we would recruit near a church. The recruitment questionnaire may also be administered by telephone or by post. Telephone or postal contact is often used if a sampling frame of the target population, for example a business directory or database, is available. The client may provide a list of possible contacts or you may have your own list, built up through knowledge of the market or subject area. Using lists or sampling frames in recruitment is sometimes referred to as *list sampling*. The quality of the sample will depend to some extent on the quality of the sampling frame. Using a network of contacts and asking these contacts to refer you to others is known as *network sampling* or *snowball sampling*. This method is useful if a list or sampling frame is not available, or if the sample is difficult to find, for example a low incidence or low visibility group. A disadvantage is that you may end up with a sample made up of people with similar characteristics. *Piggy-backing* or *multi-purposing* is another way of recruiting or identifying a sample. At the end of a study respondents are asked if they would be willing to be recontacted to take part in further research. They are contacted again at the recruitment stage of the new study to check their willingness to take part and their suitability. This sampling strategy is useful if individuals are expensive or difficult to find.

A set of good practice guidelines, including issues relating to data protection and recruitment, are contained in the Qualitative Research Guidelines published by The Market Research Society.

Sample size

Although sample sizes in qualitative studies are usually small, they should be large enough to give you the information you need to address the research problem clearly and unequivocally, and large enough to include sub-groups of relevance to the topic and to allow you to make meaningful comparisons. In choosing the sample size you should be guided by your experience (or the experience of others) in similar types of study or in similar areas or markets. One approach (common in social and academic research) is to take a 'rolling' or dynamic sample – in other words to sample until you reach 'theoretical saturation' (Bertaux and Bertaux-Wiame, 1981), until you are seeing or hearing nothing new in the data.

Chapter summary

➢ Sampling is about selecting, without bias and with as much precision as resources allow, the 'items' or elements from which or from whom we wish to collect data. In market and social research projects these elements are usually people, households or organisations, although they may be places, events or experiences.

➢ Drawing up a sampling plan is one of the most important procedures in the research process. It involves defining the target population, choosing an appropriate sampling technique, deciding on the sample size and preparing sampling instructions.

➤ There are three main approaches to sampling – probability or random sampling, semi-random sampling and non-probability sampling.

➤ Random sampling approaches include simple random sampling, systematic random sampling, stratified random sampling and multi-stage and cluster sampling. Sampling or probability theory underpins random sampling.

➤ Sampling frames are used from which to draw random samples. A sampling frame can be a database, a list, a record, a map – something that identifies all the elements of the target population. To be effective as a sampling frame, to allow you to draw a sample that is representative of the population, it must be accurate, complete and up to date. It must be easily available, convenient to use, and contain enough information to enable you to find the elements listed on it. Problems with sampling frames arise as a result of missing elements, clusters of elements, blanks or foreign elements, and duplication.

➤ Sample size is the number of elements included in the sample. It is important in terms of the precision of sample estimates but on its own does not guarantee that the results will be accurate or unbiased; the way in which the sample is chosen (the sampling technique used, the sampling frame) will affect this. Choice of sample size depends on the nature and purpose of the research enquiry, the importance of the decisions to be made on the basis of the results, and the analysis requirements (particularly of sub-groups within the sample). It needs to be large enough to provide the evidence with a degree of confidence in the findings. If the level of precision of the sample estimate or the size of the confidence level or interval required is known, the sample size can be calculated to achieve these. Time and budget constraints are also a factor in the choice.

➤ Quota sampling is the most commonly used non-probability sampling method and is used widely in market research. Information on key characteristics in the target population is used to design a sampling framework that reflects the make-up of the population on these key characteristics. The quality of a quota sample depends on the degree of randomness with which the interviewer makes selections and on how accurate and up to date is the information on which the quota controls are based.

➤ A well-designed probability or random sample should be representative of the target population in all aspects (because of randomness); a well-designed quota sample may only be representative of the population in terms of the characteristics specified in the quota – it may be unrepresentative in other ways. With probability samples we are able to estimate representativeness; with quota sampling we are not able to estimate representativeness, or even gauge the possible biases that exist.

➤ Non-probability sampling techniques are used in qualitative research – samples are typically small and notions of statistical representativeness do not apply. Representativeness is an important goal nevertheless and selecting a sample for qualitative research should be a rigorous and systematic process.

Questions and exercises

1 What is the difference between the target population and the survey population? Give examples of situations in which the two differ.

2 In what circumstances would it be preferable to conduct a census rather than a sample survey?

3 Outline the stages involved in developing a sampling plan.

4 What should you consider when deciding between a probability and a non-probability sampling approach?

5 Describe how you would select each of the following sample types:
   (a) a simple random sample;
   (b) a systematic random sample;
   (c) a stratified random sample;
   (d) a cluster sample;
   (e) a semi-random sample;
   (f) a quota sample.

6 How would you draw a representative sample for a telephone survey among telephone households in the United Kingdom?

7 Why is quota sampling popular in market research? What are its advantages and its limitations?

8 What are the main factors that determine the choice of sample size?

9 Describe the main methods you might use in generating a sample for a qualitative research study, giving examples of the types of studies in which each might be used.

10 What information would you include about your sampling plan in a report to the client?

References

Bertaux, D. and Bertaux-Wiame, I. (1981) 'Life Stories in the Bakers' Trade' in Bertaux, D. (ed.) *Biography and Society: The Life History Approach in the Social Sciences*, London: Sage.

Foreman, J. and Collins, M. (1991) 'The viability of random digit dialling in the UK', *Journal of the Market Research Society*, 33, 3, pp. 219–27.

Glaser, B. and Strauss, A. (1967) *The Discovery of Grounded Theory*, Chicago, IL: Aldine.

Kish, L. (1965) *Survey Sampling*, New York: Wiley.

Marsh, C. and Scarbrough, E. (1990) 'Testing nine hypotheses about quota sampling', *Journal of the Market Research Society*, 32, 4, pp. 485–506.

Moser, C. and Kalton, G. (1971) *Survey Methods in Social Investigation*, London: Dartmouth.

Recommended reading

Foreman, J. and Collins, M. (1991) 'The viability of random digit dialling in the UK', *Journal of the Market Research Society*, **33**, 3, pp. 219–27. A full account of the advantages and disadvantages of random digit dialling and the 'Directory plus 1' approach.

Marsh, C. and Scarbrough, E. (1990) 'Testing nine hypotheses about quota sampling', *Journal of the Market Research Society*, **32**, 4, pp. 485–506. A full account of the findings of experimental research into differences between quota and random sampling.

McIntosh, A. and Davies, R. (1970 and 1996) 'The sampling of non-domestic populations', *Journal of the Market Research Society*, **12**, 4 and **38**, 4, pp. 429–46. A very useful account of the sampling issues in industrial and business-to-business research.

Moser, C. and Kalton, G. (1971) *Survey Methods in Social Investigation*, London: Dartmouth. A comprehensive and clearly written account of sampling theory and sample design.

Mason, J. (1996) *Qualitative Researching*, London: Sage. An excellent account of the logic of sampling in qualitative research.

Qualitative recruitment: Report of the industry Working Party (1996) *Journal of the Market Research Society*, **38**, pp. 135–43. A useful review of recent practice.

Chapter 9

Collecting data on attitudes

Introduction

Attitudes are of interest to social and market researchers for their own sake and for the way in which they relate to motivation, intention and behaviour. They are 'the market researcher's favourite measurement' (Sampson, 1980). In this chapter we look at the concepts of attitudes, values, beliefs, opinions and motivations, and how quantitative and qualitative techniques can be used to gather data on attitudes.

Topics covered

➤ The concepts of attitudes, values, beliefs, opinions and motivations
➤ Relationship between attitudes and behaviour
➤ Collecting data on attitudes

Relationship to MRS Advanced Certificate Syllabus

The material in this chapter is relevant to Unit 8 – Attitude Measurement.

Learning outcomes

At the end of this chapter you should be able to:

➤ understand the concepts of attitudes, beliefs, motivations and the connection with behaviour;
➤ understand the problems involved in collecting data on attitudes;
➤ understand the role of qualitative and quantitative research in gathering data on attitudes, the methods used and their limitations.

Why are we interested in attitudes?

We are interested in attitudes for two main reasons: for what they tell us about what people think and feel; and for what they tell us about how people intend to act. A study of attitudes helps us understand people's view of the world, how individuals and groups of people differ from each other; and, because they help us understand what influences and motivates people's intentions to act, attitudes are useful in studying behaviour and understanding the ways in which we might influence it.

Attitudes are complex and difficult to research. It is important to be as clear as possible about what it is we are researching. As Tuck (1976) explains, it is important to research attitudes towards specific events and not attitudes to generalities. First we look at what is meant by the term 'attitude', to what other concepts attitudes relate, and, in particular, in what way they relate to behaviour. This is important if we are to design effective ways of collecting data on attitudes and interpreting what those data mean.

Attitudes and related concepts

Definitions of the concept 'attitude' vary but there is general agreement that holding an attitude about something means that we are predisposed or likely to respond in a particular way when we encounter the object and/or the circumstances related to that attitude. We can have attitudes about almost anything, from the seemingly mundane and everyday – frozen food or fabric conditioner – to the more serious – drug taking or religion. The attitudes we hold may reflect how we think and feel about it (so they are related to beliefs and feelings), and may influence what our intentions might be or what we might do in relation to it in certain circumstances (so they are related to action or behaviour). They may therefore provide us with a framework for responding to, and coping with, the stimuli we face in everyday situations. This is one of the reasons why market and social researchers are interested in measuring attitudes: to help understand how people think and feel and how they might behave in relation to an issue, a product or service in particular circumstances.

■ Where do attitudes come from?

We acquire attitudes in different ways and can classify them loosely according to their source or the influences on them:

➢ physiological and psychological – from biogenic, psychogenic and learnt needs and wants, and the motivation to satisfy them;
➢ sociological – from the culture and the society in which we live, from its traditions, its myth and folklore;
➢ social psychological influences, for example from the groups we belong to – primary groups such as the family, and secondary groups such as a club or society, an interest group or political party.

This classification suggests that, depending on their source, attitudes might have different properties. Those that are related to or arise from our innate needs and our personality may be more deep-rooted, more stable and less likely to be susceptible to change than those we have acquired from our day-to-day experience. Social psychologists (Oppenheim, 2000) have given labels to different 'types' of attitudes:

➤ the more superficial and the more likely to change they call 'opinions';
➤ the less superficial and less likely to change are referred to as 'attitudes';
➤ the more deep-rooted and the more immutable still are called 'values' or 'basic attitudes';
➤ the most deep-rooted and most enduring are attitudes that are a part of personality.

In market and social research we come across – and we have to collect data about – all of these types of 'attitudes'. We investigate, for example, people's opinions about events and issues, about products and brands – things that are more likely to change as a result of experience, media coverage or advertising. We also investigate issues that are connected to value systems, and to personality, and which are less likely to change, including things such as political and social attitudes, attitudes to money and finance, to cosmetics and so on. We approach these investigations in different ways: generally speaking we use quantitative techniques to measure or quantify the more superficial opinions and attitudes; and we use qualitative techniques to explore and analyse the less superficial and the more deep-rooted. In addition, qualitative techniques are used to explore and understand the context of an attitude, its relationship to needs and wants, opinions, beliefs, intentions, motivation and personality – useful information in its own right – in order to develop 'measures' for use in quantitative research. Qualitative and quantitative techniques are often used in tandem to gain an understanding of the nature of the attitude or attitude network at different levels.

Box 9.1 How do attitudes relate to needs, wants, motivation and goals?

Every human being has physiological or biogenic needs (for food and water, for example) and psychogenic needs (for self-expression, for example). These needs are innate. We also have learnt or secondary needs, related to our personality, our experiences and the society or culture in which we live (for example the need for approval or achievement). Needs can be expressed as wants (you have a need to quench your thirst, you want to drink water). Needs and wants are the basis of motivation – we are motivated to fulfil our needs and wants. Motivation is the concept that links needs and wants to action: having a need or a want may motivate us to act in order to fulfil or satisfy that need or achieve that want. Goals are the outcomes we seek by taking action: our behaviour can be said to be goal directed. Several different goals or outcomes may be available that would satisfy a particular need or want. Attitudes arise from and can influence our needs, and the motivation to fulfil these needs and the goals or outcomes we seek.

■ The relationship between attitudes and behaviour

Many social scientists, and many researchers, believe that attitudes are an indication of a predisposition to act or behave, and so can be used to understand, if not explain or predict, behaviour. At the same time it is recognised that there is no automatic link between holding an attitude to an object and taking action in relation to it. A range of intervening factors may affect both the attitude and the behaviour. For example, situational factors such as economic circumstances (you may hold positive attitudes to organic food but not buy it because it is more expensive), mood, the physical or social environment in which you find yourself (you may prefer to dress casually but if everyone else at work dresses formally you may do so, too) may have an effect. Other factors, such as the strength or depth of the attitude or its relationship to other attitudes, may dictate whether we act and the way in which we act on an attitude. It is accepted that two people can hold identical attitudes, arrived at in different ways, and that they can behave in entirely different ways. Whilst knowing a person's attitude does not allow us to predict whether he or she might take a particular action, it might tell us something about his or her pattern of behaviour.

Researching attitudes

Attitudes are difficult to research – they are complex, multi-faceted and may be dependent on particular circumstances; we may be unaware that we hold them and we may find it hard, or be unwilling, to articulate or put them into words.

■ Using quantitative techniques

It is difficult to research attitudes in a way that achieves both validity and reliability. In using quantitative techniques to measure an attitude, for example, we are relying on words to produce a set of statements and set a context for the questions. As you will see in Chapter 10, it is difficult to word questions to gather factual data or data about behaviour; it is even more difficult to construct a question or a statement to measure an attitude, which is not factual.

Capturing the essence of an attitude is almost impossible using one question or one statement: it is unlikely that we will be able to capture the complexity of the attitude, so it will lack validity; and it is unlikely that one question or statement will deliver consistent results – respondents tend to be more sensitive to the wording and the context of attitudinal questions compared to factual questions – so it will lack reliability. It is therefore unwise to measure an attitude using a single question or statement. Research shows that we can improve the validity and reliability of attitude measurement by using banks of questions or 'attitude statements' combined in an attitude scale. Validity may be improved if the question, the statements and the response sets used are designed to encompass the complexity of the attitude, and the context of it. Reliability may be improved because issues of question wording and context may be cancelled out across the range of statements. These improvements depend, of course, on ensuring that the question wording is sound, the response set is appropriate and all of the statements used reflect or measure elements of the underlying attitude.

Scales and ranking

Designing questions to measure attitudes quantitatively consists of two parts: designing and choosing the list of attitude statements or the 'item pool' for the particular attitude variable; and choosing the response format.

Designing evaluative and descriptive attitude and belief statements

According to Oppenheim (2000), an attitude statement 'is a single sentence that expresses a point of view, a belief, a preference, a judgement, an emotional feeling, a position *for or against* something [italics in original]'. The list of statements to be included in an attitude scale should be grounded in an in-depth understanding of the subject area. A study of previous research or a review of the relevant literature on the subject are good starting points. Depth interviews and group discussions among the survey's target group are invaluable – they allow us to examine the nature and complexity of the attitudes, to determine what exactly it is we want to measure, what the indicators should be, and to understand the language respondents use to express the attitudes in question.

Once a list has been generated each of the statements on the list should be carefully worded following the good practice guidelines set out in Chapter 10. You should ask the following:

➢ Is each statement clearly worded?
➢ Is each statement unambiguous?
➢ Are any statements too long?
➢ Does each statement contain one issue only?
➢ Is the list balanced – that is, are there roughly equal numbers of positive and negative items?
➢ Are the statements in a random order?

Item analysis

The item pool generated from a review of the relevant literature, through qualitative research and pilot testing, should offer a valid measure of the attitude in question. We need, however, to check that this is the case by conducting what is known as item analysis. Item analysis helps to determine which statements are indeed the most valid measures of the attitude – in other words which ones are the best to use in the scale. We have no external, measurable 'output' of the attitude against which to assess each of the attitude statements. What we do therefore is to examine how well each individual item correlates with the rest of the items in the pool, based on the assumption that the whole item pool is the best measure of the attitude in question. We calculate what is called the 'item-whole' correlation: the correlation, or strength of association, between each item and the rest of the items in the pool. (A statistical or data analysis package should be able to do these calculations for you.) Items that correlate poorly with the rest of the pool, those with low correlation coefficients, are excluded from use in the scale on the basis that they do not measure the attitude measured by the other items. The item-whole correlation can be carried out on the results of a pilot study; those items with low correlation coefficients are excluded from the final questionnaire, and so the final attitude scale. Alternatively, you can include the full item pool on the survey and calculate the correlations based on responses from the whole sample, and exclude the low correlations from the scale at the analysis stage.

The response format

Assembling an item pool is common to most scaling techniques. The techniques, however, vary in the way in which items are chosen, phrased and scored to suit particular response formats. A detailed account is beyond the scope of this book; instead we focus on one response format – the Likert Scale, which is the one you are most likely to come across. The main concern in choosing items for a Likert Scale is that all the items should measure aspects of the same underlying attitude – in other words a Likert Scale should be uni-dimensional. A further consideration is that neutral items and those at the extremes of the attitude continuum should be avoided. The response format on the Likert Scale consists of five points: 'Agree strongly', 'Agree', Neither agree nor disagree', 'Disagree' and 'Disagree strongly'. (Few researchers, however, use the Likert Scale in the way Likert intended – most use the Likert five-point response format and construct a scale from the responses.) A 'Don't know' response is added to the end of the scale, which, although not offered to the respondent, gives the interviewer a way of recording the response if it does arise.

You may find in your list of attitude statements that you have some positively phrased statements and some negatively phrased ones. Make sure that you are consistent in how you score or analyse these. If, when constructing your attitude scale, you decide that a high score means a positive attitude, score the positive statements 5 for 'Agree strongly' to 1 for 'Disagree strongly' and score the negative statements 5 for 'Disagree strongly' to 1 for 'Agree strongly'. This can be confusing to do on the questionnaire, where it is best that the response set for each statement uses the same number code; you may have to make this an instruction for data processing.

Once you have decided on the attitude statements and the response format, pilot the question and examine respondents' reactions to each of the statements. Check whether they answer at the extremes of the scale or the middle of it, or whether they answer 'Don't know'. This information should tell you whether your attitude statements are working or not. You want respondents to recognise the statements as something they would say themselves, or something that someone they know might say. You should begin to see a pattern, with respondents falling into different groups according to their responses. What you do not want is a large proportion of respondents choosing the middle response, 'Neither agree nor disagree', or saying 'Don't know' – rather you want them to choose the 'Agree' or 'Disagree' responses; this indicates that the statements are differentiating between respondents.

An example

Consider the example in Box 9.2 – it is a question from the 1999 Life and Times Survey conducted in Northern Ireland by the University of Ulster and Queen's University Belfast. A full version of the questionnaire and the data derived from this question can be downloaded from the Life and Times website at **www.ark.ac.uk/nilt**. The question is designed to measure attitudes to the teaching of citizenship in schools for children aged 11–18. It has two components:

➤ the list of attitude statements or items, for example 'It isn't the *job* of schools to teach children about politics and human rights';

➤ the fixed responses of the five-point Likert Scale, 'Strongly agree' to 'Strongly disagree'.

The attitude statements in the list were chosen to ensure that they are measuring aspects of the one underlying attitude. Extensive exploratory research was conducted, which involved a review of the literature on citizenship and education and attendance at conferences as well as a series of in-depth interviews with experts, opinion leaders and those in the target population. The survey questionnaire was pilot tested.

Reading the attitude statements you will see that some take a positive view (in favour) of teaching citizenship and others take a negative view (against it). Each response has a code assigned to it on the questionnaire, from 1 for 'Strongly agree' to 5 for 'Strongly disagree', regardless of whether it is positive or negative. At the data processing stage these codes are transformed into scores, so it will be important that on the data processing specification the list of statements is scored consistently, with, say, a high score denoting a favourable attitude and a low score a less favourable attitude. Once the scores have been assigned consistently across the statement list a total score can be calculated for each respondent across all the statements. This is the respondent's score on the *attitude scale*. It is a summary measure of the respondent's attitude to citizenship education, as measured across the list of attitude statements.

Building the scale

Say for this example that we score the favourable attitude statements from 5 = Strongly agree to 1 = Strongly disagree and the unfavourable attitudes 5 = Strongly disagree to 1 = Strongly agree. The possible range of scores on this attitude scale, excluding Don't knows, ranges from 10 (a score of 1 on each of the ten statements) to 50 (a score of 5 on each of the ten statements): these are the extremes of the scale. This type of scale is known as a linear scale. A score of 11 or 45, for example, means little except to indicate that those scoring 45 are at the more 'favourable to citizenship education' end of the scale and those with a score of 11 are at the less favourable end. The respondent's score on the attitude scale indicates the strength of their attitude to the particular subject or variable, in this case 'citizenship education' in schools. But the scores are more meaningful, and more useful, when used to compare the responses of different groups. For example, we might want to examine differences in attitude according to social class or – particularly relevant to Northern Ireland – religion (asked at Q. 22 on the survey). To compare attitudes we could, for example, work out the mean score for the Protestant respondents in the sample, the mean scores for the Catholic respondents and the mean score for other groups, such as

Box 9.2 Example: an attitude question from the Life and Times 1999 Survey

Q. 17 There has been a lot of talk recently about teaching 'Citizenship' in secondary and grammar schools in Northern Ireland. This could include classroom discussions on things like *politics and human rights in Northern Ireland.* Some people are against the idea of teaching this in schools while others are very much in favour.

How much do you agree or disagree with the following statements? SHOW CARD

	Strongly agree	Agree	Neither agree nor disagree	Disagree	Strongly disagree	(Don't know)
It isn't the *job* of schools to teach children about politics and human rights	1	2	3	4	5	8
It's about time schools started to openly tackle such difficult issues	1	2	3	4	5	8
Teaching children about politics and human rights at school is just trying to brainwash them	1	2	3	4	5	8
I doubt whether the people teaching this kind of thing would do it fairly	1	2	3	4	5	8
Our children will never be effective members of society unless we allow them to learn about human rights and politics when they are young	1	2	3	4	5	8
Schools should be a place where children are able to get away from the political problems of Northern Ireland	1	2	3	4	5	8
Teaching about human rights and politics at school will help young people become active members of their own communities	1	2	3	4	5	8
Teaching about human rights and politics at school runs the risk of encouraging children toward extreme political views	1	2	3	4	5	8
Discussions about politics and human rights will help children understand why other traditions in Northern Ireland feel hard done by	1	2	3	4	5	8
Discussions about politics and human rights at school will be too painful for a lot of children who have personally suffered during the Troubles	1	2	3	4	5	8

Source: The Life and Times Survey 1999. Used with permission.

those with no religion. We might find that these mean scores are different and conclude that one group is more positive about education for citizenship than the other; or we might find that the mean scores on the scale are the same, indicating that attitudes to citizenship education may not be dependent on the respondents' religion.

■ Other scales

The example above is an example of a linear scaling technique. As you have seen, it can be time consuming (and therefore expensive) to construct, and so may not suit every situation. Here we look briefly at two other types of scale: a semantic differential scale and a rank order scale.

Semantic differentials

The semantic differential (Osgood *et al.*, 1957) is a seven-point bi-polar rating scale (although some use a ten-point scale) with the extremes of the scale denoted by adjectives that are opposite in meaning. For example, a semantic differential might be strong and weak, or masculine and feminine, or active and passive, or rich and poor. A scale appropriate to the objects being assessed is developed and the respondent is asked to rate a series of objects (brands, for example) using the scale. Work by Osgood *et al.* (1957) shows the semantic differential to be a valid and reliable measure. It is important, though, that the elements of the scale are carefully chosen. Pilot work (a review of secondary research, qualitative exploration and quantitative testing to determine relevant factors) is extremely useful in this regard. It is also important to ensure that the adjectives used to describe the ends of the scale really are opposites. The statements should be rotated or randomised in some way to avoid order bias. The ratings for each object can be averaged across the sample and can be used to compare the perceptions held by different types of respondent to a particular object – a brand or service or organisation, its image or its attributes, for example.

Box 9.3 Examples of semantic differentials

Please tick one box for each scale

Very trustworthy							Not at all trustworthy
Modern							Old-fashioned
Unfriendly							Friendly
Reliable							Not reliable

Ranking

We can also measure opinion or attitudes to an object by asking respondents to rank a set of attitudes or opinions relevant to the object. For example we might ask, 'What, in your opinion, are the most important causes of homelessness among men in London? Please choose the five causes which in your view are the most important and number them from 1 to 5, where 1 = the most important.' Or, 'Which of these companies, in your opinion, produces the best quality products? Please choose no more than five companies and number them 1 to 5, in order of quality.' By ranking, we get an idea of the way in which a person evaluates an object on a set of criteria. One important thing to bear in mind about ranking is that we cannot say anything about the distance or intervals between the rankings. In effect, we are creating an ordinal scale and we cannot make the assumption that the distance between the intervals on the scale is equal (unlike the linear scale, in which we do assume that they are equal). For example, in rating the quality of products, it may be that first place company C rates a long way ahead of second place company A but that company B is a very close third to company A. In constructing a ranking question we must take care to ensure that the instructions are clear and unambiguous, so the respondent is clear about the basis on which to compile the ranking, and the list of items to be ranked should be limited to about ten – any more makes the task difficult to manage, for the respondent and the researcher. In addition, the criteria on which we ask respondents to rate an object must be meaningful. For completeness, it is important to include 'Other' and 'Don't know' categories in the list of criteria. As with the scores on the semantic differential, we can average the rank scores across the sample, and we can count how many first place rankings a particular criterion received, how many second place and so on, for each criterion.

Paired comparisons

Paired comparisons are a form of ranking – the respondent is presented with two objects and asked to choose between them. This approach is used in product testing, when the respondent is asked, for example, to choose between two products on the basis of taste or appearance. To get a rank order measurement from a series of objects, say a group of six products, we must present each pair combination to the respondent. This can make the use of paired comparisons for creating rank order scales unwieldy – with six items there are 15 pairs $[0.5 \times N(N - 1)]$; with eight items there are 28 pairs; with ten items there are 45 pairs and so on.

In designing any rating scale the guidelines that pertain to question wording (see Chapter 10) should be followed. Particular attention should be paid to the wording of instructions, to ensure that they are clear and easy to follow. Relevant information should be given as to the context of the required rating (for example thinking about how you use this product) and the aim of the rating scale. The rating criteria or attitude statements, the elements of the scale, should be relevant to the object being rated, should mean the same thing to all respondents and should be within the respondent's frame of reference. The response categories should be relevant to the purpose of the question – a Likert format, a semantic differential or a rank order, for example. A decision also needs to be made about the number of steps in the scale, which can vary from three to ten, and you must also decide whether or not there should be a midpoint – a neutral, 'neither/nor' category.

■ Problems with scales

You need to be aware of the 'error of central tendency' – the tendency for respondents to avoid using the extreme of the scales. This can be counteracted to some extent by ensuring that the extremes do not appear too extreme, or by combining the two (or three, depending on the number of steps in the scale) top categories at each end of the scale at the data processing stage.

Another common problem with rating scales is the 'halo effect': in responding to items on a scale a respondent's like or dislike for the object being rated may influence his or her response to each item on the scale. This may be overcome to some degree by designing the questionnaire so that the rating scales are spaced apart. Another manifestation of the halo effect is a sort of automatic response syndrome, which can occur if the scale is laid in such a way that all the positive scores line up on one side of the page and all the negative ones line up on the other, or if all the statements or items in the scale are positive or all of them are negative. If the respondent notices this pattern, he or she may be tempted to reply automatically, without really thinking about the answer. The solution is to include in the list positive and negative statements, and, if using a semantic differential scale, to make sure that the positive ends of the scale are not on the same side.

Another common problem is the problem of logical error. This type of error occurs when the respondent gives a similar rating to an object on attributes or attitudes that he or she thinks are somehow related. A way of overcoming this is to ensure that such attributes or attitudes do not occur close together on the rating scale.

■ Grids

If you want to understand how respondents describe or evaluate a product, service or brand – useful in understanding how the consumer perceives the market or the brand, and what effect marketing activity has on the perception of brands, for example – rating products or services against a set of criteria can be useful. An association grid, which allows the respondent to choose which statements he or she associates with particular brands, is a useful way of collecting a lot of information quickly and allows scope for analysing the data in a variety of ways, from calculating the proportion of the sample who associate a particular statement with a brand or product, through comparisons of the profiles of each brand across all the statements to more complex multivariate mapping techniques.

To measure the 'attitude' towards an object, a product or service, for example, the first step – as with the attitude scale – is to develop a set of evaluative or descriptive statements designed to reflect attitudes or beliefs about the object. Descriptive attitude statements can relate to particular properties of a product, service or brand, perhaps those that have been emphasised in marketing or advertising activity. Evaluative attitude statements relate to more opinion- or attitude-based characteristics, such as 'reliable', 'good quality', 'suitable for children'. Research has shown (Bird and Ehrenberg, 1970) that evaluative measures discriminate more effectively between users and non-users of a brand than do general descriptive measures, which may be worth bearing in mind.

Before choosing the statements it is therefore important to be clear about what it is you are measuring and the purpose to which the findings will be put. Are you collecting information on attitudes and beliefs – asking respondents to evaluate a list of products or brands – in order to see how people distinguish between different products, services or brands? Or are you collecting information on attitudes and beliefs in order to determine preference, or likely choice when it comes to buying or using the products, services or brands? Or both? The end use of the data should determine the choice of criteria: the thing to remember here is that those statements that distinguish between products may not necessarily be the same as those that are used to make preference or purchase decisions or those that underlie an attitude (Bird and Ehrenberg, 1970). What is important to remember in using this approach is to determine the relevant or salient beliefs about or characteristics of a product, service or brand or list of brands. If you are assessing a range of brands it is important to include attitudes and beliefs that are salient to each of the brands. Using salient beliefs will help you write much better attitude and belief statements and will give you a more sensitive understanding of the market. One way of obtaining a list of salient attitudes and beliefs is to get respondents in the target market to list (without prompting) the characteristics or attributes of a service, product or brand and their opinions of it, and to use these to develop a set of evaluative or descriptive statements (a list of 10 or 12 is manageable). Remember, in designing the statements and the questions, be specific, and put them in context.

Box 9.4 Example of a grid

	Brand L	Brand M	Brand N	Brand O	Brand P
Pleasant tasting	1	1	1	1	1
Makes you drowsy	2	2	2	2	2
Quick to take effect	3	3	3	3	3
Easy to take	4	4	4	4	4
Suitable to use throughout the day	5	5	5	5	5
Treats all the symptoms of a cold	6	6	6	6	6
Effective	7	7	7	7	7

Quantitative methods are particularly suitable for collecting data on attitudes when a less detailed understanding is required. If the measures used are grounded in solid qualitative work it is likely that they will be reasonably valid measures; if well designed they can produce reliable (repeatable and consistent) measures, which can be used in statistical analysis (in cluster and factor analysis, for example). In the course of developing attitude questions, however, there is a tendency to oversimplify and so risk losing much of the richness and detail and even some of the understanding of the nature of the attitude. Using scales and rankings can mislead us into thinking that attitudes fall on a continuum, with positive at one end and negative at the other, which may not be a useful or valid way of thinking about attitudes at all.

■ Using qualitative techniques

No matter how reliable or valid you endeavour to make quantitative attitude questions, detail, richness and complexity are sacrificed for sparseness and simplicity. If this detail, richness and complexity is important to fulfilling the aims of the research you may not want to sacrifice it; at the very least you may want to ensure that the sparse and simple quantitative questions are grounded in the detail. Thus a qualitative exploration of the attitudes is a useful precursor to any quantitative study. The detail, and the more in-depth understanding, is, however, gained (some will argue) at the expense of reliability – in terms of repeatability and consistency of the technique used and the results achieved. Nevertheless a qualitative approach is often the only way of uncovering or understanding attitudes that respondents may not be able or willing to articulate via direct questioning, or those that relate to sensitive topics or to socially desirable and undesirable attitudes. Such research can provide not only an understanding of the content of attitudes but the intensity with which they are held, the nature of the related elements – beliefs, feelings, intentions to act – the context in which they are held, or in which they might be acted upon, and the language used to describe them. This is useful information in itself, which can also be used to design effective quantitative attitude measures.

Interviewing people via group discussions can be a useful way of exploring the range of attitudes that might exist in that group. However, a respondent may want to present himself or herself in a favourable light to the moderator and to others in the group, which means that the group format may be limited in its usefulness if you need to get beyond the expression of socially acceptable attitudes and beliefs. Interviewing people individually should remove this peer group pressure and enable you to get beyond the socially acceptable, and it also enables you to explore attitudes and beliefs that may be of a more personal and sensitive nature. Even in a depth interview, however, it can be difficult to uncover or understand more deep-rooted attitudes. Using projective techniques – including association, completion, construction, expressive and choice ordering techniques – can help here. Projective techniques can be used to overcome the barriers (Oppenheim, 2000) of:

➢ awareness;
➢ irrationality;
➢ inadmissbility;
➢ self-incrimination;
➢ politeness.

There is some concern about the ability of projective techniques to produce valid and reliable findings: some believe that they are too subjective, both in terms of how the respondent uses them and in how the researcher uses and interprets them. To help overcome these concerns you should be clear about the purpose to which you put the projective technique – the technique should be chosen to suit the research objectives; and you or the researcher using them should be skilled in their use, not only in the choice of technique but in when and how to introduce it, how to apply it and how to interpret the results.

Box 9.5 Use of qualitative techniques in attitude research

A qualitative investigation is useful in order to achieve the following:

- ➤ understand the wider context of the attitude;
- ➤ determine the interconnectedness and dependencies of needs, wants, motivations, intentions, feelings, attitudes, values, culture, behaviour;
- ➤ explore deep-rooted attitudes;
- ➤ understand how people conceptualise the attitude;
- ➤ generate the language needed to design statements for quantitative research;
- ➤ determine the conceptual and perceptual frameworks and perceptual and cognitive maps of individuals.

Ultimately the choice of technique depends on the objectives of the research. If the objective of the research is to generate an in-depth understanding of particular attitudes, and their links with a person's needs, wants and motivations and with their values, beliefs and culture, a qualitative approach is recommended. A quantitative approach is appropriate if we want to measure the prevalence of the attitude and the range of attitudes in the population, and to understand how the attitudes people hold relate to other characteristics.

Chapter summary

- ➤ Attitudes are of interest to social and market researchers for their own sake and for the way in which they relate to motivation, intention and behaviour.

- ➤ Definitions vary but there is general agreement that holding an attitude about something means that we are predisposed or likely to respond in a particular way when we encounter the object and/or the circumstances related to that attitude. At the same time it is recognised that there is no automatic link between holding an attitude to an object and taking action in relation to it. A range of intervening factors may affect both the attitude and the behaviour.

- ➤ Attitudes are difficult to research in a way that achieves validity and reliability – they are complex, multi-faceted and may be dependent on particular circumstances; we may be unaware that we hold them and we may find it hard, or be unwilling, to articulate them.

➤ Capturing an attitude is almost impossible using one question or one statement: it is unlikely that we will be able to capture the complexity of it, so it will lack validity; and it is unlikely that one question or statement will deliver consistent results – respondents tend to be more sensitive to the wording and the context of attitudinal questions compared to factual questions – so it will lack reliability.

➤ The validity and reliability of attitude measurement can be improved by using banks of questions or 'attitude statements' combined in an attitude scale. Validity may be improved if the question, the statements and the response sets used are designed to encompass the complexity of the attitude, and the context of it. Reliability may be improved because issues of question wording and context may be cancelled out across the range of statements.

➤ Designing questions to measure attitudes quantitatively consists of two parts: designing and choosing the list of attitude statements or the 'item pool' for the particular attitude variable; and choosing the response format. The most common approaches include linear scaling techniques, semantic differential scales and rank order scales.

➤ Be aware of the sources of error in the design of scales – the error of central tendency, the 'halo effect', automatic response syndrome and the problem of logical error – and take steps to overcome them.

➤ An association grid allows respondents to choose which statements they associate with particular brands and is a useful way of collecting information quickly. It allows scope for analysing the data in a variety of ways, from calculating the proportion of the sample who associate a particular statement with a brand or product to comparisons of the profiles of each brand across all the statements to more complex multivariate mapping techniques.

➤ Qualitative techniques are used to explore and understand attitudes in greater detail than is possible using quantitative techniques. Qualitative research can provide not only an understanding of the content of attitudes but the intensity with which they are held, the nature of the related elements – beliefs, feelings, intentions to act – the context in which they are held, or in which they might be acted upon, and the language used to describe them. This is useful information in itself and useful for designing effective quantitative measures.

➤ The detail and the more in-depth understanding is, however, gained (some argue) at the expense of reliability – in terms of repeatability and consistency of the technique used and the results achieved.

Questions and exercises

1 What is an attitude?

2 Describe the link between needs, wants and motivation. How are these concepts related to attitudes? How are attitudes related to behaviour?

3 What influences the development of attitudes?

4 Why is qualitative research important in the study of attitudes?

5 What qualitative research techniques are used to explore and analyse attitudes?

6 Why is a single question an unsuitable way of measuring an attitude?

7 Describe how you would develop a list of attitude statements for use in a quantitative survey.

8 What is a Likert Scale?

9 What is a semantic differential?

10 What are the limitations of using: (a) quantitative research and (b) qualitative research to gather data on attitudes?

References

Bird, M. and Ehrenberg, A. (1970) 'Consumer attitudes and brand usage', *Journal of the Market Research Society*, **12**, 3, pp. 233–47.

Oppenheim, A. (2000) *Questionnaire Design, Interviewing and Attitude Measurement*, London: Continuum.

Osgood, C., Suci, G. and Tannebaum, R. (1957) *The Measurement of Meaning*, Urbana, IL.: University of Illinois Press.

Sampson, P. (1980) 'The technical revolution of the 1970s: will it happen in the 1980s?', *Journal of the Market Research Society*, **22**, 3, pp. 161–78.

Recommended reading

Ajzen, I. and Fishbein, M. (1980) *Understanding Attitudes and Predicting Social Behaviour*, New Jersey: Prentice-Hall. An account of the theory of reasoned action and its application to the measurement of attitudes. Also includes a history of attitude research.

Bird, M. and Ehrenberg, A. (1970) 'Consumer attitudes and brand usage', *Journal of the Market Research Society* **12**, 3, pp. 233–47. An account of the design and use of brand image and brand attitude statements.

Madden, M.J., Ellen, P.S. and Ajzen, I. (1992) A comparison of the theory of planned behavior and the theory of reasoned action, *Personality and Social Psychology Bulletin*, 18(1), pp. 3–9. An account of the theory of planned behaviour and the theory of reasoned action.

Oppenheim, A. (2000) *Questionnaire Design, Interviewing and Attitude Measurement*, London: Continuum. A comprehensive account of the design of attitude statements and scales and the use of projective techniques.

Tuck, M. (1976) *How People Choose*, London: Methuen. An account of why attitudes are of interest.

Chapter 10

Designing questionnaires

Introduction

The purpose of this chapter is to introduce the principles of questionnaire design. We look at why questionnaire design is important; we examine the process of planning a questionnaire and address specific issues that relate to different types of questionnaire and data collection method; and finally we look briefly at the concepts of validity and reliability in the context of questionnaire design.

It is useful to consider what we mean by the term *questionnaire*, as its use varies. Some, in particular those involved in social research, use the term *questionnaire* to describe the self-completion format used in postal, web and email surveys. The structured and semi-structured data collection instruments used in interviewer-administered surveys, those conducted face to face or by telephone, they refer to as *interview schedules*. In market research, however, the term *questionnaire* is generally used to describe any *data collection instrument* used in quantitative research or at the recruitment stage of qualitative research, regardless of whether it is self-completion or interviewer administered. This wider definition is the one that will be used here. Decisions about content, structure, wording, order of questions and layout are important to the design of both formats, self-completion and interviewer administered. Many of these issues are also important for the design of *interview guides* or *discussion guides*, the less structured data collection instruments used in qualitative research. So, although the main focus of this chapter is the design of questionnaires, the issues raised and the processes discussed should also be useful to those designing guides for qualitative data collection.

Topics covered

➢ The importance of good design
➢ The questionnaire design process
➢ Question content
➢ Question wording
➢ Question order
➢ Layout and appearance
➢ Questionnaire length
➢ Pilot testing

The material in this chapter is relevant to Unit 6 – Questionnaire Construction, specifically the following:

➢ overall approach to questionnaire construction;
➢ principles of questionnaire construction;
➢ suitability of questionnaire design for data collection method and data processing;
➢ pilot testing.

Learning outcomes

At the end of this chapter you should be able to:

➢ understand the principles of questionnaire design;
➢ develop an instrument for the collection of valid and reliable data.

The importance of good design

Good design matters. Quite simply, effective research and quality data depend on it. This means that not only should it be effective in addressing the research objectives – collecting valid and reliable data to address the research problem clearly and unambiguously – but it should also be suited to the practical tasks of data collection and data processing and analysis. The questionnaire has a huge role to play in helping the interviewer gather and record data accurately and effectively, and in helping the respondent provide accurate, complete and reliable data. It must be a workable, user-friendly tool for the interviewer, the respondent and the data analyst. It also has a role to play in representing research, and the research industry, to the wider world.

■ Questionnaire design and data quality

There are many ways in which error can creep into the research process; a poorly designed questionnaire can open the floodgates to it. Here are some of the ways in which this can happen and the sort of problems that arise as a result:

➢ A poorly designed questionnaire can result in an unpleasant experience for the respondent and a poor perception of research and the research industry, which can in turn lead to an unwillingness to take part in future research.
➢ A poor introduction or presentation of the research can lead to high levels of non-response and problems with representativeness of the sample.
➢ Poorly conceived questions not measuring what they claim to measure mean the data collected are not valid.
➢ Unsuitable or irrelevant content – questions that lie outside the respondent's frame of reference, or which relate to subjects about which he or she has little or no knowledge, or which rely too heavily on the respondent's memory to provide accurate answers, will produce inaccurate and unreliable data.

➤ Poorly worded questions (using ambiguous, vague, difficult, unusual or technical language) can be misunderstood, misinterpreted or interpreted differently by different people and will lead to unreliable and invalid data.

➤ A badly structured questionnaire (difficult, sensitive or personal questions appearing too early, before sufficient rapport has been established) can result in refusals to answer or complete the questionnaire.

➤ Poor question order may result in order bias, or contamination of later responses by earlier questions.

➤ Long, boring or repetitive questions may result in a loss of interest in answering or produce inaccurate responses.

➤ A questionnaire that is too long can lead to respondent fatigue, loss of interest and thus poor quality data; too short and it may mean that there is no time to build rapport.

➤ Inadequate or poorly written interviewer or respondent instructions can result in response and recording errors.

➤ Poor layout can lead to errors in recording and data processing.

Box 10.1 Validity and reliability

A way of understanding what these concepts mean is to think about the measurement of temperature (Kirk and Miller, 1986). We have two thermometers: we put the first thermometer into boiling water and each time it reads 82°C – it gives a reliable measurement (it is consistent) but not a valid one (it is not measuring the true temperature of the water); each time we place the second thermometer into the boiling water the readings vary around 100°C – this thermometer gives a valid measurement but an unreliable one (each time we get a different value).

Validity

We looked at the concept of internal and external validity in Chapter 4, in the context of research design. Internal validity is also an important concept in questionnaire design. In this context it refers to the ability of the specific measures or questions used in the research to measure what they claim to measure. There are three types of this 'measurement' validity:

➤ *Construct validity* is about what the question is measuring. It has to do with how it was constructed. Why did we choose to build the question in that way? On what concept is it based?

➤ *Content validity* is about the suitability of the question to measure the concept that it claims to measure. It is more subjective than construct validity.

➤ *Criterion validity* is about how well a new measure or question works in comparison to a well-established one, or how well a question works in relation to other questions that are considered meaningful measures of the characteristic or attitude being studied.

Reliability

Reliability refers to the consistency of research results. If we repeat the research, or if different interviewers undertake the fieldwork, will we get the same results? Perfect reliability

Box 10.1 continued

relies upon the same conditions pertaining each time we repeat the research, which is, of course, very unlikely in real-world situations (we have to accept as reliable results that vary within certain limits). In designing questions and putting together a questionnaire, and briefing and training interviewers in how to administer it, it is important to bear in mind that we are aiming for reliable data. There are several methods for assessing the reliability of questions – the 'test/retest' method, the alternative forms method and the split-half method:

➤ The *test/retest* method – since reliability is about the extent to which a question will produce the same result when repeated under the same conditions, one way of ensuring it is reliable is to test it and then retest it on the same subjects in the same way. There are a number of difficulties with this approach (associated with the fact that the retest is not independent of the original test) that cloud the issue of reliability. There are problems associated with the following:

➤ reassembling the same sample and creating the same conditions – for example, in the time between the test and the retest something may have occurred that leads respondents to change their views;

➤ asking the same questions of the same respondents on more than one occasion; respondents may have lost interest, with the result that their responses differ, or they may recall their answers from the original test and repeat them exactly.

➤ In the *alternative forms method* two different but *equivalent* versions of a question are administered simultaneously to the same people. Responses are examined to determine if the two measures are correlated. A high correlation would show that the two measures are measuring the same thing. Designing an equivalent question, however, is difficult, and so we have the problem of understanding how much of the difference between the two is due to unreliability or to the differences between them.

➤ The *split-half method*, a type of alternative forms test, is the most widely used test of reliability. It does not assess stability of a question over time, as does the test/retest method, but rather it assesses the internal consistency of the research. It involves splitting the sample into two matched halves and applying the alternative measures to each half. The results from each are checked using a correlation technique.

■ Questionnaire design and the respondent

Interviewing is a social process. Regardless of how structured the questionnaire or the interview format, the interviewer and the respondent interact. Even with a self-completion questionnaire there is an interaction, albeit with an invisible researcher. The interview is a sort of conversation, one in which the respondent is a willing, interested and able participant. The questionnaire should facilitate this process, not get in the way of it. In designing the questionnaire you therefore need to think about how to begin this conversation, what words to use, what order to present the questions in and how to bring it to a close. Some examples of introductions are given in Box 10.2 (your own organisation or your client may have a standard introduction that is modified to suit each project). We look at question wording and question order and how to bring the interview to a close later in the chapter.

Box 10.2 **The importance of a good introduction**

A good introduction is crucial to getting and maintaining the respondent's participation. It sets the tone of the interview. It should set out clearly the nature of the research, the topic or topics under investigation and the time needed to complete it. It is important that the introduction mentions these things not only for the dynamics of the interview but in order to establish informed consent, one of the key ethical principles in research practice. The introduction in a telephone interview in these days of call centres and tele-marketing is even more important in gaining the respondent's co-operation. It should mention why the respondent was chosen for the research and how the respondent's telephone details were obtained. In all types of interview the respondent should be assured of the bona fides (good faith) of the interviewer and the research organisation, and of the confidentiality of the information he or she supplies. The interviewer should inform the respondent that he or she can refuse to answer any question or withdraw from the interview at any time and, if he or she wishes it, that all or part of the information they give will be destroyed at once. (Chapter 15, Ethics and the practice of research, deals with these issues in more detail.)

Introduction to a telephone survey among a business sample

'Good morning/afternoon. My name is [name] from XYZ Research – we are one of the leading research companies in Europe. We are conducting research on [topic]. The research has been commissioned by ABC Services, who plan to publish a report on the findings. As an organisation involved in this field, we are interested in talking to you. We obtained your details from [source]. The interview will last about 20 minutes. The answers you give me will be treated in strictest confidence; your name or the name of your organisation will *not* be disclosed. When the research is finished we will send you a copy of the published report.'

▪ Questionnaire design and the perception of research

The questionnaire is at the front line of research – it is what the general public understands research, particularly market research, to be about. The questionnaire and the interviewer who administers it are ambassadors for the research industry. An interviewer should never be in the position of having to administer (nor a respondent to answer) a poorly designed questionnaire. With declining response rates, the onus is more than ever on the researcher to prepare a questionnaire (or discussion guide) that is clear and easy to understand and easy to administer or fill in. It should cover issues that are relevant to the respondent and it should be designed to maintain the respondent's interest throughout. The task of completing the questionnaire should not be burdensome to the respondent in any way, either in terms of the time needed or the difficulty or sensitivity of the topics covered.

The research experience should serve to bolster the credibility of the research industry and the high standards and professionalism it espouses. Effective questionnaire design can help to ensure that we do not 'spoil the field' for future research.

Box 10.3 The contribution of good design

To data quality

➤ Delivering valid and reliable data
➤ Minimising non-response – encouraging and maintaining participation
➤ Minimising error – question error, response and recording error, and data processing error.

To the interviewer's task

➤ Making the task as straightforward as possible
➤ Minimising questioning and recording errors.

To the respondent's experience

➤ Getting and maintaining interest in and willingness to participate
➤ Making it an enjoyable experience
➤ Making it as easy as possible.

The analyst's task

➤ Making data processing and analysis accurate and efficient.

To the perception of research

➤ Raising the profile of research
➤ Enhancing the professionalism and credibility of research
➤ Increasing the goodwill of the general public towards research.

The questionnaire design process

Questionnaire design follows on from a thorough and rigorous examination of the research problem and a clear understanding of the nature of the evidence needed to address it. Decisions about question content, wording and order are the end result of a process that considers the following:

➤ *What is the research problem?*
   ➤ Background to the problem
   ➤ Definition of the problem
   ➤ Research objectives
   ➤ Use to which data will be put.

➤ *What type(s) of evidence is needed to address it?*
   ➤ Exploratory
   ➤ Descriptive
   ➤ Causal or explanatory.

➤ *What ideas, concepts, variables are we measuring?*
   ➤ Content
   ➤ Definitions and indicators.

➤ *What type(s) of data is appropriate?*
   ➤ Qualitative
   ➤ Quantitative.

➤ *From whom are we collecting the data?*
   ➤ Nature of the target population or sample.

➤ *What method of data collection is most suitable?*
   ➤ Observation
   ➤ Interviews
   ➤ Interviewer administered or self-completion
   ➤ Face to face or telephone; email, web or postal.

➤ *Where will the data be collected?*
   ➤ In the street/shopping centre
   ➤ At respondent's home
   ➤ At respondent's place of work.

➤ *How will responses be captured?*
   ➤ Pen and paper
   ➤ Computer
   ➤ Audio- and/or video-recording.

➤ *What are the constraints?*
   ➤ Time
   ➤ Budget.

➤ *How will the responses be analysed?*
   ➤ Computer
   ➤ Manually.

➤ *How will we ask the questions?*

■ Overview of the process

The aim of the questionnaire design process is to convert the research objectives into meaningful questions and assemble the questions into an effective and workable questionnaire. There are several stages:

➤ clarifying what it is exactly that you need the questions to measure;
➤ wording the questions;
➤ deciding on the types of question and the response format;
➤ putting the questions into an effective and logical order;
➤ designing the layout;
➤ testing out a draft version;
➤ revising the draft and agreeing a final version.

Question content

The purpose of a questionnaire is to collect data – valid and reliable data that can be used to address the research problem. The first task in designing a questionnaire or discussion guide therefore is to clarify the research objectives – the information requirements – and agree what exactly it is that the questions need to measure.

If the research objectives are not clear it is important to spend time clarifying them. You cannot design an effective questionnaire without being crystal clear about exactly what information it has to deliver. Some exploratory research may be needed to understand the subject area from the point of view of the target population (often different from how the researcher or the client might see it) and to uncover the language used to talk about the issues. This exploratory work might involve a review of secondary data sources (previous research on the topic, for example) and/or formal or informal qualitative research. The nature of the exploratory phase, and the extent of it, will depend on the topic and your familiarity with it and the time and resources available.

■ Standard questions

As well as questions that relate directly to the research objectives, you will almost certainly need questions to determine eligibility to take part in the survey and the characteristics or circumstances of those who do. In a consumer or social survey these classification questions might include questions on age, marital status, working status, social class, total household income, housing tenure and so on. In a business-to-business survey they might include questions on type of organisation, job title, number of employees and so on. In addition, in consumer surveys in particular, you might also have questions on awareness (of products, services, brands, advertising), buying behaviour, usage and satisfaction, for example. For these commonly asked questions there is often a standard format and so no need to design them anew each time. Using standard or consistent questions not only makes questionnaire preparation easier (and, since these questions are tried and tested, more effective) but it is essential to use a standard format should you wish to compare responses to these questions across surveys conducted in different time periods, or even on different topics. It is also essential should you wish to combine or fuse data from different surveys. Research and client organisations may have their own 'standard' versions – check before designing your own. Some examples are given in Box 10.4. Q. 6 is to determine working status: the interviewer asks the question, showing the respondent a prompt or 'show card' on which possible responses are listed. Standard versions of a range of demographic questions used in government surveys have been developed by experts at the UK's Office of National Statistics. They can be inspected at its website (**www.statistics.gov.uk**).

Screening and eligibility questions

It may be that, for reasons of client confidentiality or because you believe that certain groups of people may not be typical or representative of the target group, you want to exclude those involved in a similar or related area to that being studied. For example,

Box 10.4 Examples of standard questions

Marital status

Q. 4 Marital status **CODE FIRST TO APPLY**

Single (never married)	1
Married	2
Living as married	3
Separated	4
Divorced	5
Widowed	6

Working status

Q. 6 Which of these descriptions applies to what you were doing last week, that is in the seven days ending last Sunday? **SHOW CARD**

IF ON HOLIDAY OR TEMPORARILY SICK ASK WHAT THEY ARE USUALLY DOING

Working part time	1	
Not working (seeking work)	2	Go to Q.6a
On a Government Training Scheme	3	
On ACE (Action for Community Employment)	4	
Retired	5	
Working full time	6	
In full-time education	7	Go to Q.7
Looking after the home	8	
Permanently sick or disabled	9	
Not working (and not seeking work)	10	
Caring for elderly or disabled person full time	11	
Other (Write in)	12	

Q. 6a How many hours a week do you normally work in your job?

Source: The Life and Times Survey 2001. Used with permission.

Box 10.4 continued

Awareness, purchase and usage

Q. 2   Which of these brand of X [**SHOW CARD**], if any, have you ever heard of?

Q. 3a Thinking about the last time you bought [product], which brand did you buy?

Q. 3b Which brand or brands do you buy most often?

Q. 4   Next time you need [product] how likely or unlikely are you to buy brand X?

Definitely will	1
Probably will	2
Might or might not	3
Probably will not	4
Definitely will not	5
Don't know	8

in an advertising pre-test for a hair shampoo, you may want to exclude those who work in the hair care or beauty products industry as well as those who work in marketing, advertising, public relations or journalism. You may also need a series of questions to determine if the person contacted is eligible to take part in the research. For example, if you need to interview representatives of organisations whose customers are primarily the general public (the consumer market) rather than other businesses (the business-to-business market), you will need to include a question to establish this. Some examples are given in Box 10.5.

Box 10.5 Examples of screening and eligibility questions

Q. A. Do you or anyone in your household work in any of these occupations? **SHOW CARD**

Market research	1	
Advertising	2	
Journalism	3	**CLOSE**
Public relations	4	
Marketing	5	
Petrol or oil company	6	
Motorists' shop or garage	7	
None of these	8	**CONTINUE**

Box 10.5 continued

Q. 1 I am working on a survey among motorists. Do you have a current driving licence for a car?

Yes	1	CONTINUE
No	2	CLOSE

Q. 2 Is there a car in your household that is available for you to drive?

Yes	1	CONTINUE
No	2	CLOSE

Designing questions for some topics may seem to be, or may even be, fairly straight-forward. The topic might be familiar, or you might be using standard or tried and tested questions from previous studies. There are, however, some things that are more difficult to measure, and many things that are more difficult than they at first appear. In such cases much work is needed to clarify the meaning and define clearly what is to be measured so that there is no ambiguity about what the question you design is measuring (and how the response to it is interpreted).

■ Clarifying the meaning: concepts, definitions and indicators

Being clear about what is being measured (the concept or the variable) means agreeing a definition of the concept or variable. This should happen before the questionnaire design process begins so that it is clear what the question needs to measure. For example, think about something simple such as the age of the respondent – are you measuring the respondent's age at the time of the interview or his or her age at last birthday? Take another example, the housing status of the respondent. Do you want to know the respondent's housing type, that is whether the type of dwelling he or she lives in is a detached house or an apartment, for example; or do you want to know his or her housing tenure, that is whether the house is owned (on a mortgage or outright) or rented (from a local authority, a housing association or a private landlord)?

Box 10.6 Cultural barriers and the harmonisation of research data

Graham Mytton, BBC World Service

Terms like 'household', 'occupation' and the demographic indicators of education, social class and income level are a problem to define in a way which can be compared across cultures. In Northern Nigeria, for example, where people can live in large extended family compounds, what does 'household' mean? If such a compound or *gida* is to be defined as a household it will be an important factor in making comparisons with household data from elsewhere where households may be defined differently. Different interpretations of

Box 10.6 continued

some words used in questionnaires can be problematic. Precise terms may not be understood in the same way. Even periods of time such as a week, a month or a year may have different lengths. The day may begin not at midnight, but at dawn or dusk. Collecting data on age can be a major problem. The practice of knowing one's birthday, or even birth year, is certainly not universal. One way is to try to work out the person's age by finding out events which happened at key times in the respondent's life. Can he or she remember independence or the start of the civil war or certain floods, volcanic eruptions or other events? Were these before or after puberty?

Source: adapted from Mytton, G. (1996) 'Research in new fields', *Journal of the Market Research Society* **38**, 1, pp. 19–31. Used with permission.

Concepts and conceptualisation

In some cases it is relatively easy to decide what is to be measured and relatively easy to reach an agreed definition; in other cases it is not so easy. Think, for example, how you might meaningfully measure the incidence of sexism. Before deciding how, you need to define what you mean by the term 'sexism'. You need a nominal or working definition of the fairly abstract concept of sexism and you need to specify a set of more concrete 'indicators' of it. This process of moving from the abstract to the concrete is known as conceptual ordering or conceptualisation.

Definitions

So how do you arrive at a working definition? You could, for example, using formal or informal qualitative research, ask members of the target group what sexism means to them; you could check what definitions others have used (via a search of secondary sources). Whichever method you use, the outcome should be a clear specification of exactly what it is you are going to measure with the question or set of questions you construct and exactly what you mean when you use a particular word or phrase to describe that concept (or variable). The nominal definition of sexism might be something like 'the view that one sex is inherently superior to the other and/or that particular roles or tasks are suited to one sex or the other'.

Indicators

Once you have a clear and agreed definition of the concept the next step is to develop a set of concrete 'indicators' of it. These indicators will be used in designing the question or set of questions to measure the concept. To get from the abstract concept to the concrete indicators of it you may need to think about the 'dimensions' or aspects of the concept. You might decide that really you are interested in the gender stereotyping dimension of sexism (the view that particular roles or tasks are suited to one sex or the other). You might go further and specify that you are interested in gender stereotyping in relation to home or family duties or in relation to work and job roles, or both. In making these sorts of decision you would refer back to the research objectives and the question of why you are interested in measuring the incidence of sexism in the first place. You might be interested in measuring the incidence of gender stereotyping in relation to work in order to design equality awareness courses for employees, for example. So how do you develop indicators of gender stereotyping? Again a review of the relevant literature and/or exploratory qualitative research can be useful. The indicators in relation to work roles might include a view that men are more suited to jobs with a physical aspect, or less suited to jobs involving children. A question from the Life and Times Survey 2000 in Box 10.7 shows the sort of question that you might design based on your indicators.

Box 10.7 A question of roles

Q. 2 For each of these jobs, please say whether you think it is appropriate for men only, for women only or appropriate for both men and women.

	Appropriate for men only	Appropriate for women only	Appropriate for both women and men	Don't know
Childminder	1	2	3	8
Firefighter	1	2	3	8
Primary school teacher	1	2	3	8
Midwife	1	2	3	8
Soldier in 'front line' action	1	2	3	8
Staying at home to look after the children	1	2	3	8
Priest or minister	1	2	3	8
Secretary	1	2	3	8

Source: The Life and Times Survey 2000. Used with permission.

The task does not end with the design of the question. The next step is to think about how to interpret the responses to the question. What pattern of response would indicate or could be interpreted to mean that the respondent tends to gender stereotype? You might first of all make explicit which roles you regard as traditionally male and traditionally female. For example: firefighter, soldier in 'front line' action and priest or minister – male; and childminder, midwife, staying at home to look after the children and secretary – female; and primary school teacher – both. You might then devise a scoring system or scale so that a higher score indicates a stronger tendency to gender stereotype (assigning traditionally male jobs as appropriate to men only and traditionally female jobs to women only) and a lower score indicates a weaker tendency. In reporting on the incidence of gender stereotyping you should make it clear to the audience or reader not only how you defined the concept and how you measured it but also how you analysed and interpreted the data. This is important as you could almost certainly come up with a different set of findings about gender stereotyping if you used a different definition, a different set of indicators and a different way of analysing and interpreting the data.

Box 10.8 Pursuing the meaning

The more structured the enquiry (and the more structured the data collection instrument), the more important it is to be rigorous in pursuit of the meanings we attach to the things we are measuring. In a structured (quantitative) project we design a set of questions that cannot be easily modified in the course of data collection. With a less structured (qualitative) project we may start off with several sets of meanings or dimensions of a concept. The purpose of the research may be to understand the meanings that the respondents place on these, or it may be to refine and define these further, either as an end in itself or for feeding into the next stage of a more structured piece of research. Whatever the purpose, we must start off with clear definitions of the concepts that we are measuring before we can formulate the questions, otherwise the data we get from the questions might be ambiguous at best and meaningless at worst.

Now that we know what we want to measure we have to think about how best to word the questions. We need to turn the concepts and variables we identified into meaningful, objective questions that measure what we want them to measure. In addition, we want to design questions that the respondent is willing and able to answer.

Question wording

What you are trying to achieve in wording a question is to ensure that you get valid and reliable data. To this end, each question should be worded so that the following hold:

➢ it measures what it claims to measure;
➢ it is relevant and meaningful to the respondent;
➢ it is acceptable to the respondent;
➢ the respondent (and the interviewer) understand it;
➢ it is interpreted in the way in which you intended;
➢ it is interpreted in the same way by all respondents;
➢ it elicits an accurate and meaningful response;
➢ the meaning of the response is clear and unambiguous.

Achieving all of this is far more difficult than it might at first appear, even for seemingly simple, straightforward questions, as the two examples in Box 10.9 show.

■ Vaguely worded questions

The examples in Box 10.9 highlight some of the problems that can arise when questions are *vaguely* worded and not specific enough. In seeing the responses to such

Box 10.9 What are you asking me?

Put yourself in the respondent's place. On first hearing or reading the two questions below you might think that they are fairly straightforward (if somewhat intrusive in the case of the first one). But as you start to think about your answer you might wonder, 'What exactly are you asking me?'

Q. How much money do you earn?

➢ What do they mean by 'earn'? Money earned in employment or money earned on investments or from social benefits or a total amount earned regardless of the source? What if I'm not working, say I'm retired or unemployed. Does this mean I have no 'earnings'?

➢ To what time period does this apply? Do they want to know how much I earn in a year, a month, a week? Do they want to know my earnings in the last calendar year, the last financial or tax year or the year up to the date of the interview? Do they want to know earnings before or after tax or other deductions?

Q. Do you have a personal computer?

➢ What do they mean by 'personal computer'? A computer that I personally own? Or are they referring to a type of computer, for example a desktop computer or a laptop or a handheld computer?

➢ What do they mean by 'you'? Me, personally, or the household or family unit in which I live or the organisation for which I work?

➢ What do they mean by 'have'? Do they want to know whether I own a PC or have access to one or the use of one? Do they mean at work or at home?

questions, would you be confident in knowing what it was you had measured? In hearing or reading a question, the respondent must be able to understand precisely what it is you are asking about. To achieve this you may need to provide clear and precise definitions of words or terms. It is usual for the definition to appear first, followed by the question. See the examples in Box 10.10. As well as definitions of terms, you may also need to specify a reference period. You might, for example, want to know whether respondents visit the cinema often, sometimes, rarely or never; whether they visit several times a week, about once a week and so on; or you might want to know the actual number of visits they make on average in a month; or the actual number of visits they made last month. For questions about use or behaviour that occurs frequently, a shorter reference period is usually more suitable; for use or behaviour that happens less frequently, a longer reference period is more appropriate. In asking about usage or behaviour during a particular time period, a week for example, you need to decide whether it is appropriate to ask about 'in the last week' or 'last week', or 'last week, that is, the seven days ending last Sunday'. In deciding on reference periods the degree of precision may depend on the aims of the survey, the type of usage or behaviour you are asking about and what the respondent can be reasonably expected to remember. The question – the definition or description of the topic or terms used, the question itself and the instructions to the interviewer – should be complete so that the interviewer does not have to use his or her own words or interpretation to explain the question to the respondent.

Box 10.10 Examples of definitions and reference periods

Q. And thinking about devolution as a whole – that is the creation of local assemblies in Wales and Northern Ireland and the new parliament in Scotland. Do you think that devolution has *strengthened* the UK as a whole, has it *weakened* it, or has it *made no difference*?

Q. May I just check, thinking back to the **previous** general election – that is the one in 1997 – do you remember which party you voted for then, or perhaps you didn't vote in that election? **IF YES:** Which party was that?
IF NECESSARY SAY: The one where Tony Blair won against John Major.

Q. Apart from special occasions such as weddings, funerals, baptisms and so on, how often nowadays do you attend services or meetings connected with your religion?

Source: Life and Times Survey and the National Centre for Social Research. Used with permission.

■ Other pitfalls

There are other potential pitfalls in question wording besides vague and incomplete questions. Others to be avoided include the following:

➢ Questions using words, jargon, technical language or abbreviations unlikely to be familiar to the target population:
   ➢ *Q. Have you initiated any major refurbishments in the place where you reside?*
   ➢ *Q. Now thinking hypothetically, if you were in charge of fiscal policy, which of the following options would you implement?*
   ➢ *Q. How would you rate the performance of the UNHCR?*

➢ Questions using words or phrases that are difficult to pronounce or read out:
   ➢ *'In an anonymous form'.*

➢ Double-barrelled questions – asking two questions in one:
   ➢ *Q. Do you like using email and the web?*
   ➢ *Q. Would you like to be rich and famous?*

➢ Negatively phrased questions:
   ➢ *Q. Public speeches against racism should not be allowed. Do you agree or disagree?*
   ➢ *Q. Do you agree that it is not the job of the government to take decisions about the following?*

➢ Long or convoluted questions:
   ➢ *Q. Have you personally, in the last months, travelled abroad on holiday (not including visits to friends and relatives) for a stay of four days or more?*

➤ Questions which overtax the respondent's memory:
  ➤ *Q. How many hours of television did you watch last month?*
  ➤ *Q. List the books you have read in the last year.*

➤ Leading questions:
  ➤ *Q. Do you always buy the most expensive brand?*
  ➤ *Q. Do you agree that it is right that your organisation makes donations to polit-ical party X?*

➤ Questions using sensitive or loaded 'non-neutral' words:
  ➤ *Q. What do you think of welfare for the poor?*

➤ Questions that make assumptions:
  ➤ *Q. How often do you travel to France?*
  ➤ *Q. When did you stop beating your wife?*

➤ Questions with overlapping response categories:
  ➤ *Q. How many hours did you spend in the library yesterday?*

0 to 1 hour	1
1 to 2 hours	2
3 to 4 hours	3
4 to 6 hours	4
More than 6 hours	5
Don't know	8

➤ Questions with insufficient response categories:
  ➤ *Q. How do you travel to work each day?*

By car	1
On foot	2
By bus	3
On a bicycle	4

In addition, it is wise to avoid hypothetical questions. The risk with such questions is that you get meaningless, hypothetical data. Consider the question, '*What would you do if your home was flooded?*' What the respondent thinks he or she might do and what they might actually do may be very different. Similarly, asking the hypothetical question, '*Would you like better quality public services?*' is likely to elicit a 'yes' answer from most respondents. Questions that ask the respondent to comment on someone else's experience or views, for example, '*Do you think that other people in your area are for or against the road development?*', are likely to produce data of little relevance or value.

It is important to maintain the respondent's interest throughout the questionnaire. One way of losing his or her interest is to ask irrelevant or unnecessary questions. Questions should be relevant to the research objectives (if not, they should be excluded) and relevant to the respondent's situation or experience, and on a subject that he or she can reasonably be expected to answer accurately. If a question is irrelevant to a particular subset of respondents routing instructions should be used to ensure that they are not asked the question. Including too many questions on topics that are boring or uninteresting to the respondent should be avoided in order to maintain interest.

Box 10.11 The importance of a good translation

In translating a questionnaire it is important to ensure that the words used mean the same thing in the languages used. To achieve this, it is not only necessary to understand the language but also to understand the wider cultural context and the context of the research topic within that country. This understanding should help you to find the words or phrases that give you the meaning you want. If possible, get a native speaker who is living in, or has recently been living in, the country to do the translation. As well as words and meaning, check the conventions on using scales (they may be interpreted in different ways in different countries) and asking demographic questions (social grading varies). Back-translation – retranslating into the original language – is advisable, especially in studies where consistency (and comparability) across countries is important. A native speaker of the original language should also do the back-translation. Even when words or phrases are back-translated they may miss the meaning of the original; it may be that there is no word in the language for something that needs to be translated. Consistency, although worth aiming for, may be elusive – it is certainly harder to attain than you might at first imagine.

■ Questions on sensitive topics

If not handled properly – clearly worded, in the right place on the questionnaire, the question and the answer recorded without embarrassment on the part of the interviewer – questions on sensitive or embarrassing topics can lead to refusals – refusals to answer the question or to continue with the interview, or refusal to take part in the first place. What is judged to be intrusive, embarrassing or sensitive varies enormously; and what is a straightforward issue to the researcher may be a particularly sensitive issue to the respondent, and vice versa (Lee, 1992). Subjects that tend to be sensitive to most people and in most cultures include money, voting, religion, sexual activity, criminal behaviour, and use of alcohol and drugs. One way of handling responses to sensitive questions in a face-to-face interview is to ask respondents to fill in the answers on the questionnaire themselves (on the screen or on a separate self-completion sheet). Alternatively, show cards, from which the respondent reads out a code for his or her response, can be used. (The relative anonymity of a telephone interview often makes these approaches unnecessary.)

Social desirability bias

Questions on some sensitive topics are susceptible to a form of response bias known as social desirability or prestige bias. According to Sudman and Bradburn (1983) there are three areas of questioning in which socially desirable responses, and in consequence over-reporting, occurs: questions about being a good citizen; being a well informed and cultured person; and fulfilling moral and social responsibilities. So, for example, it might arise in questions about completing accurate tax returns, driving to the speed limit, using your vote, frequency of visiting museums and art galleries and going to the theatre, giving to charity and recycling waste. Prestige bias can also affect answers to questions about age, occupation, income, and cleanliness and grooming. The flip side of social desirability, in which there is likely to be under-reporting rather than over-reporting, occurs in relation to issues such as illness, alcohol consumption, sexual activity and socially-undesirable behaviour such as criminal activity and use of illegal drugs.

In designing questions to avoid this type of bias you need to make it just as easy and painless for the respondent to give the low prestige answer as it is to give the high prestige answer. This can be done in the same way as questions about sensitive topics – via a self-completion questionnaire, or using show cards from which the

---

Box 10.12 **Examples of techniques to overcome social desirability bias**

Q. 1 Talking to people about the general election on 7 June, we have found that a lot of people didn't manage to vote. How about you – did you manage to vote in the general election?

IF NOT ELIGIBLE/TOO YOUNG TO VOTE: CODE 'NO'.

Yes, voted	1	Ask Q.1a
No	2	Go to Q.2

Q. 1a. Which party did you vote for in the general election? **DO NOT PROMPT.**

Q. May I just check, thinking back to the **previous** general election – that is the one in 1997 – do you remember which party you voted for then, or perhaps you didn't vote in that election? **IF YES:** Which party was that?
IF NECESSARY SAY: The one where Tony Blair won against John Major.

Source: British Social Attitudes Survey 2001. Used with permission.

Q. 30 What is your *personal* income before tax and national insurance contributions? Please just give me the number on the card.

SHOW CARD [Income bands plus 'I do not wish to answer this question'. The interviewer can code 'Don't know' but this response is not on the show card.]

INCLUDE ALL INCOME FROM EMPLOYMENT AND BENEFITS

Source: Life and Times Survey 2001. Used with permission.

respondent reads the relevant code. Another way is to ensure that the question is presented in such a way that all answers are allowable and equally acceptable, or that the respondent has a valid escape route. Some examples are given in Box 10.12. As with sensitive topics, the more anonymous methods of data collection – telephone and self-completion – may be better suited to collecting this type of information.

■ Question structure

Two further considerations in designing questions are whether you want to offer respondents a choice of answers or whether you want them to provide their own answers; and how you want to record the response.

Open questions

In an open or free response question the respondent gives the response in his or her own words. For example, 'What is it about X that makes you say that?' The respondent in a personal interview gives the answer verbally to the interviewer, who notes it down (or in a telephone interview or qualitative interview might record it); in a self-completion interview, he or she writes or types the answer into the space provided on the questionnaire. The responses to open questions can be 'pre-coded' or listed in the questionnaire (a list which the respondent does not see). The interviewer records the response or responses that correspond(s) to the respondent's answer. If the answer is

---

Box 10.13 Examples of open questions

Not pre-coded

Q. What can you remember about the last TV advertisement you saw for X? **RECORD ANSWER BELOW.**

Pre-coded

Q. Which brands of coffee can you think of? Any others?

	First mentioned (One code only)	Other mentions (Multi-code)
Café Noir	1	1
Maxwell House	2	2
Nescafé	3	3
Nescafé Gold Blend	4	4
… etc.	5	5
Other (Write in)	8	8
None	9	9

Box 10.13 continued

Numeric

Q. How many people do you manage or supervise? **ENTER NUMBER.**

Numeric pre-coded

Q. How many people do you manage or supervise?

None	1
1–4	2
5–9	3
10–15	4
16–20	5
21–24	6
25 or more	7
Don't know	8

not on the list, the interviewer records it under 'Other', which is usually accompanied by the instruction 'Write in' or 'Specify'.

The main advantage of open questions is that they can make respondents feel more at ease and more in control – a feeling that the interviewer or researcher wants to know exactly what they think and is not making them select a pre-formulated response. For this reason it is useful to include open questions early in the questionnaire, or at the start of a new topic, to help build rapport. In addition, open questions allow us to see a wide range of responses, rather than the more limited ones we might get using a prompted response question; we then have those responses in the words used by the respondent. An open-ended format also offers the chance in personal interviews to probe for more detail. From a design point of view open questions can be easier to word than closed questions.

As to the disadvantages, open questions require more of the respondent, the interviewer and the data processing provider and so are more time consuming and more costly to use. The respondent has to articulate a response; and the interviewer (the respondent in a self-completion format) has to record it word for word. Sometimes detail or meaning can be lost in this process – the respondent, not wanting to write or type things out in full, may shorten sentences or abbreviate words; the interviewer may not be able to write or type as fast as the respondent talks. From the responses, the data processing department has to build a code frame and assign responses to these codes, which can be expensive and difficult to do well.

Closed questions

A *closed* question offers the respondent a choice of answers. The alternatives may be read out or shown to him or her on a card (known as a show card or prompt card). In a self-completion questionnaire the respondent may be asked to tick a box corresponding to the answer, or underline or circle the response.

Closed questions can be relatively easy to administer – they take up less time than open questions and do not involve interviewer or respondent in recording detailed responses. They also make the data processing task relatively easy. The main disadvantage is that they can be difficult to formulate well, and poorly formulated questions can result in poor quality data. In addition, using a closed question means that we lose some sensitivity in measurement – what the respondent actually said is not

Box 10.14 Examples of closed questions

Q. Which, if any, of these brands of coffee have you heard of?
SHOW CARD

	Heard of (Multi-code)
Café Noir	1
Maxwell House	2
Nescafé	3
Nescafé Gold Blend	4
. . . etc.	5

Q. On these cards are some of the things that other people have said about X. Could you sort the cards into two piles – the statements that apply to you and those that do not apply to you.

Q. I am going to read out some things that other people have said about X. Using this card [**SHOW CARD**], could you tell me whether you agree or disagree with each statement?

	Strongly agree	Agree	Neither agree nor disagree	Disagree	Strongly disagree	Can't choose
Are a company you can trust	1	2	3	4	5	8
Have friendly, helpful staff	1	2	3	4	5	8
Care more about the environment than other companies	1	2	3	4	5	8
And so on	1	2	3	4	5	8

Box 10.14 continued

A version suitable for a telephone interview, using a slightly different scale:

Q. To what extent do you agree or disagree with the following statements about X? Please rate each statement from 1 to 5 where 1 means you 'Strongly disagree', 3 means you are 'Indifferent' and 5 means you 'Strongly agree'.

[1 = Strongly disagree; 2 = Disagree; 3 = Indifferent; 4 = Agree; 5 = Strongly agree]

Q. And thinking about your knowledge of health matters in general, would you say that compared with other people you know ... **READ OUT** ...

More than other people,	1
About the same as other people,	2
Or, less than other people about health matters in general?	3
Other WRITE IN	4
Don't know	8

recorded and there is no way of analysing the 'real' response. Too many closed questions in succession can be boring and repetitive for the interviewer to ask and for the respondent to answer, which also has a negative effect on data quality.

Response 'scales' are a form of closed question often used to measure attitudes, as we saw in Chapter 9. Scales are also used to measure such things as preference, likelihood to buy and satisfaction. The choice of scale and response format will depend on your information requirements, the level of sensitivity that you need in measuring the issue under investigation and the suitability for the method of data collection.

Box 10.15 Examples of response scales

Behaviour – buy or try

Definitely would
Probably would
Might/might not
Probably wouldn't
Definitely wouldn't

Rating

Very good	Much better
Good	A little better
Fair	About the same
Poor	A little worse
Very poor	Much worse

Box 10.15 continued

Preference

Prefer R
Prefer Q
Like both equally
Dislike both equally

Opinion

X treated much better	Strongly agree	Strongly in favour
X treated a bit better	Agree	In favour
Both treated equally	Indifferent	Neither in favour nor against
Y treated a bit better	Disagree	Against
Y treated much better	Strongly disagree	Strongly against

■ Probing and prompting

Probing is the term used to describe the follow-up questions that sometimes accompany open questions. The purpose of these probes is to obtain a more detailed or more fully considered answer from the respondent. Typical probes include 'What else?', 'Why do you say that?' and 'What is it about X that makes you say that?' Probing instructions or questions are usually included in the questionnaire (or script) and the interviewer is clear about when and how to apply them. It is important for reliability of the data that each interviewer applies and asks them in the same way. An example of a more specific probe is given in the question sequence in Box 10.16. Prompts are used to elicit responses to closed questions. The interviewer asks the question and follows it up by reading out or showing to the respondent, on a prompt or show card, a list of possible answers.

■ Reviewing the questions

Once you have designed a set of questions, before going any further it is useful to review them against the relevant research objectives and, if necessary, amend them. For each draft questions, ask:

➢ Does it give me the information I want?
➢ Does it answer my research objectives?
➢ Is the purpose of the question clear?
➢ Is it really necessary?
➢ What assumptions have I made in this question?

In addition, check whether the questions are suitable for the target group, for the method of data collection and for how the data are to be analysed.

Box 10.16 Examples of a probe and prompt

Q. 13 Generally speaking, do you think of yourself as a supporter of any one political party?

Yes	1	Go to Q. 15
No	2	Ask Q. 14
(Don't know)	8	

Q. 14 Do you think of yourself as a little closer to one political party than to others?

Yes	1
No	2
(Don't know)	8

Q. 15 **IF YES AT Q. 13 OR Q. 14:** Which one?

IF NO/DON'T KNOW AT Q. 13: If there were a general election tomorrow, which political party do you think you would be most likely to support?

Source: British Social Attitudes Survey 2002. Used with permission.

Target group

Is the target population made up of adults or children, consumers or business people? Review the wording of the questions to ensure that the vocabulary used is suitable for the respondents; review the response format to ensure that respondents will have no difficulty answering the questions.

Method of data collection

In a telephone interview, where the respondent cannot see the interviewer or the questionnaire, prompts or scales must be read out, and instructions on how to use them must be clear. To prevent confusion and misunderstanding it is best to avoid long questions, long scales and long descriptions.

For self-completion interviews much depends on how the questionnaire looks – it must be visually appealing (postal questionnaires should not, for example, look too thick or feel too heavy) and should create a positive first impression. It should reflect the - professionalism of the research organisation. With no interviewer present there is no chance to clarify the meaning of questions or instructions. The questionnaire must look easy to fill in and be easy to fill in. For this reason most questions will be pre-coded – to make the process relatively easy. Open questions can be used to allow respondents to comment on, explain or add to the responses given at closed questions. The questions and the instructions must be written in clear and unambiguous language; the routing must be easy to follow. Because the respondent can read the whole questionnaire it is not possible to use unfolding techniques or pre-coded lists for unprompted questions.

Box 10.17 Example of a self-completion layout

Q. Which of the following types of business does your company deal in?

Mortgages . . . .☐
Pensions . . . .☐
Life insurance . . . .☐
Health insurance . . . .☐
Motor insurance . . . .☐
Holiday/travel insurance . . . . . .☐
Investment/savings schemes . . .☐
Portfolio management . . . .☐
Other . . . .☐
PLEASE TICK AND WRITE
IN THE TYPE OF BUSINESS

Without an interviewer present it is also more difficult to establish and maintain interest. The topic and the questions should be of interest to the respondent and relevant to him or her. If they are not, the respondent may not complete the questionnaire or may give it to someone else who they think will be able to answer the questions.

Data analysis

Think about how the data are to be analysed and seek the advice of the person responsible for the data processing. The data entry and analysis software to be used may dictate the layout of the questionnaire and the way in which questions are coded.

Question order

Now that you have a set of questions that you believe address the research objectives, the next task is to put them into an effective and logical order. Remember that the interview is a conversation and to keep the respondent's interest and co-operation it must make sense; there should be no jarring non sequiturs or illogical jumps between topics. The questionnaire should create a positive impression of the particular piece of research and of research in general. The order of the topics and questions is also important in enabling the interviewer to establish and build rapport with the respondent. Asking questions on difficult or sensitive topics too early in the interview can destroy rapport and lead to withdrawal from the interview or refusal to answer particular questions; if the respondent does respond, he or she may not feel comfortable enough to give accurate answers, so data quality is compromised. The order of questions can impact on the interviewer's confidence that the questionnaire will work in practice – and research has shown that a confident interviewer will have greater success in achieving interviews.

In deciding on the order of questions it is useful to draw up a flow chart. From a list of draft questions, group together the questions that relate to each topic. Each group or set of questions is a module. Put these modules into an order – straightforward, non-challenging topics first, more difficult or sensitive topics, including classification questions on age, income and so on towards the end. To help the flow of the questionnaire it is useful to include a brief introduction to each module. For example, on the Life and Times 2001 questionnaire the module on Culture, Arts and Leisure is introduced like this: 'The next questions are about culture and the arts, and the things people do in their leisure time.' Also, in terms of the flow of the questionnaire, you need to think about the balance between the types of questions: too many closed questions or attitude scales together can be boring and repetitive for interviewer and respondent and will adversely affect the quality of the data.

Once you have decided on the order of modules you need to decide on the order of questions within each module. Moving from general questions to more specific ones – the funnel approach – is effective. Again, more difficult or sensitive questions should appear later. Bear in mind that earlier questions may bias response to later ones. For example, ask unaided or spontaneous awareness questions before asking aided or prompted awareness; ask about usage and behaviour before asking about attitudes. In asking respondents about a relatively long list of items – brands, for example, or image or attitude statements – fatigue can set in, influencing the quality of responses to items at the end of the list. A way of randomising this effect across the sample is to rotate or randomise the order in which you present the items. This can be done automatically in computer-aided interviewing and by using randomised tick starts in pen and paper interviewing.

Remember, if a question module or an individual question is not relevant to a respondent, make sure he or she is not asked it by including routing instructions that take the interviewer or the respondent to the next relevant module or question.

Layout and appearance

The layout or appearance of the questionnaire may seem unimportant but needs to be considered for several reasons. In a self-completion format the questionnaire must be laid out so that the respondent understands what is required and can fill it in easily. An interviewer-administered questionnaire must be set out so that the interviewer can read it easily, follow the routing and record the respondent's answers accurately. In adding in interviewer instructions the convention is to use capitals and bold text, as you can see in the examples here; question text and answers are in lower case, not bold. Routing instructions should appear opposite the question codes, as shown in the examples used here, and where appropriate, above the question (for example, **IF YES AT Q. 13 OR Q. 14:** Which one?) As we noted above, layout is also important from a data processing point of view and should take into consideration the requirements of the data entry and analysis software.

In finalising a questionnaire, have it checked thoroughly by a fieldwork expert and by a person involved in data processing. In particular, it should be proof-read to ensure that routing and coding instructions are clear and accurate; that there is enough space to record and code answers (and, on paper questionnaires, enough space for coders to write in codes); for manual data entry that the codes (and column numbers, if used) are where the data entry person would expect to find them. (We look at the process of questionnaire approval in Chapter 11.)

Questionnaire length

The questionnaire must be long enough to cover the research objectives; the right length to meet the research budget (the longer the questionnaire, the greater the cost); and the right length to suit the choice of data collection method. The recommended maximum length for an in-home face-to-face questionnaire is about 45 minutes to an hour; for a telephone interview it is about 20 minutes; and for a street interview about 5 or 10 minutes. It must also be of a length that allows the interviewer time to build up rapport with the respondent. On the other hand, it should not be so long that the task of completing it is burdensome to the respondent, or so long that he or she is unwilling to take part at all. Besides affecting co-operation rates, the length of the questionnaire has been shown to affect the quality of the data collected, with poorer quality data collected towards the end of a long interview, as the respondent tires of answering questions.

Pilot study

It can sometimes be difficult to assess objectively how a questionnaire or a discussion guide in which you are involved will work – being so close to it you tend to make too many assumptions. Conducting a pilot study is an invaluable way of testing it out – it will show what questions are difficult, which ones give the type of answers you were expecting and so on. A pilot is especially useful if a questionnaire is a new one and not a repeat of a previous job or similar to other questionnaires you have used with a similar sample (or if the discussion guide is on a topic that is relatively new to you). Although relatively expensive and time consuming to conduct, in the end a pilot study can save time and money by delivering a questionnaire (or discussion guide) that is efficient in collecting good quality data. Pilot studies are crucial in multi-country projects to ensure that the questionnaire has been adapted to suit the language and culture in which it is to be used. The results of the pilot tests in each country should be compared to ensure that the questions are measuring the same things, that they are gathering equivalent data.

■ Conducting a pilot study

The pilot study can be conducted at any stage in the development of the questionnaire – from the conceptualisation stage (to explore the meanings of concepts and understand the language used by the target audience) to the fully developed draft (to check if it delivers the information it is designed to deliver). The style of the pilot interview will depend on how well developed the questionnaire is. Pilot interviews undertaken in the early stages of development might take the form of an informal qualitative in-depth interview. Those undertaken with a more fully formed questionnaire are likely to resemble a formal quantitative interview (in the first instance face to face, then using the method of data collection intended for the final version).

Regardless of the style of the pilot or the stage at which the draft is being piloted, it is a good idea that you, the person involved in designing the questionnaire or discussion guide, conduct some of the pilot interviews. This can be invaluable in developing your questionnaire design skills as you hear and see for yourself how your questions work (or do not work!) with a real respondent. Once the questionnaire is close to the final draft stage interviewers from the fieldforce conducting the survey should do some pilot interviews. It is invaluable to get feedback from experienced interviewers as well as relatively new ones – each will have a different view of the interview process and the effectiveness of the pilot questionnaire. A relatively new interviewer will have insights into the way the questionnaire works from the interviewer's point of view – if it is easy to follow, if instructions are clear and so on; the more experienced interviewer will have insights into how it works from the respondent's point of view; and both will give you feedback on timing and overall manageability of the interview. If a full-scale, proper pilot study is not possible, ask some people you work with who are not directly involved in the project (and if possible who are in the target population) to do pilot interviews with you.

The pilot interviews should be conducted face to face (regardless, in the case of a questionnaire, whether the final version is designed for the telephone or as a self-completion sheet) with members of the target population. A face-to-face

Box 10.18 Pilot checklist

In conducting a pilot study, here are some things to think about:

➤ *Clarity of purpose.* Did the questions measure what they are supposed to measure? How did the respondent interpret the questions? Were the questions relevant to the respondent? Were they meaningful to the respondent?

➤ *Wording of the questions.* Were any questions too vague, unclear or ambiguous, loaded or leading? Did any use unfamiliar or difficult words, ask about more than one thing, use a double negative? Were any too long or convoluted?

➤ *Question content.* Were there any questions that discouraged the respondent from completing the questionnaire, or that were embarrassing for the interviewer to ask or the respondent to answer?

➤ *Type of questions.* Was the balance right between open and closed questions? Was the use of each type appropriate? Were the scales used suitable?

> **Box 10.18 continued**
>
> ➤ *Response alternatives*. Were the response alternatives full and complete? Was the list too long?
>
> ➤ *Order of question modules and questions within modules*. Did the questionnaire flow smoothly from question to question and from module to module? Did the order seem logical to the respondent and the interviewer? Did anything seem odd or discordant? Were more sensitive topics in the right place? Was there any evidence of order bias or order effects?
>
> ➤ *Layout/appearance of the questionnaire*. Was it suited to the method of data collection? If self-completion, did the respondent find the instructions clear and easy to follow? If interviewer administered, how easy or difficult was it? How easy or difficult was it to record responses?
>
> ➤ *Length*. How long did it take to complete? What were the interviewer's and the respondent's perceptions of the length? Was it too long, too short, about right?

interview enables the interviewer to observe and note the respondent's physical reaction to the questions. In order to get a clear picture of how a survey questionnaire works conduct at least about 12 interviews. (For a discussion guide, a relatively new qualitative interviewer should conduct about three or four pilot interviews; with more experience, one or two interviews might provide the necessary insight.) One approach is to conduct the interview as you would a 'real' interview, making notes on how the respondent reacts to the questions. At the end of the interview you might go back over each question, asking the respondent for his or her comments. Alternatively, you can ask the respondent to comment on each question as it is asked. You may even give the respondent a copy of the research objectives to enable him or her to evaluate the questions. It can be useful to tape-record pilot interviews.

■ Reviewing and revising

When the pilot study is complete, it is useful to think through how you would analyse the responses. Check the data against the research objectives to see whether you are getting the sort of information you need. For a quantitative project, it is worth preparing a coding frame based on the responses to the questions, editing the questionnaires, entering the data and producing a holecount. This allows you to check for any inconsistencies in logic or in coding that might hamper data processing. Make the necessary changes to the questionnaire or discussion guide that the pilot work suggests. If they are substantial it may be worthwhile conducting another pilot study with a new set of respondents. Finally, it will also be worthwhile to run a short pilot study using the data collection method that is to be used in the main study, in order to identify any problems that may be related to the method of data collection.

Box 10.19 Life and Times Survey 2001: changes suggested by the pilot study

Following a comprehensive face-to-face briefing, which included practice or 'mock' interviews, 60 face-to-face pilot interviews were carried out by the interviewers who would go on to conduct the full survey. The changes suggested by the pilot included changes to the wording of some questions; additions to pre-coded lists; and changes to the order of question modules. These changes are shown below. The pilot also highlighted the need to include additional questions and to remove others (either because they were not delivering valid data or they were too sensitive). The pilot also gave valuable information on the time needed to complete the survey and each of the question modules within it. You can download the version of the questionnaire used in the full survey from the Life and Times website (**www.ark.ac.uk/nilt**).

Change: pre-coded list

In the pilot, quite a few respondents said that they would go to a pharmacist for advice. This was added to the pre-coded list and the show card.

From Section 2A: Health Issues
Q. 1a Thinking about the health problem or health issue which was most important for you, where did you go to find information or advice about this?

SHOW CARD [but not for pilot]
CODE ALL THAT APPLY

	Yes	No
A doctor or other health professional	1	2
A friend or relative who is a health professional	1	2
Another friend or relative	1	2
Someone who practises alternative medicine	1	2
The Internet	1	2
Books	1	2
Leaflets	1	2
Telephone helpline	1	2
A support group	1	2
Pharmacist	1	2
Other (WRITE IN)	1	2
Don't know/Can't remember	8	

Box 10.19 continued

Change: question wording

To reflect everyday usage 'illness' replaced 'condition' and, to avoid embarrassment and to show greater sensitivity towards the respondent, mention of specific illnesses (heart disease and cancer) were removed.

From Section 2A: Health Issues

Q. 2 Suppose you go to your GP with chest pains and he or she tells you that you may have a serious *condition* [replaced with illness] *like heart disease or cancer* [removed]. The GP makes arrangements for you to have further tests. In the meantime, would you try and get more information yourself on what might be the matter or would you probably rely on the doctors to give you the information you need?

Change: order of question modules

From Section 3: Political Attitudes

Interviewers found that not enough rapport had been established at this stage of the interview to enable good quality data to be collected on political attitudes. As a result this question module was moved to later in the questionnaire.

Change: response items

From Section 4: Education

In the pilot several respondents replied that 'everyone should be treated equally'. This was added to the question's response items.

Q. 14 Some people say that particular groups of unemployed people should be given extra help with free training courses and courses to get them back to work. Are you in favour or against giving extra help like this to *lone mothers*? **SHOW CARD**

(a) And what about *ex-prisoners*?
(b) *People in their fifties who are out of work?*
(c) *People in their twenties who are out of work?*

	Strongly in favour	In favour	Neither in favour nor against	Against	Strongly against	Don't know	Everyone should be treated equally
Lone mothers	1	2	3	4	5	8	6
Ex-prisoners	1	2	3	4	5	8	6
People in their fifties	1	2	3	4	5	8	6
People in their twenties	1	2	3	4	5	8	6

Source: The Life and Times Survey Team and Research and Evaluation Services (fieldwork provider). Used with permission.

Chapter summary

➤ The questionnaire is the instrument used to collect data. Effective research and quality data depend on a well-designed questionnaire. It must be effective in addressing the research objectives – collecting valid and reliable data to address the research problem clearly and unambiguously – and it must be suited to the practical tasks of data collection and data processing and analysis. It also has a role to play in representing research, and the research industry, to the wider world.

➤ Questionnaire design follows from a thorough and rigorous examination of the research problem and a clear understanding of the nature of the evidence needed to address it.

➤ Designing questions for some topics may be fairly straightforward. The topic might be familiar, or you might be using standard or tried and tested questions from previous studies. Standard questions are essential if comparisons are to be made between surveys and if data from different surveys are to be fused. Some things are more difficult to measure, and many things are more difficult than they first appear. Much work is needed to clarify the meaning and define clearly what is to be measured so that there is no ambiguity about what the question is measuring and how the response to it is interpreted.

➤ Careful attention must be paid to question wording, to question structure – open-ended or closed response formats – to the order of question modules and questions within the modules, to the length of the questionnaire and its layout.

➤ A pilot study is invaluable in determining whether or not you are asking the right questions in the right way.

Questions and exercises

1 Discuss the importance of good questionnaire design.

2 What is involved in the questionnaire design process?

3 What is meant by the terms 'open-ended' and 'closed' questions? What are the advantages and disadvantages of each type?

4 What are the pitfalls in question wording? Give examples of some poorly worded questions.

5 Give examples of the sort of topics for which there are standard questions. Why is it important to use standard questions?

6 What is social desirability bias and how would you minimise it?

7 Why is the order in which questions appear on the questionnaire important?

8 Why is the layout and appearance of a questionnaire important?

9 What is involved in pilot testing a questionnaire? Why is it important?

10 Start collecting examples of questionnaires from as many sources as you can. For each questionnaire in your collection, ask yourself the following:

    (a) What information does the questionnaire aim to collect?
    (b) At whom is it aimed?
    (c) Is it for self-completion, or would an interviewer fill it in?
    (d) What types of questions are used?
    (e) How is the questionnaire set out?
    (f) Is it easy to fill in?
    (g) Did you understand the questions?
    (h) How long did it take you to complete?
    (i) What sort of questions come first?
    (j) Are the questions in a logical order?
    (k) Were any of the questions sensitive or too personal?
    (l) Would you feel anxious about what might be done with the information you give?

References

Kirk, J. and Miller, M. (1986) *Reliability and Validity in Qualitative Research*, Newbury Park, CA: Sage.

Lee, R. (1992) *Doing Research on Sensitive Topics*, London: Sage.

Sudman, S. and Bradburn, N. (1983) *Asking Questions*, San Francisco, CA: Jossey-Bass.

Recommended reading

There are many excellent books devoted to questionnaire design, including:

Converse, J. and Presser, S. (1988) *Survey Questions: Handcrafting the Standardized Questionnaire*, London: Sage.

Oppenheim, A. (2000) *Questionnaire Design, Interviewing and Attitude Measurement*, London: Continuum.

Payne, S. (1951) *The Art of Asking Questions*, Princeton, NJ: Princeton University Press.

Sudman, S. and Bradburn, N. (1983) *Asking Questions*, San Francisco, CA: Jossey-Bass.

Questionnaire Design Guidelines published by The Market Research Society, London.

Miles, K., Bright, D. and Kemp, J. (2000) 'Improving the research interview experience', *The Proceedings of The Market Research Society Conference*, London, The Market Research Society. An interesting and useful account of the development of a questionnaire and its effect on the respondent's experience.

Part III

Getting on and finishing up

Chapter 11

Managing a research project

Introduction

In Chapter 3 we looked at the process of starting a research project – defining the problem, preparing the brief and finally writing the proposal. We now pick up the process again, moving on to what happens once the research has been commissioned. The aim of the chapter is to take you through what is involved in running a research project, from organising fieldwork to checking and organising the data. The detail of what to do with the data – how to analyse them and present or report them – is covered in Chapters 12, 13 and 14.

Topics covered

➢ Making it happen
➢ Organising fieldwork
➢ Checking the viability of the questionnaire/discussion guide
➢ Briefing interviewers and recruiters
➢ Developing an analysis plan
➢ Organising data processing
➢ Starting the analysis
➢ Checking and reporting progress

Relationship to MRS Advanced Certificate Syllabus

The material covered in this chapter is relevant to Unit 6 – Questionnaire Construction, specifically the following:

➢ checking the suitability of a questionnaire for data collection and data processing;
➢ briefing for a fieldforce;
➢ conducting a pilot study.

In addition it will be helpful in understanding:

➢ the role of the agency researcher (Unit 1);
➢ the process of coding data from open-ended questions (Unit 9);
➢ how to prepare a data processing specification (Unit 9).

At the end of this chapter you should be able to:

➤ brief the fieldwork supplier;
➤ brief interviewers and recruiters;
➤ conduct a pilot study;
➤ brief coders and data processing executives;
➤ write an analysis specification;
➤ check data tables for accuracy;
➤ be aware of and manage the day-to-day requirements of a project.

Making it happen

It is important that what was requested in the brief and what you promised in the proposal and in discussion with the client is turned into an effective research plan that is carried out efficiently. There may be practical concerns that you could not have anticipated when you wrote the proposal. For example, the client may have requested changes that affect the cost and/or the design; your preferred fieldwork dates might clash with a major holiday period among the target population; the length of the interview or the agreed sample size may have implications for fieldwork and data processing. The role of the research executive at this stage in the process (Box 11.1) is to communicate what is needed to those who can make it happen. In other words, you need to talk to the fieldwork supplier, the data processing and

Box 11.1 Running a project: the research executive's role

Once a project gets under way the research executive becomes the pivotal person in the research team. He or she is responsible for liaising with those who commissioned the research and those who are involved in executing the fieldwork and processing the data. The level of responsibility or autonomy will depend on seniority and experience. The tasks will include the following:

➤ administering the project on a day-to-day basis, checking progress, answering queries from field, DP, the client;
➤ making contributions to discussions about questionnaire/discussion guide design;
➤ laying out the questionnaire/discussion guide;
➤ briefing and liaising with the fieldwork supplier on the set-up of fieldwork;
➤ preparing interviewer or recruiter briefing notes;
➤ briefing and liaising with the DP supplier about data entry, coding and data processing;
➤ liaising with the client about preparation and delivery of stimulus material;
➤ checking the accuracy of data tables;
➤ listening to tapes and preparing transcripts and notes;
➤ interpreting the data;
➤ preparing presentations and draft reports;
➤ liaising with the client about progress, meetings, presentation and report.

analysis supplier and other members of the research team. You need to ensure that everyone involved with the project is clear about what is required. Much of the thinking about the research design and the research plan will have been completed at the proposal stage, and the feasibility of it will have been discussed with field and data processing suppliers; the task now is to turn the thinking into action.

Organising fieldwork

Typically the first step, once a job has been commissioned and the details agreed with the client, is to brief the fieldwork supplier in detail about what is required.

■ Briefing field

When preparing the proposal you will have discussed the feasibility of the research design with the fieldwork supplier. He or she will have costed the fieldwork based on assumptions about the incidence of the target sample in the wider population; ease of identifying or approaching the target sample; the nature and length of the interview and the number of interviews that an interviewer could achieve in one shift (the strike rate); and the total number of interviews needed. Now that the proposal has been accepted it is important to confirm the details, including fieldwork start and finish dates, with the field supplier and to discuss any changes that may have been made to the original plan which may affect cost, timing or level of staffing needed. The field-work supplier should be clear about exactly what is required before the fieldwork is booked. The questions you will need to be able to answer about fieldwork are given in Box 11.2. This is not an exhaustive list – questions will arise that are specific to types of projects, for example a product or advertising test, and to individual projects.

Box 11.2 Preparing a briefing for field

➢ What type of job is it? What is the research design?
➢ Is it an *ad hoc* project or is it continuous? Does it consist of phases? For example, an exploratory qualitative phase followed by a quantitative survey?
➢ What methods of data collection are involved? Qualitative or quantitative or both? Group discussions or accompanied shopping? Face to face or telephone?
➢ What research locations are needed? If more than one country, how is this to be managed?
➢ What equipment is needed (e.g. computer workstations)?
➢ What is the target population? What is the incidence in the general population?
➢ What type of sampling procedure is to be used?
➢ What sample size is required?
➢ Is there a suitable sampling frame?
➢ How long is the questionnaire or discussion guide?
➢ What stimulus material or test product is needed? Who is to provide it?
➢ What is the turnaround time from start of fieldwork to delivery of data?
➢ Have similar jobs been done in the past? What did we learn from those?

> **Box 11.2 continued**

> ➤ If it is a repeat of a previous job, what implications does this have, for example in terms of the questionnaire or the recruitment screener, the use of sampling points or fieldwork locations, or particular interviewers?
> ➤ Is there to be a face-to-face interviewer briefing session (with client service and the client)?
> ➤ Will the client be attending or observing/listening to fieldwork?
> ➤ How will completed questionnaires or data files be transferred to the data processing supplier?

For a multi-country project or one that involves international fieldwork, to avoid any misunderstandings it is important that the briefing is as detailed and thorough as possible. The number and detail of the briefings you give may depend on how the fieldwork is to be organised. If it is to be undertaken by a local supplier in each country you may need to prepare separate, specific briefings, ensuring that you are consistent across countries if data are to be compared or combined. If it is to be co-ordinated centrally by one supplier one main briefing document may suffice, with perhaps some notes about special requirements by country.

Box 11.3 International research: central versus local

Rosemary Childs, Shell International Market Research Specialist

Many companies run their research buying centrally or locally around a set of fairly strict rules and frameworks (even prescribing questions to be asked). This ensures a high level of consistency in coverage and an ease of access to the findings from different countries at the analysis stage, and the value of these cannot be overstated. However, in my view, there are downsides too, in that by being prescriptive you risk preventing the local researchers from thinking about the issue under research, and also you may be applying an approach that is sub-optimal and simply not suitable to the local context. You risk losing some of the sensitivity of the customer understanding you are aiming to collect. My own approach has been not to aim for a set of 'rules' or prescribed questions but rather to identify the areas where research is required and to develop with colleagues in the operating companies a common core of elements to be included within these.

Where it is beneficial to do so (for reasons of speed, cost, use of proprietary techniques or specialist research suppliers, or complex or unfamiliar techniques, or if a centrally driven marketing initiative [is to be researched]), centrally co-ordinated studies are run. In these we work with a common supplier, at least for the design, co-ordination and analysis/interpretation of the research. We look to our co-ordinating suppliers to manage this process in the optimal way. They need to have fully understood the task, both from a marketing perspective and a research perspective, in order to give the best advice, choose the most suitable local fieldwork suppliers, and design the approach that will best suit the countries and cultures concerned. It is their responsibility to ensure that the local analysis is sensitive and insightful and that the overall interpretation is a fair reflection of the picture emerging from across the countries.

Box 11.3 continued

Even in centrally co-ordinated studies it is sometimes preferable to use the usual local supplier to conduct the fieldwork, under the briefing, vigilance and guidance of the co-ordinator. This has the advantage of securing a valuable element of ownership within the local [Shell] operating company. It is also appropriate where fieldwork is being locally funded. In a couple of instances we have switched from our local supplier to work with one recommended by the co-ordinating agency in the interests of project flow and effective communication, and to maximise the sensitivity and understanding that is carried through the process. Where the co-ordinating agency has a local contact with which it is used to working, the 'learning curve' is less steep and both parties have more time to concentrate on the project itself, rather than having to learn how to work together effectively.

Source: adapted from Childs, R. (1996) 'Buying international research', *Journal of the Market Research Society,* **38**, 1, pp. 63–6. Used with permission.

Once all the issues have been discussed and agreed with the fieldwork supplier you need to agree timings and contact details. It is useful to include the following information in a document, which you can circulate among all those directly involved in managing the project:

Summary of key dates for:
➢ delivery of the final approved version(s) of the questionnaire or recruitment screener;
➢ delivery of interviewer or recruiter briefing notes;
➢ interviewer/recruiter briefing session (if appropriate);
➢ attendance at fieldwork (if appropriate);
➢ arrival/dispatch of stimulus or other material;
➢ start of fieldwork;
➢ close of fieldwork;
➢ availability of data to the data processing supplier.

Contact details of the person:
➢ with day-to-day responsibility for the project;
➢ to whom completed questionnaires or data files should be sent.

■ Getting access to the target population

When fieldwork is to be conducted at a particular site, say an airport or in a particular store, it is necessary to get the permission of the site owner. Gaining access to a sample for most consumer market research projects is, however, relatively easy. Access is relatively open, there are no barriers, and so contacting potential respondents is relatively straightforward (whether they consent to take part in the research is, of course, a different matter). In other types of research, however, particularly in business, industrial and social research, the sample or population can be more difficult to access. The issue of access should not be overlooked in planning the research.

When potential respondents belong to a vulnerable group – drug users, the homeless, children, for example, or to a powerful 'elite' group – such as business executives, members of the medical and legal professions, politicians – access can be severely limited or even closed. It is often necessary in such cases to get past a 'gate-keeper', a person who protects access to the potential respondent. Negotiations with a gatekeeper may be lengthy and time consuming, and may even be fruitless. It may be necessary to use a sponsor, someone whom the target population respect and trust, who can allay any suspicions about the research, someone who can recommend the research organisation and help 'sell' the idea of being involved in research to the target group. For example, in his research among executive directors, Winkler (1987) used the Institute of Directors, a professional body representing company directors, as a sponsor in organising group discussions.

■ Organising stimulus material

Many projects, qualitative and quantitative, involve showing material to respondents – for example advertisements, photographs of products or packaging or the products themselves. Think about what stimulus material is needed for the project and discuss with the client who is going to supply or prepare it. For example, if you are researching a new product, the client will need to provide the material; if, however, you are researching an existing product it may be easier for you to shop for it yourself. Make sure that whoever is supplying the material is aware of the fieldwork deadlines so that the material arrives at the fieldwork site or with the fieldwork co-ordination unit in time to be dispatched to interviewers or moderators.

Checking the viability of the questionnaire/ discussion guide

You will have designed a questionnaire or discussion guide with the research objectives in mind, one that contains questions that are measuring what you think they are measuring and which will collect the kind of evidence you need to address the research problem. It is important to have fieldwork experts (field executive, interviewers and respondents) check it from a data collection and fieldwork management point of view; and a data processing expert check it from a data processing and analysis point of view.

■ Checking it out with the fieldwork supplier

Have the questionnaire (or discussion guide) approved by a fieldwork expert before it goes to the client for approval (and before it goes into the field). (The equivalent of the 'field' executive in qualitative research is someone with experience as a moderator or interviewer in the type of research you are planning.) Get field to check it as soon as you have what you think is a reasonable draft version. Leaving it too close to the fieldwork start date or until you have agreed a final version with the client may mean that you have little or no time to make any changes. The consequences of this could be costly and embarrassing – you may have to delay fieldwork, and your reputation may suffer. The field executive examines the questionnaire with the respondent and the interviewer in mind:

➢ Is the questionnaire the right length for achieving the strike rate on which the costing and timings are based? (If not, questions will need to be removed or modified, or the job recosted and timings renegotiated to reflect the lower strike rate.)
➢ Is it likely to overburden the respondent? Are all the questions necessary? Do they require too much effort of the respondent? Might they overtax the respondent's memory?
➢ Do the questions make sense? Are they clear and unambiguous?
➢ Is the language suitable for the sample? For example, will all the respondents in a business survey understand the jargon or technical/business language used? Will younger respondents grasp the meaning of the rating scales?
➢ Is the balance of questions right? Are there too many dull and repetitive questions? If you are using a grid, an image grid for example, it is advisable to keep the number of statements to about 12, otherwise both respondent and interviewer will be bored and data quality may be affected.
➢ Is the content relevant to the sample? Are the questions or topics within the respondent's frame of reference? Will the respondent be able to articulate an answer?
➢ Is the order or flow of questions logical, with no unexpected jumps or changes of subject?
➢ Are instructions to respondents and/or to interviewers in the right place?
➢ Are instructions to respondents and/or to interviewers easy to follow?
➢ Has the questionnaire (the program in computer-aided questionnaires) been set up so that order bias is minimised, for example by using tick starts or by rotating the start order in lists and grids?
➢ How many versions of the questionnaire are there? What are the differences between the versions and how are they to be administered?
➢ Is the self-completion questionnaire or form laid out clearly so that it is easy for the respondent to fill it in?
➢ For paper questionnaires, are the page breaks in convenient places?

■ Checking it out with DP

The questionnaire must also be checked and approved for data processing by a DP expert. It is good practice to do this as soon as you have a final draft that has been checked and/or piloted by the fieldwork specialist. There is no point asking DP to check it if there is a possibility that field might tell you that some questions will not work, for example. The DP executive will ensure that the questionnaire is coded correctly – that it contains all the information necessary to turn completed questionnaires into tables – and that it is set out in a way that makes coding and data entry as efficient as possible. If the questionnaire is to have several versions, aim to get the main version checked and approved before creating other versions. This will save you having to make changes to all versions of the questionnaire.

■ Finalising the questionnaire

It is important that the final version of a questionnaire (or discussion guide) is checked and approved for use by the client, by field and by DP. A questionnaire in particular may change a lot during the design process. It is useful to have a fresh pair of eyes check it, as those previously involved may be too used to it. If this is not possible create a checklist of comments and suggested changes, changes made throughout the design process, and refer back to this list to make sure that all of them have been implemented correctly. In addition, make a final check to ensure that the questionnaire or discussion guide addresses the objectives set out in the brief, and that each question is measuring what you think it is measuring. With a questionnaire, make sure that it meets the standards set out in Chapter 10. Check that all the necessary administration and instructional details are correct:

➢ project number;
➢ space to record serial numbers and interviewer numbers;
➢ all questions and parts of questions numbered correctly;
➢ all routing instructions complete and easy to follow;
➢ interviewer and/or respondent instructions complete and easy to follow;
➢ all codes correct;
➢ all versions correct.

Translations

On international projects the questionnaire or discussion guide should be translated once you have approval of the original version from field, data processing and the client. To make the translation process as efficient as possible try to ensure that a native speaker with a sound knowledge of research prepares the first translation of the questionnaire or discussion guide, and the back-translation.

Briefing interviewers and recruiters

The instructions that appear on a questionnaire are there to show the interviewer around the questionnaire, and to tell him or her where to probe or prompt the respondent. Most questionnaires will also be accompanied by a set of more detailed interviewer briefing notes and in some cases the field and client service executives and the client may run a face-to-face briefing. We look at both in this section.

■ Writing interviewer briefing notes

The aim of these briefing notes is to give the interviewer a greater understanding of the purpose of the research, the questionnaire as a whole and the specific questions or topics within it. Briefing notes may include information under the following headings:

➢ *Introduction and background to the research* – An introduction to the research that may include a summary of the research objectives.

➤ *Contents of the interviewers' work pack* – A list of the contents of the work pack. The nature of this list will depend on the nature of the research (product or advertising research, attitude survey, recruitment screener) and the method of data collection (telephone, face to face, CATI, CAPI). It may list, for example, 'Thank you' letters or notes for respondents, incentives, stimulus material or show cards, a quota sheet, address lists or area maps, questionnaires, contact record forms, return of work forms, pay claims.

➤ *Importance of the briefing notes* – A short statement emphasising the importance of reading the notes and being familiar with the questionnaire before starting fieldwork.

➤ *Fieldwork location and sampling area (if appropriate)* – Details of the geographic area in which the interviewer or recruiter must work, for example a particular postal district or town.

➤ *Sampling practice or procedure* – Details of how the sample is to be drawn, for example use of Kish Grids or random route, random digit dialling, details of quota controls, if appropriate, for example in terms of age, sex and social class.

➤ *Details of specific eligibility criteria* – A description of the type and range of respondents needed. For example: 'The respondent must be a domestic user of the service and not a commercial or business user; the respondent should be the person mainly or jointly responsible for making decisions about telephone and Internet Service Provider services and paying the telephone and ISP bills.'

➤ *Details of how to present the research to potential respondents* – A description of the research and information on the length of the interview and a reminder about confidentiality, anonymity and data protection issues and guidance on how to handle queries about the research, for example the end use of the research, the client's name, contact details of the fieldwork supplier.

➤ *Detailed questionnaire instructions* – A question-by-question guide to the questionnaire or screener. This should include (as appropriate) the use of show cards, stimulus material or self-completion elements, and a reiteration of questionnaire instructions including routing and skips, instructions for probing and clarification, and recording of answers verbatim, details of questions that are multiple response and those that are 'one code only'. Also include instructions for checking and editing the questionnaires at the end of each interview.

➤ *Details of incentives for participants* – A description of the incentive, and how it is to be delivered, for example whether it is included in the work pack or is being mailed out, details of when the respondent should expect to receive it.

➤ *Fieldwork timings* – Details of when to begin fieldwork and when to complete it.

➤ *Return of work arrangements* – Details of how the completed work should be returned, to whom and by what date.

➤ *Project management issues* – Contact details of the person responsible for handling any queries that might arise, for example eligibility of particular respondents, difficulties in filling a quota, queries about a particular question or topic.

➤ *Thanks* – A note of thanks for accepting the project should be included.

Box 11.4 is an extract from a set of briefing notes for a social and political attitude survey, the Life and Times Survey, which has been conducted on an annual basis in

Northern Ireland since 1998. Survey interviews are conducted face to face in the respondent's home using CAPI and a self-completion form. A copy of the questionnaire to which these notes relate, the 2001 questionnaire, can be found at the Life and Times website, **www.ark.ac.uk/nilt**. These notes should give you an idea of the type of background explanation that can be useful to interviewers.

Box 11.4 Extract from 'Notes for interviewers: Life and Times Survey 2001'

General points

This is largely a survey of attitudes so there will always be questions where the respondent really doesn't know or doesn't have a view about a particular topic. While we don't want you to *offer* the 'Don't know' option in the question itself, it is quite acceptable to code 'Don't know' answers to attitude questions, rather than try and push the respondent into one of the other answer codes.

Section 1: Introductory questions

These are general questions that are meant to provide an easy lead-in to the main body of the questionnaire. They are almost identical to those in the 1998, 1999 and 2000 surveys – the main difference is the addition of the newspaper readership questions at the end.

Section 4A: Health Issues

(Only asked of respondents with even serial numbers.)
Detail omitted.

Section 4B: Culture and the Arts

(Only asked of respondents with odd serial numbers.)
These questions are funded by the [government] Department of Culture, Arts and Leisure. This is a relatively new government department and one of their concerns is the extent to which people take part in 'culture' and the arts. What are the 'barriers' to their taking part in arts and cultural events? However, everybody has a different idea (or no idea at all!) of what is meant by 'culture'. The very first question in this section is an open question asking people: When you hear the word 'culture' what sort of activities does this make you think of? If the respondent has no idea then just type 'Don't know' or 'DK' in as an answer. The department is interested in anything and everything that comes to people's minds here. 'Culture' is whatever people think it is. It may be frustrating for some people that we don't give them examples of what 'culture' is – but subsequent questions in the section may help them to refine their own ideas. Note that Q.6 includes a set of 'SHUFFLE CARDS' with some of the things that people have said about going to cultural events and attractions. You ask the respondent to sort these into two piles – the statements which apply to them – and those which do not. You then pick up the pile of the statements which apply to them and code those on the computer.

Section 6: Background

This is largely the same as last year's survey and again includes the question on 'sexual orientation' – that is, whether people would describe themselves as heterosexual,

---

Box 11.4 continued

homosexual, or bisexual. This worked well last year but it is important that you understand exactly why we are asking the question so that you can address any concerns that the respondent may have. The 'Equality Agenda' (legislation recently introduced in Northern Ireland) now requires that public sector bodies review their efforts to help bring about equality between all sections of society. An important aspect of the new law is that it covers equality between people of different sexual orientation. Therefore, we now ask about sexual orientation for the same reason that we have always asked people what religion they are, and whether or not they have any disabilities – so that the views and experiences of all groups of people are properly represented in the survey. Knowing someone's sexual orientation, disability and gender could be important variables when analysing average incomes among different groups, priorities for government spending, and attitudes to equality issues.

Pink self-completion form

This year there is only one self-completion form and this is to be given to *all* respondents. It is short (10–15 minutes according to the pilot) and focuses mainly on Social and Family Networks. The questions on networks are part of an international survey that is also being asked in over 30 other countries in 2001 (including Britain and the Republic of Ireland). They cover the extent to which people are in contact with their friends and family – and who they turn to in times of need. They are particularly important for comparing the situation in Northern Ireland with Britain and the Republic of Ireland as well as comparing the situation of people living in rural areas with their urban counterparts.

Data protection issues

You will notice that the survey formally asks respondents if they understand the purpose of the survey and agree to take part. We must obtain this 'informed consent' in order to abide by the terms of the Data Protection Act. You must be completely open about why we are doing the survey. The survey is used *mainly* for research purposes at universities in Northern Ireland and beyond. However, we also make the results publicly available on the Internet so that everyone with an interest in public opinion can refer to them. In fact the biggest users (after university researchers and the government) are journalists, students and school children. The survey is now well recognised as an authoritative and independent source of statistical information on Northern Ireland. It is important that people understand that the results are only ever made available in an *anonymised* form.

Source: The Life and Times 2001 Survey Team at The University of Ulster and Queen's University Belfast. Used with permission.

■ Giving an interviewer briefing

Sometimes it is necessary to run a face-to-face briefing session for interviewers and/or supervisors to demonstrate sampling or recruitment procedures as well as the questionnaire. These sessions may involve the client, the field executive and the client service researcher. The client or the client service executive briefs the interviewers about the background to the project, explaining the need for the information and the use to which it will be put. He or she may also describe particular features of the product, service or brand that is the subject of the research. The field executive and/or the client service executive briefs the interviewers about the specifics of recruitment or sampling, how to get access to respondents, and how to introduce the research. They will demonstrate how to administer the questionnaire by reading out each question or by setting up a mock interview. Interviewers and/or supervisors conduct a pretend interview themselves in order to familiarise themselves with how the questions work, and to get used to handling stimulus material. Supervisors can repeat the briefing session with interviewers in their fieldwork location. Besides briefing the fieldforce, a personal briefing session is a good way of demonstrating to the client the rigorous and quality-conscious approach adopted by the supplier.

Box 11.5 The role of the co-ordinator in multi-country research

Michael Wilsdon, Apex International Research

The co-ordinator's role is analogous in many ways to a project manager in, say, the construction industry, controlling bought-in services from a range of sub-contractors, and with overall responsibility from Day 1 to completion. The role ... combines the functions of research buyer and research supplier. For the end user, the final client, the co-ordinating agency is the supplier; for the fieldwork and other sub-contractors, the co-ordinating agency is their client.

A fairly typical selection of operational matters with which the co-ordinating manager has to deal are:

➤ *Cultural diversity* – for example creating an image battery that will work in Britain, Spain, Thailand and Taiwan; careful questionnaire development and close collaboration with the local supplier are needed before fieldwork begins.

➤ *Language problems* – most are dealt with by correct translation routines but hazards can emerge.

➤ *Sampling* – most suppliers have an adequate system of achieving representative consumer samples but these sometimes come unstuck in the execution; there are problems of imposing a sampling method that the supplier does not normally use.

➤ *Fieldwork organisation* – the variety of ways of organising interviews, even within Europe, is a problem for the co-ordinator seeking a degree of uniformity in – for example – interviewer briefing.

➤ *Data preparation and entry* – it is wise to have data preparation and entry done by the local research agencies; the co-ordinator prepares the multi-country code book and writes the edit program with all the right logic checks and provides clear and detailed instructions.

Source: adapted from Wilsdon, M. (1996) 'Getting it done properly: the role of the co-ordinator in multi-country research', *Journal of the Market Research Society*, **38**, 1, pp. 67–71. Used with permission.

Developing an analysis plan

As soon as the research plan is agreed you should develop a strategy or framework for tackling the analysis of the data. Much of the thinking necessary will have been done earlier, at the exploratory phase of the research and at the research design stage. Revisit this information to clarify what approach you want to take to analysing the data. Your thinking about the issues might evolve when you see the data but the way in which you tackle the analysis is unlikely to change dramatically. We look in detail at how to plan qualitative data analysis in Chapter 12; here we look at what is involved in the planning process in general and the planning involved in quantitative analysis.

Box 11.6 Building a framework for analysis

➢ What questions is the research designed to answer? What am I looking for in the data?

➢ Is there a theory or model that might be useful in suggesting a framework or an approach?

➢ What did the exploratory research tell me? What clues did it provide?

➢ What hypotheses do I want to explore?

➢ What types or groups of respondents are of interest? On what basis could the sample be usefully classified or segmented?

➢ How will the data vary between these groups of people? What relationships or differences do I expect between different groups?

■ Planning the analysis

Using the questionnaire as your guide, plan out what tables you need, think about what statistical tests are appropriate, and what other analyses might be useful in reaching a detailed understanding of the issue, the market or respondents' attitudes or behaviour. Getting a detailed set of cross-tabulations is relatively easy (we look at how to prepare an analysis specification in the next section). It can therefore be difficult, especially when time is short, to resist the temptation to get a set of tables with every possible demographic, attitudinal and behavioural variable run as a cross-break against every question on the questionnaire. But do resist. Be selective in specifying cross-tabulations. Ask only for those tables that are relevant to the research objectives, otherwise you risk being overwhelmed by data and may lose focus in your investigation. Remember the adage, 'data rich, information poor'. Take an orderly and systematic approach. If questions arise that you cannot answer with the tables you have, think about what other tables or analyses might help and run those.

Once you have mined this background material, and thought about what it is you need the data to tell you, review the original research problem and the research objectives and write down the questions that you plan to ask of the data: this is your analysis plan.

Organising data processing

In this section we look at the four key tasks in relation to quantitative data processing:

> checking and editing questionnaires;
> coding;
> specifying the output from data processing;
> checking the output.

We look at the role of the research executive, and what the research executive needs to tell the data processing team about the project. Handling and organising qualitative data, which is more of an integral part of the qualitative research executive's work, is dealt with in Chapter 12.

■ Checking and editing questionnaires

To ensure good quality data questionnaires are typically checked and edited, first of all in the field, and then again back at the office. Have a look at Chapter 13 for detail on the sort of errors and inconsistencies that the checking and editing process aims to eliminate.

Checking and editing in the field

The process should begin as soon as possible after a questionnaire is completed. It should be checked to ensure that each question relevant to the respondent has been asked and a response coded and that no elements of the interview are missing, for example a self-completion sheet or a page from the questionnaire. Checks should be made to ensure that routing instructions have been followed correctly (particularly important for self-completion questionnaires). In computer-based data collection these sorts of checks are typically built into the program and so are handled automatically; paper questionnaires are checked by the interviewer or fieldwork supervisor or by an office-based editor. In addition to checking the completeness of the questionnaire, the quality of responses should be examined. For example, responses to open-ended questions should be reviewed in order to ensure that probing was conducted in the manner set out in the briefing notes or instructions. Checks should also be made to ensure that the respondent was eligible to take part in the research and the sample composition should be monitored on an ongoing basis and checked at the close of fieldwork, to ensure that the original sample specifications have been met. If they have not, the fieldwork supervisors can arrange for the completion of additional interviews. Editors and 'back-checkers' make further quality control checks as questionnaires are returned from the field or downloaded to the data processing server. Most organisations conduct a '100 per cent verification', that is, all codes on all questionnaires are re-entered.

If your project involves paper questionnaires discuss with the field executive and/or make a note in the interviewer briefing notes about the sort of checks you want done. For projects involving computer-based data capture check that the program contains the necessary checks; if you also want manual checks carried out specify this in the interviewer briefing notes.

Dealing with inadequate or incomplete data during data processing

You may need to give the data processing team instructions about how to handle whatever errors or inconsistencies remain in the data on completion of fieldwork. Inadequate or incomplete data can be dealt with in a number of ways. Incomplete questionnaires or those containing poor quality data can be excluded from analysis. Removing cases from the sample, however, biases the findings (the cases removed may differ significantly in profile from other cases) and if this course of action is taken the procedure should be clearly documented and the effect on the sample checked. It can be appropriate, particularly when large amounts of data or vital elements of a case are missing; and it may have a limited effect if the total sample is large and the number of cases removed relatively small. Another option is to recontact respondents to obtain the missing data or clarify responses. This can be relatively straightforward but to be effective it should be done as soon as possible, to ensure that the time lapse does not influence the response. If possible, the respondent should be recontacted or reinterviewed using the same method of data collection as was used originally. Since it may not be advisable to remove a case from the sample or possible to recontact a respondent, missing data may be dealt with during data processing, in ways outlined in Chapter 13: assigning a code to the missing value; performing a pairwise deletion; or imputing a value. If missing values remain at the end of the fieldwork checking and editing process tell the data processing department how you would like them to be treated. Decide which option is most appropriate and include details on the data processing specification (DP spec).

The data processing specification is the document that sets out the way in which you want the data from the questionnaires to be handled and in what format you want the output presented. For those questionnaires that include open-ended questions you also need to set out the way in which responses to these questions are handled or coded. We look at coding next before going on to look at preparing a DP spec.

■ Coding

Coding is the process by which responses from open-ended (non-pre-coded) questions, sometimes called 'verbatims', are analysed and labelled, given a numeric code so that they can be counted by the analysis program. A coding brief sets out how you want these data handled and a coding frame or code frame provides instructions about how open-ended questions are to be processed.

Preparing a coding brief

To write a good quality coding frame you need first of all to review the background information on the issue or research topic – this will help you to understand and interpret the responses given on the questionnaire, which can sometimes be ambiguous or unclear. If you are researching a particular market it is a good idea to familiarise yourself with the technical language or jargon that respondents might use as well as the key issues in that market. If the focus of the research is a particular product range it is worth having a look at the products or brands, even using or tasting them. If the research is about the quality of service provision find out what the key drivers are. If it involves advertising it is worth reviewing the advertisements so that you understand to which advertisement or brand a respondent is referring. If you are not directly involved with the nitty-gritty of the coding process then ensure this material is available to the coders. You may want to summarise this information in a coding brief, in which you could also include a draft coding frame, listing what you think might be important codes, to ensure that the coders are aware of the key issues to look for in the verbatims.

Sometimes respondents may not give the answer to a question when you ask it but at a later stage in the interview, in answer to another question. To ensure that no information is lost you can ask the coders to check for this (by reading through the entire questionnaire) and 'back-code' such responses to the relevant question. It may also be important in terms of the objectives of the project to get an understanding of each respondent's overall reaction to the research topic (for example an advertisement, a product, a service or a social issue). To do this the coders must read the whole questionnaire and code or classify each respondent according to their response, for example in terms of a positive, negative or neutral reaction. It is often important that the detail given at open-ended questions is preserved. You may want to ask for verbatims to be extracted and preserved whole, labelled with key (demographic) data so that you can see what type of respondent said what. Whatever your coding requirements make sure that they are clearly set out in the coding brief.

If the project is a multi-country one in which findings are to be compared on a country-by-country basis it is important to work closely with coders to produce a good quality master coding frame, one that can be used in preparing tables for all countries in the study. The master frame should be built using verbatim comments from questionnaires from all countries, with interpretation and clarification provided by those working in each country. Differences will remain but if frames were developed separately for each country comparisons would be more difficult to make.

Preparing 'extractions'

As questionnaires are returned from the field responses from each of the open-ended questions and each of the questions with an 'other – please specify' response are extracted and listed, question by question, as individual response items. (This process can be done automatically in a CAPI or CATI system.) For example, a respondent says that she has chosen to stay with her current utilities provider at the moment because 'I have had no trouble with them and I do not know the track record of other suppliers'. This statement is broken up into its two elements, 'no trouble with them' and 'do not know the track record of other suppliers', each of which is listed in the extractions. The process of extraction continues until the content of what is being extracted does not change – until saturation point is reached and further extraction is not showing new content. A list of 'extractions' from the source material forms the basis of a draft coding frame for each question.

Box 11.7 Example list of extractions

Q. 'Why have you chosen to stay with your current [utilities] supplier at the moment?'

I have had no trouble with them.
I want to find out more about the competition.
I do not know enough about other suppliers.
I am waiting to see what happens.
I am too unwell to make a decision.
I cannot be bothered to change.
They have always been my supplier.
I feel safe with them.
I don't think I'd save any money.
I do not know the track record of other suppliers.
The hassle factor.
Other suppliers may not be reliable.
They did a good job fixing a problem.
Better the devil you know.
I have not got around to finding out about the others.
The price difference is not big enough.

From draft coding frame to final coding frame

The next step is to group together similar responses. For example, in Box 11.7 several extractions refer to knowledge or lack of knowledge about other suppliers. Once grouped together these responses can be examined for differences in meaning, in particular shades of meaning that may need to be distinguished to meet the research objectives. For example, from the list of extractions in Box 11.7, '*I want to find out more about the competition*' suggests an active attitude or intention, and it may be important for the client to know what proportion of the sample say that; '*I do not know the track record of other suppliers*' suggests inertia; and it may be important to make the distinction between these. On the other hand, it may be that this difference is not important and that both statements could be coded as '*current lack of knowledge about competitors*'. Each group of extracted responses should be examined in this way and a code written to represent them. These codes are listed question by question in a draft coding frame, which is approved by the research executive and, in some cases, the client. This draft is used to code the responses from the entire sample. As coding progresses it may be that some responses do not fit into a particular code. These responses are listed as queries and a 'query listing' is sent with the draft coding frame to a query coder with specialist knowledge of the topic or to the client service executive responsible for the survey. If the queries cannot be accommodated in an existing code, a new code may be created. If, in the judgement of the query coder or the research executive, the response is unlikely to occur in many cases, or is of limited interest to the research objectives, it may be placed in an 'other' category. The draft coding frame is updated, and the coding process continues, with perhaps several updates to the frame as queries arise, until all responses from the sample are coded. The final coding frame is used in the data processing program.

Box 11.8 Example of final coding frame

Q. 'Why have you chosen to stay with your current [utilities] supplier at the moment?'

Haven't thought about it.
Want to wait and see how things develop.
Satisfied with service provided by current supplier.
Don't feel that others would offer better service.
Satisfied with the price charged by current supplier.
Don't think that there would be any financial saving.
Poor perception of other suppliers.
Don't know enough about other suppliers.
Other.

▪ Preparing a data processing specification

There are a variety of ways in which data from a questionnaire can be processed. The purpose of the DP spec is to set down clearly, unambiguously and in detail exactly how you want it done. Most organisations have their own house style, perhaps a pro forma on which you write in your requirements. A clear, well thought out DP spec helps DP process the job quickly, accurately and efficiently. In preparing a specification you need to think about how you plan to use the output. This will inform the nature of the output you ask for and the structure of it. It is therefore important to have completed your analysis plan beforehand. Getting a detailed set of cross-tabulations is relatively easy and it is often quicker to ask for all questions on the questionnaire to be tabulated against every demographic, geodemographic, attitudinal or behavioural variable. Resist the urge to do this – be selective in specifying cross-tabulations, asking only for those tables that are relevant to your analysis plan.

The questions that a DP spec must address include the following:

➢ What is the job about?
➢ Who is the client?
➢ What type of survey is it?
➢ Are there different versions of the questionnaire?
➢ What are the deadlines?
➢ Who wants the tables?
➢ Is the job/questionnaire the same as or similar to a previous one?
➢ What output is required? Cross-tabulations, descriptive statistics, multivariate analysis?

It is this last point that is the most important. You need to be clear about what it is you want so that you can communicate it clearly to others. Talk to the executives in the DP department or DP bureau in order to get an idea of what is possible – in terms of time, money and output.

Background briefing

To give the data processing executive an idea of the context of the project and the objectives of the survey, a DP spec should contain information on the background to the project. An example is given in Box 11.9. Alternatively, you can give the DP executive a copy of the project brief. This information will enable the DP executive to understand the job better and to make suggestions about processing and analysis options.

In a multi-country study cross-tabulations should be designed with the analysis plan in mind. If the aim of the research is to compare data on a country-by-country basis, tables should be set out with each country as the top break, rather than producing a separate set of tables for each country. You may need to decide whether the data should be weighted to reflect market size or population size. Also, consider whether each country will want to see data on their country in isolation or compared to all others. Consider too whether you need to produce tables in different languages.

Box 11.9 Example of the first page of a DP specification

Background to the survey

The client is conducting a review of her organisation's business strategy in order to produce a new draft business plan. The organisation is currently the main supplier in a market that has changed relatively little in the past ten years or so. Its key products and services have a market share of about 80 per cent. A new competitor, however, has recently entered the market and, although its market share is still relatively low, the client is concerned. Adoption of new technology, which was slow to take hold in the client's market, has gathered pace in the last year and most of the client's target market is now online, connected to the Internet. This presents opportunities for the client – the organisation is considering delivering some of its products and services via this channel. It also presents a threat – market intelligence shows that two competitors have a range of online products and services that are likely to threaten the market for the client's own products and services. As part of the business review and planning process the client wants to assess customer satisfaction with its products and services, and determine interest in delivery of its products and services via the Internet.

Timings

A telephone survey (CATI) is to be conducted among a sample of 400 of the organisation's target market. A copy of the final version is attached. The datafile will be available when fieldwork closes on 24 April. The coding frame will be finalised by 1 May. The research executive needs the tables on 10 May. The tables are due to go out to the client on 15 May. The presentation is scheduled for 25 May with the report a week later. Please contact Joe Bloggs at 0123 345 678 when they are ready. Thanks for your help.

General instructions

➢ Title of the survey and client's name to appear on all pages.
➢ Tables to be numbered.
➢ Questions including question numbers to appear in full on each table.
➢ Rows and columns to be labelled.
➢ Column percentages to be calculated.
➢ All tables to be based on total sample including 'Don't knows' except if stated otherwise (see below).
➢ No weighting is needed.

Cross-breaks or top headings

Specifying how you want variables such as age or social class to appear on the tables is relatively straightforward. For example, on the questionnaire the categories of the 'Age' question may have been 18–24; 25–34; 35–44; and 45–54 and this may be how you want them to be presented in the tables. You would therefore include on the analysis spec the instruction, 'Age x 4 – as questionnaire' – in other words, the age variable split into four categories, as it appears on the questionnaire. For other variables the instructions may be less straightforward and are likely to need a written or visual explanation. For example, you may want responses from a question with an Agree/Disagree scale like this:

Strongly agree	5
Agree	4
Neither agree nor disagree	3
Disagree	2
Strongly disagree	1

to appear as a top break in the tables like this:

Total agree (codes 4 or 5) – all those saying 'Agree' or 'Strongly agree'
Total disagree (codes 2 or 1) – all those saying 'Disagree' or 'Strongly disagree'.

Box 11.10 Example of a set of top breaks

Q. 1. In total, how many cars are there in your household?

		Gender			Age group				Marital status		Accommodation type		
	Total	Male	Female	<25	25–34	35–44	45+	Single	Married	House	Flat	Other
	1505	798	707	322	409	299	475	862	643	1002	471	32
	100%	100%	100%	100%	100%	100%	100%	100%	100%	100%	100%	100%
Number of cars:												
0	156	53	103	102	48	6	–	97	59	5	130	21
	10%	7%	15%	32%	12%	2%	0%	11%	9%	0%	28%	66%
1	1013	559	454	121	349	226	317	674	339	690	314	9
	67%	70%	64%	38%	85%	76%	67%	78%	53%	69%	67%	28%
2	275	151	124	99	10	52	114	91	184	249	26	–
	18%	19%	18%	31%	2%	17%	24%	11%	29%	25%	6%	0%
3	55	31	24	–	2	14	39	–	55	54	1	–
	4%	4%	3%	0%	0%	5%	8%	0%	9%	5%	0%	0%
4+	6	4	2	–	–	1	5	–	6	4	–	2
	0%	1%	0%	0%	0%	0%	1%	0%	1%	0%	0%	6%

It is important in designing the banner heading to think of the layout and appearance of the final tables. How many headings can fit across the page without looking untidy, squashed or hard to read? If the top breaks amount to more than one page, decide how you want them split and group them into meaningful sets. The order in which top breaks appear can help in reading the tables. Often it is the demographic breaks – age, sex, class and so on – that appear next to the total column. It may be more useful to have others first, such as heavy users, medium users and light users.

In addition to looking at responses to questions by the demographics or the main banner heading, you may want to see summary tables for grid questions. Summary tables are those in which the brands, for example, used in the grid appear across the top (as the column variable) and the statements appear down the side (the row variable). You may want to show the responses to several questions on one table, for example 'Heard of', and below it on the same table 'Buy now', for ease of comparison. You may want to combine the values of a variable into a summary code or overcode – for example, 'Very satisfied' and 'Fairly satisfied' to 'Totally satisfied', or a set of responses that lists 'Likes' about a service to 'Any likes'. It may be appropriate for most tables to be based on the responses of the total sample but there will be occasions when you may want some tables to be filtered on a different base, for example 'Those who buy now', or 'Those who have heard of the brand'. Remember, a filter applies to a whole table so be careful not to confuse a filter and a top break – a top break is just the column.

Summary and inferential statistics

Think about what summary statistics you want to appear on the tables. For questions with rating scales you may want the mean score; for arithmetical variables, for example annual turnover or number of employees, you may want the mean, the median and standard deviation. If you need a mean score, think about how it should be calculated. For example, if the rating scale ran from $+2$ to -2, will the mean score be calculated using this scale, or should it be changed to $+4$ to $+1$ to make comparison with other data easier, or to fit with the convention used by the client? You may want to indicate which values or variables should be tested for statistical significance (and at what level of significance). Give details if you need any further analyses, for example a factor analysis, cluster analysis or correspondence analysis.

Box 11.11 How to prepare a DP spec

Example: Questions from the self-completion questionnaire B, Life and Times Survey 2000

Q.3 Are you the person responsible for doing the general domestic duties – like cleaning, cooking, washing and so on – in your household?

The question's response format is:
  Yes, I am mainly responsible (1).
  Yes, I am equally responsible with someone else (2).
  No, someone else is mainly responsible (3).

Box 11.11 continued

DP instruction

Q.3 by main set of top breaks. Tabulate as questionnaire (codes 1 to 3) and include summary code for Mainly or Equally responsible (codes 1 or 2).
Base: Total sample (all answering).

Appearance of table

Title: Responsibility for doing the general domestic duties
Respondent mainly responsible
Respondent equally responsible with someone else
Someone else is mainly responsible
Summary: Respondent mainly or equally responsible
No answer.

Q.4 From the following list, please circle one number from each item to show how important you personally think it is in a job. How important . . . [list of items follows].

The question's response format is an importance scale:
Very important (1), Important (2), Neither/nor (3), Not important (4), Not important at all (5), Can't choose (8).

DP instruction

Q.4 Importance scale for each of the eight items in the questions by main set of top breaks. Tabulate scale as on questionnaire (codes 1 to 8) and include summary codes for Total important (codes 1 or 2) and Total not important (codes 4 or 5).
Mean score (based on values 1 to 5 where 1 = Very important).
Base: Total sample (all answering).

Appearance of table

Title: Importance rating of job security
Job security
Very important
Important
Neither important nor unimportant
Not important
Not important at all
Can't choose
Summary: Total important
Summary: Total not important
Mean score excluding 'Can't choose'.

DP instruction

Also need summary table for Q.4 – the same layout as above but this time with the item statements as top breaks.
Base: Total sample (all answering).

Box 11.11 continued

Appearance of table
Title: Summary table of importance rating re aspects of job

	Job security	High income	Good opps	Interesting job
Very important				
Important				
Neither important				
nor unimportant				
Not important				
Not important at all				
Can't choose				
Summary: Total				
important				
Summary: Total				
not important				
Mean score				

Q.8 Suppose you were working and could choose between different kinds of jobs. Which of the following would you personally choose?

The question's response format is:

(a) I would choose . . . Being an employee (1)
Being self-employed (2)
Can't choose (8).

(b) I would choose . . . Working in a small firm (1)
Working in a large firm (2)
Can't choose (8).

(c) I would choose . . . Working for a private business (1)
Working for the government or civil service (2)
Can't choose (8).

DP instruction
Q.3 Each part (a to c) by main top breaks. Tabulated as questionnaire.
Base: Total sample (all answering).
For Q.3b and Q.3c separate tables again by main top breaks and tabulated as questionnaire but this time based on those saying 'Being an employee' (code 1 at Q.3a).

Appearance of table
As above.

■ Checking the output

Data tables must be checked for accuracy before they are sent to the client or used to prepare the presentation or report. Typically, two people will check them – the data processing executive and the client service executive. Each will check them from a different perspective. The DP executive will, for example, check the holecount to make sure that the program has delivered the right tables with the correct bases, filters and weighting, that the statistics requested are complete, and that the tables are laid out properly and are readable. The client service executive will check whether the tables meet the specification he or she set out – in terms of layout, statistics, bases, filters and weighting – and will check whether the data make sense in the context of his or her knowledge of the project topic.

Box 11.12 Standard checks on tables

➤ Is the total sample as expected? In other words, have all responses been included?

➤ Does the demographic profile match the profile of the sample or the quota controls?

➤ Are the headings on the tables correct (project number, name, dates, client name, table title and so on)?

➤ Is the set of tables complete? Did you ask for a table of contents? (If so, check off all the tables against your specification and against the questionnaire.)

➤ For the main top breaks – are the cross breaks or top break headings correct?

➤ Are the top break totals correct?

➤ For each table check the following:
  ➤ that the base size is correct;
  ➤ that the question has been handled in the way set out in the specification, e.g. filtered on the correct base;
  ➤ that summary statistics – means, etc. – have been calculated correctly;
  ➤ that summary codes (overcodes) are correct (that they do not total less than any item contained in the overcode);
  ➤ that the data look right – if there are any unexpectedly high or low numbers, check them thoroughly.

Checking data derived from different versions of the questionnaire

If there are several versions of a questionnaire it is important to check in detail those tables that are derived from the questions that vary across the versions. For example, a code on one version of the questionnaire may not mean the same thing on another version. In producing a table based on all versions the program must define what each code means in all versions. There is a chance for error to creep in here, so it is worth checking a holecount for each version to determine the frequency of response on each one.

If you have a top break that is derived from a question rather than the classification data, for example 'Use brand X nowadays', it is worth checking to ensure that it is based on the right total. To do this you need to go to the question from which it is derived, for example 'Which of these brands do you use nowadays?' and check that the number of people answering 'Brand X' matches the number you have in the top break. In Table 11.1 56 per cent or 336 of the total sample use brand X, therefore the top break based on 226 is wrong. The version in Table 11.2 is correct.

Table 11.1 Brand use nowadays: incorrect version

	Total	Use brand X nowadays
Brand use nowadays	%	%
Brand X	56	100
Base: All responding	(600)	(226)

Table 11.2 Brand use nowadays: correct version

	Total	Use brand X nowadays
Brand use nowadays	%	%
Brand X	56	100
Base: All responding	(600)	(336)

Checking top breaks based on summary codes or compound variables

Check too that top breaks which are combined from different questions, or are summary codes, are correct. In the example below, 75 interviews were conducted in each country; countries were grouped together into regions as follows:

➣ central and eastern Europe (450) – Czech Republic, Slovakia, Poland, Rumania, Hungary, Russia;

➣ Asia Pacific (375) – Japan, South Korea, Malaysia, Singapore, Australia;

➣ Nordic (225) – Norway, Sweden, Finland;

➣ southern Europe (300) – Spain, Portugal, Italy, Greece.

Table 11.3, however, shows the total sample to be (1275) rather than (1350); and the total for the central and eastern europe (CEE) top break is (375) rather than (450). A quick check found that Russia had been left out of the CEE top break.

Table 11.5 also shows where it is possible for errors to occur. Table 11.5(a) is correct – all the cells are based on the right proportion of the sample. Table 11.5(b) shows how it might go wrong. The 35–44 age group has been included in error in the 25–34 age group.

Checking repeat data

If your data are repeat data, for example from a panel or tracking study or a dipstick monitor, do not assume that because the previous set of tables were correct this new set will be too. Check them as thoroughly and in the same way as you would a new set. In addition, make sure that the tables have the correct fieldwork dates, and that any changes to the questionnaire since the tables were last run have been included (for example new questions added, old ones deleted, changes to codes as a result of new brands being added to a brand list or new statements to an image grid). Check that

Table 11.3 Regional data: Incorrect version

	Total %	CEE %	S Eur %	Nordic %	Asia Pac %
Central and eastern Europe	33	100	–	–	–
Southern Europe	22	–	100	–	–
Nordic	17	–	–	100	–
Asia Pacific	28	–	–	–	100
Base: All responding	(1275)	(375)	(300)	(225)	(375)

Table 11.4 Regional data: Correct version

	Total %	CEE %	S Eur %	Nordic %	Asia Pac %
Central and eastern Europe	33	100	–	–	–
Southern Europe	22	–	100	–	–
Nordic	17	–	–	100	–
Asia Pacific	28	–	–	–	100
Base: All responding	(1350)	(450)	(300)	(225)	(375)

Table 11.5 (a) Age group: Correct version

Age group	Total %	18–34 %	35–54 %	55+ %
18–24	10	40	–	–
25–34	15	60	–	–
35–44	16	–	50	–
45–54	16	–	50	–
55–64	33	–	–	77
65+	10	–	–	23
Base: All responding	(608)	(152)	(194)	(262)

Table 11.5 (b) Age group: Incorrect version

Age group	Total %	18–34 %	35–54 %	55+ %
18–24	10	24	–	–
25–34	15	76	–	–
35–44	16	–	–	–
45–54	16	–	100	–
55–64	33	–	–	77
65+	10	–	–	23
Base: All responding	(608)	(249)	(97)	(262)

any changes in the data, any differences since the last fieldwork period, are explainable in the context of market activity.

Starting the analysis

Once you have an accurate set of tables or, for a qualitative study, a set of transcripts, tapes and notes, you can begin the main stage of your analysis:

- ➤ Select the data relevant to the research problem.
- ➤ Prepare some informal analyses (for a quantitative project – highlight interesting numbers, extreme values, anything unexpected; for a qualitative project, prepare summaries of the key themes or issues emerging from each interview or group).
- ➤ Prepare tables, charts or diagrams that summarise the findings and build in comparisons with other relevant data, where appropriate (suitable for both quantitative and qualitative data).
- ➤ Refer back to your analysis framework – what ideas or hypotheses did you formulate? Test these ideas or hypotheses using the relevant data (and, for quantitative data, the appropriate statistical tests).
- ➤ What claims can you make based on the results of the hypotheses testing?
- ➤ Look for other data that support the story or argument that is emerging and continue to develop the story.
- ➤ Compare the findings from your research with the secondary data you collected or any qualitative data you gathered in the exploratory phase of the project.
- ➤ Continue to build up the story, checking for evidence that supports the findings as well as evidence that may refute them, to ensure the robustness of your argument.

Checking and reporting progress

During the life of a project you will be expected to liaise with and answer queries from the fieldwork organiser, coders and the data processing supplier, other members of the research team and the client. You therefore need to make sure that you are well briefed about the project so that you can handle queries in a confident and professional manner and keep all members of the project team informed and up to date with progress. You may find it useful to attend a fieldwork session, to hear and/or see for yourself how respondents react to a request to take part in research, how they respond to the questions or the stimulus material, and how the interviewer handles an interview. The experience will help you to answer questions about coding, for example, and will give you insights into the data that you might otherwise miss simply by looking at the tables or reading the transcripts. It will help you build up a greater understanding and appreciation of the data collection process and should help to improve your questionnaire and discussion guide design skills. It is also worthwhile spending some time working with the data processing supplier, in particular, in checking, editing and coding questionnaires. Reading through an entire record of an interview will give you greater insight into how the respondent views the issue under investigation than you may get seeing the data in tables aggregated by question.

▪ Liaising with the client

As soon as the client agrees the proposal and gives the go-ahead for the research, plan the fieldwork and data processing schedule with your suppliers and work out a detailed project timetable listing key delivery dates. There are two examples of timetables in Chapter 3 (Figures 3.1 and 3.2) that you might find useful in designing your own. Discuss and agree this timetable, making amendments where necessary, with the client. If, as the project progresses, some of these dates will not be met, tell the client as soon as possible, explaining the reasons why. Try not to set deadlines that you know you are unlikely to meet; if possible (and it is not always possible) build in some contingency time, in case fieldwork takes longer than anticipated, for example. Make sure that the client is clear about what is happening, when it is happening, what output he or she should expect, and what input is expected of him or her, for example agreement of the final questionnaire or dispatch of stimulus material. Keep the client up to date with regular progress reports, formal or informal, depending on the nature of the project, your relationship and what you agreed in the proposal.

▪ Managing your time

At any one time you may be dealing with four or five different projects, all at different stages of the research process. For example, you may have just been briefed on one job and may need to start preparing a proposal, while another job has just gone into field and you need to start thinking about developing an analysis plan; yet another job might be at the report-writing stage. It is important to prioritise this work and manage your time effectively so that you have enough time to do each part of each job well, and meet external and internal deadlines (DP specs and so on). One way of doing this is to plan out your projects on a workplan chart, with key dates highlighted and preparation time built in. Have a look again at the workplan examples in Chapter 3; you could adapt these to suit your own project. Alternatively, you could make a list of all the tasks you must complete each day and each week.

Recording and monitoring time

Recording and monitoring the time and costs associated with a project – filling in and analysing time reports – is important. If you are involved in costing a project you can use information in the time report system to see how long various aspects of similar projects took. To be useful, however, the information in the time report system must be accurate and up to date – hence the need for accurate and timely completion of the dreaded time sheets. The information in the time report system is also useful in workload planning – those managing the work can assess how busy people are (utilisation rates) and use this information to assign projects, decide on staffing levels and determine if there is a need to develop new business. The information is also useful in reviewing individual projects, to assess how time spent on the project compares with the original costing or the fee charged to the client. If a project took longer than the original costing suggested it is important to know why, so that any pitfalls may either be avoided on future jobs or built into the costing. There are many reasons why a project might go over budget, including the following:

➤ poor communication or briefing leading to tasks taking longer than expected or having to be redone;
➤ a client asking for more than was anticipated, for example extra reports or meetings;
➤ a change in the nature of the project after the original costing that was not addressed at the time;
➤ a sample that was harder to achieve than anticipated;
➤ the need for extra analyses to understand the research problem.

Although clients are not charged for proposals, time spent on proposals, even those that are unsuccessful, should be recorded so that you can work out the time and cost involved in generating new business and incorporate this into the costing structure.

Chapter summary

➤ What was requested in the brief and promised in the proposal and in discussion with the client must be turned into an effective research plan that is carried out efficiently. The role of the research executive is pivotal in this. He or she must brief the fieldwork, data processing and analysis suppliers and other members of the research team.

➤ The research executive's role also includes the following:
  ➤ administering the project on a day-to-day basis, checking progress, answering queries from field, DP, the client;
  ➤ making contributions to questionnaire/discussion guide design;
  ➤ ensuring the questionnaire/discussion guide is suitable and ready for fieldwork and analysis;
  ➤ preparing interviewer or recruiter briefing notes;
  ➤ preparing a coding and an analysis specification;
  ➤ checking the accuracy of data tables;
  ➤ listening to tapes and preparing transcripts and notes;
  ➤ liaising with and reporting progress to the client.

➤ International and multi-country research can be centrally co-ordinated or handled locally. The aim should be to achieve consistency across markets without losing any sensitivity in understanding particular markets. The role of co-ordinator is analogous to that of project manager, liaising with both the client and the local suppliers.

➤ A skill of the researcher is to manage his or her time effectively so that all internal and external project deadlines are met, and all elements of the project are carried out to a high standard.

Questions and exercises

1 Describe the role of the research agency executive in managing a research project.

2 List the information that you would give to a fieldwork supplier to ensure that they are fully informed about the requirements of a project.

3 Make a list of the things you would look out for in checking the suitability of a questionnaire for fieldwork.

4 List the information that should be included in a detailed set of interviewer briefing notes. For the next project in which you are involved, write a detailed set of briefing notes for interviewers or recruiters. If possible, compare your version with the version used for the project.

5 Describe the two main approaches to managing a multi-country research project. What are the advantages and disadvantages of each approach?

6 What do you need to know in order to design an analysis plan?

7 What issues do you need to think about in requesting the following:
(a) a set of top breaks;
(b) a set of summary tables; and
(c) summary and inferential statistics?

8 List the checks you should make to ensure that a set of data tables are accurate and meet the requirements set out in the table specification.

9 Describe how you would start the detailed process of analysis.

10 Why is it important to monitor the time spent on projects?

Reference

Winkler, J.T. (1987) 'The fly on the wall of the inner sanctum: observing company directors at work', in G. Moyser and M. Wagstaffe (eds), *Research Methods for Elite Studies*, London: Allen Unwin.

Recommended Reading

Childs, R. (1996) 'Buying international research', *Journal of the Market Research Society*, **38**, 1, pp. 63–6.

Hornsby-Smith, M. (1993) 'Gaining access', in Gilbert, N. (ed.), *Researching Social Life*, London: Sage.

Wilsdon, M. (1996) 'Getting it done properly: the role of the co-ordinator in multi-country research', *Journal of the Market Research Society*, **38**, 1, pp. 67–72.

Chapter 12

Analysing qualitative data

Introduction

In this chapter we look at ways of analysing and making sense of qualitative data, converting a mass of raw data – notes, taped interviews, transcriptions of interviews – into meaningful findings.

Topics covered

- What is qualitative data analysis?
- Planning the analysis and developing a strategy
- Doing the analysis:

    - organising the data
    - getting to know the data
    - getting to grips with what is going on
    - making links, looking for relationships
    - pulling together the findings

- Using computers in data analysis

Relationship to MRS Advanced Certificate Syllabus

The material covered in this chapter relates to Unit 9 – Information and Data Analysis, specifically:
- the analysis of qualitative information.

Learning outcomes

At the end of this chapter you should be able to:

- understand how to approach qualitative data analysis;
- understand and evaluate the findings from qualitative research;
- undertake and manage the qualitative analysis process.

What is qualitative data analysis?

In the same way that we look for patterns in quantitative and numeric data, we examine qualitative data for patterns, themes and relationships. The process of analysis is not a discrete phase undertaken once fieldwork is completed, rather it is ongoing from the very start of the research and a lot of the ideas about what you think is going on in the data will occur to you during fieldwork. It is once fieldwork is over, however, that you get the chance to organise the data, sort through them, think about them and with them, and pull together 'the findings'.

■ Approaches to analysis

Analysis of qualitative data is difficult and time consuming. There are no standard techniques or clearly defined procedures – there are many different approaches. Most researchers have their own way of doing it – and since little has been written about how it is done, particularly in commercial market research, there are no common guidelines. Denzin and Lincoln (1994) refer to qualitative research as *bricolage*, the art of adapting and using a variety of materials and tools, and to the qualitative researcher as a *bricoleur*, someone who is skilled in the use and adaptation of the tools. Qualitative data analysis is one area of qualitative research where this *bricolage* approach is very much in evidence. Techniques for conducting qualitative research and analysing qualitative data have been drawn from a range of disciplines within the social sciences, in particular from social anthropology and sociology. The approach individual researchers take in analysing qualitative data depends on a range of factors and their interaction. These include background and training, for example in science, social science or humanities; in psychology, sociology or anthropology; in the rational or emotional schools of qualitative research; in a particular paradigm or method such as semiology, hermeneutics, symbolic interactionism, ethnomethodology or discourse analysis. The approach also depends on the following:

➢ the way his or her mind works to sort and think about things (influenced by training and perhaps the left brain/right brain split);
➢ level of experience;
➢ level of knowledge in the area under investigation;
➢ the availability of relevant theories or models;
➢ the nature of the research enquiry – exploratory, descriptive, explanatory or a combination of these;
➢ the end use of the research;
➢ the resources available – time and number of people.

With so many factors having a potential influence, and with a lack of literature describing it, it is not surprising that qualitative data analysis is idiosyncratic – there are almost as many approaches to it as there are researchers.

Inductive and deductive reasoning

There are, however, some common principles based on deductive and inductive reasoning. In a deductive approach we speculate up front, in advance of fieldwork, about what it is we think we will find and we set out in the research to test this theory or hypothesis. We design the research and approach the analysis in a way that allows us to do this. We move from the general to the specific in deductive reasoning – from a general hypothesis or theory about what might be happening to specific observations to see if what we expect is actually happening. This approach is common in quantitative research and among some qualitative researchers (Katz, 1983) who refer to it as 'analytic induction'.

Box 12.1 Analytic induction

The approach known as analytic induction (AI) works something like this. You have defined the research problem and have some ideas about what you are looking for. From this, and using your understanding of the issues and the background to the problem (what you know from other research as well as gut feeling and intuition) you develop working hypotheses about the matter under investigation. You start fieldwork and throughout it you are thinking about how what respondents are telling you fits with your initial ideas and hypotheses. You keep questioning this, asking whether you need to amend or expand the hypotheses, modify your ideas about what is happening, explore some issues in greater depth, get more examples of things that fit with and do not fit with your hypotheses and so on.

In qualitative research the tendency is to use induction rather than deduction. Using this approach means that we do not go into the fieldwork to test out assumptions or existing theories or ideas. Data are collected and from the data we identify general principles that apply to the subject under study – we move from the specific to the general – theory building rather than theory testing. One such well-documented approach, grounded theory, is outlined in Box 12.2.

Box 12.2 Grounded theory

Grounded theory is the approach to analysis of qualitative data described by Glaser and Strauss (1967) and later by Strauss and Corbin (1998). In the grounded theory approach data are examined using the 'constant comparative method' in order to identify themes and patterns; concepts and codes are developed in order to summarise what is in the data. These concepts and codes are used to build propositions, or general statements, about relationships within the data. The codes and propositions are tested out in the data to make sure that they hold up, to make sure that they fit the categories to which they were assigned and that the propositions help to explain what is being studied. 'Theoretical sampling' is used to select new 'cases' (respondents) that might help develop the emerging concepts, propositions and theory.

Although grounded theory is often cited, particularly in academic research, as the approach taken in analysis, there is evidence (Bryman and Burgess, 1994) that few use it

Box 12.2 continued

in its entirety in the way that Glaser and Strauss and Strauss and Corbin describe. Citing the grounded theory approach is more likely to mean that the analysis is data driven rather than meaning that the specific approach, for example the coding procedures, the use of the constant comparative method or theoretical sampling, is followed exactly.

As you might imagine, it is difficult to use a purely inductive approach in practice. It is difficult to keep out all other ideas and to have a completely open mind when tackling a problem. It is likely that you will have some knowledge of the product field or area under investigation, or at least some understanding of general patterns of behaviour and attitudes (from previous research or the literature). Thus in real-world research analysis it is an iterative process involving both inductive and deductive reasoning. Hypotheses and ideas emerge from the data and are tested out within the data; you might revise or change them, collect more data in which to test and develop ideas and so on.

A word of caution is appropriate here. We all have biases – ways of thinking, opinions and attitudes, ideas about the research and what we might find before we start. These might come from our life experience and general knowledge as well as from work on projects in the same area, from briefing documents and background reading and so on. It is important that these are not allowed to skew the analysis and interpretation of the data or limit it in any way. Your own thinking about the issue may mean that you see only what you want to see, or only what fits with your view of the problem. It is important in qualitative research and in analysis to think about alternative hypotheses, to be open to different ways of looking at and interpreting the evidence, and to question and challenge what we see or think we see in the data. At the outset of a project, therefore, it is important to examine what you 'know' or assume, what pre-conceptions you might be bringing to the fieldwork and analysis. Before going into the field think through how you feel about the topic. Ask yourself: What do I think about the advertising? What attitudes do I have about this issue? Make these explicit, articulate them, challenge them and then leave them to one side as much as possible.

This approach, however, does not rule out the use of existing theories or models. A good theory or model can be an invaluable aid to analysis – it can be used to help develop and expand your thinking. Speed the analysis process by giving it a framework and thus a coherence; it can suggest questions to ask and lines of enquiry to follow; and it can provide ideas for developing typologies. Used alongside a systematic testing out of ideas in the data – looking for supporting and disconfirming evidence – a model or theory can help produce a very robust analysis. In choosing a model or theory you need to examine how well founded it is – use those that are well researched and empirically based.

In analysing qualitative data remember the following:

➢ keep an open mind;
➢ do not jump to conclusions too early;
➢ separate how you see the issue from how respondents see it (to avoid imposing your views and ways of thinking on the data);
➢ do not force the data to fit with what a theory or model suggests.

■ The aim of analysis

Regardless of the approach, however, the aim of analysis is the same – to extract meaningful insights from the data and to produce valid and reliable findings that help to answer the research problem. To achieve this, analysis should be disciplined and rigorous. This does not mean that it should be entirely mechanical or prescriptive. It does mean that it should be thorough, consistent and comprehensive, systematic without being rigid, and open to the possibilities and insights that emerge as a result – intuition and creativity are a vital part of it.

The aim of this chapter is to set out some general guidelines for analysing data in a way that leads to valid and reliable findings. For ease of description the process is broken up into stages:

➤ Planning the analysis and developing a strategy.
➤ Doing the analysis:
  ➤ organising the data;
  ➤ getting to know the data;
  ➤ getting to grips with what is going on;
  ➤ making links, looking for relationships;
  ➤ pulling together the findings.

In the real-life, untidy world of qualitative analysis, however, these activities often do not always exist as distinct phases – parts of each phase may be taking place at one time. Rather than moving from one stage to the next in a neat progression it is more likely that bits of each stage will be repeated over and over again as you move through the data. What is presented here is not a prescription for qualitative data analysis but a guideline or set of techniques that you may find useful in getting to grips with your data and discovering your own approach to analysis.

Planning the analysis

In this section we look at what needs to be done before the main stage of analysis – post-fieldwork – begins. In other words, what do you need to be thinking about during the early stages of the project?

■ At the research design stage

Although the main phase of analysis happens at the tail end of fieldwork, that is not where it begins. Analysis really does start from the moment you get the brief and start thinking about the problem. Box 12.3 is a checklist designed to help you think through what implications each bit of the research process and each decision has for the analysis. There is no substitute for clear, thorough thinking at this early stage. The process of analysis will be less painful and the outcome of the analysis of much better quality if you spend time at the front end – understanding the research problem and its implications for analysis. The aims and objectives of the research drive the research design and the choice of sample, method and questions, and all of this will determine the analysis strategy. Thinking about these things at an early stage will often give you a way into the analysis, a way of tackling it, helping you to develop both a framework and a strategy.

Box 12.3 Thinking forward to the analysis

The problem

➢ Are you clear about the issues involved? Is the problem clearly defined?

➢ Is your task to explore, describe, explain or evaluate?

➢ What output is expected? How will the findings be used?

➢ What, if any, are your working hypotheses or ideas?

➢ Is there any previous research or relevant literature that might be helpful?

The sample

➢ Whom do you need to interview? How many?

➢ Have you identified different types of respondent?

➢ What implications will this have for your analysis? Do you expect to see different responses from different types of respondent? Will it be useful to compare responses among similar groups of respondents and between different groups?

The method

➢ What method have you chosen? Observation? Depth interviews? Group discussions?

➢ How will this affect the analysis process?

The questions

➢ What topics are to be covered in the interview?

➢ What questioning techniques will you use? Will you use projective or enabling techniques?

➢ What implications do these questions have for the analysis?

■ At the fieldwork stage

There is a huge overlap between fieldwork and analysis in qualitative research. You collect data, think about them all the while and collect more – perhaps using a slightly amended discussion guide or reworked stimulus material as fieldwork sheds light on the issues. The whole time your thinking about the issues is developing: ideas, hunches and insights will pop up, hypotheses will emerge that you might want to test out or explore further.

Fieldnotes

For this reason it is worth keeping a fairly detailed log of thoughts and insights as they occur to you during fieldwork. Write them down as soon as possible – you may not remember them when it comes to the main phase of analysis. Sit down as soon as possible after an interview or group is over and 'braindump' all your thoughts, feelings, ideas, impressions and insights in as much detail as possible. If you are working with a colleague review the interview or group with him or her in detail as soon as possible after it is over and make detailed notes. If you have client observers talk to them – ask them what they thought and note down what they say. Write down what you think are the key themes, relevant quotations, things that you might want to explore or think about in more detail later, anything that was said that you did not expect, for example. In other words make a note of anything that occurs to you that you think might be useful when the analysis process is in full swing. Make sure to clarify what are impressions and inferences and what are facts or more concrete observations (Boulton and Hammersley, 1996).

It is also useful at the end of an interview or group to write up a summary of the main points made by the respondent or by the group under each of the topics or questions on the interview guide (Miles and Huberman, 1994). This will help settle things in your memory and will be useful later in the analysis. It will help you develop ideas about the data and decide on an analysis strategy. It may also be a useful reference source or guide when it comes to writing up the findings in detail.

These notes and summaries can be particularly useful if more than one person is involved in the fieldwork, and if more than one person is to be involved in the analysis. Other members of the team can read them in order get to grips with data across the whole sample.

Box 12.4 Summary so far

➤ Plan out how you are going to tackle the analysis when you plan the research.

➤ Think about and evaluate what is going on while you are doing the fieldwork – what you are hearing and seeing and sensing.

➤ Braindump all your thoughts as soon as possible afterwards.

➤ Make detailed notes about what is emerging, what picture is beginning to build up; write down any particularly relevant or interesting quotations.

➤ Ask yourself what was unexpected or surprising; examine and challenge your own assumptions.

➤ Think of questions to ask of the data, comparisons that might be useful.

➤ Consider what issues need to be explored in greater depth, what new areas you need to probe.

➤ Consider what implications these early findings have for further fieldwork, and for analysis and interpretation, and make changes if necessary.

■ Developing an analysis strategy

Having thought through the research problem and completed some of the fieldwork you will have in your head – and in your notes – the basis of an analysis strategy, or plan for tackling the analysis. It is worth formalising this plan, making it explicit, especially if you are relatively new to qualitative research. It is easy to feel over-whelmed by the amount of data you have collected, and by the thought of having to find a way through them. The possible lines of inquiry in most qualitative studies are numerous, and time and resources are usually always limited. The analysis strategy should set out a way of approaching the data, and in doing so calm your fears about the size and complexity of the task and ensure that you tackle it in a systematic and rigorous way. A strategy that has been developed to suit the aims and requirements of the research should help you make the most of the time and resources available by prioritising your lines of inquiry. But having a strategy in place does not mean that you have to stick rigidly to it, whatever the data throws up – it can and should be adapted and modified to fit the circumstances.

In putting together your analysis strategy it is useful to think about the following:

➢ What are the practical considerations?
   ➢ How many are going to be involved in the analysis?
   ➢ Is the client or sponsor to be involved in the analysis process?
   ➢ How long do you have for analysis?
   ➢ Are you going to work from transcriptions, tapes or notes or a combination?
   ➢ Will you be using a computer analysis package?

➢ What are the research considerations?
   ➢ What decisions are to be taken on the basis of the research findings?
   ➢ How detailed does the analysis need to be?
   ➢ What outputs are required? Presentation, summary report, full report?
   ➢ Are the findings to be published?

➢ How are you going to tackle the task?
   ➢ By country?
   ➢ Interview by interview or group by group?
   ➢ Question by question?
   ➢ By respondent type?

There is no one way of developing a strategy – one approach is to use the research brief or the research proposal (if there is one). Start by writing down the big research questions that you have set out to answer – the objectives of the research. List the questions and the types of respondents that might help throw light on each of these and write down what it is you will be looking for in the data generated by the questions and the respondents that will help you address the research objectives. This is your analysis strategy. As your analysis and your ideas develop you might find (through a search of the relevant literature) that there is a body of knowledge that supports them – from reports of research on your topic to well-developed models and theories – from marketing science, psychology and consumer behaviour, and sociology, for example. It can often be worthwhile to make use of these models and theories – they can help you to structure the analysis, suggesting lines of enquiry, and will help you to develop your thinking. They should not be overlooked as a source of inspiration and help but neither should they be used uncritically.

Doing the analysis

The main stage of analysis usually begins when fieldwork is more or less completed. There are five main steps in this part of the process:

➤ organising the data;
➤ getting to know the data;
➤ getting to grips with what is going on;
➤ making links, looking for relationships;
➤ pulling together the findings.

■ Organising the data

Organising the data involves sorting out all the materials you need in order to get on with the analysis. Depending on the size and complexity of the project, and the way in which you like to work, you may well have accumulated a lot of 'raw materials' – a pile of tapes from interviews or group discussions; fieldnotes; transcriptions of the taped interviews; and notes about respondents' interpretations of enabling and projective exercises and copies of the output of these exercises.

It may help you to declutter your mind in readiness for the in-depth analysis process if you spend some time sorting this material into files or folders, labelling it, and generally making it easy to retrieve. It is particularly useful at this stage to make several copies of transcripts – an unadulterated master copy, a copy for cutting and pasting (if that is how you like to work), and a copy on which you make notes. Once this sorting and filing is complete you can review your field notes, listen to (or watch) your tapes, read through the transcripts and prepare how you plan to tackle the analysis.

Common reactions of novice researchers at this stage are panic and anxiety – about the mass of data and how to get started. In all likelihood you will have more thinking done than you realise, and sorting and organising your data, reviewing your notes, reading transcripts and talking to colleagues about the data will help sort things out in your mind. Do not put off getting started – look back at your analysis strategy and get stuck in. It can be a laborious process – and you must approach it in a systematic way – but you will soon find that things fall into place, and a story will start to emerge.

■ Getting to know the data

It is a good idea in the early stages of your qualitative research career (if time and teamwork considerations permit) to prepare your own transcripts. Not only will you learn a lot about your interviewing technique but it will give you the chance to get into the data, to get to know it thoroughly. If you are not able to do this make sure you listen to or watch your tapes and read through the transcripts in full. Make notes as you do this, putting faces to words, noting how things were said, what was not said, what interpretations occur to you as you go through, what ideas strike you and so on.

Although you go into this more intensive phase of analysis with some ideas, feelings and impressions about what is going on, and perhaps some ideas about what it all means, it is important not to jump to conclusions too early. You may find that until you listen to your tapes or read through the transcripts that the interviews or groups you conducted all merge into one in your mind. There is a danger that you misremember things, or give some things more importance in your mind than was actually the case. You need to protect against the selectivity and decay of your memory. This is why notes made at the time are particularly important – they are more reliable than notes made some time after fieldwork – and why listening to or viewing the tapes of the interviews is so important. When reading your notes and transcripts and listening to or watching your tapes, write down any analytic ideas and impressions that occur to you and make a note about testing them out right across the data to see if they hold up. You will need to go back through all of the data systematically and read, listen to or watch them closely to make sure that you see the whole picture, not just the bits that stuck in your mind. Test your ideas out by looking at and comparing data from different types of respondents. Do not get too attached to ideas too early – you may have to ditch them as the analysis develops. Keep your mind open throughout the process to the possibility of new or alternative explanations and new ideas.

■ Getting to grips with what is going on

This is the 'pulling apart' stage of the analysis. Once you have read your notes and transcripts and listened to/watched the tapes, and looked at the data by respondent, by type of respondent or by topic, you will start to notice patterns and themes. You will see that some things crop up a lot, or at least more than others, that there are discernible patterns in attitudes, behaviour, opinions and experiences. You may notice patterns in the way in which people express themselves about an issue and the language they use to describe things. Record all of these – in a notebook, on the transcripts, on your data analysis sheet, in the computer program – whichever you use.

Coding and summarising

To understand fully what is going on you need to dissect the data, pull them apart and scrutinise them bit by bit. This involves working through the data, identifying themes and patterns and labelling them or placing them under headings or brief descriptions summarising what they mean. This process is known as categorising or coding the data. Later in the process, when you have a thorough understanding of all the elements, you can link the data – all the coded segments – together again.

This coding process is not just a mechanical one of naming things and assigning them to categories, it is also a creative and analytic process involving dissecting and ordering the data in a meaningful way – a way that helps you think about and understand the research problem. Coding is a useful 'data handling' tool – by bringing similar bits of data together (Miles and Huberman, 1994) and by reducing them to summary codes you make the mass of data more manageable and easier to get to grips with, enabling you to see what is going on relatively quickly and easily. The process of developing codes and searching for examples, instances and occurrences of material that relate to the code, ensures that you take a rigorous and systematic approach. Codes are also a useful 'data thinking' tool. The codes you develop – and the way you lay them out – allow you to see fairly quickly and easily what similarities, differences, patterns, themes, relationships and so on exist in the data. They should lead you to question the data and what you see in them. The coding process can help you develop the bigger picture by bringing together material related to your ideas and hunches, thus enabling you to put a conceptual order (Strauss, 1987) on the data (moving from specific instances to general statements) and to make links and generate findings.

Generating codes

But how do you generate these codes in the first place? Where do they come from? You can use the topics or question areas from your discussion or interview guide (without reference to the data) as general codes or headings. For example, you might have asked respondents to describe their ideal airline flight – you could have a general code called 'ideal flight' and during the coding process bring together all the descriptions from across the groups or interviews under this code or heading, as follows (although in a live project each extract would be labelled with respondent details):

Ideal flight

'Good films, plenty of leg room, decent food. You're sitting on your own for six or eight hours, you want those things.'

'You want to feel appreciated by them. You don't want to be treated like a number.'

'Plenty of airmiles that I can use to go on holiday.'

'Nothing to annoy you – no one in front of you in the check-in queue, no delays, a seat with plenty of leg room and no one sitting beside you, decent food, clean toilets and not having to wait around for ages before your bags arrive.'

'Comfort and decent entertainment – that's it.'

'The service – the feeling that they're there to serve you.'

'There's never a queue at check-in – it's hassle-free . . .'

'A reserved car parking space, close to the terminal, that's free.'

'An efficient service from check-in right through to collecting your luggage.'

'Speed at the check-in, and not having to be there really early.'

'Comfort and plenty of room – and no one sitting beside you, that's great.'

'A fully reclinable chair and plenty of room around you.'

'Being left alone to get on with some work.'

'A good entertainment system – good head phones, comfortable ones, and your own little screen.'

'No delays or hassles – simple things like that.'

'Being able to get off the plane feeling great, not uncomfortable and exhausted.'

Remember in doing this that some people may have talked about a particular topic or answered a question later or earlier than the topic was mentioned, so you may need to search the data for all incidences of it.

Rather than imposing codes from outside the data you can go into the data and see what words or terms or concepts respondents use to describe things and use these as the codes. Remember that different people may use different language to describe the same thing so make sure that you look for this.

The coding process

The coding process itself can also be tackled in a number of ways, and different researchers will have different approaches – using pen and paper or computer. A relatively easy way of doing it if your transcripts are available in a word-processing package is to create a new document for each heading, topic or code. As you work through your transcript cut out sections of text that relate to the code and paste them into the document you have created to represent that code. In this way you can build up a store of relevant material related to that particular code or topic. Take care to label the source of each bit (respondent details, group, place in transcript) that you cut so that you know the context from which it came, and can refer back to it if necessary. And remember that one bit of data or text may fit under more than one heading or code. You could, alternatively, go through the transcript and label bits of text *in situ*, before gathering the same or similarly labelled bits in one place or under one heading.

It is likely that you will make several – at least two – coding 'passes' through the data. At the first pass you might keep the codes fairly general and keep the number to a minimum. For example, you might have identified four or five key themes in your data or you may have divided it up under several topic areas. As you work through the data a second time you can divide these big, general codes into more specific ones. In the 'ideal flight' example you might, on a second coding pass, pull apart all the aspects respondents include in their ideal flight and code or group these under headings such as 'emotional aspects' (feelings of well-being and so on), 'physical aspects' (leg room and so on), 'facilities available' or 'service'. In this second pass you might group your data extracts under each of the relevant codes as follows (note that some appear in more than one category, either because the respondent said more than one thing and you want to maintain the quotation in full or because in some cases it is not clear in which category to include them):

Emotional aspects

'You want to feel appreciated by them. You don't want to be treated like a number.'

'Nothing to annoy you – no one in front of you in the check-in queue, no delays, a seat with plenty of leg room and no one sitting beside you, decent food, clean toilets and not having to wait around for ages before your bags arrive.'

'Being left alone to get on with some work.'

'No delays or hassles – simple things like that.'

Physical aspects

'Good films, plenty of leg room, decent food. You're sitting on your own for six or eight hours, you want those things.'

'Nothing to annoy you – no one in front of you in the check-in queue, no delays, a seat with plenty of leg room and no one sitting beside you, decent food, clean toilets and not having to wait around for ages before your bags arrive.'

'Comfort and decent entertainment – that's it.'

'Comfort and plenty of room – and no one sitting beside you, that's great.'

'A fully reclinable chair and plenty of room around you.'

'Being able to get off the plane and feeling great, not uncomfortable and exhausted.'

Facilities

'Good films, plenty of leg room, decent food. You're sitting on your own for six or eight hours, you want those things.'

'Plenty of airmiles that I can use to go on holiday.'

'Nothing to annoy you – no one in front of you in the check-in queue, no delays, a seat with plenty of leg room and no one sitting beside you, decent food, clean toilets and not having to wait around for ages before your bags arrive.'

'Comfort and decent entertainment – that's it.'

'A reserved car parking space, close to the terminal, that's free.'

'A good entertainment system – good head phones, comfortable ones, and your own little screen.'

Service

'Nothing to annoy you – no one in front of you in the check-in queue, no delays, a seat with plenty of leg room and no one sitting beside you, decent food, clean toilets and not having to wait around for ages before your bags arrive.'

'The service – the feeling that they're there to serve you.'

'There's never a queue at check-in – it's hassle-free ...'

'A reserved car parking space, close to the terminal, that's free.'

'An efficient service from check-in right through to collecting your luggage.'

'Speed at the check-in, and not having to be there really early.'

'Being left alone to get on with some work.'

'No delays or hassles – simple things like that.'

Alternatively, you can code the other way round – coding everything that occurs to you as you pass through the data the first time and use the second or third pass to structure or revise these more detailed codes. There is no right or wrong way – do what feels best for you and for the data.

During the coding process do not rule out the possibility that bits of data may have multiple meanings or a meaning different from the one that you are assuming. Always check out the context of comments in order to learn more about the meaning of what was said; it may also be useful to go back to the tape. Stay open to new ideas and new ways of looking at and coding the data. Try not to jump to conclusions or close off avenues of enquiry. Do not think of the codes you have created as static or fixed – they can be expanded, split apart or even discarded if they no longer seem useful or if they do not work.

Once you have bits of data together under a heading or code the next step is to compare all the bits – looking for similarities and differences between them. This will help you refine the codes, making them more specific, and it will also help you achieve a greater understanding of the data. You might do this during the second pass at coding, or even at a third pass, depending on the time available and the level of detail and depth you need to achieve with the analysis.

At this stage you may want to extract some verbatim comments – quotations or vignettes, extended story-like quotations that illustrate a typical experience or event (Miles and Huberman, 1994) – for use in the presentation or report of the findings. In selecting these make sure that you do not oversample the responses of the more articulate respondents. You may want to choose a range of responses that illustrate a particular phenomenon, attitude, feeling or experience, putting together a sort of database of quotations. Make sure in removing them from the transcript that you provide enough context so that the meaning is clear, and ensure that they are labelled with the relevant respondent details.

Box 12.5 Approaches to coding and analysis: variations by technology

➤ *Pen and paper*: use a different coloured pen to highlight or underline comments that relate to each topic or theme; cut out verbatim comments from the transcript and paste them together with other comments relating to that topic or theme on to a separate sheet of paper.

➤ *Word processor*: use the word-processing package to highlight comments using different colours or different fonts for different topics or themes; cut and paste relevant sections of the transcriptions under headings or themes on a separate page or into a separate document.

➤ *Qualitative data analysis package*: import transcripts into an analysis package, label sections of text that relate to particular topics and themes with relevant headings or brief descriptions – 'codes' – and use the software to sort and retrieve passages of texts labelled in the same way.

During and after this 'dissection' stage you will start to see links and connections between bits of data. The next step is to put things back together again in the light of the understanding you have achieved via the dissection. The summary version of the data – the coding scheme – can make it easier to see links, connections and relationships in the data.

■ Making links and looking for relationships

You now have a very good grasp of your data. A 'story' should be emerging, and it is likely that you will have some tentative ideas or explanations about what is going on. As you have read through and listened to your data and as you have coded them you will have made notes about links between different themes or codes that overlap and you will have been asking questions of the data, testing out ideas and looking for relationships. For example, you might ask, 'Does the description of an ideal flight vary between frequent and less frequent flyers or those who usually fly club class and those who fly first class?', 'Is it only users who think x, or do non-users hold the same view?', 'Is it younger women who say that or is it all women?' or 'Is it life stage rather than age or demographics that might explain a particular pattern?' You may be able to develop typologies, categorising respondents in terms of similarities in their characteristics. You might be able to isolate several types of business flyer, for example, characterised by frequency of travel and attitude or delight in the experience; or different types of homeless people, characterised by the length of time they have been homeless and their feelings about their situation. The questions you ask of the data and the way you develop the data will be driven by the research objectives.

As you make links and connections, or see relationships, think about what might explain them and think about more than one explanation. Once you have generated some possible explanations start looking for evidence to support your ideas and interpretations as well as evidence that might not support them. At this stage you may well still be coding the data – and making the codes more detailed or refined. At the same time you may also find that you can move from the specific codes you developed to more abstract concepts and from these concepts to a greater degree of generalisation about what is going on in the data.

Box 12.6 Thinking about the data

What's going on?

Words and meaning:

➤ Look for common words and phrases.
➤ Look at the context of words – always try to get an understanding of the respondent's meaning.
➤ Always think of alternative meanings in a phrase; look at the context and the data as a whole for clarification of meaning and as an aid to understanding.

Frequency, strength and consistency of response:

➤ How common were particular responses?
➤ Was there a range of response in relation to a particular topic or question?
➤ How diverse was the response? How similar?
➤ How strongly held were opinions or attitudes?
➤ How consistent were opinions and attitudes?

Emerging ideas and hypotheses:

➤ Look for evidence that supports and evidence that disconfirms the hypothesis.
➤ Make comparisons between respondents or between groups. What does this tell you?

Box 12.6 continued

➢ Are there similarities in responses and patterns of response?
➢ Can you form categories or typologies? Do certain types of people hold similar views? Are there several people who fall into the one category? Are there exceptions? Does someone fall into a different category than you might expect?
➢ Why might that be? What is it that drives this difference?

Using charts, diagrams and maps

Using diagrams, tables, flow charts and maps to sort and present data can help you think and can help to uncover or elucidate patterns and relationships. Some people can think in and/or express ideas better in pictures and diagrams than they can in words. Reducing data to fit a diagram or table can focus the thinking on the relationships that exist in the data. The most suitable format will depend largely on what it is you are trying to understand. A perceptual map may be useful in showing how different brands lie in relation to each other and key brand attributes. Figure 12.1 shows an example.

A flow chart might be suitable to show a detailed chronology of events, for example the events leading to homelessness or a move to a hostel or shelter, or the steps involved in investment planning. A table might be useful for summarising the reactions of different groups or types of respondents to particular stimulus material – product concepts, for example, or mood boards. An example is given in Table 12.1. Key comments about each concept can be written in for each respondent.

■ Pulling together the findings

As you work through your data, immersing yourself in them, pulling them apart and building them up, questioning, testing out ideas and hypotheses, you are likely to reach a point where suddenly it all seems to fit together and make sense or produce a story. Here are a few ways of helping this along. When all of the data and ideas are in your

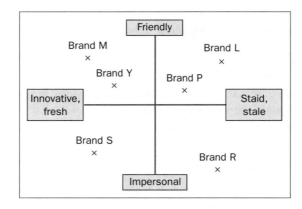

Figure 12.1 Example of a perceptual map

Table 12.1 Data analysis summary table

	Younger respondents (15–18 years) Comments			Older respondents (19–24 years) Comments		
	R1	R2	R3	R1	R2	R3
Concept code						
1						
2						
3						
4						

head it can be useful to take a break from the analysis, to let things ferment, to give things time to 'gestate'. Go and do something unrelated – exercise or listen to music – and you may find you have that 'eureka' moment. Another way is to talk about the findings out loud to someone not directly involved in the project. All he or she has to do is sit and listen and perhaps ask a few questions. Often in trying to articulate the ideas in your mind in order to speak them out loud and explain them to someone else you make connections or see a picture that you have not seen before. The other person can help by asking questions so that you have to explain your thinking and reasoning. They may ask questions that you have not asked yourself, which may help further. Yet another way is to read the literature relevant to your project, whether it is the original briefing notes or a journal article on the same topic. This may spark off fresh ideas, suggest further lines of questioning or help you make a useful connection.

During the whole of the analysis process it is important that you bear in mind the objectives of the research – do not lose sight of them as you become immersed in the data. It can be helpful after you complete the coding stage to start writing things down in some detail and, as you do so, to be constantly asking yourself how it all ties in with the research objectives. As soon as you have the story or the elements of the story clear in your mind, go back again to the research objectives. Think about what light the evidence you have uncovered sheds on the research objectives. Think about what implications the findings have – what is the 'So what?' of each of the insights the research has produced?

It is also useful to think about the quality of your findings:

➤ How plausible are they?
➤ Do they make sense?
➤ Are they intuitive or counter-intuitive? Surprising or what you might expect?
➤ How much evidence is there to support them?
➤ How credible and plausible is this evidence?
➤ How do they fit with evidence gathered elsewhere – from other research in this area, from theory, from the literature?
➤ Have you thoroughly examined the data for disconfirming evidence?
➤ Have you checked that other explanations do not fit the data better?
➤ Have you accounted for contradictions, oddities or outliers?

➢ Have you introduced any bias?

➢ Have you given more weight to what the more articulate in the sample have said at the expense of others?

➢ Have you been systematic and rigorous in looking for evidence and taking into account all views and perspectives?

➢ Are you seeing in the data what you want to see?

➢ Are you overinterpreting things?

➢ Is there anything you might have missed?

Using computers in data analysis

There is no computer program that will perform the task of data analysis for you. There are, however, many programs (including word-processing programs) that can be used for the more mechanical aspects of the process. There are programs that will store and manage data, search for and retrieve text and replicate the manual tasks of cutting, pasting and coding data. There are also programs that have mapping capabilities and some which help in building theory – linking concepts and categories. Most of this type of software has been designed by qualitative researchers in the social sciences who have worked on large-scale qualitative projects.

Computer-aided qualitative data analysis software (CAQDAS) is popular in academic research, not least because it allows an audit trail through the researcher's analysis process, which may be essential for peer review of the work. The approach is increasingly popular in social research for much the same reason – it implies a systematic approach, added rigour in the analysis process and a transparent and traceable route through the data (although most of these benefits come from how the researcher uses the software rather than the software itself). CAQDAS is little used at present in commercial market research. It can be time consuming, and most packages rely on full transcripts, which are not always produced in market research. Below we look at some of the functions available in the software.

■ Storing and organising data

All qualitative analysis packages have this capability. Word-processing packages are also useful – you can open a new document each time you want to separate out segments of transcripts under particular headings. In order to trace the segments extracted back to their original, however, you have to make sure you have indexed them or labelled them in some way.

■ Search and retrieve

Again all qualitative analysis packages offer this. Word-processing packages can be used to a limited extent to search and retrieve (more so if you can write macros). There are specially written programs that perform the task much faster than word-processing programs – they search for the word or phrase and can give you the extract in which the word is embedded (you can specify the length or spread of words either side of the key word).

■ Coding

There are programs that allow you to code or label chunks of text and allow you to search under that heading for all those bits of texts labelled with that code – rather than just searching for text that contains a particular word.

■ Content analysis

There are programs that allow you to count the frequency with which certain words or phrases occur – particularly useful if you are doing a detailed content analysis.

Qualitative data analysis packages are a good way of storing and handling data and making analysis accessible. They allow you to change how you think about the data, reworking coding schemes as new insights emerge, revisiting segments of the data quickly and easily. As you work through the data you can record all your thinking about it (the way you might make notes in the margin of a transcript, for example). They allow you to see all the bits of data plus the whole – you can move back and forward in order to see the context of extracts. The search and retrieve functions allow you to interrogate the data more easily and so more thoroughly than you might with paper transcripts – and so enable you to achieve a more in-depth understanding of the data and have greater confidence in your findings.

Ultimately, of course, any package is only as good as your own thinking and analysis skills. Do not think that by simply going through the procedures set out in the program you will end up with a good piece of analysis. The program will only carry out your instructions, it does not think for you. It will help you do the things you would normally do, and enable you to do them in more detail, more often and more thoroughly.

If you are thinking of using an analysis program it is advisable to have a good grasp of the principles of analysis before you start and you should bear in mind that despite your analytical skills there is quite a steep learning curve with most programs. In addition, most require full transcripts, which are time consuming to prepare, but once familiar with the program you may save time in the labour-intensive tasks of sorting, organising and coding the data. This is particularly true if you are working on a large project or have a complex mass of data to analyse. With smaller projects – Morgan (1998) suggests the cut-off point is six groups or less – it may not be worth the bother.

Chapter summary

➤ Qualitative data analysis involves looking for patterns, themes and relationships in the data. It is an ongoing process that begins at the start of a project and continues during fieldwork. The main work is, however, done at the end of fieldwork.

➢ It is a difficult and time-consuming task. There are no standard techniques or clearly defined procedures – there are many different approaches. Techniques are drawn from a range of disciplines within the social sciences, in particular from social anthropology and sociology. The approach individual researchers take depends, among other things, on their background and training.

➢ The aim of analysis is to extract meaningful insights from the data and produce valid and reliable findings that help answer the research problem. Analysis should be disciplined and rigorous, systematic without being rigid, and open to the possibilities and insights that emerge as a result – intuition and creativity are a vital part of it.

➢ One approach to analysis is the inductive approach – to collect data and from the data identify general principles that apply to the subject under study, moving from the specific to the general – theory building rather than theory testing. Grounded theory is an example of this approach.

➢ It is difficult to use a purely inductive approach in practice as it is likely that you will have some knowledge of the product field or area under investigation. In real-world research analysis is an iterative process involving both inductive and deductive reasoning. Hypotheses and ideas emerge from the data and are tested out within them.

➢ It is important in approaching fieldwork and analysis to be aware of our biases – ways of thinking, opinions and attitudes, ideas about the research and what we might find before we start. These should not be allowed to skew the analysis and interpretation of the data or limit it in any way. Throughout the analysis process keep an open mind, do not jump to conclusions too early; separate how you see the issue from how respondents see it.

➢ A good theory or model can be an invaluable aid to analysis, helping to develop and expand thinking; speed the process by giving it a coherence, suggesting lines of enquiry to follow and providing ideas for developing typologies. In choosing a model or theory examine how well founded it is – use those that are well researched and empirically based. Do not force the data to fit with what a theory or model suggests.

➢ The process of analysis involves organising and sorting the data, getting to know the data in detail, thinking about them and with them, pulling them apart to understand them and fitting them together, making links and looking for relationships, to produce 'the findings'.

➢ In the real-life world of qualitative analysis these activities do not always exist as distinct phases – parts of each phase may be taking place at one time. Rather than moving from one stage to the next in a neat progression it is more likely that bits of each stage will be repeated over and over again as you move through the data.

➢ The process of coding or labelling the data is an important analytical tool. It not only helps summarise the mass of data but it enables the researcher to think with the data and uncover patterns, themes and relationships.

➤ Using diagrams, tables, flow charts and maps to sort and present data can help you think and can help to uncover or elucidate patterns and relationships.

➤ Findings and the evidence on which they are based should be checked and tested in the data in a thorough and systematic way.

➤ There are many specialist computer programs for the analysis of qualitative data. The programs help with the storage, sorting, searching and retrieval of data; some facilitate theory building. The quality of the analysis produced can be greater in depth and detail but is dependent on how the researcher uses it, not on the software itself.

Questions and exercises

1 Describe the stages involved in analysing qualitative data.

2 What is coding and why is it useful in analysis?

3 Why are tables, diagrams and maps useful in analysis? Give examples of their use.

4 Describe the advantages and disadvantages of computer-aided qualitative data analysis.

5 Prepare a checklist that you might use to assess the quality of a piece of data analysis.

References

Boulton, D. and Hammersley, M. (1996) 'Analysis of unstructured data', in Sapsford, R. and Jupp, V. (eds) *Data Collection and Analysis*, London: Sage.

Bryman, A. and Burgess, R. (eds) *Analyzing Qualitative Data*, London: Routledge.

Denzin, N. and Lincoln, Y. (eds) (1994) *Handbook of Qualitative Research*, London: Sage.

Glaser, B. and Strauss, A. (1967) *The Discovery of Grounded Theory*, Chicago IL: Aldine.

Katz, J. (1983) 'A theory of qualitative methodology: the social science system of analytic field-work', in Emerson, R. (ed.) *Contemporary Field Research*, Boston, MA: Little Brown.

Miles, M. and Huberman, A. M. (1994) *Qualitative Data Analysis: An Expanded Sourcebook*, London: Sage.

Morgan, D., quoted in Krueger, R. (1998) *Analyzing and Reporting Focus Group Results*, Chapter 8, p. 93, London: Sage.

Strauss, A. (1987) *Qualitative Analysis for Social Scientists*, Cambridge: Cambridge University Press.

Strauss, A. and Corbin, J. (1998) *Basics of Qualitative Research*, London: Sage.

Recommended reading

Listed below are several excellent accounts of analysis in a social research context that serve to illustrate the process.

Casey, M. (1998) 'Analysis: honoring the stories', in Krueger, R. *Analyzing and Reporting Focus Group Results*, London: Sage.

Ritchie, J. and Spencer, L. (1992) 'Qualitative data analysis for applied policy research', in Burgess, A. and Bryman, R. (eds) *Analyzing Qualitative Data*, London: Routledge. This volume contains other interesting and useful accounts, including those involving computer aided analysis.

Taraborelli, P. (1993) 'Becoming a carer', in Gilbert, N. (ed.) *Researching Social Life*, London: Sage.

Robson, S. and Hedges, A. (1993) 'Analysis and interpretation of qualitative findings, Report of The MRS Qualitative Interest Group', *Journal of the Market Research Society* 35, 1, pp. 23–35. A review of qualitative data analysis in market research.

Wells, S. (1991) 'Wet towels and whetted appetites or a wet blanket? The role of analysis in qualitative research', *Journal of the Market Research Society* 33, 1, pp. 39–44. An account of the process in market research.

For those interested in computer-aided qualitative analysis the main applications are reviewed at the CAQDAS website, **www.surrey.ac.uk/caqdas**.

Strauss, A. and Corbin, J. (1998) *Basics of Qualitative Research*, London: Sage. A very readable account of the 'techniques and procedures for developing grounded theory'.

Miles, M. and Huberman, A. M. (1994) *Qualitative Data Analysis: An Expanded Sourcebook*, London: Sage. A very useful source of ideas and information on analysis.

Chapter 13

Analysing quantitative data

Introduction

The aim of this chapter is to introduce you to quantitative data and to the basics of quantitative data analysis. The process of analysis involves sorting, organising and summarising data collected via the questionnaire in a way that aids interpretation and reporting of findings, and ultimately the decision-making process.

Topics covered

- ➤ Understanding data
- ➤ Checking and cleaning data
- ➤ Univariate data analysis
- ➤ Bivariate data and cross-tabulations
- ➤ Filtering and use of bases
- ➤ Weighting
- ➤ Using inferential statistics
- ➤ Introduction to multivariate analysis

Relationship to MRS Advanced Certificate Syllabus

The material covered in this chapter is relevant to Unit 9 – Information and Data Analysis, specifically the analysis of quantitative data:
- ➤ understanding data;
- ➤ editing, coding and data entry;
- ➤ dealing with non-response;
- ➤ bivariate analysis;
- ➤ filtering and use of bases;
- ➤ principles of weighting;
- ➤ descriptive or summary statistics;
- ➤ using confidence intervals and significance testing.

Learning outcomes

At the end of this chapter you should be able to:
- ➤ understand quantitative data;
- ➤ conduct basic analysis of quantitative data;
- ➤ understand the role of inferential statistical tests;
- ➤ understand and evaluate the findings from quantitative research.

Understanding data

Before we look at the analysis of quantitative data it is worth spending some time describing how the responses to a questionnaire are transferred into an analysis package.

■ Data entry or data input

With computer-aided data collection there is no separate data transfer or data entry phase; the responses are captured, entered and verified almost simultaneously. The data capture program alerts the interviewer or respondent if a response is not within the bounds allowed by the question. Data collected on a paper questionnaire, however, must be transferred or entered into an analysis package. This is done either manually (responses keyed into the data entry program) or electronically (responses read by a scanner or optical mark reader). However the responses are captured and entered, the answer given by the respondent is recorded as a number at a fixed place in a data record sheet or grid. The process of assigning a number to a response is called coding. Coding means that data captured in a non-computerised form – answers marked or written on a questionnaire – are converted into number values that a computer analysis package can recognise and use. On most questionnaires you will see that opposite each response, or at the end of a question, there is a number. These numbers are codes that represent the responses to the question. In Box 13.1 is an example from the main CAPI questionnaire of the Life and Times Survey. If you were to answer in response to this question that your household's income had gone up by more than prices, the number 3 would be coded. In compiling the table for this question the analysis program will count the number of times that each response code has been entered or coded. It will count the number of respondents who said 'Fallen behind prices' or code 1; the number who said 'Kept up with prices' or code 2; the number who said 'Gone up by more than prices' or code 3; and the number who said 'Don't know'. These frequency counts will be converted to a percentage, calculated on the most suitable base for that particular question, all answering or total sample, for example, and you can ask in your data processing specification or when you write the table specification that both the percentage and the frequency count or raw number appear on the table.

Box 13.1 Response codes example: Life and Times 2000 Main Questionnaire

Q. 6 Looking back over the *last year* or so, would you say that your household's income has . . . READ OUT . . .

Fallen behind prices	1
Kept up with prices	2
Or gone up by more than prices	3
(Don't know)	8

Cases, variables and values

A complete individual unit of analysis is called a case. Typically, one questionnaire – the record of an interview with one respondent – is one case. If you have a sample of 300 completed questionnaires you have 300 cases. To identify each individual case a unique number – a serial number – is assigned. In a sample of 300 each questionnaire would be numbered, from 001 to 300. For each case, or questionnaire, the individual bits of information (questions or parts of questions) are called variables, and the answers the respondent gives to these questions are called values. Look again at Q. 6 in Box 13.1 from the Life and Times questionnaire. Respondents were asked about changes in their household income over the last year or so. The variable has been labelled HINCPAST (an abbreviation of **h**ousehold **inc**ome over the **past** year); the respondent's answer – Fallen behind; Kept up; Gone up by more; or Don't know – is the value of the variable. Here is another example. At the end of the Life and Times questionnaire there are a series of questions about the background of the respondent. One of these (Q. 4) involves the interviewer asking the marital status of the respondent. This variable – marital status – has been labelled 'RMARSTAT' (**respondent's marital status**). The values of the variable marital status are the following responses:

Single (never married)	1
Married	2
Living as married	3
Separated	4
Divorced	5
Widowed	6

In order for an analysis program to receive and understand data from the questionnaire the data must be in a regular, predictable format. For most datasets the data usually appear in a grid arrangement – this will be familiar to you if you have ever used a spreadsheet. The grid is made up of rows of cases and columns of variables. Each case makes up a line or row of data and the variables appear as columns of number codes. The purpose of data entry is to convert the answers on the questionnaire into a 'line of data' that the analysis program will accept and recognise. Table 13.1 is an illustration of how these lines of data and columns of codes would look for the answers given to Q. 1 to Q. 6 on the Life and Times questionnaire by ten respondents. The first three columns of numbers are the interviewer's identity number; the next four columns are the unique serial number or case number of that particular questionnaire – both are on the front page of the questionnaire. The subsequent columns represent the responses to Q. 1, Q. 2 and so on in sequence up to Q. 6. (You could download the questionnaire from the Life and Times website (www.ark.ac.uk/nilt) and check what responses the codes represent on the questionnaire.)

You can see from this grid how each variable or question has been coded. Numeric data entered by the interviewer, for example in response to Q. 1 'How long have you lived in the town (city, village) where you live now?' appears as it is. The respondent with serial number 0010, for example, has lived for four years in the small city or town (Q. 3 code 3) and this has been coded 04 in the grid; respondent number 0011 has

Table 13.1 Data entry grid for ten fictional respondents to the Life and Times 2000 Survey

Int No			Serial No				Q1		Q2	Q2a			Q3	Q4	Q5	Q6
1	2	3	0	0	1	0	0	4	1	1	2	2	3	1	1	3
1	2	3	0	0	1	1	3	9	2	–	–	–	5	2	3	1
1	2	3	0	0	1	2	2	4	1	2	1	1	3	1	1	2
1	2	3	0	0	1	3	1	2	1	1	1	1	3	1	1	3
1	2	3	0	0	1	4	1	9	2	–	–	–	4	3	3	3
1	2	3	0	0	1	5	0	0	1	2	2	1	4	1	1	3
0	0	7	0	0	1	6	1	1	2	–	–	–	2	1	1	3
0	0	7	0	0	1	7	0	8	2	–	–	–	2	1	1	3
0	0	7	0	0	1	8	1	5	1	1	2	1	2	1	1	2
0	0	7	0	0	1	9	0	9	1	1	2	2	1	1	1	3

lived for 39 years in the farm or home in the country (Q. 3 code 5) where he or she lives now; respondent 0015, who has lived where he or she lives now for less than a year has been coded 00, following the instructions on the questionnaire. Where the information you want to code is not a numeric value, Q. 2 to Q. 6 in the Life and Times example, the response is entered using the number code assigned as the label for that response (the value of that variable). So, for example, responses to Q. 2 'Have you ever lived outside Northern Ireland for more than six months?', 'Yes' and 'No', are coded as 'Yes' = 1 and 'No' = 2. (Note that for questions that the respondent is not eligible to answer a blank – or a space or a zero – is entered in the grid.) Remember, however, that although the code is a number it has no arithmetic value.

These number codes are what you or the data entry program transfer from the questionnaire into the analysis program in a process known as *data entry* or *data input*. Besides allowing you to enter numeric codes, most packages also allow you to enter alphanumeric codes – codes that use letters as well as numbers. Codes that use letters are called *string* variables. You might want to use a string variable to enter a brand name, for example, or to transfer responses to open-ended questions verbatim rather than coding the response in numeric form.

■ Levels of measurement

You will have noticed from the above descriptions of the use of numbers as codes that numbers do not always mean the same thing. In all cases they describe or measure something but they can represent different types or levels of measurement. Sometimes they represent numeric quantities, years lived where you live now, for example, or age or number of people in the household, or the price paid for a product. Sometimes they are merely symbols, for example, where 1 = 'Yes' and 2 = 'No' in Q. 2 in the Life and Times questionnaire. In the context of quantitative data analysis it is important to understand what level of measurement a number represents. There are four levels: nominal, ordinal, interval and ratio. Data at the nominal or ordinal levels are known as categorical or non-metric data; data at the interval or ratio level are known as continuous or metric data. Interval and ratio numbers are also known as cardinal numbers.

Nominal scale numbers

At the nominal level of measurement numbers are used to classify or label things. Other symbols would be just as suitable but numbers are used because they are familiar and easy to understand. When they are used in this way numbers have no arithmetic meaning or value. In an analysis context sex or gender is a nominal variable – we have assigned the number 1 to represent male and the number 2 to represent female; 'ever lived outside Northern Ireland for more than six months' is a nominal variable with 1 = 'Yes' or those who have; and 2 = 'No' or those who have not. These numbers have no other meaning than that – it would be meaningless to add 1 and 2 together.

Ordinal scale numbers

At the ordinal level of measurement numbers represent a category and indicate that there is a relationship between the numbered items. In other words there is an order or ranking or sequence to the numbers. House numbers on a street are ordinal numbers; your position in a race or birth order in your family – first, second, third and so on – are ordinal rankings. An example of an ordinal level variable would be opinion ratings or preference ranking in a product test: first preference; second preference and so on. An ordinal number does not represent a real amount, so, as with nominal scale numbers, arithmetic is not meaningful.

Interval scale numbers

At the interval level of measurement numbers represent numeric values, so arithmetic is meaningful. The numbers in an interval scale are ordered and the intervals between the numbers are of equal size. Temperature is measured on an interval scale. The main feature of an interval scale is that there is no absolute zero: negative amounts mean something. For example, minus 5°C is a meaningful number. Income is an example of an interval level variable – it is possible to have a negative income if one has debts, for example.

Ratio scale numbers

Ratio scale numbers have the same properties as interval scale numbers – they have a rank order, there are equal intervals between numbers, arithmetic is meaningful – but on the ratio scale there is an absolute zero. Zero on a ratio scale means that there is nothing there, whereas on the interval scale zero might mean 'low' or 'very low'. At the ratio level of measurement it is impossible to have minus numbers. Examples of ratio level variables would be elapsed time, weight, the number of times an item has been used or the number of children in a household.

But why does all this matter?

In research you will come across variables at all four levels of measurement. Interval and ratio level variables can be manipulated using a range of mathematical and statistical procedures – because they represent numeric amounts and because arithmetic is meaningful with these types of numbers. Nominal and ordinal level variables, on the other hand, because they do not represent numeric amounts, are not suitable for precise methods of analysis. So, in order to determine what type of analysis is appropriate, and the type of inferential statistical test to use when testing hypotheses, it is important to be able to recognise what kind of number or variable you have. Different tests are suitable for different levels of measurement. We look at how to choose the relevant test later in the chapter.

■ Editing and cleaning the dataset

As the data are being entered on a case-by-case basis they can be edited or cleaned to ensure that they are free of errors and inconsistencies. Such checks should be carried out by interviewers and field supervisors during fieldwork and by editors when the questionnaires are returned from the field. (With computer-aided data capture this process is incorporated into the data capture program.) During the editing and cleaning process missing values, out of range values and errors due to misrouting of questions are sorted out and the data are checked for other inconsistencies.

Missing values

If a response has been left blank it is known as a 'missing value'. Missing values can occur for all sorts of reasons – the question may not apply to the respondent, he or she may not know the answer or may refuse to answer, or the interviewer may have inadvertently forgotten to record a response. It is important to deal with missing values so that they do not contaminate the dataset and mislead the researcher or client. One way of dealing with the possibility of missing values is at the questionnaire design stage and at interviewer training and briefing sessions. In a well-designed questionnaire there will be codes for 'Don't know' and 'No answer' or 'Refused'. Interviewers should be briefed about how to handle such responses and how to code them on the questionnaire. It is also possible to avoid missing values by checking answers with respondents at the end of the interview or during quality control call-backs.

If missing values remain a code (or codes) can be added to the data entry program that will allow a missing value to be recorded. Typically a code is chosen with a value that is out of range of the possible values for that variable. Imagine that for some reason a respondent to the Life and Times Survey did not answer, or the interviewer did not ask for or record, a response to Q. 3 'Would you describe the place where you live as ... ?' The values or response codes for this question range from 1 = 'big city' to 5 = 'farm or home in the country'; you could assign a missing value code of 9 for 'No response'. If you know in more detail why the information is missing – for instance 'Doesn't apply', 'Refused to answer', or 'Don't know', and this is not already allowed for on the questionnaire, you can give each of these a different missing value code – 'Doesn't apply' could be 96; 'Refused to answer' could be 97; 'Don't know' could be 98; and 'Missing for some other reason' could be 99. There are other ways of dealing with missing values. One extreme approach, known as casewise deletion, is to remove from the dataset any case or questionnaire that contains missing values. This approach, however, results in a reduction in sample size and may lead to bias, as cases with missing values may differ from those with none. A less drastic approach is the pairwise deletion in which only those cases without missing values are used in the table or calculation. This too will affect the quality of the data, especially if the sample size is relatively small, or if there is a large number of cases with missing values.

An alternative is to replace the missing value with a real value. There are two ways of approaching this. You could calculate the mean value for the variable and use that; or you could calculate an imputed value based on either the pattern of response to other questions in the case (on that questionnaire) or the response of respondents with similar profiles to the respondent with the missing value. Substituting a mean value means that the distribution of the values for the sample does not change. We are assuming, however, that the respondent gave such a response when of course he or she may have given a more extreme answer. If we substitute an imputed value we are making assumptions and risk introducing bias.

Inconsistencies, routing errors and out of range values

Other data cleaning issues involve resolving problems that arise due to inconsistent answers, routing instructions not followed correctly, extreme answers and answers that are not valid or are outside the range of possible answers. For example, if at Q. 2 in the Life and Times Survey a respondent answered, 'No' (he or she has not lived outside Northern Ireland for more than six months), this respondent should not be asked Q. 2a but should skip to Q. 3. Only those answering 'Yes' at Q. 2 are eligible to answer Q. 3 – all others should be filtered out. If a respondent answers 'No' at Q. 2 and goes on to answer Q. 2a, the 'skip' or routing instruction has not been followed correctly and the answers at Q. 2 and Q. 2a are inconsistent. This should not happen in a CAPI survey such as the Life and Times, where the routing is handled automatically by the data capture program. Data collected via CATI, CAPI, CASI, CAWI or web-based methods are subjected to such checks automatically as data are entered – built-in editing programs and logic checks should highlight any such problems, if programmed correctly. The program alerts the user (the interviewer or the respondent) to inconsistent answers, skips to the appropriate question and can be programmed to refuse an answer or code that is out of range. Further checks on the accuracy and consistency of the data can be made at the next stage of the process, when the data are available in the form of a frequency count or 'holecount'. For example, if 406 respondents out of a total of 1,100 say that they have bought goods over the Internet, have 406 replied to a later question to which they are directed about the type of goods they bought?

Once the data have been entered, edited and verified they are in a form that can be manipulated and analysed. The next step, once variables and values have been labelled, is to explore the data using a holecount or a set of tables. We looked at how to request a set of tables in Chapter 11.

Descriptive statistics

With the clean dataset you can begin some basic analysis. The purpose of this preliminary analysis is to get to know the data. It involves summarising or describing responses using frequencies and calculations known as summary or descriptive statistics.

■ Frequency counts

A frequency count is a count of the number of times a value occurs in the dataset, the number of respondents who gave a particular answer. For example, we want to know how many people in the sample are very satisfied with the level of service provided by Bank S. A frequency count – a count of the number of people who said they are very satisfied with Bank S – tell us this. The holecount is a set of these frequency counts for each of the values of a variable; it may be the first data you see. It is useful to run a holecount before preparing a detailed analysis or table specification as it gives an overview of the dataset, allowing you to see the size of particular sub-samples, what categories of responses might be grouped together, and what weighting might be required. For example, say we have asked if respondents are users of a particular Internet banking service. The holecount or frequency count will tell us how many users we have. We can decide if it is feasible to isolate this group – to look at how the attitudes, behaviour or opinion of Internet customers compares to those of non-Internet customers, for example.

Raw numbers and percentages

A frequency count is usually expressed in raw numbers, telling us, for example, that 36 respondents are Internet customers; it does not tell us, however, what proportion of the total sample this number represents. It is therefore useful to look at percentages as well as raw numbers: a percentage tells us the relative proportion or incidence of occurrence in every 100 cases. The percentage number of Internet customers in this example is 12 per cent or 36 out of a total of 300 customers interviewed.

Including 'Don't knows' in calculating percentage figures

It is usual in expressing percentages to specify whether or not they include or exclude those who said 'Don't know' or 'No opinion'. (The number and percentage of those who 'Refused to answer' may be reported on the table.) Deciding how to handle such responses will depend on the aims of the question. It may be important to report how many respondents say 'Don't know' or 'No opinion' – for example if we are asking respondents about their likelihood of adopting new working practices in the next year; on the other hand, including them may obscure or distort the findings. Consider Tables 13.2 and 13.3. At first inspection it appears that a smaller proportion of light users is satisfied with the service provided, especially compared to those

Table 13.2 Including 'No opinion'

Q. How satisfied or dissatisfied are you overall with the service provided by your telephone company?

	Heavy users %	Medium users %	Light users %
Very or fairly satisifed	76	65	52
Very or fairly dissatisfied	16	23	19
No opinion	8	12	29
Base:	(200)	(200)	(200)

Table 13.3 Figures repercentaged excluding 'No opinion'

Q. How satisfied or dissatisfied are you overall with the service provided by your telephone company?

	Heavy users %	Medium users %	Light users %
Very or fairly satisifed	83	74	73
Very or fairly dissatisfied	17	26	27
Base:	(184)	(176)	(142)

who are medium users – but almost three out of ten light users have answered 'No opinion'. If we repercentage the figures in the table excluding the 'No opinion' group, and so including (or basing the table on) only those who expressed an opinion, a different interpretation emerges: there is no difference in rating between

Box 13.2 Manipulating variables

After an initial inspection of the data using frequency counts you may find that some variables or values of a variable are not in a form that is useful for further analysis. It is possible to change the variables or values by recoding them or manipulating them to create new variables. For example, say you asked a question about holiday destinations and you received a long list of responses. You may decide that it would be more useful to recode them into smaller groups, say by country or by continent. Or perhaps you asked respondents to give their age on their last birthday and now find that recoding the age variable into age bands or categories – 18–24; 25–34; 35–44 and so on – is more appropriate to your analysis needs. If a variable is at the interval or ratio level of measurement you can use arithmetic functions to create a new variable based on the values of the original variable or variables. For example, say you have two variables – number of adults in the household and number of children in the household. You do not, however, have a variable for the total number of people in the household. You can create this variable via the analysis program by adding the value that represents the number of adults in each household to the value that represents the number of children in the same household for each case in the dataset.

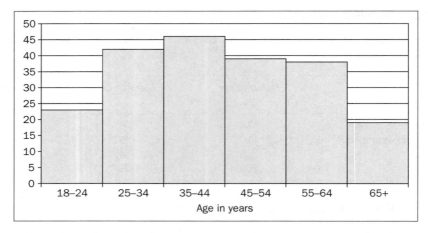

Figure 13.1 Frequency distribution bar chart

medium and light users. Deciding which way to report data will depend on the context. In most cases it can be useful to report both the percentage who said 'Don't know' or 'No opinion' and the proportion split between responses excluding 'Don't know' or 'No opinion'.

The frequency count tells us how many gave a particular answer and the percentage tells us the proportion of them in the total sample or among a particular group (whatever the base). In addition to knowing how many, we may also want to look at the spread or distribution of answers across the sample or group. For example, we might want to know what proportion of the sample falls into each social class, or each age category, or what proportion shop at particular supermarkets. One way of doing this is to plot the frequency counts for each value of the variable on a graph, giving a visual display of the distribution of the frequency count across the values of the variable (see Figure 13.1).

Another way of looking at the shape of the distribution, without having to plot a chart, is to calculate a number – a statistic – that will give us the same information. There are two sets of such statistics: measures of central tendency (sometimes called measures of location) and measures of variation (sometimes called measures of dispersion or measures of variability).

▪ Measures of central tendency

A measure of central tendency is more commonly known as an average. It is a single figure used to represent the average of a distribution or group of values. It anchors or locates the distribution on a scale of all its possible values. There are three 'averaging' statistics: the mean, the mode and the median.

The mean

The mean or arithmetic mean is the average most often used. However, it can only be used on data of at least interval level of measurement. To calculate it you add together all of the values in the sample and divide by the total number of values. For example, to work out the mean number of children in households in the sample you add together the number of children in every household in the sample and divide by the total number of households.

The mode

The mode is the most frequent response. It requires no calculation except a frequency count of all values to see which is the most commonly occurring. It can be used on data of any level of measurement. It is possible to have more than one mode in any distribution.

The median

The median is defined as the middle value when all the values are arranged in order. It can be used on all types of data except nominal level data. It has the same number of values or observations above it as it has below. If there is no one middle value – if you have an even number of values, for instance – to work out the median you take the mean of the two middle values.

Properties of the mean, the mode and the median

Each of these three averages has particular properties. The mean differs from the mode and the median in that all the values in the distribution are used in calculating it. It is an arithmetical calculation and it can be used in further calculations. It can, however, produce an 'impossible' value, for example 2.3 children, and because all values are used in its calculation outliers (extreme values) can distort its value. The median, on the other hand, is not an arithmetically derived calculation, it cannot be used in further calculations but it will usually produce a real value and it is not affected by extreme values. The mode, in referring to the most frequently occurring response, takes no other value into account, cannot be used in further calculations and always produces a real value.

So when do you use the mean, the mode or the median? Use the mean when:

➤ you need a statistic that is widely understood;
➤ you want to take into account the influence of all values, even the outliers;
➤ you need a statistic that you can use in further calculations;
➤ you do not need a 'real' value;
➤ your data are at the interval or ratio level of measurement.

For example, the mean is used for working out average household income or average spend or the average age of users of a service.

Use the median when:

➤ you want an average that is not affected by outliers;
➤ you do not need the average to calculate further statistics;
➤ the middle value has some significance;
➤ you want a more realistic representation of the average;
➤ your data are interval or ratio level.

The median can be used, for example, to describe the average breakdown rates of washing machines or in other cases where outliers might distort the value of the arithmetic mean. It can also be used to track changes in attitudes, when you want to follow changes to the middle value on an attitude scale.

Use the mode when:

➤ you do not need any further statistics based on the average;
➤ you are interested only in the most frequent value;
➤ your data are numerical (interval or ratio) or non-numerical (nominal or ordinal).

The mode is used when it is interesting to quote the most frequent response, for example the price that most people said they were willing to pay, or the most frequently cited ISP.

■ Measures of variation

The average tells us something about where the middle of a distribution is but it does not tell us about the range of values. For this we need a second group of statistics called measures of variation. The range and the standard deviation are the most commonly used measures of variation.

The range

The range is the difference between the highest value in the distribution and the lowest value. It is a useful way of determining the scope of the distribution, the range over which the values are spread. The bigger the range, the bigger the spread in values; the smaller the range the more tightly clustered the values. For example, you might be interested in establishing the range of prices paid for service A. The range is, however, a fairly crude measure because one outlier can have a huge effect on it. Consider the example in Figure 13.2. The distributions are identical save for one value. This one number increases the range from to four to ten.

The standard deviation

The standard deviation is a statistic that summarises the average distance of the values from the mean. Like the range, the bigger the standard deviation the greater the variation or spread in sample or distribution. It is a more robust calculation than the range because in calculating it we use more of the values of the distribution – not

---

Price paid for car cleaning service at nine outlets in two regions.

Prices in €

Sample A: 10, 11, 11, 12, 12, 13, 13, 13, 14   Range: 14 – 10 = 4

Sample B: 10, 11, 11, 12, 12, 13, 13, 13, 20   Range: 20 – 10 = 10

Figure 13.2 **The effect of an outlier on the range**

just two, as with the range. The first step is to work out the mean. Once you know the mean you subtract each value in the distribution from the mean – in effect working out how far each one is from the mean. These figures – some are below the mean (and so are minus numbers) and some are above it – are known as the deviations from the mean. In order to get rid of the minus numbers from the calculation the deviations are squared. These figures are known as the squared deviations. The next step is to add all these values together – giving us the sum of the squared deviations. You then divide the sum of the squared deviations by the total number of values or observations – this is the mean of the squared deviations, also known as the variance. To get the standard deviation you take the square root of the variance, in effect removing the squaring that you applied earlier. Thus the standard deviation is a summary statistic that tells you the amount of variation around the mean of the distribution.

The standard deviation is a very useful statistic, particularly when used alongside the mean. For example, you are comparing service A and service B. The mean price paid for A and B was the same at €79. The standard deviation in the price paid for service A is greater, however – €22 compared to €14. This tells you that while the average prices are the same the price of A is more variable than the price of B. The next step in your analysis might be to check why this variation exists (what might explain it) – is it due to a sub-group of service A providers charging more, or to one or two providers charging a lot more?

■ Measures of shape

Two measures can be used to describe the shape of a distribution – measures of skewness and kurtosis.

Skewness

In a symmetrical distribution, such as the normal distribution, half of all values lie below the mean and half lie above it. There is no skewness in either direction; the mean, the mode and the median take the same, or roughly the same, value. When a distribution is skewed it is off-centre or asymmetrical, with more values or observations falling to one side of the mean than the other and the mean, the mode and the median do not have the same value. If the distribution is positively skewed a greater proportion of values lie above the mean than below it; negative skewness means that a greater proportion lie below the mean than above it.

Kurtosis

Kurtosis is a measure of how flat or how peaked a distribution is relative to the normal distribution. The kurtosis of the normal curve is zero. If a distribution is more peaked than a normal distribution the kurtosis is positive; if it is flatter than the normal curve the kurtosis is negative.

In terms of analysis we now have a reasonable armoury with which to explore the data: frequency counts and percentages tell us how many gave each answer; and

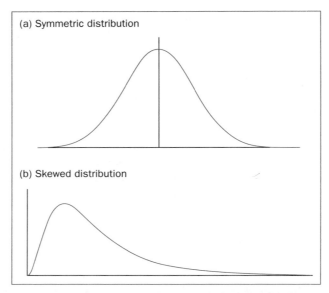

Figure 13.3 A symmetric and a skewed distribution

the measures of central tendency and variation tell us something about the spread of the whole group of answers. At this level of analysis, however, we are looking at only one variable and/or one value at a time. This level of analysis is called univariate analysis and there is only so much of the story that we can tell using it. In most research we are interested in comparing the responses of different groups of people to see if they vary, and examining the relationship between variables. For example, are those with different demographic or geodemographic profiles more or less likely to buy product X or service Y; is there a relationship between type or size of business and use of e-commerce; are women more likely to visit a general practitioner than are men? To answer these sorts of questions we need bivariate (and multivariate) analysis – analysis that involves examining the relationships between two (or more variables) – and this involves cross-tabulations.

Cross-tabulations

Most quantitative data analysis involves inspecting data laid out in a grid or table format known as a cross-tabulation. This is the most convenient way of reading the responses of the sample and relevant groups of respondents within it. For example, we may need to know what the total sample's view of a product is, as well as what a particular type or group of consumers thinks – whether the product appeals more to men or women, or to different age groups or different geodemographic groups, for instance. Each table or cross-tab sets out the answers to a question by the total sample and by particular groups or sub-sets within the sample that are relevant to the aims of the research. Table 13.4 is an example of a cross-tab.

Table 13.4 Example of a cross-tabulation

Q. 7 Have you contacted your supplier in the last six months for any of these reasons?

| | Total % | Payment frequency | | | | Annual household income (€000s) | | | |
		Annual %	Qrtrly %	Mthly %	Varies %	To 20 %	21–40 %	41–60 %	61+ %
No contact	57	49	70	45	56	57	57	39	52
Problem/query with service	28	34	17	35	33	28	28	39	22
Problem/query with bill	14	13	8	18	22	13	16	18	9
Change of address	1	2	1	1	–	1	–	–	–
Special offer	8	8	5	12	6	4	11	14	17
Base:	(852)	(106)	(340)	(320)	(36)	(282)	(174)	(112)	(46)

■ Which variables as top breaks?

The convention in preparing a cross-tabulation is to use the independent or explanatory variable as the cross-break or column variable and to calculate percentages within this variable. This means that percentages are read down the column variable and the responses of different groups can be compared side by side for each value.

The type and number of variables used in the top break or banner (those that define the columns) should be chosen with the objectives of the research in mind. The variables commonly used fall into three groups: demographic and geodemographic, attitudinal and behavioural. Demographic variables include age, sex, class, working status, region; geodemographic variables are composite variables that include location and demographic measures. If the research objectives involve determining the profile of users of a product or service, for example, or finding out whether different groups vary in terms of their attitudes or opinions, then it will be worth including the relevant variables as a top break. Attitudinal variables describe attitudes, for example liberal or conservative social attitudes, or attitudes to health, or level of satisfaction with a service or product. Behavioural variables describe behaviour or usage, for example users of Internet banking services or frequent buyers of ground coffee or those who visit a gym at least once a week. Looking at the data through the eyes of those with different attitudes or who behave in different ways can help us understand what motivates or influences different types of people and can help us build up a picture of the dynamics of a market. Are those with liberal social attitudes more or less likely to favour government funding of religious schools than those with conservative social attitudes? Are those who are concerned about their health more likely to buy organic food than those who do not worry about their health? Are those who visit the gym once a week more or less likely to buy exercise equipment than those who do not visit the gym? What other drinks do frequent buyers of ground coffee buy? What is it about the service that Internet banking customers receive that makes them more likely to be satisfied with their bank than traditional account customers?

Box 13.3 The dependent and the independent variable

In formulating ideas and hypotheses and talking about relationships between variables we often designate one variable as the dependent variable and the other as the independent variable. The dependent variable is the one that we predict will change as a result of the other – for example, satisfaction is dependent on type of banking service used. The independent or explanatory variable is the one that we think explains the change in the dependent variable – the level of satisfaction is explained by the type of banking service used. When we ask, 'Are those who are concerned about their health more likely to buy organic food than those who do not worry about their health?' we are suggesting or hypothesising that the purchase of organic food is dependent on or influenced by attitudes to health; or, put another way, we believe that attitude to health might explain likelihood to buy organic food. Attitude to health is the independent variable and propensity to buy organic food is the dependent variable. Similarly when we ask, 'Are those who visit the gym once a week more or less likely to buy exercise equipment than those who do not visit the gym?' the dependent variable is likelihood to buy exercise equipment and the independent or explanatory variable is gym attendance. In other words our hypothesis is that attendance or lack of attendance at a gym might explain buying behaviour in the exercise equipment market.

In a single response question the column per cent should add to 100. Due to rounding of proportions it may sum to slightly more or less than 100. If respondents were able to give more than one answer to the question, as in Table 13.5 or, for example, in answer to the question, 'Which of the following gyms have you ever used?', the column per cents may add to more than 100 because respondents in this case may have used several different gyms (or, in Table 13.4, have contacted their supplier for more than one reason in the last six months). From Table 13.5 we can see that 43 per cent of those who attend the gym at least once a week say they are unlikely to buy exercise equipment in the next three months; among those who attend less often the figure is 33 per cent. Each column of data is based on the total number of people in that particular group, which is determined by the number of people who gave that answer or group of answers to the question or questions from which it is derived. For example, the column 'attend gym at least once a week' is based on all those in the sample saying that they visit the gym at least once a week, which you can see in Table 13.5 is 123 people. We know that 43 per cent of this group say they are very unlikely to buy exercise equipment in the next three months. With a base size of 123, we therefore know that about 53 people who attend the gym at least once a week are very unlikely to buy exercise equipment in the next three months.

Table 13.5 Likelihood to buy equipment in next three months by gym attendance

	Q. 3 Frequency of attendance at gym	
Exercise equipment	At least once a week %	Less often than once a week %
Q. 7 Likelihood to buy in next three months		
Very likely	8	6
Fairly likely	17	22
Fairly unlikely	28	32
Very unlikely	43	33
Don't know/not sure	4	7
No answer	–	–
Base:	(123)	(279)

■ Use of bases and filtering

Each table is usually based on those in the sample eligible to answer the question to which it relates. Not all questions are asked of the total sample, however, and analysis based on total sample is not always relevant. Those that are will be based on the total sample; those that are not will be based on the relevant sub-sample. For example, in a survey of the use of e-commerce, we might ask all respondents whether or not their organisation uses automated voice technology (Q. 7, say). Those who say 'Yes' are asked a bank of questions (Q. 8a to Q. 8f) related to this; those who say 'No' are filtered out and routed to the next relevant question (Q. 9). When the data tables are run it would be misleading to base the tables that relate to these questions on the total sample if the purpose of the table is to show the responses of users of the service. The tables should be based on those who were eligible to answer the questions, in other words those saying 'Yes' at Q. 7. The tables for Q. 8a to Q. 8f that relate to automated voice technology are said to be based on those using automated voice technology (those saying 'Yes' at Q. 7). The table that relates to Q. 7 is said to be based on the total sample. In designing tables it is important to think about what base is relevant to the aims of your analysis.

If you have a particularly large or unwieldy dataset and you do not need to look at responses from the total sample, 'filtering' the data, excluding some types of respondents or basing tables on the relevant sub-sample can make analysis more efficient and safer. For example, your preliminary analysis of data from a usage and attitude survey in the deodorants market involved an overview of the total sample. Your next objective is to examine the women's deodorant market. In the interests of efficiency and safety, it may be worthwhile to have the tables rerun based on the sub-set of women only.

■ Labelling tables

Cross-tabulations should be clearly laid out and easy to read – it makes the whole task of thinking about the findings much easier. Each table should have a heading that describes the content of the table, and should contain the question number to which it refers and, in full or in summary, the question(s) or variable(s) on which it is based. The base on which percentages are calculated should be clearly shown and it should be indicated whether percentages are based on the column or the row variable or both.

■ Weighting the data

Weighting is used to adjust sample data in order to make them more representative of the target population on particular characteristics, including, for example, demographics and product or service usage. The procedure involves adjusting the profile of the sample data in order to bring it into line with the population profile, to ensure that the relative importance of the characteristics within the dataset reflects that within the target population. For example, say that in the usage and attitude survey the final sample comprises 60 per cent women and 40 per cent men. Census data tell us that the proportion should be 52 per cent women and 48 per cent men. To bring the sample data in line with the population profile indicated by the Census data we apply weights to the gender profile. The overrepresented group – the women – are down-weighted and the underrepresented group, the men, are up-weighted. Multiplying the sample percentage by the weighting factor (Table 13.6) will achieve the target population proportion. To calculate the weighting factor divide the population percentage by the sample percentage. Any weighting procedure used should be clearly indicated and data tables should show unweighted and weighted data.

■ More than two variables?

What happens when you want to look at the relationship between more than two variables at one time? Three variables are manageable within a cross-tabulation. In fact a third variable can clarify the analysis by further explaining the relationship between the original variables. For example, in an examination of employment patterns among young people aged 18–34 we find by cross-tabulating employment status by sex (Table 13.7) that, among other things, a similar proportion of men and women are in full-time employment. We are interested in going further and determining if employment patterns among men and women vary by age.

We split the two groups on the age variable into men aged 18–24 and men aged 25–34 and women aged 18–24 and women aged 25–34. This new table, Table 13.8, reveals that while the proportions of men and women aged 18–24 in full-time employment are similar, proportions among the older age group are different – a smaller proportion of women compared to men are in full-time employment. A possible explanation for this finding is that women in the 25–34 age band may

Table 13.6 Applying a weighting factor

Group	% of the sample	% in target population	Weighting factor
Women	60	52	0.87
Men	40	48	1.20

Table 13.7 Employment status by sex

Q. 25 Employment status	Men %	Women %
Full time	68	62
Part time	16	30
Unemployed	11	5
Other	4	2
No answer	–	1
Base:	(250)	(250)

Table 13.8 Employment status by age within sex

Q. 25 Employment status	Men		Women	
	18–24 %	25–34 %	18–24 %	25–34 %
Full time	64	72	67	58
Part time	17	16	24	35
Unemployed	13	9	3	6
Other	6	3	4	1
No answer	–	–	2	–
Base:	(112)	(138)	(120)	(130)

have children and that this is the reason they are not working full time. To explore this further we could compare employment patterns among women in each group with children and those without.

Using inferential statistical tests

There is a battery of inferential statistical tests and procedures that allow us to determine if the relationships between variables or the differences between means or proportions or percentages are real or whether they are more likely to have occurred by chance. For example, is the mean score among women on an attitude to the environment scale significantly different from the mean score among men? Is the proportion of those who buy product A significantly greater than the proportion who buy product B? The choice of test will depend on the type of data and on the level of measurement.

But why are these tests necessary at all? Most research uses samples rather than populations. When we talk about our findings we want to generalise – we want to talk about our findings in terms of the population and not just the sample. We can do this with some conviction if we know that our sample is truly representative of its population. With any sample, however, there is a chance that it is not truly representative. As a result we cannot be certain that the findings apply to the population. For example, we conduct a series of opinion polls among a nationally representative sample of voters of each European Union member state. In our findings we may want to talk about how the opinions of German voters compare to those of French voters. We want to know if the two groups of voters really differ. We compare opinions on a range of issues. There are some big differences and some small differences. Are these differences due to chance or do they represent real differences in opinions? We use inferential statistical tests to tell us if the differences are real rather than due to chance. But we cannot say this for certain. The tests tell us what the probability is that the differences could have arisen by chance. If there is a relatively low probability that the differences have arisen by chance then we can say that the differences we see between the samples of German voters and French voters are *statistically significant* – real differences that are likely to exist in the population and not just in the sample we have studied.

■ Significance levels

As we saw in Chapter 8, the question then arises: at what point or level of probability do we accept that a difference is statistically significant or real? The significance level is the point at which the sample finding or statistic differs too much from the population expectation for it to have occurred by chance – the difference cannot be explained by random error or sampling variation and is accepted as a true or statistical difference. At the 5 per cent significance level there is a 5 per cent probability or a 1 in 20 chance that the result or finding has occurred by chance. This is the lowest acceptable level in most market and social research projects.

■ Testing the hypothesis

At the analysis and interpretation stage of the project you will want to test whether the hypotheses you have devised hold up. Because you cannot prove an empirical assertion but you can disprove it, you test the null hypothesis – the hypothesis of no difference. If the test tells you that you can reject the null hypothesis then you can accept the alternative or research hypothesis; if you fail to reject the null then you cannot accept the research hypothesis.

Procedure for hypothesis testing

➤ Formulate a specific research hypothesis (for example that there is a difference in men's and women's attitudes to the environment).
➤ State the null hypothesis (for example that there is no difference in men's and women's attitudes to the environment).
➤ Set the significance level.
➤ Choose the appropriate statistical test.
➤ Apply the test and get the test statistic.

➤ Interpret the test statistic (determine the probability associated with it or the critical value of it).

➤ Accept or reject the null hypothesis.

➤ State the finding in the context of the research hypothesis and the research problem.

➤ Draw conclusion.

■ What test?

It is important to choose the correct test for the data otherwise you risk either ending up with a test result and a finding that are meaningless or you miss an interesting and useful finding. First of all you must determine what it is you are testing for – a difference or a relationship? Next check the level of measurement of the data involved; and finally check whether the data are derived from one sample or two and, if two, whether the samples are related or unrelated.

■ A difference or a relationship?

Hypothesis testing can be applied to test differences or to test associations or relationships. You might want to test the difference between means or proportions or rankings. For example, you may want to find out whether the average price independent retailers charge for product X is significantly different from that charged by multiple retailers; or you may want to find out if the mean number of breakdowns reported by owners of brand X washing machines is really different from the mean number reported by owners of brand Y machines; or you might want to find out if the proportion of students achieving a first class honours degree differs significantly between university A and university B. Alternatively, you might want to test for associations or relationships – for example you may want to know whether there is a relationship between use of your product or service and gender – is it more likely to be used by men than women?

■ The data: what level of measurement?

For interval and ratio level or metric data you can use a parametric or a non-parametric test, depending on how precise or powerful you need the test to be in detecting differences at any given level of significance. Parametric tests are the more powerful – power refers to the test's efficiency or precision in detecting differences. Parametric tests are more powerful because they make Type II errors (see Chapter 8) on fewer occasions – they are more discriminating than non-parametric tests. They have, however, greater restrictions on their use. Besides being suitable for metric data only, the data must be normally distributed. For non-metric data you are restricted to using non-parametric tests. Non-parametric tests are relatively free of any conditions on their use and are suitable for use on data at any level of measurement. The downside is that they lack precision or statistical power.

One sample or two and unrelated or related?

When we talk about one sample what we mean is that we are comparing the statistic – the mean or the proportion or percentage from a sample – against a known population parameter or standard. For example, we know the incidence nationally of reported violent crime; we want to determine if the incidence in a particular city is significantly different. We have two unrelated or independent samples when we have two groups that are not related in any way – the values of one group have no effect or no relationship to the values of the second group. For example, we want to know if there is a significant difference between Japanese and German organisations in the proportion of their profits reinvested for research and development. The two samples – Japanese organisations and German organisations – are unrelated. We are dealing with related samples (sometimes called paired samples), for example, when we ask a group or a sample of respondents to rate product S and product R. We may calculate the mean score for product S and the mean score for product R but the same respondents are involved in each one, so, although we have two groups, they are not independent of each other.

Box 13.4 What test?

Type of analysis: testing for *difference* or *association/relationship*?

If testing for *difference*: data categorical/non-metric or continuous/metric?

➤ If non-metric: from one sample or two or more samples?
➤ If one sample: chi-square and binomial.
➤ If two related samples: Sign test, Wilcoxon test and chi-square.
➤ If two unrelated samples: Mann-Whitney *U* test, chi-square, Kruskal-Wallis, ANOVA.

➤ If metric: from one sample or two or more samples?
➤ If one sample: *z* test and *t* test.
➤ If two or more unrelated samples: *z* test, *t* test, ANOVA.
➤ If two or more related samples: paired *t* test.

If testing for *association*: level of measurement of dependent variable (DV) and independent variable (IV)?

➤ Both DV and IV categorical: measures of association chi-square, tau b (and others).
➤ DV continuous and IV categorical: ANOVA.
➤ IV and DV continuous: regression and correlation.

■ Testing for difference

In testing for difference we are dealing with proportions or percentages and means, and statistical testing involves testing for differences between two proportions or percentages or means.

Example of a one sample test

Z and *t* tests are used to determine whether the mean of the sample differs significantly from the mean of the population. For example, a survey shows that the average annual income of those holding an Internet account with bank X is £40,000; the average annual income of all of bank X's customers is £32,000. Do those holding Internet accounts with the bank really earn more or is the difference caused by chance? The research hypothesis (H1) is that those holding Internet accounts have a greater annual income than the population of the bank's customers. The null hypothesis (H0) is that there is no difference in annual income between the sample of Internet account holders and the population of the customers of the bank. To test the null hypothesis – to determine if there is a significant difference between the sample of Internet account holders and the population of the bank's customers – we use a *z* or a *t* test. To use a *z* test besides the information we have already we need to know the standard deviation of the annual income of the bank's customers. If this is not available, or we cannot work it out, we can use a *t* test. The calculations in the *z* and the *t* test produce a value. Using standard normal tables – statistical tables based on the normal distribution – the probability of getting the particular value produced by the test can be determined. This probability level is compared to the significance or probability level you set for the test (for example, *p* is 0.05). If it is greater than this value we must accept the null hypothesis; if it falls below this value we can reject the null hypothesis (that there is no difference) and accept the research hypothesis that there is a difference. We can say that the difference is statistically significant at the 5 per cent significance level. In other words there is a 1 in 20 chance that it is not a real difference and a 95 per cent chance that the difference is real and that the mean annual income of Internet account customers is significantly greater than the mean annual income of the bank's customers.

The end result of most tests is a statistic. This statistic is not meaningful in itself. For it to tell us anything about the difference it has tested we have to compare it against a set of possible values (given in a set of tables specially derived for that test statistic) at a given level of probability.

Example of a paired or related samples test

For example, the client would like to say that his product is better rated than the product of his competitor. You design a blind paired comparison product test. Each respondent rates the client's beer and the competitor's beer. Half the sample tries the client's beer first and half tries the competitor's beer first. Respondents are asked to rate each on a score of one to ten. This is an example of a related samples or paired samples situation and so a related *t* test such as the Sign test or the Wilcoxon *T* test would be appropriate.

▪ Testing for association

The test you choose will depend on the nature of the data – the level of measurement of the variables.

Chi square

If you want to see whether there is a relationship between categorical variables – those at the nominal or ordinal level of measurement – the first step is to create a cross-tabulation using raw numbers (not percentages). For example, you want to establish if there is a relationship between type of bank account and level of satisfaction; your hypothesis is that the type of bank account influences the level of satisfaction with the service provided; the null hypothesis is that there is no relationship. The dependent variable is level of satisfaction; the independent variable is type of bank account. As we noted above, it is common practice to use the independent or explanatory variable as the column variable and the dependent variable as the row variable in a cross-tabulation. Thus a cross-tabulation of bank account type by satisfaction would look as shown in Table 13.9.

A test for measure of association such as a chi-square test computes the frequency distribution it expects to see between the variables as if there were no association between them and compares these expected frequencies with what is observed, that is, the data in the table, to produce the chi-square statistic. The greater the difference between the expected and the observed frequencies the larger the chi-square statistic. To find out if the difference is a real difference, and not one that could have arisen by chance, the probability of finding a chi-square statistic of that value or larger is esti-mated using special tables for the distribution of chi-square values and the degrees of freedom (the number of observations minus the number of constraints needed to calculate the statistic) – in this case the number of rows minus one times the number of columns minus one. We can reject the null hypothesis that there is no relationship (and accept the research hypothesis that there is a relationship) if the value of the chi-square statistic is greater than the critical value of the chi-square distribution at the particular degrees of freedom. If the null hypothesis is rejected we can say that there is a relationship between type of account and level of satisfaction, that signifi-cantly more of those with an Internet account are satisfied with the service provided.

The contingency coefficient, which has a range of values between 0 and 1, tells us the strength of the association between the variables – 0 indicates no relationship. Other coefficients you might come across include the phi coefficient, which gives the strength of association in 2 × 2 tables, and Cramer's V, which gives the strength of the correlation in tables larger than 2 × 2. Tau b and tau c and gamma are test statistics that can be applied to variables at the ordinal level of measurement.

Table 13.9 Example of a 2 × 2 contingency table for a chi-square test

Level of satisfaction with service	Type of bank account		Total
	Internet current account	Traditional current account	
Satisfied	172	396	568
Not satisfied	28	204	232
Total	200	600	800

Analysis of variance

You may want to find out if there is a relationship between a categorical variable and a continuous variable. For example, you may be interested in the price variations in a product by outlet type, or variations in income by social class or by gender, or differences in crime rates in different types of cities. The procedure or test used for this sort of analysis is called analysis of variance (ANOVA). ANOVA compares the amount of variation between the categories of the independent variable with the amount of variation within them. For example, say we want to examine the price variations on a brand of whisky in independent outlets and in multiple or large retailers. Using ANOVA we determine the amount of variation in the price of the whisky *across* the different types of outlet and the variation in price *within* each type of outlet. If there is a greater variation between the outlet types than within each type we can say that there is a relationship between price and sales outlet.

Correlation and regression

If you have two continuous variables, for example temperature and sales of soft drinks, life expectancy and income, or years in education and earnings, and you want to establish if there is a relationship between them, the most appropriate procedures are correlation and regression. The first stage in establishing whether there is a relationship is to plot the values of the variables on a scatterplot – this will show visually any pattern that might exist in the data. A line of best fit through the data can be calculated mathematically. The statistic associated with this calculation is r – the correlation coefficient. It tells us the strength of association between the two variables. The value of r ranges from -1 to $+1$, where -1 tells us that there is a strong negative correlation between the variables (for example, as the price of X rises sales of X fall); $+1$ tells us that there is a strong positive correlation (for example, the greater the income the greater is life expectancy); when r is zero it means there is no linear relationship between the two variables. R^2 (the coefficient of determination) tells us the proportion of variation in one variable that is explained by the other. For example, if r is $+0.2$ we have a fairly weak positive correlation, say between temperature and sales of soft drinks; if r is $+0.2$ then R^2 is 0.04, which tells us that 4 per cent of the variation in sales is explained by temperature. The statistical significance of the relationship between the variables as measured by r can be tested.

Beyond cross-tabulations: multivariate analysis

It is possible to examine four or more variables in a cross-tab but it becomes increasingly difficult, and of course the more cells you generate in the table, the more you divide up the sample, the smaller the sample size becomes and the less robust and reliable the analysis. Another way of approaching such multivariate analysis is to use techniques designed to handle multiple variables at the same time. Examples of such techniques include factor analysis, cluster analysis, mapping (correspondence analysis and principal component analysis), multiple regression and conjoint analysis. A discussion of these techniques is beyond the scope of this book. To give you a flavour of what is involved, however, a brief description of three of the more commonly used techniques is given below.

■ Factor analysis

The aim of factor analysis is to reduce or summarise a large number of variables into a smaller set of factors. The analysis does this by looking for correlations or similarities between all of the variables in the particular set of data. For example, in a study to evaluate customer perceptions of the service provided by a telecommunications company, respondents were asked to rate the organisation on 16 different attributes. The factor analysis examines the relationships between all of these attributes and summarises or reduces these to a smaller set of factors that tell us what is driving perceptions of the service. Factor analysis can be used whenever it is useful to group respondents or attributes into smaller segments. It is widely used in, among other things, product testing research, to determine which features of a product drives preference, and market segmentation studies, to identify factors on which to group or cluster respondents.

■ Cluster analysis

The aim of a cluster analysis is to divide a sample (of at least 100) into distinct, homogeneous groups or clusters. Each cluster will contain respondents with similar characteristics or values on particular variables; each cluster will be different from all other clusters. Attitudinal data are often used to build the clusters. For example, clusters can be developed based on social and political attitudes, or based on attitudes to the adoption of new technology in an organisation. The analysis identifies a number of distinct clusters in the sample by analysing the relationships between the variables and each cluster is given a name that reflects its most important attribute. Respondents should fall into one particular cluster; the output of the analysis gives details of the proportion of the sample that falls into each one and the proportion of variation in the sample accounted for by each cluster. Cluster analysis can be used simply to generate clusters in order to describe groups within the data. It can also be used to reduce data into more manageable and meaningful units; the clusters can be used as cross-breaks in further analysis. Cluster analysis is often used to help understand the make-up of a particular market and the needs and preferences of segments within that market. For example, a cluster analysis based on questions about the range or repertoire of brands bought will help identify what types of consumers buy what group of brands and may help determine if there is a gap in the market that a new brand might fill. A cluster analysis using attributes that respondents consider important in choosing a supplier of office equipment might help determine whether there is a market for different types and levels of service.

■ Correspondence analysis

Correspondence analysis is a multidimensional scaling or mapping technique. The aim of correspondence analysis is to produce a map showing in two dimensions how variables and items relate to each other. To use a correspondence analysis your data must be derived from an association matrix, a grid of image or attribute statements by a list of supermarket brands, marques of car or brands of beer, for example. The variables (the statements) and the items (the brand) are shown as points on a map. From the map it is possible to say something about the relationship between the items and the attributes and so the positioning of items or brands in relation to the attributes and to each other. The analysis determines what proportion of variation between the items is accounted for by the dimensions included. Correspondence analysis is useful in understanding markets, how they are segmented, how consumers perceive brands, how effective advertising has been in positioning a brand, or where there might be a gap that a new product could fill.

Chapter summary

➤ Data are transferred from a questionnaire to an analysis package in a process known as data entry. This process is handled automatically in computer-aided data capture.

➤ Once entered the data are checked and edited – missing values, out of range values and errors due to misrouting of questions are sorted out and the data are checked for other inconsistencies.

➤ A complete individual unit of analysis is called a case. Typically, one questionnaire – the record of an interview with one respondent – is one case. The individual bits of information on the questionnaire (questions or parts of questions) are called variables and the answers the respondent gives to these questions are called values.

➤ Data exist at several levels of measurement: nominal, ordinal, interval and ratio. Data at the nominal or ordinal levels are non-metric data; data at the interval or ratio level are metric data. To determine what type of analysis is appropriate, and the type of inferential statistical test to use, it is important to be able to recognise what kind of data you have.

➤ Data can be explored using a 'holecount' – a frequency count of the responses to each question. A frequency count is usually expressed in raw numbers. It is useful to look at percentages as well as raw numbers – a percentage gives the relative proportion or incidence of occurrence per 100 cases. It is usual in expressing percentages to specify whether or not they include or exclude those who said 'Don't know' or 'No opinion'. Deciding how to handle such responses will depend on the aims of the question.

➤ The spread or distribution of answers across the sample or group may be important. One way of examining this is to plot frequency counts for each value of the variable on a graph; another way is to calculate statistics that will give the same information. These statistics are called descriptive statistics. There are two sets: measures of central tendency or measures of location – the mean, the mode and the median – and measures of variation – the range and the standard deviation.

➤ Analysis involving one variable at a time is called univariate analysis. Bivariate and multivariate analyses involve examining the relationships between two or more variables.

➤ Cross-tabulations or data tables are used to facilitate bivariate and multivariate analysis – they are the most convenient way of reading the responses of the sample and relevant groups of respondents within it. The independent or explanatory variable typically appears as the column variable and the dependent variable as the row variable, allowing responses of different sub-groups to be compared side by side.

➤ Tables may be based on those in the sample eligible to answer the question to which it relates. Not all questions are asked of the total sample, however, and analysis based on total sample may not always be relevant. In such cases tables may be filtered – based on the responses to a particular question rather than on the total sample.

➤ Weighting is used to adjust sample data in order to make them more representative of the target population on particular characteristics and to ensure that the relative importance of the characteristics within the dataset reflects that within the target population.

➤ Inferential statistical tests enable us to determine if relationships between variables or the differences between means or proportions or percentages are real or whether they are more likely to have occurred by chance. The choice of test will depend on what you are testing for (a difference or a relationship), the level of measurement of the data involved and whether the data are derived from one sample or two and, if two, whether the samples are related or unrelated.

➤ There are techniques designed to handle multivariate analysis. These include factor analysis, cluster analysis and correspondence analysis.

Questions and exercises

1 Describe what is meant by the following: (a) a case, (b) a variable, (c) a value.

2 Describe the process of transferring responses from a questionnaire to a data entry package.

3 What is involved in data editing?

4 How are missing data handled?

5 Why is it necessary to weight data? Describe how weighting is carried out.

6 What is a holecount and why is it useful?

7 What do descriptive statistics tell you? Why are they useful? Give examples.

8 What are cross-tabulations and why are they useful?

9 What is meant by 'filtering' the data?

10 What do inferential statistics tell you? Describe how you select an appropriate test.

Recommended reading

Clegg, F. (1991) *Simple Statistics*, Cambridge: Cambridge University Press. A clear and accessible book on descriptive and inferential statistics.

Ehrenberg, A. (1982) *A Primer in Data Reduction*, London: Wiley. A classic text introducing statistics and data analysis.

Chapter 14

Communicating and reviewing the findings

Introduction

The final stage in the research process involves, on one side, communicating the findings of the research and, on the other, reviewing what is presented to you. Findings are communicated via an oral presentation or a written report or both. The purpose of this chapter is to give you some guidance on how to communicate the findings clearly, accurately and effectively in a presentation or a report, and to set out guidelines for reviewing the output.

Topics covered

➢ Preparing a presentation
➢ Writing a report
➢ Reviewing the research

Relationship to MRS Advanced Certificate Syllabus

The material covered in this chapter is relevant to Unit 10 – Reporting the Results, specifically the following:

➢ the principles of reporting;
➢ methods of presenting and displaying data;
➢ approach to report writing;
➢ approach to oral presentation.

Learning outcomes

At the end of this chapter you should be able to:

➢ communicate the findings of research via an oral presentation and a written report;
➢ review the quality of the output.

Communicating the findings: presentations and reports

It is obvious but worth saying nevertheless that research is a pointless exercise if the findings are not disseminated in some way. The two most common methods of disseminating the findings are via an oral presentation and a written report. Both a presentation and a written report are prepared for most projects. In some projects findings may be written up for publication in journals and books. Presentations and reports are important to the research process for several reasons:

➢ as a means of crystallising the thinking about the research findings;

➢ as a channel for communicating and disseminating the findings;

➢ as a way of influencing and persuading the client in a course of action;

➢ as a way of selling the skills and expertise of the researcher.

Presentations are also important because they offer a chance for two-way communication to take place – they give the client and the researcher an opportunity to discuss the findings and explore their implications. Reports too have their own particular strengths. The report brings together in one document the detail of the research project – from the original definition of the problem to the findings and implications, and so acts as a record for the work completed. Many of those who read the report or attend the presentation will not have been involved at any other stage of the project – the presentation or the report *is* the project for them. In commissioning further work the client or the client researcher may look back at a report or presentation document as a way of evaluating the quality of the research and the quality of the research supplier.

The written report can precede or follow the presentation. If a full and detailed presentation of the findings and their implications is made the client may feel that a full report is not necessary and may opt for a summary report, sometimes called a management summary report. Alternatively, the client may prefer a full report in advance of a presentation, allowing him or her to get to know the data, the findings and the implications. A presentation may or may not follow. Some clients prefer a draft report in advance of the presentation, using the presentation to discuss and debate the implications, and the action to be taken; following the presentation the researcher prepares a final report to reflect the discussion and to record the conclusions reached. Presentations and reports are sometimes delivered during the course of a project. In large-scale or multi-stage projects the researcher may present interim findings, findings from the exploratory qualitative stage, for instance, or the results of the quantitative pilot study, with the aim of getting input or sharing ownership or simply updating the project team.

■ Communication

Before looking in detail at what is involved in preparing presentations and writing reports it is worth thinking about the art of communication. What is communication about? What does it involve? The aim of communication is to transmit 'stuff' – data, information, knowledge, ideas – in order to inform or influence or persuade. It involves four components:

> the sender or a source, the originator of the message;
> the message;
> the channel or the medium of delivery;
> the receiver or the audience.

To deliver effective communication, whether it is a presentation or a report, it is important to understand the role of these four components and their interaction. You need to know what you want to say, you need to be clear what the message is, you need to know the audience and how that message relates to the audience and why it is important to them. The aim is to match the message with the audience, and make use of the sender or source and the channel to enhance the delivery of it. More specifically, in a research context, you need to make research 'come alive ... *The goal is to create a dialogue between the consumer and the marketer*' (Biel, 1994).

■ Planning a presentation or report

In planning a presentation or writing a report the first step is to think about what you want to achieve. What is the purpose of it? Why did the client commission the research in the first place? What was the problem they came to you with? What help are they expecting the research to give them?

The objective

Focus on the client's needs, think yourself into his or her shoes. What end result do you want to achieve? What do you want the client to do as a result of what you have said or written? Do you want, for example, the client to tailor his or her service provision to suit the needs of customers better? How do you do that? What evidence did the research provide about this? Did it provide insight into what customers need and want? Perhaps you want the client to choose Ad A rather than Ad B for his or her new advertising campaign. How do you do that? Show how and why Ad A works more effectively at communicating brand values than Ad B? Always approach the presentation or report with the client's needs in mind. Think of it in terms of taking the audience or the reader on a journey from where they are with their problem to where you – as a result of the research – want them to be. At the end of the presentation or the report the audience should be clear about what action is needed, about what the next steps are. Do not approach a presentation or report by thinking about how much data you can pass on in the time or space available. Data are not what the client is interested in. They are interested in information and knowledge, evidence to help them make better decisions. The content of the presentation or the report should be driven by the end result, the objective, and not by the pile of data the research has produced. Develop the message in order to meet the objective of the presentation. Aim to deliver to the client the relevant findings and the implications of the findings for his or her business. You do not want the client saying 'So what?' at the end of the presentation or report. You must think of the 'So whats' when you are preparing so that at the end of the presentation or the report the client is clear about what action to take.

Clearing up assumptions

To do this effectively you need to know the client's needs, you need to know the nature of the decision-making process and the decision-making environment. You need to know the audience. So think about what you really know and what you are assuming you know. Think again about why the research was done, about how the findings are to be used, about the decision the client has to take, about what is going on in the client's mind. Think about the assumptions you are making about all of this. What problems or issues is he or she facing? What attitudes or opinions does he or she have about the research, about the problem, about the decision to be made? What does he or she know about research practice or research techniques? Will there be people in the audience with different perspectives? If in doubt, ask these questions before or as you are preparing the presentation or report. You need this information in order to be able to craft the message to fit the audience and achieve your objective.

Box 14.1 Who is the audience or the reader?

➤ How big will it be?
➤ Who are they?
➤ Where are they?
➤ How senior are they?
➤ How familiar are they with research?
➤ How familiar are they with the problem?

The audience may be a diverse lot and there may be underlying political currents. Try to find out what these might be. If this is not possible, just be aware that everyone in the room may not be thinking along the same lines or may not be envisaging the same outcomes. You may need to decide whom you most need to influence, and aim the presentation or report and target the message at that person or group of people. You may even need to prepare separate reports or give separate presentations to meet the needs of different audiences.

Preparing and delivering a presentation

You know the audience – you have done your background research on who will be present – how do you design the presentation to get them interested and keep them interested?

■ The medium

The source of the message is you and the channel or the medium of delivery is the visual aids. The choice of medium will affect the way in which the message is received – it may enhance the delivery of the message or it may even get in the way of the message. It can add to or detract from the credibility of the source and the message. Your choice of visual aids will depend on three things: the setting (the type and size of the room and the audience); availability of the equipment; and your own preferences.

Choice of visual aids

Choose the method which best allows you to communicate your message to that particular audience in the particular venue. Low technology methods such as handouts, flip charts or overhead projector (OHP) slides can be just as effective in the right situation as high-technology methods such as a computer projector and multimedia presentations.

Although handouts are easy to prepare and offer a permanent record of the material presented they are low in impact as a main presentation tool. If they are handed out to accompany the presentation they can distract the audience's attention. They are perhaps best given to the audience when the presentation ends. Flip charts are most suitable for very small audiences. They are easy to prepare but can have little impact with a large audience or in a big room (especially if the writing is small and unclear).

Overhead projector slides (sometimes called charts, acetates or transparencies) are easy to prepare on a word processor or presentation software package and most venues have an OHP. They can have high impact if well designed – for example, not too much text, text of a readable size, a background that enhances rather than detracts from the text – but they can be difficult to use well. If they have a paper backing remember to remove this before going to the presentation, the sound and the action of ripping it off are distracting to both audience and presenter.

If the equipment is available, the presentation can be run directly from a personal computer via projector on to a screen. Make sure that you are comfortable using it. If you are bringing your own projector make sure that the facilities can cope. This approach has high impact – it is easy to give a professional gloss to any set of charts. In addition, the software allows handouts to be prepared easily. However, there are some drawbacks. It is not as flexible as the OHP approach, for example if you want to refer back to a particular slide (best to have a copy of it at the relevant points in the presentation); and the equipment can fail. It is always wise to have a contingency plan – a set of paper charts, for example – for such circumstances. The technology is widely available to allow you to design a multimedia presentation in which you can incorporate audio or video clips or still photographs as well as text. If you do this make sure it is appropriate to the material and the audience, and that you are confident in using the technology and getting it to work.

Chart design

In designing individual charts think about the way in which people assimilate information: some prefer numbers, some words, others pictures and diagrams. It is a good idea in any presentation (and in a report) to use a combination – to break up the style, to ensure that the presentation does not become monotonous. Make sure, however, that the choice is suitable to the material. We look at the design of charts and the display of data in more detail later.

Integrate your visual aids into the presentation. Remember, they are only aids, they are not the presentation, so do not let them dominate it. Do not put a full script of your presentation on to the charts or handouts you use. This will take the focus of the audience's attention away from what you are saying. Use the visual aids to emphasise and enhance the message, to draw attention to key elements of it. Point out what the audience should look for on your charts or handouts and talk around them.

■ Content and structure

Edit the content ruthlessly. Present only those data or findings that shed light on the issue. Think about ways of presenting the material that clarify your argument or your interpretation – using two-sided arguments, or summaries, repetition and reinforcement, by citing evidence from other data sources or other research you have conducted, for example. Structure the presentation in a way that is relevant to the project or the client. For example, you might want to start with an overview or summary of the findings and move on to the detail, or start with the conclusions and then show the evidence that supports the conclusions.

Think about the order in which you present the main findings. Remember that you need to keep the audience's attention – build the story so that it leads clearly to the most important finding or implication. If bad news is to be delivered talk about the good news first – this generally tends to help the audience accept the bad news and the overall message. Include signposts or placeholders in the presentation so that the audience knows where the story is going and can make links between different bits.

■ Preparation and practice

Make sure that you are well prepared. Know your material inside out. Do a timed practice run. Ask some colleagues to sit in, watch and listen, ask questions and give you feedback. In particular, ask them to give you feedback on:

➢ audibility;
➢ tone of voice;
➢ pace/speed;
➢ body language;
➢ audience connection;
➢ handling of visual aids;
➢ quality of visual aids;
➢ mastery of the material;
➢ ease of following the logic of the presentation;
➢ signposting;

> timing;
> illustration of points made;
> opening and closing;
> handling of questions and discussion.

If you cannot get a practice audience run through the presentation on your own out loud anyway. Having to say it out loud means you take fewer short cuts than when you run through it mentally. Just hearing your own voice speak the words out loud is very helpful in judging what works and what does not, for example where your links between sections or your line of argument are weak.

Think of the sort of questions that your presentation might raise. Depending on your role and the type of presentation you should prepare yourself to address two types of questions: technical or methodological questions; and questions about your interpretation, your recommendations or your insight or wisdom about the issue or its wider business or social context.

■The logistics

Check how much time has been allocated for the entire presentation meeting, for the presentation itself, for discussion time, and for other items, and tailor the presentation accordingly. Do not let the volume of data you have dictate the length of the presentation. People will not concentrate for much longer than 45 minutes. Time the presentation and cut back as necessary. If you have been allocated 45 minutes design the presentation to last about 30 minutes – you may be slowed down by interruptions or questions or a late arrival delaying the start of the meeting but you will be expected to finish on time anyway. In making the presentation shorter than the allotted time you give yourself some leeway should such situations arise.

Check the technical details – make sure that the room in which you are presenting has the equipment you need and that the room layout and size is suitable for the audience and the method of delivery. Make sure you are comfortable with the equipment and that if anything breaks down or does not work you or someone with you knows how to put it right. Have a back-up set of OHP slides or a presentation document – if the equipment fails you can at least run through an OHP or a paper version of the presentation.

Settling in

Arrive at the presentation venue in plenty of time to give yourself a chance to get settled and organised and to familiarise yourself with the room (you may want to rearrange the seating to suit your needs). Make sure that the room is neither too cold nor too hot – an overheated room can send people into lethargy and a cold room can make them fidgety and unable to concentrate. You will probably be a bit nervous, most people are. The adrenalin generated will help you perform. Try to relax by slowing down your breathing. Think positive thoughts – you are well prepared, you have practised, you have a good story to tell. Your nerves will probably disappear as soon as you get into your stride, and once you get into the flow of the presentation.

Getting started

Put your watch on the desk or podium in front of you so that you can glance at it unobtrusively. Wait until everyone is settled. Find out if everyone can hear you and see your slides. Make the necessary adjustments if they cannot, then begin. Make a conscious effort to speak slowly and clearly. It is very easy when you are nervous to talk too fast, and in a higher pitch than normal. Be aware of the tone of your voice – try to vary it, make it conversational rather than monotonous. Remember, you are aiming to establish and maintain a connection with the audience, to get their attention and maintain their interest in what you are saying – not how you are saying it. Keep your body language open and friendly. Look at the audience, make eye contact with all of the people in your audience, to include them in what you are saying. Try not to look down at the PC or OHP and do not turn your back on the audience. Try to avoid making gestures that might distract people, for example tapping or playing with a pen or a pointer, putting your hands in and out of your pockets, pacing up and down or rocking back and forward, or playing with jewellery. If you are using a PC and a presentation software package you can call up notes on the screen; you may have notes on the podium or desk. Do not read these notes verbatim – use them as a guide only, as an aide-memoire – in reading them out your voice may sound monotonous. Talk *to* the audience, not *at* them.

If some audience members' first language is not the same as your own make sure that you speak clearly, avoid using too many idioms and ensure all your main points are clearly set out on your charts or handouts. Most people using a second language find it easier to follow written materials than speech.

■ Getting interest: the opening

How do you get people interested and motivated enough to listen to your presentation (or read your report)? This should be relatively straightforward if you have thought your way inside their heads – if you have designed the presentation to target the needs of the audience. People are more likely to remember messages that interest them and that are relevant to their needs. A good opening is important – you need to establish a connection with the audience. The main purpose of the opening is to prepare the ground, to set the scene, to get the audience ready for the message. You can use the opening to relax the audience. Tell them something they already know – use the opening to tell them why there was a need for the research, for example. If you have reviewed the background to the issue move on to demonstrate, for example, the gap in knowledge and how the research findings will address it. Another way of opening is to acknowledge the options available, or the difficulties involved in the client's decision. You can follow this with a statement of how you think the research findings will help. Research findings are often full of stories and anecdotes; using one of these can be an interesting and engaging way of starting the presentation. Choose one that ties in well with your overall message, or one that gets the audience to think in a different way about the issue, a way they may not have considered.

Depending on the audience and the nature of the project, it might be useful to describe the research methodology, including a description of the sample, but keep this brief. It is unlikely that many people will be interested in a lot of methodological detail at this stage. They are there to hear the findings and, although the methodological details give them an understanding of the validity and reliability of the research it is not appropriate to go into detail by starting with something that may be unfamiliar or difficult to understand. Keep it simple – do not risk losing the audience by overwhelming them or boring them with methodological detail. Also, be wary of saying anything contentious, it may be too distracting at such an early stage and cause the audience's attention to wander. However, do say something contentious if you need to challenge the audience's thinking about the topic or to get their attention.

Whatever opening you use make sure it captures the audience's attention and lays the way for the main focus of the presentation. Give a map of the presentation – an outline of the structure of the presentation, the issues or findings that you will deal with – so that the audience knows what is involved and where the presentation will take them. There are some housekeeping tasks that can be dealt with here too. Tell the audience how long the presentation will last, whether you will take questions during it or at the end; and let them know whether you are providing handouts, so that they can decide whether or not to take notes.

■ Keeping interest alive

Once the presentation is under way you need to work at maintaining the audience's interest and your connection to them. All elements of the presentation should contribute to this. You know yourself from attending presentations and lectures why your attention sometimes wanders. Here are some of the most common problems – make sure in preparing and delivering your presentation that you avoid them.

The structure and content of the message
➢ You lose track of where the presentation is going.
➢ You lose track of the relevance of the content.
➢ The content is dull and uninteresting.
➢ It is hard to follow and difficult to understand.
➢ It is not clear what particular findings you should be focusing on, what the important elements are and what is padding or just 'nice to know'.

The source: the presenter
➢ Speaks in a monotonous voice.
➢ Reads from a script or from notes.
➢ Distracts you by fiddling with clothing or jewellery.

➤ Does not engage the audience with appropriate eye contact or body language.

➤ Talks down to the screen or his or her notes rather than to the audience.

The medium: the visual aids

➤ The charts are not in the right order.

➤ There are problems with the equipment.

➤ The text on the charts is difficult to read.

■ Bringing the presentation to an end

Signal clearly to the audience that the presentation is coming to an end. In most research presentations the end involves a summary and some concluding remarks and/or recommendations. Summarising the main points of the message – in effect restating the main message or the key issues in short form – can help consolidate the audience's awareness and understanding of the issues. Conclusions should be based on the evidence you have included in your presentation; do not introduce new material at this stage. If appropriate to the project and the setting, make recommendations for future action. This may just mean clarifying the next steps, suggesting further research, inviting audience members to contact you for further analyses or queries about the findings, or even arranging a meeting to evaluate the research or the research contribution to the project. Make sure to finish on time. If you are running over time skip some of the detail of the findings and move to the ending.

■ The discussion/question and answer session

In many presentations the discussion or question and answer session begins when the presentation ends. When answering questions take your time, do not rush to give an answer. Do not be afraid of pauses – they often seem longer to you than they do to the audience – do not rush to fill the silence. Repeat the question in order to clarify your understanding of what is being asked, in case some people may not have heard it, and to give yourself some thinking time. If someone from your organisation is attending the presentation ask him or her to note down the questions asked and the comments made so that you can follow them up if necessary. When you answer a question address the entire audience, not just the questioner. Keep the answer to the question relevant – do not use it as an opportunity to talk about something that has just come into your head. If someone wants to know something in detail that may not be relevant to the whole audience, or not wholly relevant to the main issue, tell them that you will talk to them about it at length at the end of the meeting.

■ Getting feedback

Once the presentation is over ask colleagues and clients for feedback; think about what you did well and what you would do differently, or what you could improve on.

Writing the report

Although the medium is different, the aim in writing a report is the same as the aim in giving a presentation – to communicate the results of the research clearly and effectively. Plan out the report in detail. Before starting to write be clear about what you want the report to achieve. Why is it being written? What is the objective of the report? Who are the readers? What do they expect to read? What do you want to tell them or get them to do as a result of reading the report? Once you have established the objective of the report and the audience for it, start writing.

Box 14.2 Establishing the objective of the report: checklist

Think of the reader and ask yourself the following questions:

> ➤ Why am I writing it?
> ➤ What do I want to achieve?
> ➤ Who will read it?
> ➤ Why will they want to read it?
> ➤ What do they want to know? What do they know already?

■ Preparing an outline

It can be helpful to prepare a report outline – a map of what is to be included in the report. Collect all the data and information you need and write down all the main ideas, issues, key findings, interesting facts. Do not pay too much attention to order or style – just get it all together in one document or on one large sheet of paper. Read through it all and start grouping the ideas, issues and so on under headings of themes or topics. Refer back to the objective of the report (and to the research objectives and your analysis framework if necessary) – what is the message that you are trying to communicate? Begin to add some structure by ordering and numbering the themes or topics in a way relevant to the aim. The document you have now is your report outline or map. You can now get stuck into the main writing task.

■ The report layout

The layout, the visual appearance of what is put down on paper, is a major contributor to the reader's enthusiasm and ability to understand the report. Make good use of white space. Keep print size and style consistent. Use headings to label and identify the structure. Use a simple numbering system to direct the reader. Keep diagrams and tables as close as possible to the relevant text. If you refer to a table or diagram in several places in the text, repeat it so that the reader does not have to refer back to it. Most reports follow a similar structure that consists basically of an introduction,

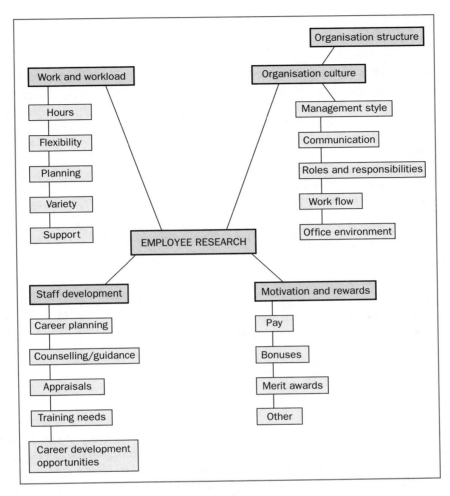

Figure 14.1 Example of a report outline

a methodology chapter, a findings chapter and a summary, conclusions and recommendations chapter. There are variations on this depending on the house style of the organisation or the specific needs or requests of the reader. A more detailed structure or contents list is given in Box 14.3.

Box 14.3 Report headings

➢ Title
➢ Abstract or management summary
➢ Table of contents
➢ Background and introduction

Box 14.3 continued

➢ Literature review

➢ Problem identification (see Chapter 3)

➢ Terms of reference (what the research needs to deliver, research objectives) (see Chapter 3)

➢ Methodology or approach to the research:
  ➢ research design
  ➢ sample
  ➢ method of data collection
  ➢ questionnaire/discussion guide development
  ➢ limitations of the research

➢ Analysis or findings

➢ Discussion and interpretation

➢ Conclusions

➢ Recommendations

➢ Appendices:
  ➢ technical details, e.g. of sample
  ➢ questionnaire/discussion guide in full
  ➢ organisation details
  ➢ CVs of team members

Title

The title of the report is important, particularly if the report is to have a wide circulation or is to be published. It must catch the reader's attention, spark interest in and inform the reader of the main focus or storyline of the report. Coming up with a title that does all this is not as easy as it might seem. It is usually best to use a draft or working title during the preparation of the report and wait until the report is almost complete before deciding on the final title – something in the write-up may suggest something suitable. A brainstorming session or a competition among project team members (with suggestions posted on the website or circulated via email) is a useful way of generating a title. The title can have two parts – a catchy main title that creates interest and a more descriptive sub-title that informs.

Abstract

An abstract is a short, easy to read summary or map of the entire report, typically no more than 500 words long and usually about 150–300. It is common (usually essential) in journal articles or more academic reports but it is good practice to include one in every report you write – it may be the only bit that a busy reader reads. It should inform the reader of the salient facts, allowing him or her to decide whether to read on; and for those who do read on, it sets the scene. It should include the following:

➣ the research problem or research questions;
➣ why this is being researched;
➣ how the research was conducted, the methods used;
➣ the main findings; and
➣ the implications or conclusions.

Although an abstract is best written once the report is finished, you can draft it out as soon as you have done your report outline (see above). This is a useful exercise – it will help you ensure that you are clear about what the message of the report really is. Preparing an accurate, brief but clear abstract is not easy – you may need to prepare several drafts. Instead of an abstract you may need to write a longer summary of the key findings.

Box 14.4 Example of an abstract

Misbehaviour by survey interviewers includes actions forbidden either explicitly or implicitly in codes of ethics, interviewer training or interviewing instructions. As examples of misbehaviour, interviewers can reword questions, answer questions when interviewees refuse to respond or fabricate answers to entire questionnaires. This study investigates the nature and incidence of such interviewer actions in telephone surveys, currently the most popular mode of data collection in marketing research in the United States. It uses both a mail survey and field experiment with samples of survey interviewers to investigate four factors hypothesised to influence misbehaviour by telephone interviewers. Results indicate that misbehaviour by telephone interviewers is ordinary and normal. Recommendations for reducing interviewer actions classified as misbehaviour are provided for research suppliers, marketing managers and marketing academics.

Source: adapted from Kiecker, P. and Nelson, J. (1996) 'Do interviewers follow telephone survey instructions?', *Journal of the Market Research Society* **38**, 2, p. 161. Used with permission.

Table of contents

Make sure you have a clear, logical and well-presented table of contents. It will help readers understand the scope and coverage of the report as well as helping them find relevant sections.

Background and introduction

The purpose of this chapter of a report is to set the scene and describe the wider context of the research problem. You may have already prepared a similar section for the proposal but things may have changed since then, so write the background and introduction from the point of view of having now done the work.

Literature review

The project may have involved a literature review or a review of previous research on the topic. A literature review chapter should be a synopsis and assessment of that literature or the previous research, with a particular focus on material that has informed the research design, the analysis of the data or the interpretation of the findings.

Do not use it merely to show that you know 'the area', and do not write a literature review without some critical thinking. It should achieve the following:

➤ provide background information on the topic and its wider context;
➤ provide a brief synopsis and assessment of the findings of previous research and their implications;
➤ highlight any gaps in knowledge or understanding;
➤ show why this research is worth doing.

Methodology

This chapter should set out details of how you went about the research, your research design and the methods you used. You should address the following questions:

➤ What is the structure or design of the research?
➤ What is the target population and how did you identify it?
➤ On what basis did you draw your sample and why?
➤ What are the characteristics of the people you interviewed?
➤ What data collection methods did you use and why?
➤ How did you translate the research objectives into a questionnaire or interview guide?
➤ How did you handle the data?
➤ How did you approach the analysis of the data?
➤ What difficulties arose during the research and how were these addressed?
➤ What are the limitations of the research and the data presented?

Analysis of findings

You can tackle the write-up of your findings in one chapter with sections for each of your main themes or areas, or you can write up each bit in a separate chapter. Whichever way you do it make sure that you plan out the sequence of your sections and chapters in advance of writing anything. Constantly review this report outline to make sure that it addresses the aim of the report, that the sequence is logical, and that the reader can follow the story clearly.

Discussion

The purpose of this chapter is to bring together your original research questions, your findings, the previous work discussed in the literature review and the wider context of the research problem as outlined in the introduction. In other words in this chapter you aim to establish the implications of the research findings for the original research problem and the wider business issues. You may also want to make some suggestions about further research that might follow from your findings. In addition you may want to set out here what you would do differently (and why) if you were doing the research over again.

Conclusions and recommendations

You may want to include the conclusions and recommendations in the discussion chapter. Alternatively, you may want to create a separate chapter. The decision will depend on your readership or on house style. Readers are generally busy people with limited time and they may decide to read only the abstract or summary, the introduction and the conclusions and recommendations. The summary, conclusions and recommendations may come at the beginning, even before the introduction, or before the main findings section. Remember – the summary is a short version of the main findings; the conclusion summarises the facts and arguments presented. Do not include any new facts or opinions in the conclusion that have not appeared in the report. Together with the introduction the conclusion should give the reader the gist of the report. In the recommendations section put your points of action – these must follow directly from the rest of the report. Where the conclusion gives an objective view of the information presented, in the recommendations section you may give your suggestions for action.

Box 14.5 Summary, conclusions and recommendations: example

Summary

The research shows that housing exerts a critical influence on older people's well-being. There are several aspects of housing that we found to be important:

➢ the dwelling – the quality of the building itself;
➢ the location;
➢ the house as an asset or form of wealth;
  ➢ as a source of income;
  ➢ as a bequest.

Dwellings provide shelter and comfort, but they also locate their occupants in relation to relatives, neighbours and services; they are often valuable assets, they are usually the main form of the older person's wealth, and they can be important in the family dynamics because of their potential as bequests to heirs.

Conclusions

Housing is a critical factor in the quality of life of older people. Many older Irish people are in a paradoxical situation . . . : they are housing poor and housing rich at the same time – many live in houses that are no longer suitable for their needs but which are worth a substantial amount of money . . .

Recommendations

Market solutions might include the following:

➢ the provision of suitable housing in towns, which allows older people to trade sideways, or down;
➢ equity release schemes to free capital tied up in the property;
➢ clawback schemes – where local authorities renovate a property but can reclaim some or all of the cost of doing so if the owner dies within a certain time period and the house is passed on to the next generation.

Source: adapted from Fahey, T. (2001) 'Housing, social interaction and participation among older Irish people', in McGivern, Y. (ed.), *Towards a Society for All Ages*, Dublin: National Council on Ageing and Older People. © 2001 National Council on Ageing and Older People. Used with permission.

Appendices

The purpose of an appendix is to hold all the information that is not directly relevant to the story but may be important to readers who need more detail (to evaluate the quality of the work, or to replicate it, for example). It should contain technical and methodological details, for example the sampling procedure and the sample, how the data were handled, what weighting, if any, was used. It should also contain a full version of the questionnaire or discussion guide; and details of the organisation(s) that carried out the work, perhaps even CVs or résumés of team members. Depending on the type of report the appendix may also contain a full bibliography of references cited and used. Data tables, transcriptions of interviews, field notes or coding schemes may be contained in an appendix but are more usually presented separately, if at all.

■ Starting to write

It is likely that you will write about three or four draft versions of the report before you are satisfied that it gets your message across. No one gets it right first time. The important thing is not trying to get it right first time but to start writing. Do not be afraid to start. No one may even see the first draft. It is not the final product. In an early draft you are still formulating your ideas and crystallising your thinking. You can start writing before you have the data. Start with the background to the problem or the problem definition. Starting with fairly straightforward sections that you may have covered in the proposal will help you write your way into it. It will also help you establish the aim and focus of the issues and it may make you better and more efficient at interrogating the data when you get them.

Structure

When the data tables and analyses or the tapes and transcripts arrive, work through them systematically. Once you get to grips with the data and understand what they are saying start putting down all your thoughts and ideas – as you work through the research results write down what is interesting, meaningful and relevant, including thoughts and insights that pop into your head. Do not be concerned about how crafted or polished the language is at this stage, or the order of ideas or themes. Once you have dumped down all your ideas you can then start working through them to structure the material and give it a logical order in line with the report's objective. There are lots of ways of organising the flow of a report – there is no one right way. To help you structure it you can write all your major themes down on separate cards, or in boxes on a flow chart, and move them around to see how they best fit together to make the story flow.

Vary the length of sentences, and in writing and editing them remember that a sentence is a unit of thought and so should contain one idea only. A paragraph is a theme, a group of related sentences, so separate your themes into paragraphs – it will help make the reading easy and clear. Build a map into your report by making the first sentence in a paragraph and the first paragraph in a section a summary of what you are going to say in the subsequent sentences and paragraphs. This makes the report more readable, and enables the reader to get to grips with content relatively easily.

Language

Once you have the structure more or less sorted out you can tackle the language. Sorting out the structure will have helped you to clarify the ideas and the message; editing the language will help you take this a stage further. Use the language that you use every day and use the active voice rather than the passive. Reports are hard to read when they contain too many sentences in the passive voice, or too many long words, too much jargon, and too many long sentences and long paragraphs. Get rid of redundant words and phrases, including unnecessary adjectives and adverbs. It will have the effect of making your ideas sharper and more focused.

Getting feedback

Is it readable? Is it understandable? Give a draft to a colleague and ask him or her to read it and give you feedback. The problems feedback might uncover at this stage are that your ideas and your expression of them and the logic are not yet clear. If at this stage someone starts picking on your choice of words or your sentence construction remember it for later, but ignore it now. Now is the time to get the ideas and the message or argument clear. There should be a thread or storyline that runs through the report which leads the reader to your conclusions and to the overall picture. Read your draft out loud and see what the language sounds like. It should be easy on the ear. If it jars, rewrite it. Rewriting should focus on achieving brevity and adding clarity while at the same time maintaining accuracy.

When it is done, let it go. It is often assumed that taking more time is better than taking less time. That is not always the case, and time spent at the end polishing is usually better spent up front thinking about the objective of the report, planning it out and devising a structure and a logical order.

Box 14.6 Checking a report draft

☐ Is the table of contents complete?
☐ Are all the chapters/sections present?
☐ Is the structure clear?
☐ Are the topics within each chapter in a logical order?
☐ Are there good links between sections?
☐ Is there anything that would be better off in an appendix?
☐ How informative and attention getting is the title?
☐ Is the abstract an accurate summary of the entire report?
☐ Does the background set the scene in enough detail? Does it contain enough information for a newcomer to the topic to understand the issues and the need for research?
☐ Have you clearly stated the research objectives?
☐ Does the literature review present relevant material?
☐ Have you explained the research design and methods clearly?
☐ Are the limitations of the research (and the findings) identified?
☐ Have you distinguished clearly between findings and interpretation, between 'facts' and speculation or opinion?
☐ Have all (and only) the relevant data been used?

Presenting data in tables, diagrams and charts

The ability to reduce the mass of data in your data tables or from tapes and transcripts and display them in summary form (as short written summary statements or in summary tables, charts or diagrams) in a way that tells the story is an important skill. The aim of data display is twofold: to reduce the amount of data; and to present data in such a way that it becomes information.

■ Written summary statements

Some types of data are best presented as written statements. Written summary statements are useful for drawing the audience's or the reader's attention to key messages in the presentation or report. If well written they are easy to understand and can be used to convey the meaning of complex data. For a presentation, however, they can lack the impact of a good graphic or visual display. Here are some guidelines that will help you obtain maximum impact from any written chart, even summaries contained in a report:

Text
➢ the text should be easy to read;
➢ the typeface should be large enough for most people to read easily;
➢ the typeface should be easy on the eye (if different typefaces are used on the same chart they should complement each other, otherwise the end result may look untidy);

➤ the text should be in a colour that does not clash with or fade into the background.

Words and grammar
➤ avoid too many abbreviations;
➤ do not reduce sentences so much that the meaning is unclear;
➤ give each chart a title that clearly explains its content.

Layout
➤ make use of space – avoid using too much text or text too tightly bunched.

■ Data tables

The data tables you receive from data processing should not be used in their unadulterated form in a presentation or a report. Invariably they contain too much data, much of which is likely to be irrelevant to the particular point you are trying to make. The data from these tables should be reviewed with the objectives of the report or presentation in mind, and only those data extracted that address these objectives.

Summary tables

The tables used in a presentation or report should be designed so that the reader or viewer does not have to work hard to get the message or see the finding. Each table should have a title that is short but informative. In a report the tables should be numbered. Text describing the content of columns and rows should be clear, and not abbreviated so much that they are hard to understand. The units of measurement of the numbers in the table should be clearly displayed, with base sizes and summary statistics (such as means and standard deviations) included when appropriate.

The layout should make reading the table easy. If numbers are to be compared make sure they are in columns side by side rather than in rows. Avoid cluttering the table with too many lines, or too much text, or using shading or colouring that makes it difficult to read. Make sure the spacing between numbers is consistent and that numbers line up. Keep the numbers in a consistent style; for example, if some numbers have two decimal places and others have one, decide which is more appropriate and use that. Arrange rows and columns in an order that tells a story. For example, a simple rank ordering in terms of content or value often does the trick. Consider Tables 14.1 and 14.2, which show fictional data on medication for colds derived from an association grid. With Table 14.1 it takes a while to work out what the data are saying. It is not immediately clear which brand is associated with which attributes, or which attributes seem to be more important.

In Table 14.2 a simple reordering and the addition of another line of data makes the finding more obvious. The two most popular brands, L and M, are considered by most people in the sample to be effective, suitable for use throughout the day, to treat all the symptoms and quick to take effect. More people find M compared to L easy to take and pleasant tasting. Brand N is the third most popular in terms of claimed purchase. It appears to share some characteristics with L and M – effective, treats all the

Table 14.1 Data from brand attribute association grid

Attribute	Brand L %	Brand M %	Brand N %	Brand O %	Brand P %
Pleasant tasting	27	67	84	72	78
Makes you drowsy	62	19	25	78	82
Quick to take effect	24	79	76	69	74
Easy to take	38	66	79	79	76
Suitable to use throughout the day	25	83	84	22	29
Treats all the symptoms of a cold	22	82	76	56	79
Effective	27	89	72	62	74
Mean of attribute ratings	32	69	71	63	70

Table 14.2 Data from brand attribute association grid – modified version

	Brand M %	Brand N %	Brand P %	Brand O %	Brand L %
Buy now	**82**	**71**	**52**	**38**	**11**
Effective	89	72	74	62	27
Suitable to use throughout the day	83	84	29	22	25
Treats all the symptoms of a cold	82	76	79	56	22
Quick to take effect	79	76	74	69	24
Pleasant tasting	67	84	78	72	42
Easy to take	66	79	76	79	38
Makes you drowsy	19	25	82	78	62
Mean of attribute ratings	69	71	70	63	32

symptoms, quick to take effect; and it is similar to M in that similar proportions say that it is pleasant tasting and easy to take. It differs, however, from both L and M in that a large proportion say that it makes you drowsy and a relatively small proportion, in comparison to L or M, say that it is suitable to use throughout the day. A smaller proportion compared to L, M or N sees Brand O, which shares the 'makes you drowsy' attribute with N and P, as effective or as treating all the symptoms of a cold. Relatively few respondents associate Brand P with any of the attributes, with the exception of 'makes you drowsy'.

Detailed tables

It is sometimes necessary to provide more detailed tables in a report or in an appendix to a report. In preparing these tables all the above guidelines should be followed. In addition you may want to add in explanatory notes, explaining terms used in the table, the source of the data or a commentary on the findings.

Types of numbers in tables: using indices, ratios and percentage change

If you want to show trends over time it can be useful to transform the data into an index by expressing it as a percentage or proportion of the earliest figure in the time sequence. Table 14.3 shows the unit sales for three products from 1999 to 2003.

Table 14.3 Unit sales (millions) 1999–2003

	2003	2002	2001	2000	1999
Product X	376	320	298	246	202
Product Y	499	348	306	298	288
Product Z	636	588	542	322	288

Table 14.4(a) Unit sales 1999–2003 (1999 = 100) – original version

	2003	2002	2001	2000	1999
Product X	186	158	148	122	100
Product Y	173	121	106	103	100
Product Z	221	204	188	119	100

Table 14.4(b) Unit sales 1999–2003 (1999 = 100) – revised version

	1999	2000	2001	2002	2003
Product X	100	122	148	158	186
Product Y	100	103	106	121	173
Product Z	100	119	188	204	221

To get a clearer picture of the relative changes in sales since 1999 we can index the figures to 1999. If we divide the 1999 figure for each product by itself and multiply it by 100 we get 100. To transform each of the figures from 2000 to 2003 we do the same – divide the figure for each year by the 1999 figure for that product and multiply it by 100 to express it in the same units as the 1999 figure. In Table 14.4(a) the data are thus transformed, making the finding clearer. It is now easy to see that, for example, while sales of products Y and Z were the same in 1999, sales of product Z grew faster. Table 14.4(b) is easier to read because the order in which the years appear has been reversed so that the table reads from left to right rather than right to left.

Ratios are a useful way to highlight differences between two or three figures. Here is a fictional example: for every $1 spent on advertising by the anti-drink drive lobby, alcohol manufacturers spend $10 sponsoring motor racing.

It may be useful to show the change – the gain or loss – between two figures as a percentage of the gain. If you do this make sure that the base or sample size on which the percentage change is calculated is large enough, otherwise the results might be misleading, as the example in Table 14.5 shows. The percentage gain/loss figures in the last column of Table 14.5 show that Model W has seen the greatest increase in sales – 71 per cent compared to 53 per cent for Model U. Sales for Model W were relatively low to begin with and the percentage gain is exaggerated – it only looks big

Table 14.5 **First and second quarter sales for four models of luxury car**

Model	1st qtr	2nd qtr	Change	% gain/loss
Model R	192	79	−113	−59
Model S	440	460	+20	+5
Model U	204	312	+108	+53
Model W	42	72	+30	+71

because of this small base. When base size or sub-sample sizes are small be wary of using percentages – they are misleading, especially when used in comparison with percentages based on more robust base sizes, and in many cases are meaningless.

■ Charts and diagrams

A well-designed chart can make the material in reports and presentations more interesting, easier to get through and easier to understand or take in; it can convey quickly and easily a lot of detailed, even complex data. Designing such charts, however, is not easy. The format must be suitable for the material; and the chart or diagram should convey the message clearly and accurately – the message should jump out at the audience or the reader. Before we look in detail at different chart formats, and how to decide if a format will suit your material, here are some general guidelines that apply to all charts and diagrams:

➢ Avoid anything that makes reading and understanding charts difficult.
➢ The title should explain the content clearly and succinctly.
➢ The text should be large enough to read easily (on a presentation chart about 32-point; in a report, 12-point).
➢ The text should stand out from the background (the colour should enhance the text, not distract from it or make it look blurred).
➢ The chart design should be as plain as possible (avoid distracting designs, vertical lines and shading, especially cross-hatching, which can be hard on the eye; in fact, avoid shading at all if possible).
➢ Label sections or elements of the chart rather than use a legend or key to which the audience or reader have to refer to understand the chart.
➢ Ensure that scales are labelled with units of measurement and that the scale does not exaggerate relationships or mislead.
➢ Do not overcrowd or obscure the chart with labels – it should contain only the text and numbering necessary for interpretation.
➢ The text included should tell the reader or viewer how to read the chart and should direct attention to the relevant finding.
➢ Labels and other text should not be abbreviated so much that their meaning is difficult to decipher.

It is important that all aspects of the chart are integrated so that reading it and understanding the message is easy and straightforward – the chart designer has done all the work and the reader is able to see what is going on almost immediately.

Choosing a format

Pie charts

In choosing a suitable format it is important to consider the type of data you have. If you want to show how the whole of something divides up into parts a pie chart is useful. For example, if you want to show the breakdown of support for the political parties in an election, a pie chart is a reasonable way of doing this. Each segment or slice of the pie will represent the proportion of the electorate (the sample) which supports that party. The slices should be ordered logically in a clockwise direction. If you want to highlight a particular segment you can 'explode' that segment, removing it slightly from the rest of the pie. Pie charts are not a good choice of format if you have a lot of segments (more than four or five make the chart look messy and can be difficult to read). Although two pie charts side by side are sometimes used to demonstrate the relative breakdown of two sets of data or 'wholes', having to move back and forth between pies to compare segments can be hard work.

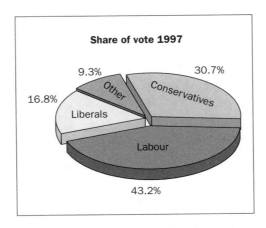

Figure 14.2 Example of a pie chart

Pictograms

Pictograms are charts in which pictures or drawings are used to represent quantities. The picture used should be relevant to the data it represents. For example, if you wanted to demonstrate the quantity of beer consumed by men and women, you could use a drawing of a beer glass foaming with beer (see Figure 14.3).

Figure 14.3 Example of a pictogram

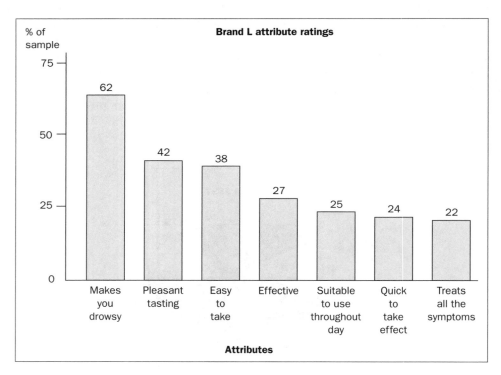

Figure 14.4 Example of a simple bar chart

Bar charts, histograms and line charts

If you have one variable or one category, or you want to compare the frequencies of two or more values or variables, bar charts, histograms and line charts are useful. Bar charts and histograms are often confused. Use a bar chart when the data are nominal or ordinal (caetgorical variables, non-metric data); use a histogram when the data are interval or ratio (cardinal numbers, metric data, continuous variables).

The horizontal or x-axis of the bar chart in Figure 14.4 is used to display the categories; the vertical or y-axis is used to display the frequency or number of observations or responses in each category – the height of the bar represents the frequency. The categories or bars should be ordered in a way that draws out the meaning or the finding. Figure 14.4 shows what percentage of the sample associates each attribute with brand L.

There are several ways of displaying bar charts. The bars can be displayed vertically, as well as horizontally as in Figure 14.4. Two or more sets of bars can be displayed on the one chart, with each set clustered or grouped together, for example to show the responses of the sample to different brands as in Figure 14.5 (a) and (b).

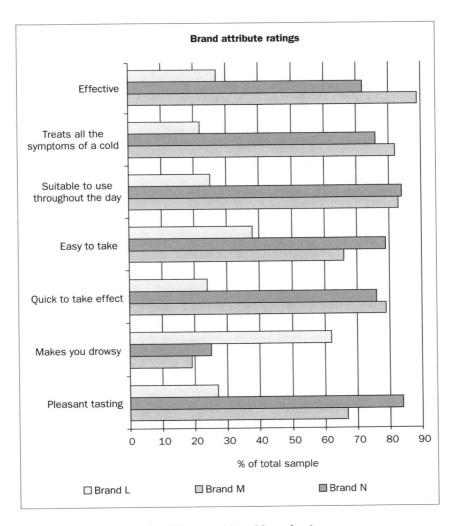

Figure 14.5 (a) Example of 'grouped bars' bar charts

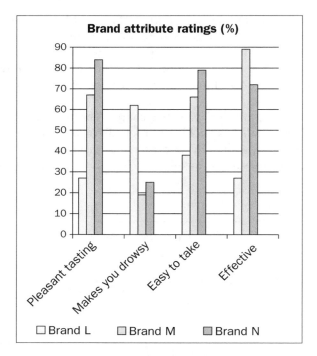

Figure 14.5(b) Vertical grouped bars

A bar can be divided up into sections, with each section representing measurements that relate to each other in some way. Figure 14.6 shows a stacked bar chart with one section showing the percentage rating the brand effective and the other showing the percentage who 'buy nowadays'. In this example each component of the bar represents the proportion of the total sample giving that response; Figure 14.7 shows a component bar chart in which the total bar represents the whole sample and each component represents the percentage or frequency of that particular response.

Histogram

A histogram looks like a bar chart without the spaces in between the bars. The reason there are no spaces, the reason the bars are touching, is because the histogram is displaying continuous data at the interval or ratio level of measurement – age bands, for example, or income groups – and not data that can be grouped in discrete categories, such as male and female or social class. The width of the bar represents the size of the interval covered by the band or group of responses and so the area of each bar on the histogram is proportional to the frequency of responses for that group (see Figure 14.8).

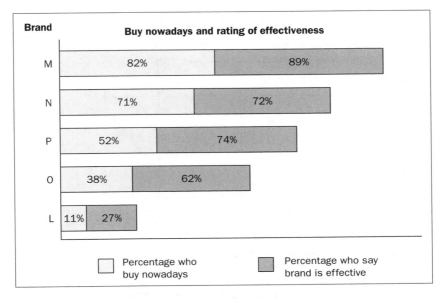

Figure 14.6 **Example of stacked bar chart**

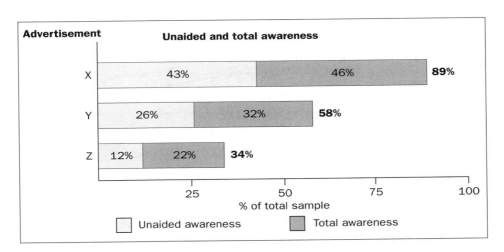

Figure 14.7 **Example of component bar chart**

Line charts

Line charts or graphs are a useful way of displaying changes in a measurement over time. Care should be taken, as with all charts, in deciding on the scales for the x- and y-axis. If the vertical or y-axis is exaggerated in scale in relation to the x-axis, the effect will be to pull the graph upwards and make increases over the length of the x-axis seem bigger than they might otherwise appear. If, on the other hand, the y-axis is compressed, differences over the length of the x-axis may appear flatter than is

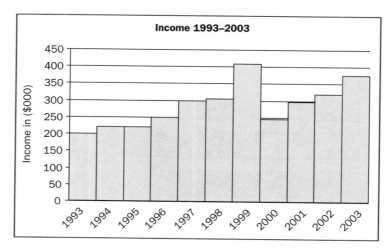

Figure 14.8 Example of a histogram

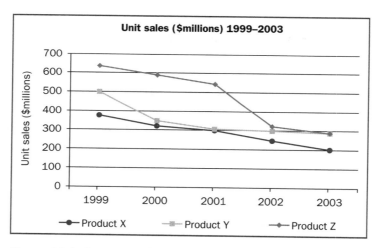

Figure 14.9 Example of a line chart

the case. Tufte (2001) has examined many cases, investigated the geometry and the aesthetics of shape and, taking the advice of Tukey (1977), recommends a shape that is wider than it is tall. He cites as benefits the ease of reading along the horizontal and of labelling on an extended horizontal axis (see Figure 14.9).

Scatterplots

When you want to display bivariate rather than univariate data, scatterplots or graphs are appropriate. These can be used to show the relationship between a dependent and an independent variable. The independent or explanatory variable is plotted on the x-axis; the dependent variable on the y-axis. Scatterplots are often produced as the first step in a correlation and regression exercise. The visual display of the data allows the

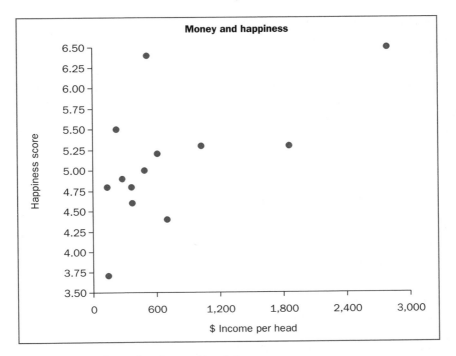

Figure 14.10 Example of a scatterplot

researcher to check by eye whether or not the two variables are related. A line of best fit can be calculated and drawn on the plot. The same guidelines for deciding on the scale of the axes, given above for line charts, apply to scatterplots and graphs.

Geographical maps can be used as the basis of a chart with, for example, the incidence of specific groups or attitudes or behaviour superimposed or denoted by colour or density of shading. Maps can be derived from multivariate techniques such as correspondence analysis and can be built using qualitative data and are a useful way of displaying data in three or more dimensions.

Evaluating the quality of research

Throughout the book we have discussed the things you need to do in order to commission or conduct high-quality research. Imagine now that the research has been completed and the findings delivered. Assuming you were happy with the proposal and the research design proposed in it, you now need to review how the research was executed and how the findings were delivered.

■ Did you get what you asked for?

First of all consider: did you get what you asked for in the brief or what you were promised in the proposal? If there were problems, what steps were taken to resolve them? Was the problem brought to your attention in a timely manner? For example, if the sample was not achieved, did the researcher explain why? Is the explanation credible? Is it clear what effect this might have on the overall robustness or credibility of the data? Are you satisfied with this explanation? If the recruitment for a group discussion did not match the criteria set down, or the group did not work particularly well, did the researcher continue with the group? Did the researcher include findings from that group in the analysis? Did he or she recruit or offer to recruit a replacement group (Lovett, 2001)? Are you satisfied that the researcher did all he or she could?

Execution of the research

In choosing a research supplier you may have reviewed how well they conducted research for others (via a credentials pitch, an office visit, informal soundings or discussions and so on). But how was their research for you? The evidence may be found in the end product; you may also have had a chance to see for yourself during the research process. Think about how you would rate the following:

➢ the fieldwork briefing or briefing notes;
➢ the fieldwork and fieldwork supervision;
➢ quality control and back-checking procedures;
➢ data entry, verification, editing and coding and data analysis;
➢ the level of expertise and experience of the providers.

For example: Did the interviewers follow the sampling instructions and/or the questionnaire instructions? Did you get detail in responses to open-ended questions? Were there a lot of 'No responses' or 'Don't knows'? Was the coding frame a good reflection of the verbatim comments? Were the data tables error free? Were there any discrepancies between data in tables and data in the presentation or report?

Project management and the relationship/interface

From a project management point of view there are some tangibles and some intangibles. Ask yourself these questions:

➢ How satisfied are you with how the project was managed?
➢ Was the senior researcher who took the brief involved throughout the project?
➢ How well were you kept informed of progress?
➢ Were key deadlines met?
➢ How well did the researchers handle any problems that arose?
➢ Did the researchers provide added value – anything above and beyond what was expected?
➢ Were they aware of the issues facing your industry/area?
➢ Did they show interest in the decisions that you have to make? Were they enthusiastic?
➢ Was the service provided value for money?

Delivery and interpretation

Review the report using the checklist in Box 14.6. Review the presentation: how effectively were the findings communicated? In reviewing both presentation and report ask yourself the following:

➤ Is it clear what action is to be taken, what the next steps are, or are you left saying 'So what?'
➤ Did you get information or data? Did the researcher relate the findings to the research problem and the wider business problem?
➤ Has the researcher understood the problem and how it relates to the wider context of your business?
➤ Is there a clear distinction between facts or other data and opinion and speculation?
➤ What is the researcher interpretation of the evidence? Are other possible interpretations given?
➤ Does the researcher give a clear line of argument? Is that argument solid – is it backed up by evidence?
➤ Is there evidence against the argument? How has that been handled?
➤ Is the researcher aware or does he or she state the assumptions underlying the approach or solution to the problem?
➤ Based on the data you have seen (tables, transcripts or tapes) would you have made the same interpretation and reached the same conclusion based on this evidence and your knowledge of the issues? Do the findings match your own understanding or knowledge of the issues? Is there anything odd or unusual? If so, is there a plausible and credible explanation for it?

Quality and suitability of the evidence for its end use

Ask the end users of the research:

➤ Was the research of value in producing evidence for decision making?
➤ Was the evidence robust enough?
➤ Was it complete – did it cover the issues?
➤ What other evidence did you wish you had? Why was it not there? Was it in the brief and not addressed or was it not included?

Chapter summary

➤ Presentations and reports are important as a means of crystallising the thinking about the findings; as a channel for disseminating the findings; as a way of influencing the client in a course of action; and as a way of selling the expertise of the researcher. Presentations give client and researcher an opportunity to discuss the findings and explore their implications; the report brings together in one document the detail of the project and so acts as a record for the work completed.

Reports and presentations are useful in evaluating the quality of research and research supplier.

➤ In both presentation and report the aim is to communicate the findings clearly, accurately and effectively. Be clear about what you are trying to achieve. Think of the audience and tailor the message to them. Edit the content ruthlessly; present only those data or findings that shed light on the issue.

➤ Prepare thoroughly for a presentation – know the material inside out; practise your delivery. Choose and design your visual aids to enhance the message. Think about the logistics – the equipment, the size of the room, the size of the audience.

➤ Clarify the aim of the report, prepare an outline of the content and the structure and start writing. Use everyday language. Develop a storyline that runs through the report leading the reader to your conclusions. Review the draft yourself and give it to a colleague to review.

➤ Design tables, charts and graphs so that they are easy to read and their message is clear.

➤ Review the research to determine how useful it was in addressing the decision makers' problem. Review the findings – check if you would have reached the same conclusions. Review the process to determine how well managed and how well executed the research was.

Questions and exercises

1 What do you need to consider in planning a presentation or a report?

2 Outline what is involved in preparing and delivering a presentation.

3 Review some of the reports you have written. What changes, if any, would you make in the light of the report writing guidelines given above? Look at some of the articles published in the *Journal of the Market Research Society*. How well written are they?

4 Draw up a guideline for the preparation of charts and graphs.

5 Prepare a checklist of questions for use in reviewing a piece of research.

References

Biel, A. (1994) 'The utilisation barrier: the need to make research come alive', *Admap*, September.

Tukey, J. (1977) *Exploratory Data Analysis*, Reading, MA: Addison Wesley.

Tufte, E. (2001) *The Visual Display of Quantitative Information*, Cheshire, CT: Graphics Press.

Recommended reading

Becker, H. (1986) *Writing for Social Scientists*; Chicago, IL: University of Chicago Press. An excellent guide to starting and finishing articles, reports and theses.

Tufte, E. (2001) *The Visual Display of Quantitative Information*; Cheshire, CT: Graphics Press. A beautiful and instructive book for those interested in designing charts and graphs.

Waterhouse, K. (1994) *English, Our English (and How to Sing It)*, London: Penguin. An excellent book on grammar and style.

Chapter 15

Ethics and the practice of research

Introduction

In this chapter we look, first of all, at the ethical principles that underpin research. We examine the more formal framing of these principles in the codes of conduct of professional bodies, in particular The Market Research Society Code of Conduct. Finally, we look at data protection legislation and its implications for research practice.

Topics covered

➢ Ethics and the practice of research
➢ The Market Research Society Code of Conduct
➢ Data protection legislation and its implications for research practice

Relationship to MRS Advanced Certificate Syllabus

The material covered in this chapter is relevant to Unit 1 – Introduction and Problem Definition, specifically the following:

➢ ethical issues in research;
➢ The Market Research Society Code of Conduct;
➢ 1998 UK Data Protection Act.

Learning outcomes

At the end of this chapter you should be able to:

➢ understand the ethical issues involved in research;
➢ demonstrate knowledge, understanding and application of the MRS Code of Conduct to the practice of research;
➢ understand the implications of the Data Protection Act for the practice of research.

Ethics and the practice of research

Ethics are moral principles that are used to guide behaviour. The study of ethics is the study of standards of conduct, of the rights and wrongs of the behaviour of a particular person or group. Ethical principles are used to set standards of conduct for groups or professions in how they deal with people. The research profession is no exception. Ethical standards are important in a research context in order that those involved in research – researchers, research participants, clients and other users of research and the wider community – know what is and what is not acceptable behaviour in the conduct of research. A researcher's ethical code extends to the treatment of clients, in relation to, for example, recommending research that is unnecessary, or misreporting findings, or to the disclosure of confidential client data, and to the treatment of other researchers and their work. The primary focus of most ethical codes, however, is the setting of standards of behaviour in relation to the treatment of research participants, on whom research depends.

■ Getting co-operation

Why do people agree to take part in research? We ask a lot of research participants and we give them little in return. We intrude into their lives – we observe, measure and question their behaviour, their attitudes and their opinions, and we analyse, interpret and report what they tell us. We often ask them to divulge personal, sometimes sensitive, information – and to someone who is a stranger to them. There is little tangible or intangible reward for taking part – it is rare that research directly serves the interest of the individual respondent. Given these circumstances it is unlikely that people would willingly co-operate in research if they felt that they could not trust the researcher. One way of creating trust is to ensure, and demonstrate, that research is conducted in an acceptable and ethical way. We do this by publishing and promoting a formal code of conduct by which research practitioners agree to abide. We will look at one such code, The Market Research Society Code of Conduct, in detail later in this chapter. First of all we need to look at the ethical principles that underlie such codes.

■ Ethical principles in the treatment of research participants

The ethical principles that are the basis of most standards of conduct in relation to research participants are as follows:

➤ voluntary participation;
➤ no harm to the participants;
➤ informed consent;
➤ anonymity, confidentiality (privacy);
➤ transparency;
➤ not deceiving subjects.

Voluntary participation

Voluntary participation is the cornerstone of an ethical code: it requires that no one should be forced or deceived into taking part in research. The researcher should obtain an individual's or an organisation's consent and this consent should be based on a clear understanding of what the research will involve and how the data collected will be used. The participant should be told that he or she has the right to withdraw from the research at any time and is under no obligation to answer any of the questions asked.

No harm to the participants

At all times during the conduct of research participants should be treated with respect and sensitivity. The onus is on the researcher to ensure respondents' emotional as well as physical well-being and to assure respondents that *they will not be adversely affected or embarrassed in any way as a direct result of having participated in the research*' (MRS Code of Conduct, July 1999). It should be relatively easy to recognise what might cause physical harm to respondents, and to avoid it. For example, if the research involves a respondent testing a product, the client and the researcher should take steps to ensure the safe use of the product, for instance by providing clear instructions about its use. It is more difficult to recognise what might cause people emotional harm, however. There are many possible causes – the very fact of being researched can cause anxiety and stress (Gordon and Robson, 1980). Intruding on respondents at unsuitable or inconvenient times can cause annoyance and distress. Asking questions about sensitive topics can embarrass and distress respondents. Reporting or publishing the findings of research in which individuals or research settings are identifiable can cause embarrassment or distress, and may damage participants' self-image or public reputation (Lee, 1992).

Informed consent

The principles of voluntary participation and no harm to participants form the basis of informed consent. Research should not proceed without the informed consent of the participants. Respondents should be clearly and unambiguously informed about what is involved and how the data they provide will be used. It is the researcher's responsibility to ensure that the nature of the research is not misrepresented in any way. We revisit the principle of informed consent in the discussion about data protection legislation later in this chapter.

Anonymity and confidentiality

Ensuring the anonymity and confidentiality of participants and the data they provide are two ways in which the well-being and interests of respondents can be protected. Anonymity and confidentiality are often confused, and sometimes taken to mean the same thing. They are different, and it is important to remember this when such assurances are given to a participant. If you promise confidentiality it means that, while you can identify a particular response with a particular respondent, you agree not to do so publicly. If, however, you promise anonymity it means that you cannot identify a response with a particular respondent. Promises of anonymity are not always possible in market research. In most projects personal data are collected for quality control and verification purposes and they remain attached to the data record at least until quality checks have been made. Respondents are therefore not anonymous. Data records can be anonymised – by removing all identifying information – and it is good practice to do this as soon as possible after quality checks on the data have been made. If it is necessary to recontact a respondent, his or her personal data should be stored separately from the data record (and only those involved in the research should have access to that information). If respondents are promised anonymity – in some projects it may be necessary to do this in order to secure co-operation (for example studies of sexual behaviour, illegal drug taking or criminal activity) – no personal data should be recorded on the data record that could identify them with their responses. This will mean that quality or verification checks cannot be made. If you assure a respondent of confidentiality or anonymity you would be acting unethically if you were to breach that assurance. For example, say you give the respondent's data to the client to add to or enhance his or her customer database, or you write up your findings for publication and the description of a respondent makes him or her identifiable, you would be in breach of your agreement with the respondent, and so you would be acting unethically. If it is not your intention to keep data confidential you should not promise confidentiality, nor describe the research as confidential. You must tell potential respondents what the purpose of data collection really is. If you assure the respondent that the postal survey in which he or she is taking part will be anonymous, and you print the respondent's staff number, for example, on the questionnaire, then the data record is not anonymous. You have breached your assurance to the respondent. If you do not inform respondents honestly about the nature and purpose of the research you may not have complied with the principle of informed consent and you may be guilty of deceiving them.

Transparency

Research can be conducted without the promise of either anonymity or confidentiality. For example, data can be collected on an attributable basis. This, however, can be done only with the consent of the participant and the data can only be used for the purpose described to the participant at the time of collection. The person or organisation collecting the data must be transparent about the purpose of the research, the end use of the data and the fact that anonymity or confidentiality is not promised.

Not deceiving subjects

Deceiving subjects in order to get them to take part in research is unethical. For example, it would be unethical to tell a respondent that the interview will take 15 minutes if you know that it will take 45 minutes. Deceiving subjects into thinking that they are taking part in research when they are not is unethical. The reputation of research has been harmed, and co-operation rates have declined, as a result of the practice of '*sugging*' or selling under the guise of research (and '*frugging*', fund raising under the guise of research). Subjects should not be misled or deceived in any way;

it should be made clear to them (transparency again) that they are taking part in bona fide research and they should be informed honestly about what that research involves.

■ Ambiguities in the interpretation and application of ethical principles

The principles outlined above are widely accepted – most researchers would agree that informed consent should be obtained, that respondents should not be deceived or coerced into taking part in research, nor deceived about the use of the data they provide, and that data should be treated in confidence unless agreed otherwise. It all seems fairly straightforward at first glance. There are complications, however. Here are some things to think about.

➢ How far do you go in encouraging the unwilling to take part? If you try to persuade a subject to take part have you violated the principle of voluntary participation? Does it depend on what you say or do in order to persuade? If only those who are willing actually take part what implications does this have in terms of representativeness of the sample (and so the external validity of the research)?

➢ If you do not get the subject's consent at the start of the data collection process is participation really voluntary, or are you deceiving the subject into participating? Does it depend on the type of research situation? In observation exercises, such as mystery shopping, where the validity of the research relies on the subject not knowing that he or she is being observed, is it justifiable not to get the subject's permission before data collection begins?

➢ How much should you tell subjects about the research in order to comply with the principle of informed consent (Robson, 1991)? Should you tell them everything about it? What is everything anyway? Is it justifiable to withhold some of the details about the research where you believe that they might bias the respondent's answers, or is this deception, and/or a compromise of the principle of informed consent? For example, what do you do if you are conducting a customer satisfaction study in which the services of several organisations are being compared and you feel that telling the respondent the name of the client might bias his or her responses?

➢ You promise participants in a video-recorded group discussion that the data they provide and the recording of the group will be treated in confidence and used for research purposes only. Is it justifiable to use the video recording in a research training session? Does this use of the material count as research? Have you broken your promise of confidentiality? Have you deceived participants about the use of their data?

➢ You are researching the experiences of employees in a relatively small organisation and the client (the employer) wants to know if experiences vary by department and grade. Will individuals be identifiable in the data if their names are not used but either their department or grade is? You interview the employees at convenient breaks in their working day. Will colleagues, or those involved in commissioning the research, be able to determine who was interviewed? In these circumstances can you promise respondents confidentiality or anonymity? Are there implications for the quality of the data if respondents feel that confidentiality might be compromised? Will the openness and honesty of their answers be limited by their perception of the confidentiality of the project? Can you be sure that no harm will come to respondents as a result of their participation in the research?

➤ A further question for consideration is that of who owns the data collected and whether research participants have rights to their data. If participants have rights to their data do they have the right to give or withdraw consent for how the data are used? What implications does this have for confidentiality and anonymity? Do they have rights to their data record once it has been anonymised?

As these questions and dilemmas show, ethical issues are rarely clear cut. Questions about how to apply ethical principles will always arise. It is to address such questions, and to ensure a professional and consistent standard of practice, that professional bodies, such as ESOMAR and the MRS, have developed formal codes of conduct.

■ Ethical considerations to clients and the research community

Researchers' ethical responsibilities do not rest only with respondents; they also have ethical responsibilities to the clients or the funders of the research (Lovett, 2001), to fellow researchers and to the wider community. As a result, researchers have an ethical responsibility to behave in a way that does not cause the public or the business community to lose confidence in research or the research profession. They should not recommend or undertake unnecessary research. They should not make claims about their qualifications or experience that are untrue, for example. In conducting a research project researchers are entrusted with confidential and commercially sensitive information – they have an ethical responsibility not to disclose this information. When proposing or conducting research or reporting on the findings of research, researchers have an ethical responsibility to be open and honest about the way in which research will be or was conducted, and its limitations or shortcomings. If difficulties are encountered, or mistakes made, these should be pointed out – in order to allow others to learn from them, and for the wider research community to benefit, and to allow others to judge the validity and reliability of the research. Researchers also have an ethical responsibility to ensure that research results – whether positive or negative – are reported accurately and honestly and that they are not used to mislead in any way. They have a responsibility to ensure that they do not use or take advantage of the work of another researcher without that researcher's permission.

Professional codes of conduct

As we have seen, many issues and circumstances that arise in the practice of research are ambiguous and open to interpretation from an ethical point of view – what one person judges to be ethical behaviour in a particular situation another may not. In order to define clearly what is and what is not ethical or acceptable in the conduct of research professional bodies that represent researchers have developed formal codes of conduct. The purpose of these codes is to establish good practice among their members. They aim to do this by ensuring that important ethical issues are identified and addressed and by trying to clear up any ambiguity in the interpretation of ethical principles. Most codes cover three areas: the researcher's responsibilities to research participants, to those who fund the research, and to other researchers. Members of ESOMAR, the professional body representing researchers worldwide, are bound by the International Chambers of Commerce (ICC)/ESOMAR International Code of Marketing and Social Research Practice. Members of The Market Research Society are bound by its Code of Conduct, which incorporates the ICC/ESOMAR Code. The Social Research Association publishes *Ethical Guidelines*. The codes and guidelines are self-regulatory and, although they may incorporate principles that are covered by legislation, they do not replace or take precedence over legislation.

■ The Market Research Society's Code of Conduct

The aim of the MRS Code is '*to ensure that professional standards are maintained, that knowledge is communicated, and that the value of research is appreciated by the business community and the public at large*'. It was first published in 1954 and has been revised and updated regularly to take account of changes in research practice and in legislation. Compliance with the Code should ensure that research is conducted in compliance with the UK's Data Protection Act (1998). The principles of the MRS Code are given in Box 15.1. The Code sets out the professional responsibilities of researchers, the responsibilities of its members to other members, and to respondents and clients, and the responsibilities of clients to researchers. It addresses all of the fundamental ethical principles that were described earlier – voluntary participation, no harm to participants, informed consent, confidentiality and anonymity, transparency and no deception. A full version of the Code, which contains notes about its interpretation, is available at the MRS website (**www.mrs.org.uk**). To give researchers a more detailed framework for the interpretation of the principles of its Code of Conduct the MRS also publishes a series of Guidelines (also available at the MRS website). These Guidelines interpret the Code for the practice of different types of research – mystery shopping, Internet and employee research, for example, and research among children and young people.

Box 15.1 Principles of the MRS Code of Conduct

Research is founded upon the willing co-operation of the public and of business organisations. It depends upon their confidence that it is conducted honestly, objectively, without unwelcome intrusion and without harm to respondents. Its purpose is to collect and analyse information, and not directly to create sales or to influence the opinions of anyone participating in it. It is in this spirit that the Code of Conduct has been devised.

Box 15.1 continued

The general public and other interested parties shall be entitled to complete assurance that every research project is carried out strictly in accordance with this Code, and that their rights of privacy are respected. In particular they must be assured that no information that could be used to identify them will be made available without their agreement to anyone outside the agency responsible for conducting the research. They must also be assured that the information they supply will not be used for any purposes other than research and that they will not be adversely affected or embarrassed as a direct result of their participation in a research project.

Wherever possible respondents must be informed as to the purpose of the research and the likely length of time necessary for the collection of the information.

Finally, the research findings themselves must always be reported accurately and never used to mislead anyone, in any way.

Source: The Market Research Society. Used with permission.

■ Applying the MRS Code: Codeline

The MRS operates an advice service called Codeline, which is staffed by research experts. The purpose of Codeline is to provide practical advice to respondents, researchers, clients and other interested parties about the MRS Code of Conduct and the Guidelines series. You can submit a query to the Codeline experts by email at **standards@mrs.org.uk**. To give you some understanding of how the Code of Conduct works in practice, and to help you understand better the application of it to real research problems, set out in Box 15.2 is a range of queries from the Codeline service. They are presented here with the advice provided by the Codeline's experts. There is a caveat: the advice given here was correct at the time of publication. Advice can, however, become out of date with the introduction of new legislation and/or the updating of the Code of Conduct and the Guidelines. In making decisions about how to proceed with an issue of your own always consult the most up-to-date version of the Code of Conduct.

Box 15.2 A selection of queries from Problem Corner in *Research* magazine

April 2001

1 An agency's client's project involves interviewing the client's own staff members on a confidential basis. Does the agency need individual staff members' consent?

Denis Pirie: Staff members have the same rights to agree or refuse to take part in research as any other type of respondent, but prior publicity by the management about the purpose and objectives of the study should improve response rates, especially if it is stressed that responses will be treated anonymously.

Box 15.2 continued

May 2001

2 A research agency is conducting a customer satisfaction survey for a car dealership client. The client wants the questionnaire to have a section asking respondents if they wish to be recontacted directly by the client for marketing or promotional purposes. The respondents' names will be forwarded to the client for these purposes. Is this permissible?

Denis Pirie: Certainly not! Market research respondents and their responses must not be used for such non-research purposes as sales or promotions as these are strictly forbidden by A13 of the Code. If the client wishes to sell or promote to survey respondents this activity must not be classified as market research and respondents must also be clear that this is not market research.

June 2001

3 An agency is conducting mystery shopping where shoppers purchase a service via a telephone call centre using either credit or debit cards. The agency is concerned that if all mystery shoppers then cancel the service and payment this could constitute an unacceptable waste of time of the mystery shopped company and the card payment service companies. Is this potentially a breach of guidelines?

Denis Pirie: I think a rule of thumb when mystery shopping is to try and match, as closely as possible, the 'real' pattern of shopping. Thus, while some shoppers would reconsider and cancel their service purchase others would make their purchase with a few possibly cancelling later. Accordingly, why not instruct the mystery shoppers to make a percentage of actual purchases such as to minimise or balance out inconveniences to those services that have been mystery shopped.

June 2001

4 A member of the public complains about a telephone interviewer asking for 'a minute of your time', when the interview took 30 minutes. They ask if this deceit is permissible or should interviewers have to tell the truth about the time involved?

Denis Pirie: Section A8 of the Code insists that market research interviewers keep to all assurances or promises made at the outset – including those relating to interview length. The data collection guidelines call for the maximum times to be given, these must be adhered to. The subject will also be referred to in the questionnaire design guidelines (time-consuming repetitive questions). Members of the public must be aware of the efforts being made by the profession to retain the goodwill of respondents and ensure rules and guidelines are adhered to. The public are advised to monitor their further market research participation. If assurances given by interviewers are not kept they can raise the matter urgently with the agencies concerned so that bad practice can be eliminated.

Box 15.2 continued

June 2001

5 A client wishes to have snippets from some group discussion videos combined into a short edited version to demonstrate respondents' interest in the product to their trade clients. Can group videos be used in this way?

Denis Pirie: No, video recordings of groups are for market research use only. Using them for sales or promotional purposes breaches both A13 of the Code as well as the Second Principle of the Data Protection Act (1998) on 'specified purposes' for data collection.

July 2001

6 Can you confirm that passing individual comments arising from an independent market research interview to the client is not permitted, even if a respondent asks us to.

Denis Pirie: Verbatim comments from any interview can be passed to a client as long as the source is not identified. Identified verbatim comments can be passed to the client at the express wish of the respondent (without prompting from the interviewer), and if such identifiable responses are to be fed back the content must be agreed by the respondent.

July 2001

7 A third party wishes to query aspects of research the agency did for a client and has requested copies of the questionnaire, which the client prefers the agency not to release. B14 of the Code says that researchers must make validation details available while B21c says that the questionnaire is the property of the client who pays for its development. Which clause applies?

Denis Pirie: If an agency's methodological competence has been questioned that agency has the right, if not the duty, to provide such information about segments of the questionnaire used and the broad range of responses to those segments, to reassure the questioner that any inferences made in a report overtly published by the client have been properly made. However, this applies only where a report prepared for the client has been published by the client and its contents are in the public domain and can thus be criticised by third parties. If no part of a report published for a client has been made public by the client, then it cannot be reasonably challenged by an external third party. Only information that has been made public can be challenged for validity by third parties.

August 2001

8 An agency wants to evaluate a direct mail campaign from the client's customer database by conducting groups with customers/respondents. Is this a problem?

Denis Pirie: It needn't be. The caller can select a sample of those to whom the client has sent direct mail, noting when it was sent and using this sample to recruit the groups. The topic guide items for these groups will be issues related to the respondents' receipt of and attitudes to direct mail.

Box 15.2 continued

September 2001

9 Are emailed surveys classified as spamming? Would it be better to set up panels or get respondents' consent before sending a survey?

Brian Bates: Internet research and research using email addresses are just alternative methods of data collection. All the rules relating to the rights of respondents – as set out in the MRS Code – apply in full to any research project conducted using the Internet or email. It is permissible to send unsolicited email to potential respondents if the email contains all the relevant information necessary for the potential respondent to make an informed decision about whether to participate. This concept is similar to the initial contact made for a conventional face-to-face interview, and the same rules apply. Any approach made in this way is not regarded as spamming. An email invitation should be kept as short as possible to minimise inconvenience or annoyance to the potential respondent, but it should include relevant data, especially concerning data privacy and guarantees that the data will only be used for MR.

September 2001

10 A market research agency has recently completed a project for a client. The researcher has learnt that the results of the study appear in a press release (which has subsequently appeared in the press) that states the correct figures from the report but presents them in a misleading way. Can and should the researcher query these differences with the client?

Denis Pirie: Clause B14 of the Code states that researchers must not knowingly allow the dissemination of conclusions from a market research project that are not adequately supported by the data. Clause B27 states that if the client publishes any of the findings of a research project, it is their responsibility to ensure that the findings are not misleading. In addition, the researcher must be consulted and agree in advance the form and content of publication, and must take action to correct any misleading statements about the research and its findings. Clause B29 states that researchers must ensure that clients are aware of the existence of the Code and of the need to comply with its requirements.

Thus, the Code makes it clear that researchers who are aware of a prima facie case of misrepresentation of research conclusions, i.e. between the results of a survey and the conclusions drawn from those contents, have obligations under all of these clauses to bring this matter to the client's urgent attention, and to seek and obtain either a fully satisfactory explanation or justification of these differences or the withdrawal of the misleading documentation and its substitution by one which properly reflects the content of the project.

To omit raising these issues with the client would imply the market research agency's collusion with the client to distort the views of the respondents, which would damage not only the market research agency's reputation but that of the entire market research profession.

Source: The Market Research Society (Professional Standards). Used with permission.

Data protection legislation

In 1995 the European Union adopted the Data Protection Directive. One of its aims, stated in Article One, was to *'protect the fundamental rights and freedoms of natural persons, and in particular their right to privacy with respect to the processing of personal data'*. Individual EU member states introduced legislation to comply with this Directive. In the United Kingdom the legislation is the 1998 Data Protection Act. The ethical principles discussed earlier are incorporated in this data protection legislation – in particular the principle of informed consent and the principle of confidentiality.

Box 15.3 Notification under the 1998 UK Data Protection Act

In order to hold or use personal data or receive information on customers from a data owner (a client, for example) and remain within the law, a researcher must notify the relevant data protection authority in the country in which the personal data are collected and processed. Under the UK's 1998 Data Protection Act the data protection authority is the Office of the Information Commissioner (OIC). In addition, if a researcher receives data from a data owner he or she must confirm with the data owner that the data owner is legally allowed to pass these data on. To do so legally the data owner must also be notified with the OIC to hold and use personal data in this way (that is, for research purposes).

Notification involves providing information about personal data held, use of personal data, arrangements for the protection of personal data and details of transfer of data outside the European Economic Area (EEA – the European Union member states as well as Norway, Iceland and Liechtenstein). The organisation or individual must provide details of all the personal data it holds and uses, including data in paper files, on microfiche, on audio or video tape and in electronic form, no matter how small or large the data holding. (If data are held in paper files only notification is not required but a voluntary notification can be made.) Details of security arrangements for the protection of the data must be provided. (To ensure best practice in protecting data the OIC recommends use of British Standard BS7799. The British Standards Institute provides information on BS7799 at its website, **www.bsi.org.uk**). Details of any transfer of data outside the EEA must also be provided.

If there are any changes to any of the details of a notification – for example changes in the use of the data – during the period to which it applies (one year), the notification entry must be updated. An out-of-date notification entry is against the law. Those who have notified the OIC are included on the Data Protection Register, which is available for consultation at the Register's website, **www.dpr.gov.uk**.

■ Informed consent and data protection legislation

Informed consent in the collection of personal data is the key tenet of the data protection legislation. The two pillars that support informed consent are *transparency* and *consent*.

What does this mean for the practice of research? To comply with the *transparency* requirement the person responsible for collecting the data must ensure that those from whom the data are collected have a clear understanding of both the purpose or purposes for which the data are collected and the way in which the data will be used. At the time of data collection the person involved must give his or her *consent* for the data to be collected and must be given the chance to opt out of any further uses of the data. The EU Directive describes *consent* as *'a freely given and informed agreement by a person to the processing of his or her personal data'*. The 1998 Data Protection Act gives individuals the right to withdraw consent at any time and allows them to attach any condition to the consent that he or she deems appropriate. If sensitive data are being collected the Act states that consent must be based on a detailed explanation of how the data will be used. Sensitive data are defined as data relating to *'race or ethnic origin; political opinions and religious beliefs; membership of a trade union; physical or mental health; sexual life; and the commission or alleged commission of an offence or any proceedings for an offence committed and the outcome'*.

If a sample has been derived from a client database, a membership list for example, and a respondent asks how the interviewer obtained these personal details, to comply with the legislation the interviewer must give the respondent this information at some stage during the interview. If a further interview with the same respondent is needed at some point in the future the interviewer must get the respondent's consent for this interview at the initial interview, and not at a later stage. If further interviews are likely to be carried out by a different organisation the respondent must be told this when he or she is asked for consent. The respondent should also be told the identity of the organisation collecting the data at a suitable point in the data collection process.

■ The scope of the 1998 Data Protection Act: personal data only

The aim of the Act is to ensure confidentiality in the collection and use of *personal data*. In the context of the Act, personal data are data that can be used to identify a living natural person (children and adults). An identifiable person is someone who can be identified by *'an identification number or by physical, physiological, mental, economic, cultural or social characteristics, either directly or indirectly'*.

Rights of access to personal data

When personal data are attached to a data record such as a questionnaire the data subject – the respondent to the questionnaire – has, under the Act, the right to request access to these personal data (see Box 15.4). This right, however, does not apply once the data have been depersonalised – once personal identifiers have been removed from the data record. It is worth considering therefore how soon in the data handling process data can be depersonalised. In many research projects personal data are collected and held for quality control purposes – to verify that the research has been conducted. Once quality control checks have been made personal data can be deleted from the data record. The MRS Code of Conduct advises that primary data records should be kept for one year if there are no contractual agreements in place that require otherwise. In order to avoid having to fulfil potentially burdensome access requests from respondents, however, the MRS advises members to use much shorter retention periods than the one-year period for identifiable data such as questionnaires.

Storing personal data

Compliance with the Act does not mean that data should be depersonalised in order for it to be stored. In fact the Act states that personal data can be kept indefinitely as long as this does not conflict with the Fifth Principle of the Act, which says that personal data must not be kept beyond fulfilling the purpose for which they are collected. This is particularly relevant for attributable research where the issue of depersonalising the data does not arise. The issue for researchers therefore is not the need to depersonalise the data (although this is certainly advisable from an administrative point of view) but to ensure that the data are held securely and that unauthorised access is prevented.

Box 15.4 Respondents' rights of access to personal data: researcher's responsibilities

Under data protection legislation respondents have rights of access to their personal data. This means that if a respondent asks to see the data held on him or her the researcher should give him or her contact details of the data owner, and/or the researcher must notify the data owner within 40 days of the respondent's request. If the respondent asks that he or she be removed from the database, or requests that incorrect data are corrected or removed from the data record, or asks the data owner to contact him or her, the researcher should give the respondent contact details of the data owner, and/or notify the data owner within 40 days of the respondent's request. The researcher should inform the respondent of any action he or she has taken on the respondent's behalf.

■ The treatment of personal data

There are eight principles that govern the treatment of personal data under the 1998 Data Protection Act:

➢ *First principle*: personal data must be processed fairly and lawfully.
➢ *Second principle*: personal data must only be used for the specified, lawful purposes for which it was collected.
➢ *Third principle*: personal data shall be adequate, relevant and not excessive.
➢ *Fourth principle*: personal data shall be accurate and kept up to date.
➢ *Fifth principle*: personal data must not be kept beyond fulfilling the purpose for which it was collected.
➢ *Sixth principle*: personal data shall be processed in accordance with the rights of the data subjects.
➢ *Seventh principle*: personal data must be kept secure.
➢ *Eighth principle*: personal data shall not be transferred from the European Economic Area unless adequate protections are in place.

Processing personal data

In the context of the 1998 Act the term *processing* means obtaining, recording or holding data; it refers to any operation conducted on the data, such as organising, adapting or altering them. It also covers the processes involved with retrieving and consulting the data or using the data. It covers the processes involved in disclosing data by transmitting or disseminating them and any process involved in destroying the data.

Box 15.5 Responsibility for personal data: the role of the data controller

The data controller is the owner of the data and the person responsible for determining the purposes for which personal data are processed, how they are processed and how they are stored. It is his or her responsibility to ensure that his or her organisation complies with the notification procedures (see Box 15.3) set out in the 1998 Act. If data are to be processed by someone other than the data controller (a data processing contractor, for example), the data controller must have a written agreement with this person or organisation. The purpose of this agreement is to ensure that the contractor will handle personal data in accordance with the data controller's instructions and so ensure that the data are securely stored and remain confidential. If data are to be given to a third party who is not a data processor the data controller must be sure that the data subjects have agreed to this.

The data controller in a client organisation must ensure that any personal level data given to him or her by a researcher are used only for the purpose or purposes for which the respondent gave informed consent. The researcher must make sure that the client or list broker from whom he or she receives data or rents a list, for example to use as a sampling frame, is complying with the Data Protection Act (1998). The researcher should clarify with the data owner that market research is included in its notification for the use of the data, and that in collecting the data respondents gave consent for their use. The researcher should also make sure that any individuals who asked that their data should not be used for market research have been removed from the database.

Each time the database is used for sampling purposes the data controller should record on the database if an individual was interviewed, if an interview was attempted, or if the person refused to be interviewed. Each time an individual is contacted his or her details should be checked in order to ensure that the database is kept up to date.

If a researcher rents a list or uses a client database for sampling purposes the researcher does not become the data controller for that data; the data owner remains the data controller. However, if a researcher buys a list, or acquires rights to one, or creates a new list or database, he or she becomes the data controller of that list or database. A new database can be one that is generated from scratch or one that is created by combining client-supplied personal data and research data. It is the data controller's responsibility to make sure that personal data on a database are up to date.

If other research data are held on an identifiable basis, for example for use as a sampling frame or for recontacting respondents on a panel, the organisation that holds these personalised data is the data controller. If interviewers or recruiters use personal information collected or used in one project to build or create a database for use in other projects, the individuals who are included in this database must have given their consent for their personal data to be used in this way. The interviewer or recruiter compiling and holding this database is the data controller and must be notified with the OIC. There is a further complication in that using personal information gathered in one project to compile a list for use in other projects may violate a contract between the owner of the original list and the user of the list, the interviewer's employer.

Treatment of personal data for research purposes

The 1998 UK Act treats the processing of personal data for research purposes in a special way. It allows for personal data to be reprocessed if the purpose of this further processing is in line with the original purpose as described to the respondent. It allows personal data to be kept indefinitely, as long as this does not conflict with the Fifth Principle of the Act (that personal data must not be kept beyond fulfilling the purpose for which they were collected). As we saw earlier, whilst data subjects have the right to request a copy of their data record if it contains information that could identify them, they do not have the right to request access once any personal identifiers have been removed. To be eligible to be treated this way, however, three conditions must be met:

➢ Data must be used for research purposes *only.*

➢ Data should not be used in a way that would cause substantial damage or distress to the data subject.

➢ Data should not be used to support actions or decisions in relation to particular individuals.

It is this last condition that caused a rethink of what can be classed as research. As we noted in Chapter 5, there has been huge growth in the use of databases, particularly customer databases, and an attendant rise in research using these databases for sampling. This raises issues in relation to data protection legislation. If researchers use databases for sampling purposes, can they pass on information from the individual to the data owner? Can they pass on information about the individual to the database owner? For what purposes can the data owner use that information? In other words, what feedback is allowed under the Act?

Box 15.6 What feedback is allowed?

➢ The client has a relatively small database of customers and wants to make sure that the same customers do not take part in research more than once a year. What sort of feedback can you give the client about the individuals contacted?

➢ During the sampling process for a project you discover that some of the personal information on the database from which the sample was taken is incorrect or out of date. What sort of feedback can you give your client?

➢ During the data collection stage of a project a respondent complains about the level of service he received from the client and he wants you to tell the client. Can you do his?

➢ In the course of research you gather a lot of non-personal information about customers. What sort of feedback can you give to clients so that they can update the non-personal information they have on customers?

■ The treatment or classification of market research

In order to clarify the type and extent of feedback allowed from research projects under the 1998 Act, The Market Research Society agreed a classification of research projects with the Office of the Information Commissioner. The classification divides projects into six categories. Five of the categories are described as *classic* research; the sixth category contains projects that do not meet the requirements of classic research. One way of distinguishing classic and non-classic research projects is to think about the purpose for which the data are collected, or the end use of the data. Data gathered in classic research projects – those in Categories One to Five – are used to understand and predict attitudes and behaviour; data gathered in Category Six projects are used to take action – direct marketing, for example, aimed at the individuals identified. The categories are not mutually exclusive – a project could be classified as belonging to more than one category, depending, for example, on the source of the sample and the end use of the data.

Box 15.7 MRS classification of research projects

➤ *Category One* covers classic confidential research in which there is no feedback of any personal data except to those involved in the project who are bound by the MRS Code of Conduct and agree to use the data for research purposes only.

➤ *Category Two* covers projects that use samples drawn from client customer databases or other third party owned lists. To comply with the Fourth Principle of the 1998 Data Protection Act – that personal data shall be kept accurate and up to date – those using the database or list (the researcher) can notify its owner where an individual is either 'no longer at this address' (but not of any new address) or has died.

➤ *Category Three* also covers projects that use client or third party owned customer databases or lists for sampling. To prevent the over-researching of individuals on a database or list, the researcher can give the database owner names or identification numbers of those contacted, including those who declined to be interviewed on that occasion, solely for the purpose of setting up a '*do not select for research*' marker.

➤ *Category Four* covers projects that involve feedback about specific complaints. A respondent or the client can request that interviewers give details of specific complaints to the client for investigation. The respondent must give his or her consent to the principle of this feedback happening and to the content of the complaint (to ensure accuracy). The only details given to the client are the respondent's contact details plus a description of the complaint. The client can use the information to deal only with the issue raised and for no other purpose.

➤ In *Category Five* projects the client gets the results of the research at an individual respondent level (for example, a videotape of a group discussion) with the condition that the data at this personal level are used for research purposes only. This must be part of the project contract between researcher and client. These sorts of projects are described in the MRS guidelines as collecting data for *attributable* purposes.

Implications for research practice in general

What implications does this have for the practice of research? Classic research – projects in Categories One to Five – meets the strict terms of the MRS Code of Conduct. In conducting classic research, the MRS Code of Conduct requires the following:

➤ respondents give informed consent to their personal data being used for specified other purposes;
➤ they have the opportunity to opt out of any follow-up activities;
➤ if sensitive data are being collected, consent is based on a detailed explanation of how the data will be used.

There is a sixth category of projects in which data are collected for purposes other than, or in addition to, research. In these sorts of project the MRS Interviewer Identity (IID) Cards and standard 'Thank you' leaflets must not be used; reference should not be made to the MRS Code of Conduct (nor to the MRS Freephone service) as the MRS Code of Conduct does not cover these sorts of projects. The MRS recommends that anyone carrying out such projects should make sure that they are registered in the appropriate way with the OIC. Respondents in Category Six projects may be allowed to prevent the processing or use of their personal data for direct marketing purposes. As a result, the MRS advises that those working on Category Six projects with a direct marketing purpose in the United Kingdom should also be familiar with the Direct Marketing Association Code of Conduct.

Implications for business-to-business research

The 1998 Act applies to personal data on individuals, and so covers partnerships and sole traders (in England and Wales). It does not apply to data on organisations. Business-to-business research, however, can often involve collecting and processing data about individuals in organisations who may be identifiable on the basis of the data collected. In such cases the data should be treated in the same way as other individually identifiable data.

International research

The EU Data Protection Directive says that data controllers should comply with the law of the EU member state in which they are based and in which data processing is carried out. If a data controller is responsible for several EU countries he or she must ensure that data protection procedures are in compliance with the law in each of the member states in which data processing takes place. Transfer of data is allowed within the European Economic Area, and to other countries deemed to have 'adequate' data protection legislation. A list of such countries is published on the UK Information Commissioner's website (**www.dataprotection.gov.uk**) and at the time of writing included Hungary, Canada and Switzerland. It does not include the United States. There is, however, a 'safe harbour' agreement between the United States and the EU; US companies registered under this agreement should meet EU data protection standards and so can receive data. If not, it is possible to transfer data legally if a data transfer contract is drawn up. Copies of standard data transfer contracts can be obtained from the EU website (**www.europa.eu/comm/internal_market/en/datprot/news/index.htm**).

Data can also be legally transferred outside the EEA under certain conditions. These include where the following apply:

➤ contractual obligations create an adequate level of security to permit transfer;
➤ unambiguous consent of the data subject has been obtained;
➤ there is a contract between the data subject and the data controller, or a contract concluded in the interest of the data subject;
➤ transfers are legally required on public interest grounds or for the establishment, exercise or defence of legal claims;
➤ transfers are needed to protect the vital interests of the data subject;
➤ transfers from a register established under laws or regulations are open to consultation by the general public or anyone with a legitimate interest.

A list of data protection commissioners around the world and a list of contacts in EEA countries who can provide information on the implementation of the EU Data Protection Directive within that specific country is published by the OIC on its website (**www.dataprotection.gov.uk**).

Box 15.8 Data transfer

Under the 1998 Act the term data transfer means the following:

➤ access to personal data held in EEA countries from countries outside the EEA, including electronic access via a multinational organisation's computer network;
➤ access to data held in an EEA country by an employee of an EEA-based organisation via a mobile computing device whilst travelling outside the EEA;
➤ placing personal data on a website;
➤ faxing or using the telephone to pass personal data from an EEA country to a country outside the EEA, which will be entered into a computer.

Implications for Internet research

If customer data for use in research have been collected via a client's website the data controller must make sure that the data were collected with the customers' knowledge. Customers should be informed about the type of information being collected about them, and the purpose for which it is being collected, or the purpose to which it will be put. Email addresses are classified as personal data where they refer to a data subject. They should be protected in the same way as other personal identifiers. The data controller should ensure that data provided by clients, for example, are protected from unauthorised access by encryption or via a firewall. If data are being sent via the Internet to another country the data controller must make sure that the transfer is allowable (see Box 15.8).

Implications for qualitative research

Audio and video records in which individuals can be identified are classed as personal data and should be treated accordingly. Respondents should be informed before the start of a group discussion or in-depth interview about the purpose and use of any audio or video recordings and transcripts made, and about the presence of any observers. Consent should be given in the full knowledge of the conditions under which the interview takes place and the use to which the data will be put. If the audio and video records are to be used for purposes other than research – for example for training purposes (an example of a Category six project), respondents must give their informed consent at the recruitment stage of the project. Video, audio or transcripts from which individuals could be identified should not be used for purposes other than research if this specific consent has not been given. Any observers at a group must be informed by the researcher of their responsibilities under the 1998 Act and the MRS Code of Conduct to ensure that any personal information they glean remains confidential.

Anyone involved in managing or creating a database of respondents must ensure that they are notified with the OIC and must be clear about their responsibilities in processing and storing data. The data must be stored securely so that unauthorised access is prevented.

Implications for observational research

If an organisation uses or intends to use observational research techniques, including mystery shopping, it must tell its employees. If closed circuit television (CCTV) is used to collect data the user must notify under the 1998 Act as a data controller. A CCTV Code of Practice is available from the OIC. The MRS guideline on observation is available from the MRS website (**www.mrs.org.uk**).

■ The impact of other legislation: UK Human Rights Act (1998)

The 1998 Human Rights Act may have implications for research practice. The Act contains Articles that may strengthen the 1998 Data Protection Act. For example, Article 8 discusses the right to respect for private and family life, home and correspondence; the 1998 Data Protection Act covers rights concerning personal data only.

Chapter summary

> Ethics are moral principles that are used to guide behaviour. Ethical principles are used to set standards of conduct for groups or professions in how they deal with people. They are important in a research context in order that those involved in research – researchers, research participants, clients and other users of research and the wider community – know what is and what is not acceptable in the conduct of research.

➤ The ethical principles that are the basis of most standards of conduct in relation to research participants are the following:
  ➤ voluntary participation
  ➤ no harm to the participants
  ➤ informed consent
  ➤ anonymity, confidentiality (privacy)
  ➤ transparency
  ➤ not deceiving subjects

➤ Ethical issues are rarely clear-cut. Questions about how to apply ethical principles will always arise. It is to address such questions, and to ensure a professional and consistent standard of practice, that professional bodies such as ESOMAR and the MRS have developed formal codes of conduct. These codes help to create trust between the research profession and those who take part in research by demonstrating that research is conducted in an acceptable and ethical way.

➤ The codes and guidelines are self-regulatory, and although they may incorporate principles that are covered by legislation they do not replace or take precedence over legislation.

➤ The aim of the MRS Code is '*to ensure that professional standards are maintained, that knowledge is communicated, and that the value of research is appreciated by the business community and the public at large*'. It is revised and updated regularly to take account of changes in both research practice and legislation. Compliance with the Code should ensure that research is conducted in compliance with the UK's Data Protection Act (1998).

➤ There are eight principles that govern the treatment of personal data under the 1988 Data Protection Act:
  ➤ *First principle*: personal data must be processed fairly and lawfully.
  ➤ *Second principle*: personal data must only be used for the specified, lawful purposes for which it was collected.
  ➤ *Third principle*: personal data shall be adequate, relevant and not excessive.
  ➤ *Fourth principle*: personal data shall be accurate and kept up to date.
  ➤ *Fifth principle*: personal data must not be kept beyond fulfilling the purpose for which it was collected.
  ➤ *Sixth principle*: personal data shall be processed in accordance with the rights of the data subjects.
  ➤ *Seventh principle*: personal data must be kept secure.
  ➤ *Eighth principle*: personal data shall not be transferred from the European Economic Area (EEA) unless adequate protections are in place.

➤ To clarify the type and extent of feedback allowed from research projects under the 1998 Act, the MRS agreed a classification of research projects with the OIC, dividing projects into six categories. Five are described as *classic* research; the sixth contains projects that do not meet the requirements of classic research. The categories are not mutually exclusive – a project could be classified as belonging to more than one category, depending, for example, on the source of the sample and the end use of the data.

➢ Category Six has been introduced to describe projects where survey research methods are used to collect data but the results at an individual respondent level are provided to the client for purposes such as direct marketing. These types of project are outside the definition of confidential market research, which underpins the MRS Code of Conduct, but they are still subject to the Data Protection Act 1998.

Questions and exercises

1 Why are ethical standards of conduct important in the practice of research?

2 Describe the researcher's ethical responsibilities to participants in research.

3 Why are professional codes of conduct necessary?

4 What are the key principles of The Market Research Society's Code of Conduct?

5 Describe an ethical dilemma you have faced in conducting research. How did you resolve it?

6 What are the key principles of the 1998 UK Data Protection Act?

7 What is 'notification'? Who should be notified under the 1998 Act?

8 What is the role of the data controller?

9 Describe what is meant by 'classic research'. What types of projects are not included in the 'classic research' definition?

10 Describe the implications of the 1998 Data Protection Act for the following:
   (a) qualitative research;
   (b) international research;
   (c) business-to-business research.

References

Gordon, W. and Robson, S. (1980) 'Respondent through the looking glass: towards a better understanding of the qualitative interviewing process', *Proceedings of The Market Research Society Conference*, London: The Market Research Society.

Lovett, P. (2001) 'Ethics shmethics! As long as you get the next job. A moral dilemma', *Proceedings of The Market Research Society Conference*, London: The Market Research Society.

Robson, S. (1991) 'Ethics: informed consent or misinformed compliance?', *Journal of the Market Research Society*, 33, 1, pp. 19–28.

The MRS Code of Conduct (July 1999) (**www.mrs.org.uk**).

Recommended reading

Bulmer, M. (1982) (ed.) *Social Research Ethics*, London: Macmillan. Includes detailed discussions of ethics in a variety of social research contexts.

The Market Research Society Code of Conduct (**www.mrs.org.uk**).

The MRS Guidelines Series. The application of the Code to aspects of research practice.

The ICC/ESOMAR International Code of Marketing and Social Research Practice (**www.esomar.nl**).

The Social Research Association Ethical Guidelines (**www.the-sra.org.uk**).

The 'Problem Corner' feature in *Research* magazine (**www.research-live.com**). Provides expert opinion on ethical dilemmas that you might come across in your own work.

The MRS *Guide to the Data Protection Act 1998* and *The Data Protection Act 1998 and Market Research: Guidance for MRS Members* (**www.mrs.org.uk**). Give details about the Act and its implications for research.

Lovett, P. (2001) 'Ethics shmethics! As long as you get the next job. A moral dilemma', *Proceedings of the Market Research Society Conference, London*: The Market Research Society. An interesting account of the response of researchers to some ethical dilemmas in business practice.

Robson, S. (1991) 'Ethics: informed consent or misinformed compliance?', *Journal of the Market Research Society*, 33, 1, pp. 19–28. A very useful discussion of ethical issues in qualitative research.

Bibliography

Accenture (2001) *The Unexpected eEurope*, London: Accenture.

Adriaenssens, C. and Cadman, L. (1999) 'An adaptation of moderated e-mail focus groups to assess the potential for a new online (Internet) financial services offer in the UK', *Journal of the Market Research Society*, **41**, 4, pp. 417–24.

Ajzen, I. and Fishbein, M. (1980) *Understanding attitudes and predicting social behaviour*, Englewood Cliffs, NJ: Prentice-Hall.

Baez Ortega, D. and Romo Costamaillere, G. (1997) 'Geodemographics and its application to the study of consumers', *ESOMAR Conference Proceedings, The Dynamics of Change in Latin America*, Amsterdam: ESOMAR.

Bagozzi, R. (1988) 'The rebirth of attitude research in marketing', *Journal of the Market Research Society*, **30**, 2, pp. 163–95.

Bairfelt, S. and Spurgeon, F. (1998) *Plenty of Data, but are we doing enough to fill the Information Gap?*, Amsterdam: ESOMAR.

Barnard, P. (1999) 'The expanding universe of market research', *Admap*, April.

Becker, H. (1986) *Writing for Social Scientists*, Chicago, IL: University of Chicago Press.

Bertaux, D. and Bertaux-Wiame, I. (1981) 'Life Stories in the Bakers' Trade', in Bertaux, D. (ed.) *Biography and Society: The Life History Approach in the Social Sciences*, London: Sage.

Biel, A. (1994) 'The utilisation barrier – the need to make research come alive', *Admap*, September.

Bijapurkar, R. (1995) *Does Market Research Really Contribute to Decision Making?*, Amsterdam: ESOMAR.

Bird, M. and Ehrenberg, A. (1970) 'Consumer attitudes and brand usage', *Journal of the Market Research Society*, **12**, 3, pp. 233–47.

Boulton, D. and Hammersley, M. (1996) 'Analysis of unstructured data', in Sapsford, R. and Jupp, V. (eds) *Data Collection and Analysis*, London: Sage.

Bristol, T. and Fern, E. (1996) 'Exploring the atmosphere created by focus group interviews: comparing consumers' feelings across qualitative techniques', *Journal of the Market Research Society*, **38**, 2, pp. 185–95.

Bulmer, M. (ed.) (1982) *Social Research Ethics*, London: Macmillan.

Burgess, R. (1984) *In the Field: An Introduction to Field Research*, London: Allen & Unwin.

Callingham, M. (1991) 'The role of qualitative notions in company decision making', *Journal of the Market Research Society*, **33**, 1, pp. 45–50.

Casey, M. (1998) 'Analysis: honoring the stories', in Krueger, R. (ed.), *Analyzing and Reporting Focus Group Results*, London: Sage.

Chisnall, P. (1997) *Marketing Research*, London: McGraw-Hill.

Clegg, F. (1991) *Simple Statistics*, Cambridge: Cambridge University Press.

Collins, L. (1991) 'Everything is true but in a different sense: a new perspective on qualitative research', *Journal of the Market Research Society*, **33**, 1, pp. 31–8.

Colwell, J. (1990) 'Qualitative market research: a conceptual analysis and review of practitioner criteria', *Journal of the Market Research Society*, **32**, 1, pp. 13–36.

Comley, P. (1999) 'Moderated Email Groups: Computing Magazine case study', *Proceedings of the ESOMAR Net Effects Conference*, London.

Converse, J. and Presser, S. (1986) *Survey Questions: Handcrafting the Standardized Questionnaire*, London: Sage.

Cooper, P. and Branthwaite, A. (1977) 'Qualitative technology: new perspectives on measurement and meaning through qualitative research', *Proceedings of The Market Research Society Conference*, London: The Market Research Society.

Cooper, P. and Tower, R. (1992) 'Inside the consumer mind: consumer attitudes to the arts', *Journal of the Market Research Society*, **34**, 4, pp. 299–311.

Cowan, D. (1995) 'The importance of good consumer information: information – generals can't do without it. Why do CEOs think they can?', *Admap*, July.

Dale, A., Arber, S. and Procter, M. (1988) *Doing Secondary Analysis*, London: Unwin Hyman.

De Mooij, M. (1998) *Global Marketing and Advertising: Understanding Cultural Paradoxes*, London: Sage.

Denzin, N. and Lincoln, Y. (eds) (1994) *A Handbook of Qualitative Research*, London: Sage.

De Vaus, D. (2001) *Research Design in Social Research*, London: Sage.

Dilly, R. (1996) *Data Mining: An Introduction, www.qub.ac.uk/pcc*.

Doole, I., Lowe, R. and Phillips, C. (1994) *International Marketing Strategy: Analysis, development and implementation*, London: Thomson.

Ehrenberg, A. (1982) *A Primer in Data Reduction*, London: Wiley.

Elliott, R. and Jobber, D. (1995) 'Expanding the market for market research: changing beliefs, attitudes and corporate culture', *Journal of the Market Research Society*, **37**, 2, pp. 143–58.

ESOMAR (2001) *Annual Study on the Market Research Industry*, Amsterdam: ESOMAR.

Farr, D. and McKenzie, J. (1990) '"…And what sex will you be next birthday?": The Market Research Week Survey Revisited', *Proceedings of The Market Research Society Conference*, London: The Market Research Society.

Fawcett, J. and Laird, A. (2001) 'Bottoms up! Consultees' views on consultation', *Proceedings of The Market Research Society Conference*, London: The Market Research Society.

Fishbein, M. (ed.) (1967) *Readings in Attitude Theory and Measurement*, New York: Wiley.

Fishbein, M. and Ajzen, I. (1975) *Belief, Attitude, Intention and Behaviour*, Reading, MA: Addison-Wesley.

Foreman, J. and Collins, M. (1991) 'The viability of random digit dialling in the UK', *Journal of the Market Research Society*, **33**, 3, pp. 219–27.

Gabriel, C. (1990) 'The validity of qualitative market research', *Journal of the Market Research Society*, **32**, 4, pp. 507–20.

Glaser, B. and Strauss, A. (1967) *The Discovery of Grounded Theory*, Chicago, IL: Aldine.

Gordon, W. (1999) *Goodthinking: A Guide to Qualitative Research*, Henley-on-Thames: Admap.

Gordon, W. and Robson, S. (1980) 'Respondent through the looking glass: towards a better understanding of the qualitative interviewing process', *Proceedings of The Market Research Society Conference*, London: The Market Research Society.

Gosschalk, B. (1999) 'Opinion formers' views on market research', *Admap*, April.

Hakim, C. (1982) *Secondary Analysis in Social Research*, London: Allen & Unwin.

Hammersley, M. and Atkinson, P. (1995) *Ethnography: Principles in Practice*, London: Routledge.

Harvey, M. and Evans, M. (2001) 'Decoding competitive propositions: a semiotic alternative to traditional advertising research', *Proceedings of The Market Research Society Conference*, London: The Market Research Society.

Hedges, A. (1994) *Commissioning Social Research: A Good Practice Guide*, London: Social Research Association.

Holmes, D. (1998) *Market research: A backroom support function or vanguard of knowledge management*, Amsterdam: ESOMAR.

Hornsby-Smith, M. (1993) 'Gaining access', in Gilbert, N. (ed.) *Researching Social Life*, London: Sage.

Katz, J. (1983) 'A theory of qualitative methodology: the social science system of analytic fieldwork', in Emerson, R. (ed.) *Contemporary Field Research*, Boston, MA: Little Brown.

Kaushik, M. and Sen, A. (1990) 'Semiotics and qualitative research', *Journal of the Market Research Society*, 32, 2, pp. 227–42.

Kirk, J. and Miller, M. (1986) *Reliability and Validity in Qualitative Research*, Newbury Park, CA: Sage.

Kish, L. (1949) 'A procedure for objective respondent selection within the household', *Journal of the American Statistical Association*, **44**, pp. 380–7.

Kish, L. (1965) *Survey Sampling*, New York: Wiley.

Kreinczes, G. (1990) 'Why research is undervalued', *Admap*, March.

Krueger, R. (1998) *Moderating Focus Groups*, London: Sage.

Lee, R. (1992) *Doing Research on Sensitive Topics*, London: Sage.

Leventhal, B. (1997) 'An approach to fusing market research with database marketing', *Journal of the Market Research Society*, **39**, 4, pp. 545–58.

Lovett, P. (2001) 'Ethics shmethics! As long as you get the next job. A moral dilemma', *Proceedings of The Market Research Society Conference*, London: The Market Research Society.

McIntosh, A. and Davies, R. (1970 and 1996) 'The sampling of non-domestic populations', *Journal of the Market Research Society*, **12**, 4, pp. 217–32 and 38, 4, pp. 429–46.

Marks, L. (ed.) (2000) *Qualitative Research in Context*, Henley-on-Thames: Admap.

Marsh, C. and Scarbrough, E. (1990) 'Testing nine hypotheses about quota sampling', *Journal of the Market Research Society*, **32**, 4, pp. 485–506.

Mason, J. (1996) *Qualitative Researching*, London: Sage.

Miles, K., Bright, D. and Kemp, J. (2000) 'Improving the research interview experience', *Proceedings of The Market Research Society Conference*, London: The Market Research Society.

Miles, M. and Huberman, A. M. (1994) *Qualitative Data Analysis: An Expanded Sourcebook*, London: Sage.

Morris, D. (1994) *Bodytalk: A World Guide to Gestures*, London: Jonathan Cape.

Moser, C. A. and Kalton, G. (1971) *Survey Methods in Social Investigation*, 2nd edn, Alder-shot: Dartmouth.

O'Connor, J. and Seymour, J. (1993) *Introducing NLP*, London: HarperCollins.

Oppenheim, A. (2000) *Questionnaire Design, Interviewing and Attitude Measurement*, London: Continuum.

Osgood, C., Suci, G. and Tannebaum, R. (1957) *The Measurement of Meaning*, Urbana, IL: University of Illinois Press.

Page, B. and Wojtowicz, T. (2000) 'Benchmarking on a global scale: a case study illustrating experiences and implications of the use of the Internet', *Proceedings of the ESOMAR Net Effects Conference*, Dublin.

Payne, S. (1951) *The Art of Asking Questions*, Princeton, NJ: Princeton University Press.

Procter, M. (1993) 'Analyzing other researchers' data', in Gilbert, N. (ed.) *Researching Social Life*, London: Sage.

Punch, K. (2000) *Developing Effective Research Proposals*, London: Sage.

Pyke, A. (2000) 'It's all in the brief', *Proceedings of The Market Research Society Conference*, London: The Market Research Society.

Qualitative recruitment: Report of the Industry Working Party (1996) *Journal of the Market Research Society*, **38**, pp. 135–43.

Quinn Patton, M. (1986) *Utilization-focused Evaluation*, London: Sage.

Ritchie, J. and Spencer, L. (1992) 'Qualitative data analysis for applied policy research', in Burgess, A. and Bryman, R. (eds) *Analyzing Qualitative Data*, London: Routledge.

Robson, S. (1991) 'Ethics: informed consent or misinformed compliance?', *Journal of the Market Research Society*, **33**, 1, pp. 19–28.

Robson, S. and Hedges, A. (1993) 'Analysis and interpretation of qualitative findings: Report of the MRS Qualitative Interest Group', *Journal of the Market Research Society*, **35**, 1, pp. 23–35.

Rose, J., Sykes, L. and Woodcock, D. (1995) 'Qualitative recruitment: the industry working party report', *Proceedings of The Market Research Society Conference*, London: The Market Research Society.

Rubin, H. and Rubin, I. (1995) *Qualitative Interviewing: The Art of Hearing Data*, London: Sage.

Sampson, P. (1967 and 1996) 'Commonsense in qualitative research', *Journal of the Market Research Society*, **9**, 1, pp. 30–8 and **38**, 4, pp. 331–9.

Sampson, P. (1980) 'The technical revolution of the 1970s: will it happen in the 1980s?', *Journal of the Market Research Society*, **22**, 3, pp. 161–78.

Sampson, P. (1985) 'Qualitative research in Europe: the state of the art and the art of the state', ESOMAR Congress, Wiesbaden.

Sampson, P. and Harris, P. (1970) 'A users' guide to Fishbein', *Journal of the Market Research Society*, **12**, 3, pp. 145–68.

Schlackman, W. (1984) 'A discussion of the use of sensitivity panels in market research', *Proceedings of The Market Research Society Conference*, London: The Market Research Society.

Shipman, M. (1997) *The Limitations of Social Research*, London: Longman.

Smith, D. and Fletcher, J. (2001) *Inside Information: Making Sense of Marketing Data*, London: Wiley.

Spackman, N. (1993) 'Judging the value of research', *Admap*, January.

Sparre, M. and Steen, J. (2000) 'Advantages of conducting employee research on the Internet: a case study', *Proceedings of the ESOMAR Net Effects Conference*, Dublin.

Stoker, S. (1999a) 'Good data housekeeping', in *DM Direct*, August, *www.dmreview.com/dmdirect*.

Stoker, S. (1999b) 'Building an information warehouse', in *DM Direct*, December, *www.dmreview.com/dmdirect*.

Strauss, A. (1987) *Qualitative Analysis for Social Scientists*, Cambridge: Cambridge University Press.

Strauss, A. and Corbin, J. (1998) *Basics of Qualitative Research*, London: Sage.

Sudman, S. and Bradburn, N. (1983) *Asking Questions*, San Francisco, CA: Jossey-Bass.

Sykes, W. (1990) 'Validity and reliability in qualitative market research: a review of the literature', *Journal of the Market Research Society*, **32**, 3, pp. 289–328.

Taraborelli, P. (1993) 'Becoming a carer', in Gilbert, N. (ed) *Researching Social Life*, London: Sage.

Taylor, S. and Bogdan, R. (1998) *Introduction to Qualitative Research Methods*, London: Wiley.

The ICC/ESOMAR International Code of Marketing and Social Research Practice (*www.esomar.nl*).

The EU Data Protection Directive (Directive 95/46/EC of the European Parliament and of the Council) (1995), *Official Journal of the European Communities*, No L. **281**, p. 31, November.

The Market Research Society Guidelines on Qualitative Research available from the MRS and at the MRS website (*www.mrs.org.uk*).

The MRS Code of Conduct (July 1999) (*www.mrs.org.uk*).

The Research and Development sub-committee on Qualitative Research (1979) 'Qualitative research: a summary of the concepts involved', *Journal of the Market Research Society*, **21**, 2, pp. 107–24.

The *Research Works* series: papers from the AMSO (now BMRA) Research Effectiveness Awards, Henley-on-Thames: NTC.

Tuck, M. (1976) *How People Choose*, London: Methuen.

Tufte, E. (2001) *The Visual Display of Quantitative Information*, Cheshire, CT: Graphics Press.

Tukey, J. (1977) *Exploratory Data Analysis*, Reading, MA: Addison Wesley.

Warren, M. (1991) 'Another day, another debrief: the use and assessment of qualitative research', *Journal of the Market Research Society*, **33**, 1, pp. 13–18.

Waterhouse, K. (1994) *English, Our English (and How to Sing It)*, London: Penguin.

Wells, S. (1991) 'Wet towels and whetted appetites or a wet blanket? The role of analysis in qualitative research', *Journal of the Market Research Society*, **33**, 1, pp. 39–44.

Winkler, J. T. (1987) 'The fly on the wall of the inner sanctum: observing company directors at work', in G. Moyser and M. Wagstaffe (eds), *Research Methods for Elite Studies*, London: Allen Unwin.

Wissing, A. (2000) 'Using the Internet to measure advertising effectiveness', *Proceedings of the ESOMAR Net Effects Conference*, Dublin.

Yu, J. and Cooper, H. (1983) 'A quantitative review of research design effects on response rates to questionnaires', *Journal of the Market Research Society*, **20**, 1, pp. 36–44.

Index